M/
I

Between Slavery and Free Labor

JOHNS HOPKINS STUDIES IN ATLANTIC HISTORY AND CULTURE
Richard Price, General Editor

Sponsored by the Joint Committee
on Latin American Studies
of the Social Science Research Council
and the American Council of Learned Societies

Between Slavery and Free Labor: The Spanish-Speaking Caribbean in the Nineteenth Century

Edited by
Manuel Moreno Fraginals,
Frank Moya Pons,
and Stanley L. Engerman

THE JOHNS HOPKINS UNIVERSITY PRESS • BALTIMORE AND LONDON

© 1985 The Social Science Research Council
All rights reserved
Printed in the United States of America

The Johns Hopkins University Press, 701 West 40th Street,
Baltimore, Maryland 21211
The Johns Hopkins Press Ltd, London.

The paper in this book is acid-free and meets the guidelines for
permanence and durability of the Committee on Production Guidelines
for Book Longevity of the Council on Library Resources.

Library of Congress Cataloging in Publication Data
Main entry under title:

Between slavery and free labor.

(Johns Hopkins studies in Atlantic history and culture)
Based on papers presented at the Conference on Problems of
Transition from Slavery to Free Labor in the Caribbean, held at the Museo
del Hombre Dominicano in Santo Domingo, Dominican Republic, June
11–13, 1981; sponsored by the Fondo para el Avance de las Ciencias
Sociales, Santo Domingo, and the Social Science Research Council,
New York.
Includes index.
1. Slavery—Caribbean Area—Emancipation—History—
19th century—Congresses. 2. Slave labor—Caribbean Area—History—
19th century—Congresses. 3. Labor supply—Caribbean Area—
History—19th century—Congresses. 4. Sugar—Manufacture and
refining—Caribbean Area—History—19th century—Congresses.
I. Moreno Fraginals, Manuel. II. Moya Pons, Frank, 1944–
III. Engerman, Stanley L. IV. Conference on Problems of Transition
from Slavery to Free Labor in the Caribbean (1981 : Museo del Hombre
Dominicano) V. Fondo para el Avance de las Ciencias Sociales.
VI. Social Science Research Council (U.S.) VII. Series.
HT1073.B48 1985 306′.362′09729 84-23379
ISBN 0-8018-3224-1 (alk. paper)

Contents

PART FOUR: DOMINICAN REPUBLIC

PART FIVE: PERSPECTIVES

Tables

Illustrations

Preface

This volume is based on papers presented at the Conference on Problems of Transition from Slavery to Free Labor in the Caribbean, held at the Museo del Hombre Dominicano in Santo Domingo, Dominican Republic, June 11–13, 1981. The conference was sponsored by the Fondo para el Avance de las Ciencias Sociales (Santo Domingo) and the Social Science Research Council (New York).

The idea of holding this seminar arose during a postgraduate course given by Manuel Moreno Fraginals at Columbia University in 1978–79. The presence of an outstanding group of students—some North Americans, others from different areas of the Caribbean and Latin America—continually forced the consideration of bases for comparisons among the different regions of the area. In the long run this course on the Caribbean became a course in comparative history, thanks to the excellent work of the students and the contributions of the distinguished scholars who were invited to the meetings: Herbert Gutman, Herbert Klein, Sidney Mintz, and Helen Safa.

In establishing regional differences, there was agreement that the development of what can be called the Spanish Caribbean (composed of Cuba, the Dominican Republic, and Puerto Rico) presented characteristics that were not found in the islands colonized by the English or French, to say nothing of the Dutch, Swedish, or Danish. Although some of these differences have been pointed out by various authors (e.g., Frank Tannenbaum, Herbert Klein, Fernando Ortiz, Franklin Knight), no single coherent study analyzed the region in a global form, exposing the similarities and differences in depth and explaining their past significance and the potential repercussions.

In the comparative study of the Spanish with the English and French Caribbean, seven major differences became immediately evident:

1. Differences of size. The size of Cuba, the Dominican Republic, and Puerto Rico permitted a level of economic activity impossible in the

rest of the island Caribbean, with the exception of Jamaica. In
the time of Cromwell, Barbados was "the most precious jewel of the
British Empire," but Puerto Rico is 21 times larger than Barbados, the
Dominican Republic 113 times larger, and Cuba 266 times larger.

2. Differences in the colonizing process. With the exception of the early
sixteenth century, Spain placed no emphasis on the exploitation of the
economic possibilities of the islands. Its attention directed toward the
continent, Spain regarded its islands in the Caribbean as having the
fundamental mission of ports of call, serving as communication and
military enclaves with an emphasis on the provision of services.

3. Differences in the timing of the development of the plantation economy. The plantation economy, typical of the Caribbean, did not acquire preponderance in the Spanish islands until the end of the
eighteenth century and the beginning of the nineteenth century, precisely when the great decline and disintegration of the English and
French slave-based plantation system had begun.

4. Differences in demographic patterns. As a result of the chronological
disjunction described in point 3, as well as the size of Cuba, the
Dominican Republic, and Puerto Rico, at no point did the number of
slaves exceed the free population, nor did the number of black inhabitants or mestizos of African origin surpass the white or "whitened"
population.

5. Differences in the colonial relationship. In no period in the nineteenth century did Spain play the role of a modern metropolis in the
sense of the English or French capitalist colonial exploiters. This was
not because of religious or moral reasons (though these are undeniable factors) but because of the naval incapacity to transport the
volume of sugar and coffee produced by Cuba and Puerto Rico, the
industrial incapacity to process these raw materials, the incapacity of
the internal market to consume them, and the incapacity in international commerce to reexport them.

6. Differences in sociopolitical development. Lacking a modern economic metropolis, the plantation system developed on the basis of
internal forces and investments of locally accumulated capital. And
these internal forces also developed extended national, or at the very
least native, oligarchies and a magnified set of political and ideological contests. In this way the Spanish Caribbean articulated different
national programs and waged important battles to concretize them.
Bloody wars of independence were fought by the Dominican Republic
against Haiti and Spain, and by Cuba against Spain.

7. Differences in economic development. Lacking an economic metropolis, but with a typical colonial structure, Cuba, the Dominican Republic, and Puerto Rico were inevitably incorporated into the North
American neocolonial orbit, long before the English or French Carib-

bean. In this process the new plantation system played a special role that, while maintaining many of the aspects of the old system, differed in essential ways.

Although many other differences were noted during the course, numerous similarities were pointed out: colonialism and neocolonialism, dependence on only one product and only one market, persistent poverty among a large strata of the population, and strong pressures for emigration, among others. How can one properly analyze and discuss these analogies and differences? How would this contribute to an understanding of the Caribbean? One distinct proposal was holding periodic meetings among specialists with experience in the Spanish islands (without excluding the presence of those familiar with the rest of the region) and initiating a series of basic investigations. The first of these conferences has dealt only with some antecedents of the problem and included a number of themes that were considered essential as historical points of departure. Special attention was given to problems such as the late abolition of slavery in Puerto Rico and Cuba and the transition from slavery to salaried labor; problems of land and work in the Dominican Republic during the nineteenth century; the growth of the modern sugar industry; and the transition from a decadent Spanish colonialism to the modern forms of North American neocolonial domination. Needless to say, not all of the themes could be expounded on to an equal extent, and we hope that there will be further conferences, dealing with other periods and other topics; for example, one would begin with the period of the Cuban-Spanish-North American War and go through the period of the 1929–39 depression, and another on the politics of North America in the Caribbean from the New Deal to the Caribbean Basin Initiative.

We wish to make some points regarding the conference held in Santo Domingo and those planned for the future. All of us who participated in their organization have thought of them as small meetings, carefully prepared and without a public audience: in sum, a group of specialists rigorously discussing and analyzing, in an open but cordial manner, all the problems that interest and strike us. To achieve this, it was imperative that the group contain a broad regional coverage as well as a good ideological balance. Both were achieved, with the presence of well-known North American, Puerto Rican, and Dominican specialists and a Cuban representation. The discussion at the conference was most lively and informative. We have decided, however, not to publish any of the commentary, because we felt that the best arrangement of the published volume differed from that at the conference. We do wish to acknowledge the help of commentators Lambros Comitas, Gervasio Luis García, Franklin Knight, Sidney Mintz, and Stuart Schwartz, as well as the other participants at the conference, Carlos Dore y Cabral and Rubén Silié, for their contributions. This volume includes all but one of the papers presented at the conference; two papers plus the epilogue, by Sidney Mintz, have been added.

The conference was able to achieve its ends and emerge in published forms thanks to the financial support and enthusiastic collaboration of institutions and persons too numerous to mention here. Nonetheless, there are names that cannot be omitted and to whom we wish to express our gratitude:

- The Social Science Research Council, which welcomed the project, assigned funds, and performed an excellent job of organization. Reid Andrews, the director of the Latin American Program at the time and a highly capable administrator, is responsible for a fundamental part of the project's success. His successors, Brooke Larson and Joan Dassin, also provided considerable help and encouragement.
- The Fondo para el Avance de las Ciencias Sociales, for material and organizational support and for the hospitality with which we were received.
- The Museo del Hombre Dominicano and its director, Lic. Bernardo Vega.
- The Fundación García Arevalo and its director, Manuel García Arevalo.
- Professor Carmen Rafucci, who acted as organization secretary throughout the preliminary stage of the project, and Professor Herbert Klein, who collaborated from the initial organizational stage through the publication of this volume.
- The University of Rochester Department of Economics.
- Stephanie McCurry for help with editing the manuscripts, Elizabeth Ann Castle for the typing of several drafts of the volume, Maria Carmen Garcés Ramón for periodic aid in translations from the Spanish, Judith Evans for help in translating an earlier draft of this Preface (the translators of those essays originally in Spanish are acknowledged in each essay), and James Irwin for work done in the final stages of the manuscript preparation.
- Franklin Knight, for help in obtaining maps and other assistance throughout the preparation of the volume. We also wish to thank him, as well as the University of Wisconsin Press and the Oxford University Press for permission to use maps from his books, *Slave Society in Cuba during the Nineteenth Century* and *The Caribbean: The Genesis of a Fragmented Nationalism*, as the basis for two maps in this volume. The originals for two of the other maps were obtained from the Library of Congress.
- Gerald P. Cooper and Anita Matthews, of the Photo/Illustration Service of the University of Rochester, for drawing the figures and maps.

- Richard Price, the editor of the series in which this volume has been published.
- The Johns Hopkins University Press, in particular Henry Tom, George Thompson, Mary Lou Kenney, and for her excellent copy editing, Ann E. Petty. The index was prepared by Joyce Taylor Snow.

Finally, Moreno Fraginals wishes to express gratitude to the Tinker Foundation and Columbia University for the magnificent opportunity for professional work during the year 1978–79, when the plans for this conference originated; to the administrators of his center of work in Cuba, the Instituto Superior del Arte, for permitting him to divert so much time to these labors; and to Dr. Francisco López Segrera, his most intimate collaborator, for his efficiency, enthusiasm, abilities, and uncontainable optimism for every undertaking, no matter how difficult.

Part One
Overview

The Caribbean

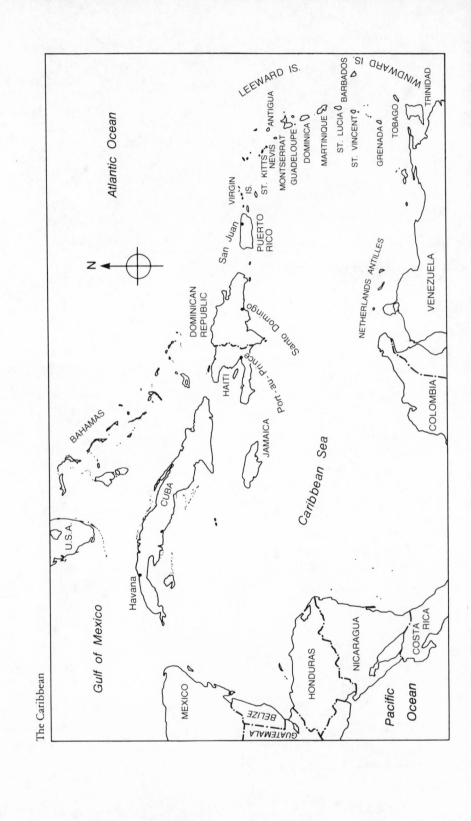

1. Plantations in the Caribbean: Cuba, Puerto Rico, and the Dominican Republic in the Late Nineteenth Century

Manuel Moreno Fraginals

Historical phenomena, obviously, have never been static; but there are certain periods in which transformations occur slowly, and others in which the rate of change is such that in a few short years everything seems different. An example of this may be found in the industrial history of the Caribbean.

During the eighteenth century and the first half of the nineteenth, the patterns of sugar production and commerce changed very little, and what changes occurred were either geographical (shifts in production from one island to another) or determined by the partial adoption of certain technologies. On the other hand, starting about 1860 and within not more than thirty years, the centuries-old structure of the sugar industry was shattered, to be replaced by completely new forms of production and commerce and even by a new form of the final product itself, a sugar produced to different standards and shipped in different packaging. It is no exaggeration to say that as regards sugar in the Caribbean, in the nineties everything was completely different from what existed in the sixties.

It is almost impossible to list the successive developments in the sugar world from the 1860s on, and even more so to establish causal relationships among these developments in order to follow them like a chain reaction. These changes equally affected sugar producers, merchants, and consumers; they modified human and labor relations and altered age-old habits of consumption. This great transformation was at once the cause and the consequence of other economic, social, and political factors and was at the same time connected by innumerable links to other world events such as the crisis of the Spanish colonialism, the emergence of the United States as a world power, the rapid developments in science and technology, the universal increase in population, and the new systems of communications.

CHANGES IN THE SUGAR INDUSTRY

Technical Changes

An overview of the process allows us to point out that, in the first place, from a technical point of view, Caribbean sugar-producing methods changed completely in the last thirty years of the nineteenth century. A series of radical innovations sprung up at every stage of the sugar-making process, causing the old manual machines (run by untrained workers) to be junked and replaced by highly sophisticated machinery that required skilled operators and efficient technical supervision.

The installing of this new machinery required an extremely large economic investment and the scrapping of the existing production lines and even of most of the buildings constructed under the previous system. Consequently, the new enterprise cannot be considered an old mill that had been modernized (as was the case with the introduction of the first steam engines into the sugar mills); rather, the old sugar mill was demolished, and in its place—or elsewhere—new buildings were erected to house new machinery run by new types of workers. The only holdovers of the old sugar mill complex were, in general, certain structures for social use, the communications infrastructure, and the cane fields, which in any case supplied only a small part of the new production center's needs: obviously, to be profitable, the new industrial plant had to process much greater quantities of cane than the old sugar mill.

This was the case when the new industrial plantation (the central or centralized factory, as it came to be known at the end of the nineteenth century) was set up in the zone previously occupied by one or more *ingenios*, the old sugar mills. One other solution, also quite typical, was for the organizers of the new central to seek out fertile new low-priced lands.

This change is both quantitative and qualitative. From the point of view of quantity, the old central differed from the old *ingenio* both in grinding capacity and a higher rate of extraction of sugar from the cane that it ground. For example, the so-called modern mechanized sugar mills of 1860 ground, on an average, the cane from 30 to 35 *caballerías* of land (roughly 400 to 500 hectares or about 1,000 to 1,250 acres); the central of 1890 could handle the production of 100 to 120 *caballerías* and those that could grind the cane from up to 150 or 200 *caballerías* were not uncommon. But production increased at an even greater rate than milling capacity because the new factories could extract almost twice the amount of sugar from the same amount of cane as the old mill.

This increase in production capacity accelerated the process of consolidation. In 1860 there were 1,318 sugar mills in Cuba producing some 515,000 metric tons of sugar; by 1895 the number had decreased to 250 while production was up to almost 1 million tons. In Puerto Rico, where a similar process began somewhat later, there were 550 mills in 1870 producing about 100,000 tons, the highest figure achieved there in the nineteenth century; by 1910, fifteen centrales were producing 233,000 tons.

This consolidation affected landowning practices from a legal standpoint and brought about the emergence of the sugar latifundia in Cuba and Puerto Rico; socially, the consolidation process undermined the old class of slaveowning planters, who were replaced to a great extent by a new type of industrial entrepreneur. In Cuba, by 1895 only 17 percent of the owners of centrales came from the old plantationowning families.

This industrial revolution in the sugar industry also made it necessary to transform labor relations over the next thirty years, having finally triggered the crisis of the slave system on which the old *ingenio* had been based. But the industrial revolution of the Caribbean was not accompanied by a complementary agricultural revolution. On the contrary, the agricultural side of the sugar industry (planting, cultivation, and harvesting) retained its traditional backwardness, which had originated in slaveowning cultural patterns, though under a new political climate, for by 1873 (in Puerto Rico) and 1881 (in Cuba) slavery had been abolished.

Thus a technological gap arose between the industrial sector and its agricultural base. In contrast to the modernity of the central, the agricultural sector retained its obsolete ways: within a few years the law of diminishing returns (which applies where, as in this case, no efforts were made to improve crop yields by modern methods of cultivation) made its appearance, marked by the trend toward smaller cane yields.

The first response to this situation, aggravated by other social and legal factors, was to create an administrative separation between the manufacture of sugar (the industrial sector) and the supply of raw material, cane (the agricultural sector). The relationship between these two sectors was to be a permanent source of conflict from the end of the nineteenth century. The old Creole sugar oligarchy, the sugarocracy of Cuba and Puerto Rico, was for the most part forced out of the manufacturing side of the industry, but in many cases stayed on as owners of cane plantations.

As a result of the industrialization process, the productivity of the industrial worker in the central rose steeply; but the productivity of the agricultural worker, especially that of the cane cutter, remained the same, for, as mentioned, the methods of cultivation and harvesting had not evolved. In order to take advantage of the enormous capacities of the new industrial installations, the *zafras*, or cane harvests, became bigger and bigger but were carried out in shorter periods, generally starting in January and ending in April.

This, in turn, created two problems of far-reaching magnitude: one with labor, the other with the amortization and the optimal utilization of the expensive industrial equipment. With respect to labor, the amount of cane required by the modern industry made it necessary to employ hundreds of thousands of agricultural workers (cane cutters) simultaneously in Cuba, Puerto Rico, and Santo Domingo for a period of three to four months of the year. Thus there arose, in all its tragic dimensions, the problem of seasonal employment during four months of the year, which for the majority of the laborers meant seasonal unemployment for eight months of the year. This situation had not occurred previously because with unskilled slave labor (which in any case had to be supported all year round), rudimentary manufacturing equipment, small daily millings, and long harvest seasons, there was almost always work for all hands. But the modern plantation required, for its optimal running, the existence of an army of unemployed workers, ideally located off the *ingenio* grounds but subjected to economic pressure that forced them to sell their services cheaply and with a minimum of social benefits, as cane cutters. These workers made up a migratory mass, and their migration could be either internal (from one part of the country to another) or external (from one country to another). A mixture of both kinds became the normal pattern.

The other problem created by the installation of modern industrial equipment was the need to find additional sources of income, not necessarily connected with the sugar industry, that would help to amortize the enormous economic investment. Certain double-purpose equipment (railways, power plants, foundries, etc.), as well as some specific services, became "independent" enterprises, with autonomous economic existence. Thus in typical centrales the cane-hauling railway also offered passenger services; the power plant provided electricity for the centrales facilities as well as for the nearby settlements that would pay for it; the foundry made items ranging from park benches to manhole covers for the municipality— and all at high prices because the central enjoyed a monopoly of these services in its region, besides decisive economic and political influence. The typical Cuban central of the nineties controlled the general store where laborers bought, the hotels, house, and barracks, either permanent or temporary, the barbershop, the butcher, the drugstore, and sometimes even the gaming house and the brothel.

Partly for its own financial benefit and partly for increased control on all the surrounding region, the centrales issued their own coinage, in the form of tokens, as legal tender. By this system of private coinage, Cuba, Puerto Rico, and the Dominican Republic reproduced, under conditions of colonialism and underdevelopment, one of the most typical aspects of the English Industrial Revolution. There were two ways in which the sugar token was employed. One was for the central to pay its workers in tokens. These tokens were legal tender in all the shops and facilities around the mill and could be redeemed there, though at a discount (often this was the result of a "secret" agreement between the management of the mill and the owner or manager of the store), which was the equivalent of a wage reduction. The other system was for the central to pay wages monthly in official currency; but since workers had to pay for their daily needs from their first day on the job, the storeowner would advance them small loans in tokens that could be spent only in his store or in the establishments of other members of the group. The storeowner would notify the management of the central of the advances made to each worker, and the totals would be automatically docked from his wages at the end of the month. In cases of illness or layoff, the mill would immediately notify the shopowners to withhold credit. Payrolls for Cuban and Puerto Rican mills show that at the end of the month many workers received only 10 percent of their wages in cash, the balance having been advanced.

In 1892, the Santa Lucía sugar mill in Gibara, Cuba, ran as subsidiaries five general stores, seven grocery stores, one shoe shop, one distillery, three barbershops, one drugstore, nine bars, one school, one confectioner's, two eating houses, three blacksmiths, three bakers, three clothing stores, two tailor shops, and one leather goods or saddlery. All of these accepted payment in the nickel tokens issued by the central. And what made this case even more unusual was that the official paper currency issued by the Bank of Spain was not accepted by these establishments; it had to be exchanged for Santa Lucía company tokens—at more than 10 percent off face value.

Within this group of transformations, there was one further and extremely important change that has been little noticed: the end product, the sugar produced by the new-style industry, was as different from the previous product as the central was different from the old slave-run *ingenio*. Indeed, it is enough to glance at any market report of the 1860s, in any market or colonial products to see that they do not give the prices for *sugar* (in the singular) but for *sugars* (in the plural). The Colleges of Brokers of Havana and Puerto Rico (up to the sixties, the Havana market played a key role in fixing world sugar prices) daily quoted prices for fourteen different types of sugar. And the Dutch Standard (Tipo Holandes in Spanish-speaking countries), which was accepted worldwide as the most suitable set of standards for trading in sugar, listed twenty-one different grades, based on color, where grade 1 was practically muscovado and 21 was powdered white sugar.

This plethora of kinds of sugar was the logical consequence of sugar's being manufactured with primitive equipment, set up in different ways in hundreds of small factories throughout the Caribbean: mills in which the quality of sugar depended on natural factors (the degree of ripeness of the cane), on the purity of the cane juice obtained by manual operations, on the intensity of the fire that heated the boilers (a fire fed by slaves who might throw more wood or less wood on), and, in the final event, on the skill of a maestro (generally illiterate) who was guided only by his senses (smell, taste, touch, hearing), by his long experience, and by orally transmitted tradition.

On the other hand, the industrial processes of the sugar mills of the nineties were standard, supervised by technically trained professionals, who were aided by internationally recognized analytical methods carried out on modern laboratory equipment. Thanks to these controls, by the end of the century all the Caribbean mills were producing centrifugal sugar Pol 95 degrees. In the first few years of this century a sugar purity of Pol 95 degrees became the standard.

The different types of sugar produced in the preindustrial stage required at least three types of packing: the box, the hogshead, and the bag. This last was little-used in the sixties (only 4 percent of total New York market sales), but by 1890 the situation had changed completely, with more than 95 percent of U.S. sugar imports in bags. By the beginning of the twentieth century the box and the *bocoy* (the hogshead) were virtually museum pieces.

One type of sugar, one type of packing: these factors influenced the transformation of the sugar trade. The Pol 95 degrees sugar of the new industrial period, as we have seen, was a standardized product, whose source (cane or beet) or region of origin (Cuba, Puerto Rico, Java, Australia, Mauritius, Brazil, or whatever place in the sugar-producing world) was impossible to determine. It was also a long-lasting product, that packed in bags could be stacked and stored cheaply. In contrast, the muscovadoes of the sixties differed widely in quality and spoiled easily; the hogsheads in which they were shipped could be stacked only three high without those on the bottom bursting. There were other essential differences: the hogshead was expensive, the bag was cheap; the hogshead was heavy (10 to 14 percent of the weight of the sugar it contained), the bag light (less than 1 percent); the hogshead was hard to handle and raised shipping costs enormously, the bag was easy to handle.

Commercial Changes

All these factors brought about a new commercial practice that had hitherto been little observed: the storing of large surpluses from successive sugar crops. As the new-type centrifugal sugar came more and more to be packed in bags, it became feasible to store it indefinitely. This was the beginning of a new dimension of the problem of initial stocks as a factor affecting sugar prices. Sugar traders had always taken initial stocks into account in fixing their prices, so it was not a new phenomenon: what changed was its magnitude. Before 1860, stocks on hand rarely were as much as 10 percent of the estimated annual consumption; by the nineties it was common for them to run over 50 percent of estimated consumption, and the trend was constantly upward. The bigger the stocks sugar importers had in their warehouses, the more pressure they could bring to bear on the producers to lower their prices.

All these new conditions (uniform product, packing in bags, worldwide standards, large on-hand stocks) inevitably led to what can be called the revolution of the sugar trade. This commercial revolution was in part the result of the factors already detailed, but it was also caused by other features of the world's economy in the last third of the century. There were several significant dates in the sixties and seventies. For example, historians point to 1871 as the year in which the tonnage carried by sailing ships, subject to the whims of the winds, was first surpassed by that shipped in steamers—fast, punctual, and with low freight rates. A steamer could carry five times the cargo that a sailing ship of the same displacement could. In addition, the opening of the Suez Canal had eliminated sailing ships from the regular Europe–Far East runs. In general, freight rates between America and Europe fell, on the average, 25 percent between 1860 and 1880, while those between Europe and the eastern sugar colonies (India, Java, Mauritius, Philippines) fell 63 percent. As a result, sugar could finally breach the wall that high freight rates had built around the colonies, thereby limiting their development. At the same time, sugar from Hawaii began to reach California.

So far, these new factors affected those countries that produced cane sugar. But simultaneously the last decades of the century saw a tremendous boom in beet sugar. In 1860 the 352,000 tons of beet sugar produced made up 20 percent of total world sugar production. By 1890, however, beet sugar production was up to 3.7 million tons, for a total of 59 percent of the world's production. From being a net importer of sugar, Europe became an exporter. And logically what had resulted was not by any means "fair competition": an immensely intricate protectionist system, complemented by every sort of subsidy and direct aid, brought beet sugar prices below any possible competition and drove Cuban, Puerto Rican, and Dominican sugar off the European markets.

The three Spanish-speaking countries (of which two were still Spanish colonies) had only one customer left for their sugar, the United States. Java increased its sugar production thanks to the protected Dutch market; India and Mauritius benefited, to a certain degree, from English protectionism, as did Reunion (formerly Bourbon Island) from French policy. Cuba and Puerto Rico (and the Philippines), on the other hand, never had a protected market: of all the colonial countries of Europe, Spain had the lowest sugar consumption per capita, and, besides, its poor commercial and maritime development did not allow it to become a re-exporter of its colonies' raw materials. Santo Domingo's sugar was also in the hands of its almost exclusive customer, the United States.

By 1890 the commercial sugar world had required the same characteristics it was to keep until 1960. On one hand were the beet sugar-producing countries, highly developed and defended by protectionist barriers. On the other were the colonial countries that produced cane sugar (except Cuba, Puerto Rico, and the Philippines) with the protected markets offered by their respective mother countries (Hawaii, at this time a colony, must be included in this group). The difference between total European sugar consumption and the supply of local beet sugar plus the cane sugar from protected colonies made up the prize that Cuba, Puerto Rico, Santo Domingo, and Brazil, principally, competed for. This minimal breach in the protectionist barrier—irregular, unstable, and residual—was to receive, in the twentieth century, the imposing name of *free market*.

As may be seen, then, at the end of the nineteenth century the European market for sugar imports was characterized by its lack of elasticity: only to a very limited degree (the "free" or residual market) can we speak of free competition or of the interplay of supply and demand. The foregoing, obviously, refers to the European market. At that time the other great importer was the United States, which possessed characteristics of a free market in that its local producers, benefiting from protectionism, supplied a minimal percentage of the country's needs. Cuba was its principal supplier: in the 1860s Cuban sugar exports to the United States covered more than 60 percent of that country's consumption and the share was a rising one. The balance was supplied mainly by Puerto Rico and Brazil and to a lesser degree by Santo Domingo.

This overall picture shows a key fact: the European beet sugar producers were industrial powers (independently of sugar), countries with solid economies, a high degree of culture, and extraordinary political development. They thus met all the conditions necessary for being able to establish effective protectionist policies and, further, to set up a system of subsidies, the Sugar Bounties, that permitted beet sugar to compete all the more advantageously with cane sugar. For example, French and German raws drove sugar from Cuba, Puerto Rico, Santo Domingo, and Brazil off the British domestic market. In the eighties French refined sugar was selling in London at 15 percent under its cost of production.

Cuba, Puerto Rico, and Santo Domingo were colonial countries (even though Santo Domingo had become an independent country in the second half of the century, from an economic point of view it must be considered a colony), poor, tied to a single major crop and a single major export to a single major market, and completely lacked the means of economic self-defense. Nor did they have the remotest chance of forming a producers' pool to safeguard the prices of their raw materials. It was not until far into the twentieth century that the developing sugar-producing countries were able to bring about the holding of the first international sugar conference, which would set forth their points of view.

Since the cane sugar–producing countries were virtually defenseless, the sugar trade was rapidly dominated by the great international trade interests that drove out even the local traders: these became simple intermediaries of the great international firms. There was a corresponding shift in the location of the price-setting markets: in 1884 the FOB Hamburg price played a more decisive part in commercial decisions than the FOB Havana quotations. Another important development, moreover, marked the coming of a new age to the sugar trade.

Until the sixties sugar prices were fixed in the market. But until that time the concept of the *market* was a strictly physical one: it referred to the geographical, urban region where warehouses were located and where the traders carried out their operations. In London it was Mincing Lane; in New York, lower Wall Street; in Le Havre, the great square where the Exchange Building stands today; in Havana, the dock area near the College of Brokers, where the principal trading firms—Drake and Brothers, Sama and Company, Ajuria and Brothers, and others—were located. What was meant by market prices were the highs and lows of the day's most important sales, that is, the maximum and minimum spot prices paid for sugar for immediate (fast or prompt) delivery. Payment for purchases was generally made on delivery (although it was also customary to ship sugar on consignment to European or U.S. markets to be sold through agents there, again for immediate delivery).

In this world of commerce, physical and tangible, the parameters to be fixed were equally objective and concrete, requiring the trader's personal attention in the solution of specific problems rather than the theoretical analysis of market conditions and trends. The trader's calculations were done with elementary arithmetic—thus the figure of the rich but illiterate sugar merchant. Just as the old slave-operated sugar factories were swept away by the modern industry, this type of trading (and consequently this type of trader) would be replaced by new firms, using new methods, in the last thirty years of the nineteenth century. There was a simple physical reality: the old trading organizations could no longer cope with the multiple factors that went into the making of a sugar sales agreement, or dealing with futures, on the exchanges of New York, Paris, London, or Hamburg.

In brief, then, the modern sugar industry of the late nineteenth century—an intricate economic complex with an enormous volume of production that had to meet international standards of quality—came into being in a world that since the sixties was being constantly shaken by new developments: the rise of monopolistic world capitalism, the ever-increasing speed of transport, and the radical techniques of handling information.

The application of mathematics to business (especially sampling surveys, the concept of indexes, the improvement of economic statistics); modern data processing (the decimal classification system, other coding and retrieval systems, punched cards); new methods of transmitting information (the telegraph, telegraphic codes, the telephone, the Atlantic cable, the stock ticker); the concept of marketing; new methods for evaluating the efficacy of management and for manipulating public opinion; the use of sociological and anthropological studies to help the incipient international trusts achieve economic domination—all of this can be found in the large-scale sugar speculation of the last years of the nineteenth century. In that sense, the sugar trade led the field in international trade.

For example, the German firm of F. O. Licht, founded in 1861, was the first firm of sugar brokers to use successfully, and on a large scale, sampling to predict world sugar production. Licht's figures, published in the famous "Monthly Report of Sugar" from 1868 on, were a fundamental tool of the big sugar speculators. C. Czarnikow Ltd., of London, did similar work to Licht but concentrated on the Caribbean. In 1897 this firm opened in New York a branch office that was to play a decisive role in the sugar trade of Cuba, Puerto Rico, and Santo Domingo: merging with the New York–based Cuban broker Manuel Rionda in 1909 as the Czarnikow-Rionda Company, within a few years it had so dominated the market that it could act as sole broker for the Cuban crops of the war years (1914–18) and for some 80 percent of both Puerto Rican and Dominican crops of the same period.

These and similar firms functioned simultaneously as market researchers, trade publishers, and brokers and acted as agents for certain powerful sugar interests, although this last was done more or less discretely: for example, Willet and Hallem (later Willet and Gray Inc.) acted for the American Sugar Refining Company, at one time one of the world's largest trusts.

In the last thirty years of the nineteenth century, the world sugar market fell into the hands of a small group of refiners and bankers, who used the most up-to-date big business methods to control the producers of raw sugar and eliminate the old traders. In this struggle the key strategy was to create a price-fixing mechanism that while appearing to observe the rules of supply and demand, would allow them to take over the market. The commodity exchanges played a fundamental role, opening a new era in the trade of colonial products. For the West Indies, especially Cuba, Puerto Rico, and Santo Domingo, the London Sugar Exchange and the New York Produce Exchange (which later became the famous New York Coffee and Sugar Exchange) were especially significant.

These exchanges, in theory at least, were of ancient origin: some scholars claimed that they were the direct descendants of the medieval bourses. But whatever the kinship, the similarity was only skin-deep. Commodity exchanges, before this commercial revolution, had been organizations made up jointly of buyers and sellers, a kind of organized market where the forces of supply and demand would meet to carry out commercial transaction. But the new exchanges were marked by an essential difference: here the products were not sold directly; the transactions carried out were exclusively speculative. Briefly stated, the commodity operations consisted of signing sales contracts in which one party undertook to supply a certain amount of sugar on a certain date: that is, a sale was made at the prices of the day for future delivery. When the date of delivery arrived, no sugar was delivered. The price of the sugar involved was calculated on the basis of the prices in effect on the delivery date, and the difference between the two prices was paid by one party to the other, in cash, less a commission paid to the exchange for its services. As there were many such operations daily, the exchange provided the means for setting the transaction: that is, it acted as a clearinghouse. Only in less than 1 percent of the deals did any sugar actually change hands. Thus the exchange did not replace the real market in which the actual sugar was bought and sold: it simply dominated it, imposing prices and terms. It is clear why in the nineties London's authoritative *Economist* described the London Sugar Exchange as "Monte Carlo in Mincing Lane."

As stated, however, the exchanges were not only places where one could gamble in commodity prices but also the brain children of economically dominant groups, whose purpose was to consolidate and broaden their control of the market. Appearing before a U.S. Senate hearing that was investigating a great sugar antitrust scandal, Theodore Havemeyer, president of the American Sugar Refining Company, stated that he used the stock exchange to bribe government officials and the commodities exchange to impose the prices that he wanted on the raw sugars of Cuba, Santo Domingo, and Puerto Rico.

As may be expected, in the last decade of the nineteenth century there was little regulation of the activities of the commodity exchanges. This allowed the carrying out, daily, of operations that could not even be attempted on today's exchanges. It must be remembered that data gathering and handling were new phenomena at the time and that there were no regulations affecting relations between different exchanges; it was possible to take advantage of the five-hour time difference between England and the East Coast to learn London's closing prices before the New York Exchange opened (thanks to the international telegraph, which was also poorly regulated and, furthermore, controlled by a group of speculators) and use this information advantageously. In general, in the United States (practically the only market for Cuban, Puerto Rican, and Dominican sugar at the time) sales of sugar futures lacked any regulatory legislation until the incredible speculating of 1920–21 led to the controversial Futures Trading Act of August 24, 1921, which was declared unconstitutional shortly afterward, though passed again, with minor changes, on September 21, 1922.

An interesting commentary on the changes at this time may be found in the following, first published in 1888: "In the good old days merchandise seldom arrived to a loss, except in time of severe panic: dealers, when they speculated at all, had visible evidence of the goods in warehouses and docks, and prudence, foresight and intelligence reaped their reward. The

introduction of steamships changed all this, and the telegraph completed
the revolution. . . ."[1]

CUBA AND PUERTO RICO: GROWTH OF PRODUCTION

Throughout the nineteenth century Cuba's sugar production increased
steadily, year by year, until 1875, when the slave plantations, which for
some time had been showing clear signs of crisis, started on the path to their
definite disintegration. Plotted on a graph, the fortunes of the sugar industry would show marked fluctuations, especially for the 1876–89 period,
reflecting the transition from the old *ingenio* to the modern central. By the
nineties, however, Cuba had regained its scepter as the world's largest sugar
producer, with five successive crops of over or just under a million tons, only
to fall into the great slump brought about by the War of Independence and
the subsequent U.S. occupation of the island.

Puerto Rico, on the contrary, maintained its upward economic trend only
until the fifties, when the series of ups and downs started that bore witness
to the instability of its slave-based production. In 1873 (before Cuba,
notwithstanding the fact that both islands were Spanish colonies) slavery
was abolished in Puerto Rico. This occurred during a period marked by
large harvests; but abolition in Puerto Rico was not accompanied by a
general process of modernization, and production fell sharply in the nineties.

Diverse factors contributed to the dissimilar development of these two
colonies of the same mother country and therefore with the same form of
government, countries with similar climate and in the same geographical
region. In the first place, historically they had different pasts. From the
sixteenth to the eighteenth centuries and into the first two decades of the
nineteenth, Cuba was a center of defense of the Spanish Empire, a main
maritime base (for both the navy and the merchant fleets), and an important productive region. Due to these factors, there developed on the island
an oligarchy that came to wield almost unique political power and from the
start accumulated large sums of capital derived from the service sector
(trade, shipbuilding for the Spanish state, building of forts, etc.). This
capital was subsequently invested in agroindustrial resources: tobacco, coffee, and sugar. The Cubans took advantage of the favorable conditions of
foreign trade, which had been upset by the 1791 revolution in Haiti (until
then the largest sugar producer in the world), emerging in the first third of
the nineteenth century as the possessor of an important sugar complex that
by 1829 was outproducing all the British West Indies together.

During the long process of formation of the Cuban oligarchy, its accumulated wealth and political experience also led to a cultural development of
the highest order. In addition, it was able to impose, uniquely, its own

terms on the home government: for example, the right to trade freely and directly with any foreign port and in ships of any nationality was a privilege won by the native oligarchy in 1792 (though officially recognized only from 1818 on).

Unlike the French or English West Indian colonies, in Cuba the sugar mills were the result of native investments, and with very few exceptions they were never the property of absentee owners. These owners, on the contrary, lived in Cuba and as a general rule at the beginning of the sugar harvest would move into their *ingenios* to watch over and manage their interests directly. Like modern entrepreneurs, they kept up to date regarding world technological developments and quite rapidly incorporated into the Cuban sugar complex those items of equipment and technical advances that could improve the capacity or the profitability of the industry.

As early as 1796 these native businessmen carried out the first experiments in adapting the steam engine to the cane mill; in 1837 they inaugurated the world's first railway devoted to hauling sugar and molasses from the mills to the ports (and the first railway of any kind in Latin America); in 1842 they started using vacuum evaporation for obtaining sugar; in 1844 (the same year as in the United States) they put up the first telegraph wires; in 1849 they installed sugar centrifuges. Cuba, a colonial possession, outpaced all the other Latin American countries in technological developments during the nineteenth century. Under the influence of legislative privileges and a dynamic class of entrepreneurs, and helped by extraordinarily favorable natural conditions (highly fertile lands, ideal weather conditions, large forestry resources, etc.), Cuba understandably was the world's largest sugar producer from 1829 to 1883. (Puerto Rico, which did not share these characteristics, was a much smaller producer.)

With the arrival of the sixties, however, both Cuban and Puerto Rican plantations began to show the first symptoms of a crisis. Put briefly, the crisis was a structural one, provoked by the steadily decreasing profitability of slave-based labor and by the difficulties resulting from the adoption of the new technologies.

Thus there came into being a state of permanent instability in which the principal problem faced by the producers—and therefore by officialdom—was to find a viable solution to the transition from slavery to wage-earning labor. The objective of the producers was to obtain from Spain a law of abolition that would include indemnification to allow them to recoup the capital that they had invested in slaves for reinvesting in modern equipment. They also hoped for related legislation that would provide a cheap and constant supply of free laborers (by *free* meaning semienslaved, obliged to work 12 hours a day for starvation wages and then laid off at the end of the harvest). In Cuba in 1863 over 95 percent of all sugar properties were mortgaged. Economic studies of the period showed that the 300 million pesos invested in the sugar industry bore 200 million pesos in mortgages. That is to say, two-thirds of the sugar industry was in the hands of merchants who in Cuba and Puerto Rico carried out the functions of bankers.

In the sixties this critical situation on the two islands abruptly entered a stage wherein a series of external events acted favorably, not by solving the inherent structural difficulties (for the slave plantation had exhausted all possibilities of internal reform) but by extending the system's lease on life. The U.S. Civil War and the Franco-Prussian War for years created their classical effect of upsetting market conditions, bringing about increased demand and very high prices. In Cuba, the Ten Years' War (1868–78), the first gigantic struggle for independence, also heightened the panic in the sugar trade and extended favorable market conditions. There were almost ten years of good harvests and high prices (even though most of these, in Cuba, occurred during the Ten Years' War), which allowed the Cuban sugar producers to pay off a great part of their mortgages, and their Puerto Rican counterparts to begin the mechanization of their sugar mills, which in general lagged behind Cuba in this respect. But this period was an exception to the trend, and once it had passed, the crisis made itself felt stronger than ever.

In Puerto Rico the process of disintegration of the old-style sugar plantations was extremely rapid. In 1870 there were 550 mills with a total production of 96,000 tons; by 1880 there were 325, producing 50,000 tons. Due to the existing backwardness, the crisis in production was matched by a crisis in quality, and many U.S. importers refused to buy the Puerto Rican raw sugars that were rejected by refiners. But there was a more significant reason for the island's crisis: the basic problem was that Puerto Rico lacked the necessary physical and economic infrastructure on which to base its industrialization. Without investment capital or an adequate railway system, without concerted action by the producers, without what might be called the vision of sugar, the few efforts made were individual and for the most part limited to the purchase of machines (which were not always logically installed) and to the building of a few centrales that until the end of the century alternated between good and bad years, and generally with heavy debts. To cite but one example, Central San Vicente, in Vega Baja, founded by Leonardo Igaravidez, Marquis of Cabo Caribe, by 1873 had taken over the larger surrounding plantations to ensure a supply of cane for his mill and was using the services of as many as several hundred cane cutters. But by 1879 his debts were over a million pesos (one peso = one dollar), an incredible amount for the time. In 1880, besides the San Vicente, there were four other centrales: the Luisa, San Francisco, Coloso, and Canovanas. All through the nineteenth century, from the economic point of view, their histories were the same.

Another key point that limited the development of Puerto Rico's sugar industry was the failure to find a successful means of transition from slavery to free labor. It is generally said that slavery was abolished in Puerto Rico in 1873, but this is true only in the legal sense. In fact, the institution of slavery had for a long time been in a state of collapse, and by the seventies the island lacked a labor force that could be subjected to the conditions that the plantation owners considered necessary. Unlike Cuba, in Puerto Rico there was no significant influx of migrant labor: only small numbers of coolies came in from China; efforts to set up a system of migrant workers from Spain (colorfully known at the time as *golondrinos*—swallows) met with no success; and the experiment of importing laborers from the British West Indies ended with a handful of groups that settled on offshore Vieques and on the sugar mills of Ponce, Humacao, Loiza, and Carolina.

The Cuban case was different. The great sugar boom took place in regions that had easy access to ports that by midcentury were already served by an excellent rail network. In general, this railway system, originally designed to carry hogsheads and boxes of sugar, turned out to be exceptionally useful for carrying cane from the fields to the mills. As far as the labor force was concerned, 1847 saw the beginning of an impressive immigration of coolies that probably reached as high as 150,000 by the end of the century. Another source of labor for Cuba's sugar mills had an unusual origin. The Spanish regular army being needed at home for the Carlist Wars, garrisons in Cuba were manned chiefly by *quintos*, or conscripts from Spain. A series of Cuban regulations—which were considered thoroughly illegal in Spain—gave the draftee the choice of serving out his full term as a soldier or of signing on as a hand in a sugar mill. The Ten Years' War being fought in Cuba at the time, many *quintos* not unnaturally became cane cutters. And in the eighties the owners of the new centrales were able to set up an efficient flow of migrant workers, who would arrive in Cuba at the beginning of January and leave at the end of April, from the Canary Islands and from the Spanish provinces of Galicia and Asturias, where there were extremely low standards of living, overpopulation, and high rates of unemployment.

Large sums of capital being available, many Spanish merchants and some families belonging to the old *criollo* (Cuban-born) oligarchy invested in centrales, especially from the eighties. From an economic point of view, Cuba's bloody Ten Years' War for independence turned out to be profitable for the modernized sugar industry. The war, which was fought mainly at the eastern end of the island, destroyed over a hundred old sugar mills, all of which were technologically backward and unproductive. The western part of the country where the new "giant" mills were located, and which produced 80 percent of Cuban sugar, did not suffer the ravages of the war.

Moreover, the *Banco Colonial* and the *Banco Español de la Isla de Cuba*, both controlled by the big Spanish merchants and some members of the Cuban oligarchy, had been charged with the financing of the war by the Spanish government, and this turned out to be an enormously profitable deal. Cuban-Spanish shipping and railway companies handled the transportation of military supplies. With a military colonial administration and under the psychological state-of-war pressures, legitimate business and shady deals of all types were made, and illicit enrichment became the norm. It is evident that at the end of the war these groups would have the necessary liquid capital to invest in the great "new" (i.e., radically modernized) sugar industry.

There were still other factors. With a sugar-oriented background and political experience, united by long-time common interests, the Cuban producers were well aware of the needs of the times and began to create a group of institutions to steer the new industry. In this way came into being the *Asociación de Hacendados de la Isla de Cuba* (Association of Mill Owners of the Island of Cuba) in 1879 for the purpose of coordinating the action of the principal brains (and capital) in the sugar world. From its beginnings, the association guided the activities of the producers, promoted projects for bringing in migrant workers, set up agricultural and industrial training schools, sponsored research, set up direct communications with the sugar exchanges in New York and London, published a widely read magazine, and formed a powerful lobby to defend the industry's interests. During this period arose many similar but local associations of *colonos* or cane planters.

Slavery was abolished in Cuba in 1881 (eight years later than in Puerto Rico). The concept of the abolition of slavery may suggest to many the picture of a mass of people, chattels subjected to their masters' every whim who suddenly, at a given point in time, find themselves free and in full possession of civil rights and responsibilities. Had this really been so, the abolition of slavery would have brought the total collapse of the sugar industry, for as late as 1877 (the last year for which reliable statistics on Cuban slavery are available) more than 70 percent of sugar production was based on slave labor. That this did not occur was due to the simple fact that the Law of Abolition was merely the de jure recognition of a situation characterized by the de facto disintegration of the slave system.

As a matter of fact, as early as the 1860s, and much more so in the seventies, the term *slavery* covered a wide range of means of exploiting labor. To begin with, there was the "pure" slave, physically forced to work on the sugar mill. Next to him was the hired slave. These slaves were subject to totally different conditions from the first type: physical punishments were banned, and they received part of the money paid for their hire. There was the *jornalero* or wage earner, a variant of the preceding, the slave who personally signed on at a sugar mill for a certain figure and who periodically handed part of his wages to his nominal owner as payment for the status of a semifreedman with the right to sell his services freely. There was the salaried slave (a very common feature of the time), whose wages were generally 50 to 70 percent of those of a freedman. Many slaves of all types enjoyed usufruct of small plots of land where they grew produce and raised animals, selling part to the *ingenio*. With them worked free blacks and whites, Chinese and contract laborers from the Yucatán (virtual slaves themselves), and, at times, convicts whom the state provided to the mills and who were paid a small wage. This anomalous situation in the labor supply acted as a break on capitalistic industrial development: the Law of Abolition was a means to the end of rationalizing the confused labor system efficiently.

Thus, the essence of the changes brought about in Cuban sugar production from the eighties were much more economic and social than technical. This does not mean that there were no significant improvements in equipment and processes—there were. But the complete renovation of the process of production was not a mere question of installing modern industrial equipment (which had begun in numerous Cuban sugar mills since the middle of the century); it also implied a renovation on the social, institutional level that could simply not be carried out by slaveowners. The more reactionary among these retained and exploited their slaves as long as they could: clinging to a past that was doomed to disappear, they held on to their slaves because they considered them part of their investment. Perhaps, for them, there was no alternative.

One other key point refers to the process of consolidation in Cuba. Industrialization, as we have seen, led to the early disappearance of the less efficient units. In Matanzas, Cuba's most important sugar region, there were 517 mills in 1877, producing some 350,000 tons; in 1895 the number of mills was down to 99, but production was almost doubled, at 600,000 tons.

During these last years of the nineteenth century, however, the concentration of production in fewer but larger mills did not find a counterpart in land ownership. Possibly the liens and other obligations of land ownership (especially the unredeemable and indivisible type of *censo* or living pledge) conspired against all efforts to bring about a consolidation of lands that would complement industrial concentration. This led to a broad discrepancy between agriculture and industry and in part explains the backwardness of cane planting in a period of industrial and technological advance.

From the point of view of direct ownership, either of land or of mills, there are a few signs of the presence of U.S. capital in the Cuban sugar industry of the nineteenth century. There were, of course, individual American millowners, just as there were French, Canadians, and Germans. The figures of the U.S. forces, which occupied the island in 1898, show that at the time 93.5 percent of the sugar mills belonged to Cuban and Spanish capital, and only the remaining 6.5 percent belonged to foreigners, including U.S. citizens. Moreover, many of the mills then listed as American really belonged to native Cubans and Spaniards who had only recently acquired U.S. citizenship.

The preceding, in the main, has referred to the behavior of those internal factors that shaped the development of the Cuban sugar industry during the last decades of the nineteenth century. But external factors also played a decisive role in the process. Thus, the statement about the lack of a U.S. presence in the sugar period refers exclusively to an internal situation. But from the point of view of international trade, the United States had long exercised hegemony. By the 1870s the Golden Age of Competition had disappeared from that country, at least where sugar was concerned: there existed an oligopolistic structure that, though legally established in 1887, had in fact come into being a decade before. The Sugar Act of 1871 was the first legislative tool of neocolonial domination forged in the United States, under pressure of the East Coast refiners, for the specific purpose of economically dominating Cuba, Puerto Rico, and Santo Domingo. By the eighties all three islands were selling virtually all their sugar to the United States, dealing with one sole firm in the market; their sugar was shipped in U.S. vessels; the sugar prices were fixed by the New York Produce Exchange; island planters and millowners got their market prices and production estimates from Willet and Gray, in news items reported by Associated Press and carried by Western Union. Without direct investment in lands or mills, the economic annexation of the three islands was underway: physical annexation by forcible means would come a few years later.

Cuban sugar development suffered an abrupt interruption. On February 24, 1895, in the middle of the harvest season, a new war of independence broke out, one that unlike the Ten Years' War was fought over the entire island. The magnitude of the war may be gathered from a few figures: Spain moved 400,000 soldiers, the largest army ever to cross the Atlantic until the days of World War II. This signified one Spanish soldier for each three inhabitants of the island. During the War of Independence (1895–98) thousands of hectares of cane fields were repeatedly set afire (cane is an easy crop to burn). An indeterminate number of sugar mills were also destroyed. Unfortunately, quantitative documentation is lacking that would allow an exact appreciation of war damages inflicted on the sugar industry. From the point of view of production, the last five years of the century are presented in table 1.1. Using these figures as their basis, traditional Cuban historiography, influenced by the interests of the sugar magnates, created the myth of the total destruction of the sugar industry during the war. As no censuses of sugar plantations were taken during the period, the theory of total ruin still prevails among modern historians.

But painstaking qualitative studies, which analyzed thousands of dispersed sources, would seem to prove that although an enormous drop in production was evident in cane production (the result of repeated burnings), the industrial sector, on the contrary, received much less damage. Of the fifty largest centrales to grind in 1895, only seven were destroyed during the war, four received some damage, and thirty-nine remained standing,

Table 1.1 Cuban Sugar Production, 1895–99 (unit: metric tons)

1895	983,265
1896	286,229
1897	271,505
1898	259,331
1899[a]	322,337

Source: Manuel Moreno Fraginals, *El ingenio* (Havana: Editorial de Ciencias Sociales, 1978), 3:38.

[a] First year of peace.

ready to start a new grinding season. It is probable that the effective overall loss suffered by the industry was 20 to 25 percent of installed producing capacity, as a maximum. To start up the industry anew required an extensive program of cane planting at a time when the traditional farm laborers had been widely dispersed (the war had completely changed the pattern of settlements in many areas). This explains the drop in production in the war and immediate postwar years and why, within three years after the war, sugar production reached almost a million tons, which was about the total installed capacity in 1895.

NOTES

This paper draws on work that will be published in more detail and with full documentation elsewhere. The translation was done by Arturo Ross.

1. "The London Produce Clearing House," *Financial News* (London), as reprinted in *The Sugar Cane* (Manchester), July 2, 1888, pp. 350ff.

Part Two
Cuba

Cuba, 1861

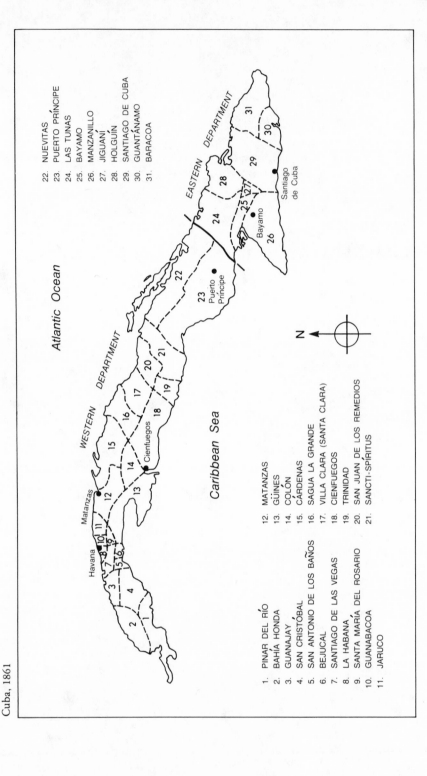

Atlantic Ocean

WESTERN DEPARTMENT

EASTERN DEPARTMENT

Caribbean Sea

N

Havana

Matanzas

Cienfuegos

Puerto Príncipe

Bayamo

Santiago de Cuba

1. PINAR DEL RÍO
2. BAHÍA HONDA
3. GUANAJAY
4. SAN CRISTÓBAL
5. SAN ANTONIO DE LOS BAÑOS
6. BEJUCAL
7. SANTIAGO DE LAS VEGAS
8. LA HABANA
9. SANTA MARÍA DEL ROSARIO
10. GUANABACOA
11. JARUCO

12. MATANZAS
13. GÜINES
14. COLÓN
15. CÁRDENAS
16. SAGUA LA GRANDE
17. VILLA CLARA (SANTA CLARA)
18. CIENFUEGOS
19. TRINIDAD
20. SAN JUAN DE LOS REMEDIOS
21. SANCTI-SPÍRITUS

22. NUEVITAS
23. PUERTO PRÍNCIPE
24. LAS TUNAS
25. BAYAMO
26. MANZANILLO
27. JIGUANÍ
28. HOLGUÍN
29. SANTIAGO DE CUBA
30. GUANTÁNAMO
31. BARACOA

2. Explaining Abolition: Contradiction, Adaptation, and Challenge in Cuban Slave Society, 1860–1886

Rebecca J. Scott

In the middle decades of the nineteenth century, as slavery was disappearing elsewhere in the New World, slave-based plantation production of sugar in Cuba reached remarkable heights of technological sophistication and output. In 1868 Cuba produced 720,250 metric tons of sugar, more than 40 percent of the cane sugar reaching the world market in that year.[1] Yet just as production reached these levels, the abolition of slavery in Cuba was initiated, beginning a process of slave emancipation that was to last nearly twenty years. This concurrence of events raises the questions: What was the relationship between slavery and the development of sugar production? Why did emancipation in Cuba take place when and as it did?

My analysis of these questions takes a comparative perspective in two respects. First, it is partly in implicit comparison to other New World slave societies that the very late abolition of slavery in Cuba—1886—poses a problem of explanation. Second, and more important, an explicitly comparative analysis of the course of emancipation in distinct regions *within* Cuba can help to identify the forces that advanced, and those that retarded, emancipation, and thus can contribute to a fuller interpretation of the causes and nature of abolition.

The predominant explanations generally put forward for Cuban abolition invoke large-scale forces and internal contradictions. One argument, enunciated most fully by Cuban historian Manuel Moreno Fraginals, goes roughly as follows. There was a contradiction between slave-based production and necessary technological innovation. For the sugar industry to advance, it had to break free of this outmoded organization of production. Indeed, as the industry advanced, slavery itself decayed. Formal abolition was thus merely the de jure recognition of a de facto disintegration of slavery.[2] A complementary argument has been made about the attitudes of Cuban slave holders. Eugene Genovese compares planters in the United States with those in Cuba and concludes that major Cuban planters had only an economic attachment to the institution of slavery and were quite prepared to abandon it in order to advance and modernize.[3]

An alternative hypothesis, advanced by Arthur Corwin in his study of Spain and Cuba, sees abolition as part of a worldwide political and diplomatic campaign resulting from a basic ideological shift away from bound labor. Cuban abolition, in this view, results from Spanish colonial policies designed to end the institution of slavery, thus protecting the colonies from outside interference while bringing Spain in line with what were seen as more advanced and civilized modes of labor organization.[4]

The underlying explanatory problem posed is a challenging one, not so much because it has historiographical implications but because it obliges one to look at large-scale explanations and then at small-scale patterns of events and ask how well the explanations actually account for the patterns observed. The point is not simply to juxtapose the particularities or uniqueness of a given case against the large-scale explanation and conclude that one must reject simplifying generalities. Rather, it is to hypothesize appropriate links between the different levels at which the historical explanation might operate and then to determine whether the observed patterns of historical reality generally match the patterns anticipated from the explanation. For example, if it is the case that "mechanization, the conversion of manufacture into large industry, unquestionably brings about the abolition of slavery,"[5] then technologically advanced areas might be expected to shift toward free labor first, with the most advanced estates giving up the use of slave labor. If, on the other hand, abolition were the result of colonial policy, then emancipation might be expected to occur more or less evenly across provinces, closely tied chronologically to key legal changes.

THE CHRONOLOGY AND GEOGRAPHY OF ABOLITION

Let us begin with the background to abolition and the key events that marked the ending of slavery. In 1860 the island of Cuba was the world's largest producer of cane sugar and contained some 1,400 sugar mills. The majority of Cuban mills operated by steam power, and a minority (located primarily in the central province of Matanzas) also used advanced processing equipment.[6] The slave population was approximately 370,000, and by far the largest single occupation of slaves was that of sugar worker.[7] Production increased rapidly in the decade of the sixties, growing from 428,800 metric tons in 1860 to 720,250 tons in 1868.[8]

Despite the apparent prosperity and productivity of the sugar industry, problems were rising to the surface. The slave trade, illegal since 1817 according to a treaty between Spain and England, had nonetheless flourished as a vigorous contraband. But after a large upswing in slave imports in the latter part of the 1850s, the 1860s saw a rapid and permanent decline as British pressure and changing United States policy finally blocked off the trade.[9] Since the Cuban slave population did not fully reproduce itself, the work force would necessarily decline in size unless other steps were taken. One response to the labor supply problem was to import indentured Chinese workers, but this practice was halted by a treaty between Spain and China in the 1870s. Another was to institute a policy of what was referred to as "good treatment," intended to encourage slave reproduction. This was to some extent successful, though not enough so as to maintain the size of the slave labor force.

The impact of these problems over the short term should not be exaggerated, however. Profits continued to be made in Cuban sugar production, and world prices for sugar remained relatively steady in the 1860s and early 1870s. Though planters had difficulties with agricultural credit, and resorted to extensive mortgaging, output continued to climb. Despite competition from beet sugar, Cuba's share of the world market in sugar remained about 25 percent.[10] In the minds of larger planters, moreover, there were strong forces supporting both slavery and colonialism. Slavery was a form of labor organization that permitted the exaction of an extraordinary amount of labor from the men, women, and children who toiled under it. Planters were unsure whether free persons would willingly labor under the grueling regime prevalent in the cane fields and sugar-boiling houses of Cuba. At the same time, to most planters in the sugar areas Spanish colonialism was a known quantity, an extractive presence but a protective one, a bulwark against social disruption, and the ultimate guarantor of peace on the plantations.

It was in this environment that the rebellion of 1868, later to be called the Ten Years' War, broke out. Small-scale planters in the eastern end of the island, provoked by heavy new taxes and by a financial crisis in 1867, rose in rebellion against Spanish domination. The insurrection, begun by relatively conservative men, some sympathetic to the possibility of annexation to the United States, rapidly became more radical as its social base expanded. Though the rebellion was not successful, three results significant for the future of slavery emerged from the conflict.[11]

First, in order to gain the support of slaves and free blacks, the insurgents declared the qualified freedom of slaves under their control, a measure that quickly went beyond the limited aims of its initiators and undermined the social relations of slavery throughout the war zone. Second, because the Spanish hoped to capture the apparent moral high ground and avoid appearing as retrograde defenders of slavery in the eyes of potential black recruits to the insurrection, as well as to potential international allies of the insurgents, Spain in 1870 adopted the Moret Law. This measure declared free all children born after 1868 and all slaves over the age of sixty and also promised some form of emancipation of the rest when Cuban deputies were seated in the Spanish parliament once the war was over. This was an extremely cautious form of gradual abolition and did not generally affect those of working age, but it did signal Spain's intention eventually to abolish the institution. Third, the 1878 peace treaty ending the Ten Years' War freed those slaves who had fought on either side. The Spanish government saw this policy as a necessary precondition for pacification—there would be little reason otherwise for slaves among the insurgents to lay down arms—but it was both controversial and disruptive.[12]

The following year, in 1879, the remaining slaves in the eastern provinces unexpectedly challenged their masters, refusing to work unless they were granted freedom *como los convenidos*—like those freed by the peace treaty. Eastern planters backed down, promising freedom in four years and wages during the interim. The Spanish government, already under pressure from abolitionists in Spain, backed down as well and declared both the end of slavery and the immediate transformation of slaves into "apprentices" called *patrocinados*.[13] This intermediate status, under which former slaves were obliged to work for their former masters, was intended to last until 1888. Attacked by Spanish abolitionists and by the handful of Cuban abolitionists, and undermined by the behavior of masters and apprentices themselves, the interim arrangement was instead ended prematurely in 1886, finishing the legal process of abolition.

This, in effect, is the political sequence of events that comprised the abolition of slavery in Cuba. If we turn the search for underlying causes and mechanisms to examining the phenomenon regionally and demographically, however, it becomes clear that the process of emancipation, the actual achievement of legal freedom by slaves, followed a pattern quite different from abolition.

The rate of decay of slavery varied widely from province to province (tables 2.1 and 2.2). Matanzas and Santa Clara, the major sugar provinces and the ones with most of the technically advanced mills, showed the greatest persistence of slavery into the early 1880s. Pinar del Río, in the west, where about one-third of the slaves in 1862 were living on tobacco farms and slightly over one-third on sugar plantations, showed a similar pattern. Havana, a province that contained the island's major urban area (about 25,000 slaves lived in the city of Havana in 1862) showed a substantially more rapid decline. By 1877 it held less than half of its 1862 slave population; by 1883, about one-fifth. The eastern provinces of Puerto Príncipe, a cattle area, and Santiago de Cuba, an area of some backward sugar mills and much small-scale farming and coffee growing, lost slave population very rapidly after 1867. These were the two provinces most involved in the Ten Years' War, which led to the destruction, both direct and indirect, of many plantations. Some had to cease operation for want of

Table 2.1 Slave and *Patrocinado* Population by Province, 1862–86

Province	1862	1867	1871	1877	1883	1885	1886
Pinar del Río	46,027	44,879	36,031	29,129	13,885	8,110	3,937
Havana	86,241	84,769	63,312	41,716	18,427	10,419	5,693
Matanzas	98,496	102,661	87,858	70,849	38,620	19,997	9,264
Santa Clara	72,116	68,680	56,535	42,049	23,260	12,987	5,648
Puerto Príncipe	14,807	14,889	7,167	2,290	246	153	101
Santiago de Cuba	50,863	47,410	36,717	13,061	5,128	1,715	738
Total	368,550	363,288	287,620	199,094	99,566	53,381	25,381

Source: See appendix to chapter 2.

labor when their slaves fled; others were burned, which often resulted in de facto freedom for the slaves.

This pattern reveals that the course of emancipation was by no means uniform across the island, suggesting that the pace of achievement of freedom was determined by factors other than Spanish colonial policy. Moreover, the result of the unequal rates of emancipation was to concentrate slavery increasingly in the more technologically advanced sugar zones. In 1862 Matanzas and Santa Clara had 46 percent of Cuba's slave population; by 1883 they had 62 percent of the *patrocinados*. The freeing of slaves thus cannot be attributed solely to the requirements of the advanced sugar plantations, either, for as emancipation proceeded these plantations held proportionately more, not fewer, of Cuba's slaves.[14]

The chronology of the process is also significant. During the 1860s and 1870s, whatever the "contradictions" facing the sugar industry, the major sugar areas were holding on to their slaves. In Matanzas in 1862 the slave population was around 98,500. About 20 percent of those slaves would have been under the age of ten or over the age of sixty, leaving approximately 78,800 between those ages.[15] In 1877 all slaves were by definition between the ages of nine and fifty-nine, as a result of the Moret Law, but about 70,850 slaves remained in Matanzas. The slave population of working age had indeed fallen in the intervening fifteen years but only about 10

Table 2.2 Slave and *Patrocinado* Population Retained, Percentage by Province, 1862–86 (1862 = 100)

Province	1862	1867	1871	1877	1883	1885	1886
Pinar del Río	100	98	78	63	30	18	9
Havana	100	98	73	48	21	12	7
Matanzas	100	104	89	72	39	20	9
Santa Clara	100	95	78	58	32	18	8
Puerto Príncipe	100	101	48	15	2	1	1
Santiago de Cuba	100	93	72	26	10	3	1
Total	100	99	78	54	27	14	7

Source: See appendix to chapter 2.

percent, an amount plausibly attributable to deaths and a shift in the age structure, partially counteracted by some in-migration. There is no support in these figures for the idea of large-scale abandonment of slaves or of slavery by the owners of plantations in Matanzas.

There was significant decline, however, in the areas of backward technology and political unrest—Puerto Príncipe and Santiago de Cuba—where slaves and insurgents fought directly for an end to slavery. Decline was also marked in the province containing a large city, Havana, where lawsuits and self-purchase by slaves were facilitated by access to courts and by money earned through hiring out. Official tabulations of appeals by slaves for *coartación* (partial self-purchase) and freedom show disproportionate representation for the city of Havana.[16]

The strong persistence of slavery through the 1870s in major sugar areas suggests that the notion of an irreconcilable conflict between the existence of slavery and the technological advancement of plantations needs revision. Sugar production expanded in the 1860s and 1870s as planters with capital bought vacuum pans and other modern processing apparatus, increasing the output of sugar per unit of land planted. Additional workers appeared on estates. (The Chinese population of Cuba increased 35 percent between 1862 and 1877, while the island's total population grew only slightly.) Some discharged Spanish soldiers and other Spanish immigrants also worked on the plantations. But the slave population, though diminishing, remained crucial. In enumerating the *dotaciones* (labor forces) of sugar estates, the 1877 agricultural census found 90,516 slaves working on the estates of their owners, 20,726 *alquilados y libres* (hired and free), and 14,597 Chinese. Slaves thus comprised at least 72 percent of the *dotaciones*, and quite probably more, since the category *alquilados y libres* included not only hired laborers but rented slaves and some young and elderly former slaves who had been freed by the Moret Law and were not full-time workers.[17]

The regional and chronological pattern of persistence of the slave population suggests that the strategy of large planters was to maintain continued control over their slaves, even while expanding their labor force in other ways—to adapt, rather than repudiate, slavery. Thus the contradictions of Cuban slavery (of which the failure of the slave population to maintain its numbers was the most urgent) did not have to impel abolition as such. An observer sympathetic to Cuban planters noted dryly in 1873: "The slave-owners in Cuba are convinced of the necessity of manumitting their slaves; but readily as they acknowledge the evils of the slave system, they are not persuaded of the wisdom of any measure by which it may be brought to an end." He described planters' advocacy of a gradual substitution of free labor for the declining slave population, rather than support for actual suppression of the institution of slavery.[18]

THE PLANTATION WORK FORCE

The most distinctive characteristic of the plantation work force in the mid-1870s, then, was its diversity. Plantation slaves, rented slaves, indentured Asians, and black, white, and mulatto wage workers all labored on the estates. Plantation employers did not face a homogeneous supply of labor but rather a segmented labor force, with different forms and quantities of payment due different types of worker. Wages were paid by the day, the task, the month, the trimester, or the year; the amount paid varied widely; workers sometimes did and sometimes did not receive maintenance; compensation occurred in coin, bills, credit, goods, or shares.[19]

This is the situation that has been interpreted as chaotic, symptomatic of the internal collapse of slavery.[20] But one must examine carefully the argument that the diversity of forms of labor in the 1870s was indicative of a disintegration of Cuban slavery in the face of unavoidable contradictions.

The argument has several parts. One claim is, in a sense, definitional: that the slave who received a bonus, cultivated a provision ground, or was rewarded for learning a skill was in some sense no longer a true slave and that these developments were symptomatic of the disintegration of slavery. Although such concessions certainly affected slaves' lives, and in some cases hastened self-purchase, they had appeared in many slave systems long before abolition and do not, by definition or otherwise, necessarily constitute disintegration. They were attempts to resolve a variety of problems within slavery, but they certainly did not need to lead to its demise.[21]

A second claim deals with the response of planters to the reduction in the slave trade. Aware that their supply of labor was being cut off, some Cuban planters had resolved to take better care of their existing slaves and to encourage reproduction. But, it has been argued, the policy of "good treatment" inevitably led to a decline in the productivity of the slave work force because the proportion of the very young and the very old increased, eventually making the enterprise unprofitable. Moreno Fraginals's study of plantation records shows convincingly that the proportion of slaves of working age did decline on some Cuban estates through the first half of the nineteenth century.[22] But even if one accepts the argument that maintaining a self-reproducing slave labor force would eventually have undermined profitability for Cuban planters (in a way that it apparently did not, for example, in the American South), the question remains: Given the very late cessation of the contraband slave trade to Cuba, how far had this process actually proceeded on Cuban plantations by the time of abolition?

Though plantation lists for an adequately representative range of estates in the 1870s have not survived, there is an extremely comprehensive source for one district: the manuscript returns of an 1875 slave count from Santa Isabel de las Lajas in the province of Santa Clara. Lajas was a prosperous area

in the jurisdiction of Cienfuegos and contained both old and new plantations. In 1861 the district had a slave population of 1,930 and contained
seventeen *ingenios* (plantations, including fields and mill). In 1875, when
the manuscript listing was drawn up, there were fifteen *ingenios* and a slave
population of 1,852.[23] The exceptional persistence of slavery in the region
was no doubt due in part to the presence of estate owners, such as Tomás
Terry and Agustín Goytisolo, who were both prosperous and tied to the
slave trade. The district is thus not typical of the island as a whole, but
analysis of its population reflects the labor situation facing large and small
planters in an important sugar area in the midseventies.

Of the slaves on *ingenios* in Lajas in 1875, 58 percent had been born in
Cuba and 42 percent in Africa; 61 percent were male and 39 percent
female. It was a population that plainly had relied recently and heavily on
imported slaves, probably during the boom in the contraband trade in the
1850s. The age structure of the plantation population is also quite striking,
considering the date—just five years before the legal abolition of slavery
and the establishment of apprenticeship. It was not an aged population:
while 28 percent were between the ages of thirty-one and forty, only 6
percent were between the ages of fifty-one and sixty, even though one
might have expected this latter group to include some slaves over age sixty
whose ages had been falsified by their masters to evade the Moret Law. Nor
was there a high proportion of young slave children. Those born since
September 1868 were technically free, and those between the ages of six
and ten constituted only 7.5 percent of the population. Even though those
born since 1868 were still the responsibility of the plantation, the total
burden was probably relatively small, for in some instances slave parents
maintained their *liberto* children directly or later reimbursed the master for
their maintenance. What is most significant is that the sixteen-to-forty age
group, of prime working age, constituted fully 63 percent of the plantation
slave population and 66 percent of the males (see table 2.3 and figure 2.1).
One can contrast this with the situation in the coffee-producing municipality of Vassouras in Brazil, where the age fifteen-to-forty sector of the plantation population fell from a high of 62 percent of the total labor force during
1830–49 to a low of 35 percent in the last eight years of slavery, thus
bringing about a true age-related crisis of labor supply.[24]

The plantation population of Lajas was, at least potentially, a quite productive one. The Moret Law had so streamlined it that 100 percent of the
legally enslaved population was between the ages of six and sixty, and
between those limits the population was further weighted toward those of
working age. The largest single groups consisted of males aged thirty-one
through forty and twenty-one through thirty. Lajas plantations were not
carrying a terrible burden of young and old slaves. Masters were not sustain-
ing the full cost of reproduction of their work force. They were still operat-

Table 2.3   Ages of Slaves on *Ingenios* in Santa Isabel de las Lajas, 1875

Ages	Males	Females	All Slaves	Percentage of Total
6–10[a]	49	51	100	7.5
11–15	56	61	117	8.8
16–20	51	58	109	8.2
21–25	108	69	177	13.3
26–30	120	64	184	13.8
31–35	132	72	204	15.3
36–40	124	46	170	12.8
41–45	69	44	113	8.5
46–50	45	24	69	5.2
51–55	31	15	46	3.5
56–60	29	10	39	2.9
61–65[a]	2	1	3	0.2
Total	816	515	1,331	100.0

Source: Archivo Nacional de Cuba, Misc. de Expedientes, leg. 3748, exp. B, Capitanía Pedánea de Santa Isabel de las Lajas, núm. 3, Padrón general de esclavos, 1875.

[a] All of those under age six or over age sixty should legally have been free under the Moret Law. Some of those age six were free.

Figure 2.1   Age Pyramid for Slaves on *Ingenios* in Santa Isabel de las Lajas, 1875

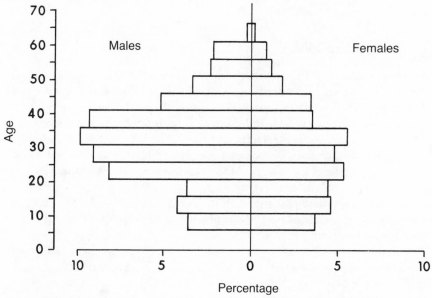

Source: See table 2.3.

ing with a carefully selected labor force built up primarily through purchase. The difficult future of slavery now that the trade had ended was apparent in the small number coming up through the ranks—there were less than half as many males aged eleven through twenty as aged twenty-one through thirty (see table 2.3). But this problem would not be expected to make itself fully felt until some years later.

Though they were also using some Chinese laborers, free workers, and rented slaves, sugar plantations in Lajas remained heavily committed to slavery. Indeed, if one can trust the ambiguous figures from the 1877 agricultural census, the large Lajas plantations relied even more heavily on slave labor than the small. The Santa Catalina, Caracas, San Agustín, Amalia, and San Isidro estates, each with a work force of over 100, had a total of 701 slaves, 161 *alquilados y libres* (which could include *libertos* and rented slaves as well as free workers), and 89 Chinese. The smaller plantations of Sacramento, Dos Hermanas, Adelaida, Santa Elena, Maguaraya, and Destino together had 235 slaves and 105 *alquilados y libres*.[25]

Large planters in Lajas were not yet facing an internal collapse of slavery. Though the demographic structure of their slave populations indicated trouble in the long run, suggesting that free laborers would have to be attracted sooner or later, this fact motivated only a theoretical acceptance of an eventual transition, not a willingness to give up control over the existing work force. It is therefore not surprising that the *hacendados* of Cienfuegos, like those elsewhere in the western part of the island, held meetings during the 1870s to oppose immediate abolition.[26]

SLAVERY AND TECHNOLOGY

A further element in the argument for the internal dissolution of slavery is the positing of an incompatibility between slave labor and the needs of technology. This is often stated as a contradiction between slave labor, which is seen as brute labor, and advanced machinery, which is thought to require the motivations characteristic of free labor.[27] This argument also fits the image of a labor force whose quality was steadily deteriorating, based on the concept of slaves as instruments of production whose productivity depended simply on physical strength and whose value therefore dropped sharply once they were past their prime. The argument is coherent but not necessarily empirically correct. One needs to ask how slaves actually behaved and how they were viewed by planters.

It is suggestive that an owner of 300 slaves in Cuba, in a pamphlet addressed to the Spanish colonial minister in 1868, estimated the average value of male slaves aged thirty-one to fifty as *higher* than that of slaves aged sixteen to thirty, remarking that in the older group were those with skills, such as machinists, carpenters, masons, blacksmiths, and *paileros* (those who worked with boiling pans), among others.[28] Corroboration of this portrait would require an analysis of actual sale prices to determine the effect of various factors on the market value of slaves. But the statement does suggest that a slave work force with an age structure similar to that in Lajas was not necessarily experiencing sharply declining productivity and that planters did not invariably regard slaves as mere brute labor.

A more important challenge to the incompatibility thesis is the direct evidence that slaves were used extensively in the large advanced mills. The *ingenio* España, for example, was one of the most advanced plantations in Cuba in the 1870s. Its work force in 1873 was composed of 530 slaves, 86 Asians, and just 19 whites. That is, the work force was more than 80 percent slave, and 97 percent unfree labor, if the Chinese were indentured, as is likely. The *ingenio* Álava, whose technological apparatus Moreno Fraginals has used to illustrate the industrial revolution on Cuban plantations, was operating in 1877 with 550 slaves and 71 Asians. It listed no free wage workers or rented slaves.[29] The Las Cañas plantation has been described as "Cuba's most modern mill in 1850," in which, up to 1880, new machinery was being added "in a continuous system of renovation." Its work force in 1873 numbered 450 slaves, 230 Asians, and 27 whites. Again, the number of free white workers was very small, and they held the same jobs that they had always held on Cuban plantations: administrator, *mayordomo*, machinist, and so forth. On Las Cañas, the Asians do seem to have been treated differently from slaves and were concentrated in the processing sector.[30]

These examples do not really test the claim that technological advancement encouraged a shift to free labor—for that, one would need reliable statistics on the work forces of a large sample of Cuban plantations and detailed data on the internal division of labor. But these cases do suggest that major technological advances did not require the extensive use of fully free labor. In fact, the only substantial concession to the supposed necessity of a shift to free labor made on some major Cuban plantations in the 1870s involved the employment of Chinese. This was a limited step, for although the structure of incentives and motivations for the indentured Chinese, working on eight-year contracts bought and sold by planters, was somewhat different from that of slaves, it was not that of free wage workers.[31]

One could go further and argue that technological innovation is, under certain circumstances, quite compatible with a labor force that for one reason or another lacks motivation or elements of internalized industrial labor discipline. One economist has suggested that "process-centered" industrial activities—of which sugar manufacture is a good example—which are often capital intensive, can be appropriate to a less socialized labor force because to some extent the machinery itself provides a pace and discipline to the work.[32] Although this hypothesis is not immediately adaptable to the circumstances of slavery, it does imply that the introduction of technology may cut both ways: advanced machinery can facilitate the labor and the pacing of labor of less experienced or less willing workers, even if at the same time it requires higher levels of skill and motivation for the performance of certain associated tasks.

Both slavery and indentured Asian labor did make labor costs in part a form of fixed capital, reducing the amount of capital immediately available from internal sources for investment in machinery. But the total available for further capital investment would depend on profitability and access to credit, which might in fact be facilitated by the purchase of slaves. Furthermore, individual planters often used rented slaves in order to mitigate the problem of fixed labor costs within the system of slavery. Rental permitted the shifting of the existing slave labor supply to areas of greatest profitability; it did not necessarily weaken slavery as an institution or loosen the bonds on slaves.[33]

Plantation records reveal the range of adaptations utilized on Cuban *ingenios* in the 1870s and convey a sense of the nature and tempo of change. The *ingenio* Angelita, for example, owned by J. A. Argudín and located in the jurisdiction of Cienfuegos, enumerated its work force several times between 1868 and 1877. On June 10, 1868, the plantation had 414 slaves; 20 "employees and workers of the estate," most of them white; and 35 *colonos*, in this case indentured Chinese laborers. By September 1868 the work force had increased with the addition of more Chinese workers, bringing their total to 74. In 1870 an epidemic of cholera hit, resulting in many deaths, and by September of that year the *dotación* consisted of 397 slaves and 58 Asians (see table 2.4).

Another document lists the Angelita work force in January 1877, and an accompanying inventory confirms the impression that it was a mechanized plantation, complete with steam-powered grinding apparatus and vacuum pans, centrifuges, and the older Jamaica trains for processing. By this date the number of slaves had fallen to 247, although there were also 37 *libertos* over age sixty and 29 children under age eight, clearly still part of the plantation population, who were not counted because of the Moret Law. The total comparable to the 1870 figure of 397 slaves would thus be 313, a drop of 84 in six years. The work force also now included 8 free blacks, all apparently former slaves of Argudín, and 6 rented slaves. There were the usual 20 or so white employees, but also about 20 *movilizados*, soldiers presumably stationed on the plantation or released for employment there. A new category, *partidario* (sharecropper) had appeared by 1877 and included 11 heads of family and numerous family members. Forty-five *colonos asiáticos* were employed at the time of the count, and at harvest time additional gangs of Asians were hired to cut cane (see table 2.4).

Despite the increase in the complexity and variety of the work force on Angelita by 1877, the importance of the nucleus of 247 slaves between the ages of nine and fifty-nine remains apparent. The sharecroppers, though included in the plantation population, seem primarily to have been en-

Table 2.4   Work Force on the *Ingenio* Angelita, June 1868 and January 1877

1868		1877	
	Employees		
Administrator	1	Administrator	1
Doctor	1	*Mayordomo*	1
Overseer	1	Accountant	1
Mayordomos	2	Overseer	1
Machinist	1	Nurse (male)	1
Cattle handlers	2	Machinist	1
Carpenters	3	Carpenter	1
Distiller	1	Sugarmaster	1
[Illegible]	2	*Maestro de tacho*	1
Tachero		Plowmen	2
(works the *tacho*, or boiling pan)	1	Cattle handler	1
Sugarmasters	2	Overseer of the *batey* (mill area)	1
Mason	1	Supervisor of *colonos*	1
Montero	1	Mason	1
Asian, job unspecified	1	Barrel makers	2
		Overseer of the *potrero*	1
		Montero	1
		Messenger	1
		Head of the volunteers	1
		Movilizados (soldiers)	23
Total employees:	20	Total employees:	44
	Slaves		
Males	212	Males	126
Females	202	Females	121
Total slaves:	414	Total slaves:	247
(all ages)		(excludes 29 children and 37 elderly)	
	Chinese Laborers		
Total Chinese:	35	Total Chinese:	45
	Others		
		Free blacks (jobs unspecified)	8
		Rented slaves (owned by	
		administrator)	6
		Sharecroppers	11
		(93 family members)	
Total:	469	Total:	361
		(454 including families)	

Sources: Archivo Nacional de Cuba, Misc. de Libros, núm. 11536, Libro Diario del Ingenio "Angelita" de la propiedad de Sr. J. A. Argudín, 1868–71, pp. 1–13; Archivo Nacional de Cuba, Misc. de Libros, núm. 10789, Libro Diario del Ingenio Angelita Argudín, 1877, pp. 2, 3, 17, 18.

gaged in supplying food to the plantation rather than working in cane, though the evidence is not unequivocal. The increase in the number of free workers suggests that they were making inroads into some areas previously dominated by slaves, but it seems unlikely that either the temporary *movilizados* or the sharecroppers were performing any of the more technical tasks. Nor does it seem likely that all of the Asians worked in the more mechanized sectors, since this too was a fluctuating population, often rented out from the *depósito de cimarrones*, and prone to flight. In short, it seems that at Angelita it was not the introduction of technology but the death of slaves—and the necessity of replacing them—that initially brought the increased use of free labor.

After 1877 the decline in forced labor at Angelita accelerated. Asians persisted in fleeing, and replacements were not always available. Slaves became more likely to purchase their freedom. Although in the late 1860s such purchases were infrequent (just one man and his daughter obtained their freedom between June 1868 and September 1870), by the late 1870s they had become more common. In February 1878 four women and two children freed themselves, apparently after having visited the *síndico* (protector of slaves) to have their prices set. In April, Secundina, a thirty-year-old Creole, paid 750 pesos for herself and another 187 pesos to free her *liberto* children. That same month the slave Gervasia went to Cienfuegos to have her price set at 700 pesos, and in August her mother, Jacoba Lucumí, age fifty, made a down payment of 500 pesos on that amount. As this was going on, the plantation began to increase the rewards given to slaves. At the beginning of the 1878 grinding season, tobacco, money, and bread were distributed.[34]

Reading through the daybook, one gets the sense that relations within the plantation were shifting as slaves, particularly women, found ways to buy their freedom and as the plantation increased the use of monetary incentives. Most of the money that slaves used for self-purchase probably came from their sales of pork and crops to the plantation, and such sales are frequently recorded. When the plantation accepted 700 pesos from a slave as payment for freedom, it was thus recouping some of what had been paid to that slave for goods produced, as well as recovering part of the investment in the slave. The master, unsurprisingly, might well come out ahead. But a circuit of money exchanges had been introduced—and not necessarily at the planter's initiative.

The records of other plantations in the 1870s show many of these same characteristics. Multiple forms of labor gathered around a slowly diminishing core of slave workers; "gratuities" were paid to slaves more frequently; rental of slaves and the contracting of Asians provided considerable flexibility. None of these adaptations, however, suggests a repudiation of slavery, only a search for supplementary forms of labor and some modifications of the slave regime. Nor do the moves toward wages and compensation appear to be correlated closely with work on machinery—they are as likely to be payment simply for Sunday work or as a general incentive at the beginning of the harvest. Indeed, the repudiation of forced labor in the 1870s comes largely not from planters but from the slaves and Chinese indentured laborers themselves, through self-purchase and through flight.[35]

As late as 1879 most sugar planters appear to have remained strongly attached to the control that slavery gave them over their work force, though they were increasingly obliged by political circumstances to contemplate some shifts in its form. The Spanish government, however, had by 1879 come under pressure from domestic abolitionists, from rebels in Cuba, and from slaves in the east who refused to work. An apparent solution was to abolish the name of slavery, while keeping much of its substance.[36]

THE *PATRONATO*

In February 1880 the Spanish parliament decreed the end of slavery and the beginning of apprenticeship, or *patronato*. All slaves were henceforth to be called *patrocinados* and remained obliged to work for their former masters until freed. Masters owed a stipend of one to three pesos monthly to their former slaves, and *patrocinados* could purchase their freedom for a specified and gradually diminishing amount. Limited rights were granted to *patrocinados*, such as the right to charge one's master with a violation of the regulations, with full freedom the reward if he were convicted. But masters also retained substantial prerogatives, including control over physical mobility, the setting of hours and conditions of labor, and, until 1883, the right to use corporal punishment. Beginning in 1885, one-quarter of the remaining *patrocinados* were to be freed each year, in descending order of age, under a complex system that was to conclude in 1888.

The previous discussion of the evolution of the nature and organization of labor in the 1870s suggests why planters might grudgingly accede to, though they did not initiate, such a gradualist solution. They wished to find substitutes for the diminishing slave work force, and nominal abolition might help attract new laborers, since European emigrants were believed to prefer nonslave societies. Both landowners and the government also wished if possible to defuse the emotional issue of abolition. At the same time, many planters sought to maintain the essentials of slavery and to keep their slaves on the plantation, which the *patronato*, in theory, would allow them to do.

The conservative nature of the law establishing the *patronato* meant that May 8, 1880, the date it went into effect, could come and go without an immediate impact on the plantations. Administrators shifted from paying irregular bonuses to paying stipends, increasing their need for cash but not severely disrupting the routine. Indeed, it appeared initially that a considerable degree of continuity was possible. For instance, while in the British

West Indies masters had often withdrawn traditional indulgences from
slaves when apprenticeship was established, on some Cuban plantations the
old rhythm of holidays and rewards was maintained. On the *ingenio* Nueva
Teresa, the New Year arrived just as the 1881–82 harvest was about to
begin. On December 30 an ox was slaughtered, and the *dotación*, which
included approximately 175 *patrocinados*, was given the day off. The following day, fresh meat, bread (a luxury), and salt were distributed, and
criollitos were baptized in the *casa de vivienda* (plantation house). The first
two days of January were also given as holidays; on the fourth and fifth the
workers began to cut and haul cane; and at six o'clock on the morning of
the sixth day the grinding began.[37]

Patronos may have felt it appropriate to observe these customs in order to
maintain their own sense of legitimacy or to encourage productivity among
the *patrocinados*. Since the government regulations were not being strictly
enforced, masters may also have been less seized by a spirit of vengeance
than their British West Indian counterparts. The usual rewards of the harvest could be maintained because the usual level of exploitation was being
maintained. During the harvest of 1880–81 on Nueva Teresa, Sunday rest
was ignored, and *patrocinados* received only one day of respite between
March 17 and April 15. At the end of May, the harvest ended, and a cow
was killed for the *dotación*, a calf for additional hired hands. Stipends for
the *patrocinados*, due weeks earlier, were finally paid. The withholding of
stipends seems clearly to have been a means for maintaining work discipline, not a problem of cash flow; the man who regularly brought the
money for stipends from Havana had arrived at the estate three weeks
before.[38]

The law of 1880 nonetheless changed the rules of the game, and after a
certain lag the impact began to be felt on plantations. By the 1882–83
harvest the administration on Nueva Teresa was becoming more scrupulous
about paying stipends on time. At the same time, *patrocinados* were beginning to obtain full freedom on their own by self-purchase. This was to have
a complicated effect on the economics of running a plantation. On the one
hand, working *patrocinados* who obtained their freedom would have to be
paid wages or replaced by hired hands. On the other, the purchase of
freedom of children, the aged, or the infirm could be a net financial gain to
the estate. In any event, such purchases subsidized the wage bill: on the
ingenio Nueva Teresa, deposits made for purchases of freedom covered
almost 70 percent of the amount paid in stipends during 1883–84, and
between 1882 and 1886 approximately eighty *patrocinados* and *libertos* on
the estate obtained full legal freedom through payment.[39]

On the *ingenio* Mapos in Sancti Spíritus, the number of working *patrocinados* initially fell only slightly. Early in 1882, however, a group of thirty-
five *patrocinados* fled the estate to present their grievances to the local Junta
de Patronato, the board established to oversee the enforcement of the 1880

Table 2.5 *Patrocinados* Legally Achieving Full Freedom, May 1881–May 1886, by Category and Year

Year (May to May)	Mutual Accord	Renunciation by Master	Indemnification by *Patrocinado*	Master's Failure to Fulfill Article 4[a]	Other Causes	By Article 8[b] (1885 and 1886 only)	Total[c]
1881–82	3,476	3,229	2,001	406	1,137	—	10,249
	(34)	(32)	(20)	(4)	(11)	—	(100)
1882–83	6,954	3,714	3,341	1,596	1,813	—	17,418
	(40)	(21)	(19)	(9)	(10)	—	(100)
1883–84	9,453	3,925	3,452	1,764	7,923	—	26,517
	(36)	(15)	(13)	(7)	(30)	—	(100)
1884–85	7,360	4,405	2,459	2,431	2,514	15,119	34,288
	(21)	(13)	(7)	(7)	(7)	(44)	(100)
1885–86	7,859	3,553	1,750	1,226	837	10,190	25,415
	(31)	(14)	(7)	(5)	(3)	(40)	(100)
Total	35,102	18,826	13,003	7,423	14,224	25,309	113,887
	(31)	(17)	(11)	(7)	(12)	(22)	(100)

Sources: Archivo Histórico Nacional, Madrid, Ultramar, leg. 4814, exp. 273 and exp. 289; ibid., leg. 4926, exp. 144; Manuel Villanova, *Estadística de la abolición de la esclavitud* (Havana, 1885).

[a] Article 4 of the 1880 law listed the obligations of the *patrono:* to maintain his *patrocinados,* clothe them, assist them when ill, pay the specified monthly stipend, educate minors, and feed, clothe, and assist in illness the children of his *patrocinados.*

[b] Article 8 called for one in four of the *patrocinados* of each master to be freed in 1885, and one in three in 1886, in descending order of age. In the event that several *patrocinados* were of the same age, a lottery was to be held.

[c] Some rows do not add to 100 percent because of rounding.

law. They returned to the plantation, but a year later the effect of the challenge appeared when the estate's *patrocinado* population fell abruptly by almost one-quarter, as more than sixty *patrocinados* were freed by order of the junta, some on the grounds of age, others through self-purchase. The success of these initiatives, combined with the ever-lengthening period during which *patrocinados* could be accumulating funds, led to a steady stream of self-purchases after the harvest of 1883. By August 1884, Mapos retained only 135 of its original 277 *patrocinados.*[40]

The acceleration of emancipation throughout the island in the 1880s, well before the gradual freeings by age began, is evident in the figures gathered by the Juntas de Patronato. In the first year 6,000 *patrocinados* obtained full freedom; in the second 10,000; in the third 17,000; in the fourth 27,000 (see table 2.5). Evidently many *patrocinados* learned to use the new situation to hasten their own emancipation. Some purchased their freedom; some brought charges against their masters; some found that they were unregistered and sued for freedom on those grounds. Even in rural Matanzas province more than 2,000 *patrocinados* successfully charged their

Table 2.6 *Patrocinados* Legally Achieving Full Freedom, May 1881–May 1886, Percentage by Province and Category

Terms of Freedom	Number Freed	Pinar del Río	Havana	Matanzas	Santa Clara	Puerto Príncipe	Santiago de Cuba
Mutual accord	35,102	9	10	43	32	0	6
Renunciation	18,826	15	36	19	19	1	10
Indemnification of services	13,003	16	16	27	24	0	17
Master's failure to fulfill Article 4	7,423	14	46	28	6	1	5
Other causes	14,224	13	21	31	23	1	11
Article 8 (1885 and 1886 only)	25,309	17	14	41	25	0	3
Total freed	113,887	13	20	34	25	1	8

Source: Same as table 2.5.
Note: Some rows do not add to 100 percent because of rounding.

masters with failure to fulfill the obligations of the 1880 law, and more than 3,000 others obtained their freedom through self-purchase between May 1881 and May 1886.[41]

Many masters tried to block such initiatives, through isolation, threats, or legal measures. The institution of the plantation store, for example, though a harbinger of controls that would be imposed on wage labor, helped for the moment to sustain the *patronato* system. In the 1880s local shopkeepers initiated a debate on the tax status of such stores, an occurrence interesting primarily for the attitudes it reveals among planters. Freely acknowledging that the main purpose of the stores was control, planters from several sugar areas made it clear that they wished to prevent their workers and particularly their *patrocinados* from setting foot off the plantation. They were not prepared to accept the physical mobility associated with fully free labor.[42]

Other masters, however, tried to come to some kind of agreement with *patrocinados* on the terms of freedom, which could include informal payment by the *patrocinado*, or an arrangement concerning future wages, resulting in emancipation by "mutual accord." Some masters actually renounced their rights over individual *patrocinados*, and a few of these were acclaimed in the liberal press for their benevolence. Such manumissions, however, declined in relative importance after 1881–82, and renunciation was generally most frequent not in the sugar areas of Matanzas or Santa Clara but in the province of Havana. Freedom in Santa Clara or Matanzas was more likely to come through "mutual accord," as masters exacted concessions in return (see tables 2.5 and 2.6).[43]

By 1883 the total number of *patrocinados* on the island had fallen to about 99,600 (half of the number of slaves six years earlier) even though the gradual freeings by age had yet to begin. In an 1884 debate within the Consejo de Administración in Havana, two councillors argued that the *patronato* had led to the worst of both worlds, providing neither the stimulus of corporal punishment nor the fear of dismissal. They urged that the system be ended, claiming that there was a labor surplus and that, if freed, *patrocinados* would work for their former masters for low wages. The majority of the councillors rejected the argument for abolition of the *patronato*, however, and clung to the compulsion that it provided.[44]

A look at the municipality of Lajas may suggest why. Lajas recorded 1,852 slaves in 1875 and 1,137 *patrocinados* in 1883.[45] Approximately a hundred slaves would probably have obtained their freedom in the interval on reaching age sixty; thus other losses through emancipation and death had been kept to only about one-third. For those in areas like Lajas, where the line had been held, extraeconomic control over this nucleus of the labor force was still worth defending.

Simply retaining legal control over *patrocinados* was not enough, however. On the *ingenio* Nueva Teresa, for example, which in 1884 still held 150 *patrocinados*, it was necessary to use new incentives tied to productivity. In February 1884, apparently for the first time, the *patrocinado* Evaristo was paid six pesos as first prize for the quantity of cane hauled, and others received amounts in decreasing size for second through fifth prize. In March prizes were given to the first ten *patrocinados*, and again in April prizes appeared.[46] By the 1884–85 harvest, the picture at Nueva Teresa had changed still further, and the mobilization of labor began strongly to foreshadow postabolition arrangements. About a dozen tenants brought cane and wood to the mill, drew supplies on credit, and in some cases hired laborers from the estate. Gangs of Chinese workers contracted to perform specific tasks, particularly in the *casa de calderas* (boiling house). Many *patrocinados* purchased their freedom, and some hired on as free workers at eighteen pesos monthly for women and twenty pesos for men, plus rations. The work force was increasingly seasonal, with Chinese contract laborers providing much of the flexibility, whether they wanted to or not. The harvest of 1885 ended on August 16, and on September 4 the *cuadrilla* (gang) of Chinese found themselves "expelled" by order of the administrator. Maintenance off season was no longer the planter's responsibility.[47]

By 1885, the year the gradual freeings by age were to begin, the *patronato* was already in a state of decay. Only 53,381 *patrocinados* remained in the island, about half of the number two years before, and many fewer than had been anticipated in the original plan. In 1883–84, 26,517 *patrocinados* had obtained their freedom, 36 percent through mutual accord, 15 percent through renunciation by the *patronato*, 13 percent through formal self-purchase, 7 percent through successfully charging their masters with violation of the laws, and 30 percent through other means, probably including proof of nonregistration. The process of emancipation had gained sufficient momentum that the interim institution could not possibly last. The financial crisis of 1884, brought on in part by a drop in sugar prices, may have further encouraged the abandonment of slavery, though renunciation still accounted for fewer than 15 percent of the freeings in the island between 1884 and 1886 (see table 2.5).

By the time of the harvest of 1885–86, the number of *patrocinados* on Nueva Teresa, for example, had fallen to fifty or sixty. The estate contracted out an increasing proportion of the cutting and hauling of cane, and paid by the cartload, while similarly contracting for wood. The contractors, generally white, took their pay in money and in sugar. Some of the estate's former slaves continued to be directly employed there at a monthly wage of seventeen to twenty pesos, but not as many as had received their freedom. A Chinese contractor provided workers to serve in the field and at the centrifuges, and they were paid both by weight of sugar processed and by the month (at forty pesos). Individual Chinese workers hired on at about thirty-five pesos and rations, as did gangs of wage workers of unspecified origin.[48]

On October 7, 1886, a royal decree, following a parliamentary resolution, abolished the *patronato*. When definitive abolition finally arrived, it merely confirmed an existing state of affairs. The number of *patrocinados* had fallen to about 25,000, and almost everyone, including the Planters' Association, was willing to see the *patronato* go.[49] The reality that the law ratified, however, had to a considerable extent been brought about in the immediately preceding years by the slaves and *patrocinados* themselves, both directly—through self-purchase, flight, and suits before the juntas— and indirectly—through the negotiation of agreements of mutual accord. Sheer abandonment of slavery by masters was not the main source of freedom for slaves and *patrocinados*.

CONCLUSIONS

At the beginning of this chapter it was suggested that a careful regional and chronological examination of the pattern of transition could help one to evaluate alternative explanations of the process of slave emancipation in Cuba. The evidence and arguments presented show that what is needed is a blending of elements from several hypotheses. The challenge is to make this blending coherent rather than eclectic and ad hoc.

It is true that Cuban slaveholders by the late 1870s had relatively little emotional attachment to the formal institution of slavery. Though some of their representatives continued to defend the institution as a benevolent one, the possibility of a controlled, gradual abolition did not put them up in arms.[50] The Moret Law had already in 1870 guaranteed the eventual demise of slavery by freeing the children of slaves, and demographic patterns were pushing in the same direction. There would not be enough slave workers to replenish the system; new sources and forms of labor had to be found.

This decay of the slave system during the 1870s must, however, be interpreted with great care. Young and elderly slaves achieved formal freedom by decree; assertive slaves, particularly in cities and in the east, sometimes obtained their freedom through litigation or self-purchase; many slaves died or became free as a result of war. The gaps thereby created were often filled with free workers. Mixed work forces were indeed common, but it does not appear, as has sometimes been argued, that the plantations invariably were driven to free labor either by the needs of the new technology or by a decline in the quality of the slave labor force caused by an excess of the young and the aged. Large plantations with available capital had often purchased Africans in the last years of the slave trade and still had substantial *dotaciones* of African and Creole slaves. An essential core of slaves of working age continued to be held in bondage in the major sugar areas, helping to maintain high levels of production during the 1870s despite the sharp drop in the total number of slaves.

If Cuba's planters by the end of the 1870s were no longer fully committed to the indefinite maintenance of an institution called slavery, they remained committed to many of the realities of slavery: its work rhythms, social relations, and power relations. They still extracted labor from substantial numbers of workers through extraeconomic compulsion. This is why they wanted the control afforded by the *patronato* and why they generally did not engage in mass manumissions.

The *patronato*, however, contained contradictions of its own, particularly in the granting of limited rights and partial access to redress. The social relations of slavery are by their nature difficult to maintain. Alterations in the relative bargaining power and legal rights of masters and slaves may weaken those relations irreparably. In this sense, the passage of the 1880 law was not merely a reflection in law of an existing state of affairs. Mechanisms provided by the law, however inadvertently, emerged as significant for the actual process of emancipation. But it was the shifting interests and resources of apprentices and their masters, not the legislature's intentions, that determined the uses to which they were put.

What, then, remains of the internal contradiction argument? It does contain a key insight concerning the difficulty of achieving capital-intensive development with forced labor, the maintenance expense of which must be borne year-round. But even this contradiction, though perceived by some planters, did not push them to the abandonment of slavery. They sought instead to segment the labor force: to add flexibility through slave rentals, to add workers through immigration, and to maintain as much control as possible over their existing slaves. Their use of Chinese laborers, contract workers, convicts, and rented slaves is sometimes cited as proof that the slave system was dissolving in the 1870s. But one could just as easily see this as evidence of its resilience. That such mixtures of forms of labor were brought together *without* the abandonment of slavery is striking. And that the men who ran these mixed plantations continued to oppose abolition is further evidence of the gap between the seeming contradictions within slavery and the forces actually driving abolition forward.

It may have come as something of a surprise to planters that their strategy could not work indefinitely. But there is a sense in which these continued improvisations and innovations did undermine slavery. It is a social one, a kind of second-order contradiction. Free labor and indentured labor were *economically* complementary to slavery: indentured Chinese workers often dealt with the centrifuges while slaves handled other tasks; white woodcutters on contract relieved the plantation of direct responsibility for providing fuel; the employment of free workers during the harvest diminished the problem of year-round maintenance of all workers. But the use of these complementary forms of labor had indirect effects on the social structure necessary to sustain slavery. Plantation slavery as a social system depended to a large degree on isolation. The incorporation of free workers, beyond those supervisors and artisans rigidly and traditionally separated from the slave work force, broke some of that isolation. It made obvious to slaves the existence of alternatives, created new sources of information, and made possible new alliances—both of individuals and of groups. Such alliances could be a matter of a union between a slave woman and a Chinese man, both interested in freedom for their children; of communication between free black workers and those who remained enslaved; of assistance from a newly freed slave to other members of the family. These alliances and examples aided slaves in their efforts at challenge and self-purchase and, in extreme cases (as in the east during the Ten Years' War), encouraged flight and rebellion.

This should not imply that slavery in Cuba inherently was always socially brittle. But in this specific political context, when abolition was already on the agenda, when insurgency was a reality, and when there was division within the white population, innovations and adaptations carried serious risks.

The abolition of slavery in Cuba, then, should not be seen simply as an imposition from the metropolitan power nor as the result of an inevitable collapse of the system of bondage in the face of internal economic contradictions. The planters' desire to maintain a high degree of control over their work force meant that as a practical matter most of them inhibited, rather than facilitated, emancipation, up to the very last years of the eighteen-year process. Slaves and *patrocinados*, on the other hand, took advantage of the legal openings provided in the 1870 and 1880 legislation and in other ways resisted submitting to their masters' control. Their initiatives served in part as a countervailing force and tended to accelerate emancipation. Thus the actual course of emancipation can be fully perceived only through an understanding of the interaction of the groups involved. Emancipation was, throughout, a social process in which the struggle between master and slave, *patrono* and *patrocinado*, employer and worker, shaped the character, the timing, and the terms of the transition from slavery to free labor.

Although these internal dynamics may be the most interesting part of the story of Cuban abolition, one ought to return, at least momentarily, to the search for large-scale explanations and ask how one would begin to reconstruct an explanation from what remains of the original hypotheses about causation. This chapter therefore concludes with a few observations about three aspects of such a large-scale explanation: the importance of political pressures, the nature of slaveholder attitudes, and the relationship between slavery and technology. For each of these three aspects, what was initially proposed as a primary cause has emerged as a complicated kind of contributing factor, not in the simple sense of yet another in a great list of factors mechanically bringing about abolition but rather as a conditioning circumstance that determined the constraints under which the process of emancipation would operate.

First, there is no question but that international diplomacy and domestic political unrest narrowed the options of Cuban slaveholders. The ending of the transatlantic slave trade—an event explicable almost entirely in terms of forces external to Cuba, crucial among them British diplomacy and the outcome of the Civil War in the United States—set in motion a long-term problem of labor supply. As long as Cuba's slave population was not fully self-reproducing, then new labor forms would have to be found. And to the extent that the existence of slavery inhibited the free immigration that might provide such laborers, a powerful argument against slavery would continue to build, even before the actual demographic crisis of labor supply had made itself felt. At the same time, domestically, the existence of an anticolonial rebellion that took on abolition as a rallying cry, however opportunistically, changed the climate in which slavery existed. The insurrection opened new options, while creating new stresses.

What has become clear through an examination of the process of abolition is that both kinds of political forces—international and domestic—could to some extent be contained and that for most of the eighteen years of gradual emancipation neither planters nor policy makers were prepared to deal with them by making substantial concessions. But these forces nonetheless conditioned the environment in which both slaves and slaveholders adopted strategies and sought to maintain or further their interests.

This brings us to a second general question involved in the search for large-scale explanations: the issue of slaveholder attitudes. It would be wrong to see modernizing Cuban planters as the prime movers behind abolition itself. The initiative simply did not come from them. Though most Cuban planters were not willing to give up slavery in pursuit of economic modernization, however, they were prepared to add free workers to their plantation work forces and to acquiesce in schemes of gradual emancipation, if these seemed to guarantee continuity of authority. Because they thought that they could control the inevitable through very gradual emancipation, they did not mount a last-ditch stand against it. They were to an extent wrong in the expectation that they could control the transition to free labor, and they were certainly wrong in thinking that they could fully control emancipation itself. But the fact that they were not utterly intransigent was a crucial circumstance as partial concessions grew beyond their intended dimensions.

Finally, on the issue of slavery and technology, there is a kind of irony in the postemancipation history of the Cuban sugar industry. I have rejected the assumption that abolition was, or was even seen as, inherently necessary in order to adopt new technologies. Yet soon after abolition there was a rapid adoption of new modes of organization of production, including the extensive use of advanced processing equipment. The early 1890s saw a dramatic increase in capital investment in machinery, extensive consolidation of estates, and a great boom in sugar production. Several external factors having little to do with abolition stimulated this boom—including the fall in the prices of steel rails that made cane transport cheaper over long distances and shifts in the United States tariff policy that favored Cuban sugar. So the rapid development of central mills with very modern equipment, processing cane from several sources, cannot be fully attributed to the elimination of slavery. Even more important, the boom was by no means uniformly advantageous for former slave holders. Many found their estates swallowed up in the new central mills and either lost their land entirely or became growers of cane rather than producers of sugar. It is not surprising that those who foresaw that abolition might be followed by such a change in their status would have opposed emancipation. But even those who stood to benefit from the development of central mills saw no reason for relinquishing any control over their workers along the way.[51]

The unfolding of emancipation and the development of postemancipation society were processes so complex that one cannot infer from the postemancipation experience of technological innovation and growth that a perceived need for such innovation actually motivated abolition. Moreover, as one moves away from the invocation of internal contradictions or diplomatic pressures as explanations for abolition, and shifts the focus to the dialectic of, on the one hand, stalling and improvisation by slaveowners and, on the other, pressure and initiatives from slaves, gradual emancipation emerges as a form of social change largely controlled by planters and the state, but which nonetheless drew much of its character and timing from slaves and insurgents. Large-scale explanations and small-scale historical events can thus be linked in the case of Cuban abolition, but only by multiple threads of interaction and adaptation, woven together over time.

APPENDIX: NOTES ON CENSUS DATA USED IN TABLES 2.1 AND 2.2

The figures cited in tables 2.1 and 2.2 are based on several official tabulations. Those for 1862 are from Cuba, Centro de Estadística, *Noticias estadísticas de la isla de Cuba en 1862* (Havana, 1864). I have derived provincial totals by aggregating the population figures for the 1862 *jurisdicciones* to match the provincial boundaries established in 1878. (For details on redistricting and the method of compilation, see Rebecca J. Scott, "Slave Emancipation and the Transition to Free Labor in Cuba, 1868-1895" [Ph.D. dissertation, Princeton University, 1982], ch. 4, note 2.) Returns from the 1867 slave count are neither reliable nor consistent and are included here only for the purpose of comparison. They can be found, divided by jurisdiction, in the "Resumen general de los esclavos que segun el censo de 1867 . . . existían a la terminación de ese censo en las jurisdicciones que componían el territorio de la Isla," in the Archivo Histórico Nacional, Madrid, Sección de Ultramar (hereinafter AHN, Ultramar), legajo 4884, tomo 8, expediente 160. The 1871 figures are from the "Resumen de los esclavos comprendidos en el padrón de 1871 . . . ," in AHN, Ultramar, leg. 4882, tomo 4. The 1877 census has often been considered unreliable, but the article by Fe Iglesias García, "El censo cubano de 1877 y sus diferentes versiones," *Santiago* 34 (June 1979): 167-211, presents new evidence that in its final version the census was more accurate than previously imagined. I have used her totals for 1877. The figures for the 1880s are from AHN, Ultramar, leg. 4926, exp. 144, and leg. 4814, exp 289, and are based on records of the provincial Juntas de Patronato.

NOTES

This essay is part of a larger project that was funded by the Social Science Research Council, the Fulbright-Hays Program, and the Latin American Program of Princeton University. The author would like to thank David Davis, Seymour Drescher, Stanley Engerman, Albert Hirschman, Thomas Holt, Franklin Knight, Sidney Mintz, Magnus Mörner, David Murray, Stuart Schwartz, and Gavin Wright for their comments, and Manuel Moreno Fraginals for numerous discussions of the issue of slavery and abolition. This essay first appeared in *Comparative Studies in Society and History* 26 (January 1984): 83-111. Parts will appear in Rebecca Scott, *Slave Emancipation in Cuba: The Transition to Free Labor, 1860-1899*, to be published in 1985 by the Princeton University Press. It is reprinted by permission of both Cambridge University Press and Princeton University Press.

1. Manuel Moreno Fraginals, *El ingenio: complejo económico social cubano del azúcar*, 3 vols. (Havana: Editorial de Ciencias Sociales, 1978), 3:37.
2. The thesis of the incompatibility of slave labor and technology is argued by Moreno Fraginals in *El ingenio*, and he expresses it succinctly in several articles, including "El esclavo y la mecanización de los ingenios," *Bohemia* (June 13, 1969): 98-99, and "Desgarramiento azucarero e integración nacional," *Casa de las Américas* 11 (September-October 1970): 6-22.
3. Eugene D. Genovese, *The World the Slaveholders Made: Two Essays in*

Interpretation (New York: Random House, Vintage Books ed., 1971), pp. 69–70.

4. Arthur F. Corwin, *Spain and the Abolition of Slavery in Cuba, 1817–1886* (Austin: University of Texas Press, 1967).

5. Moreno Fraginals, "El esclavo y la mecanización de los ingenios," pp. 98–99.

6. Carlos Rebello, *Estados relativos a la producción azucarera de la isla de Cuba* (Havana: n.p., 1860).

7. Cuba, Centro de Estadística, *Noticias estadísticas de la isla de Cuba, en 1862* (Havana: Imprenta del Gobierno, 1864).

8. Moreno Fraginals, *El ingenio*, 3:36–37.

9. David R. Murray, *Odious Commerce: Britain, Spain and the Abolition of the Cuban Slave Trade* (Cambridge: Cambridge University Press, 1980).

10. Moreno Fraginals, *El ingenio*, 3:36–37.

11. The best analyses of the Ten Years' War are to be found in Raúl Cepero Bonilla, *Azúcar y abolición* (Havana: Editorial Cenit, 1948); Ramiro Guerra y Sánchez, *Guerra de los Diez Años* (Havana: Cultural, 1950–52); and Franklin Knight, *Slave Society in Cuba during the Nineteenth Century* (Madison: University of Wisconsin Press, 1970).

12. For a fuller analysis of the effects of the war on slavery, see Rebecca J. Scott, *Slave Emancipation in Cuba: The Transition to Free Labor, 1860–1899* (Princeton: Princeton University Press, 1985), ch. 2.

13. For evidence on the events of 1879, see the opinion of José Bueno y Blanco in Archivo Histórico Nacional, Madrid, Sección de Ultramar (hereafter AHN, Ultramar), leg. 4882, tomo 5, "Documentos de la Comisión . . . 1879," and AHN, Ultramar, leg. 4882, tomo 3, exp. 76, Telegram from the Governor General to the Minister of Ultramar, September 11, 1879. José Martí vividly described the pressure on Spain from rebellious slaves in the east of Cuba and the double-edged response of abolition and increased military presence. See José Martí's speech given in Steck Hall, New York, January 24, 1880, printed in Hortensia Pichardo, ed., *Documentos para la historia de Cuba*, 2 vols. (Havana: Editorial de Ciencias Sociales, 1976, 1977) 1:424–49.

14. For these and other provincial totals, see Appendix.

15. The figure of 20 percent was derived by using the age distribution of slaves in Cuba in the 1862 census. Of those listed, around 22 percent were over age sixty or under age ten (Cuba, *Noticias*). I have assumed that the proportion would be somewhat smaller in a plantation area, which would have a higher concentration of imported Africans. This estimate also coincides with the age pyramids derived by Moreno Fraginals from plantation accounts. Moreno Fraginals, *El ingenio*, 2:90.

16. See Archivo Nacional de Cuba (hereafter ANC), Misc. de Expendientes, leg. 3814, exp. A, Expediente promovido por este Gob° Gral para conocer las operaciones practicadas en todas las Sindicaturas de la Isla durante el quinquenio de 1873 a 1877. Of the 3,359 *coartaciones* in the island, 1,413 were in the city of Havana.

17. For area planted in cane, see Rebello, *Estados*, and the *Revista de Agricultura* (Havana), 3 (March 31, 1879), 75. Population figures are from the 1862 census and from Fe Iglesias García, "El censo cubano de 1877 y sus diferentes versiones," *Santiago* (Santiago de Cuba) 34 (June 1979): 167–211. On the categories of workers in sugar, see the *Revista de Agricultura* cited earlier.

18. A. Gallenga, *The Pearl of the Antilles* (London: Chapman & Hall, 1873), pp. 96, 105.

19. This picture emerges from censuses, account books, and observers' reports. See the 1877 agricultural census, the plantation records cited in notes 33–35 and F. de Zayas, "Estudios de agricultura: II. El trabajador, el jornal," *Revista de Agricultura* 1 (April 30, 1879): 83.

20. Moreno Fraginals puts forward this argument in "Abolición o desintegración? Algunas preguntas en torno a un centenario," *Granma* (Havana) (January 23, 1980), and in "Plantations in the Caribbean: Cuba, Puerto Rico, and the Dominican Republic in the Late Nineteenth Century," in this volume.

21. For an examination of the ways in which "contradictions" within slavery are resolved, and in some cases give rise to new contradictions, see Sidney Mintz, "Slavery and the Rise of Peasantries," in Michael Craton, ed., *Roots and Branches: Current Directions in Slave Studies* (Toronto: Pergamon, 1979), pp. 213–42. The point is that such things as bonuses and provision grounds may or may not signal disintegration, depending on the surrounding circumstances. In some cases, they may even strengthen slavery.

22. Moreno Fraginals, *El ingenio*, 2: 83–90. He states that the conscious policy of "good treatment," aimed at creating a self-reproducing slave work force, was "the most visible symptom of the dissolution of slavery" (p. 90).

23. See the 1862 census and Enrique Edo y Llop, *Memoria histórica de Cienfuegos y su jurisdicción* (Cienfuegos: Imprenta nueva de J. Andreu, 1888), appendix, pp. 5–6. The manuscript slave list is in ANC, Misc. de Expendientes, leg. 3748, exp. B, Capitanía Pedánea de Santa Isabel de las Lajas, núm. 3, Padrón general de esclavos, 1875.

24. Stanley J. Stein, *Vassouras: A Brazilian Coffee County, 1850–1900* (New York: Atheneum, 1974), p. 78.

25. See *Revista Económica* (Havana) 2 (June 7, 1878): 13. The Armantina and Manaca estates, excluded from the comparisons because their 1875 slave data are incomplete, had 122 slaves and 17 *alquilados y libres*.

26. Edo y Llop, *Memoria histórica*, p. 629. For evidence of planter hostility to abolition in the 1870s, see Corwin, *Spain and Abolition of Slavery*, ch. 14.

27. In Cuba, this argument dates at least to Ramón de la Sagra in the mid-nineteenth century and is repeated by Moreno Fraginals. See *El ingenio*, 2:30.

28. AHN, Ultramar, leg. 4759, exp. 85, "Exposición del Excmo. Señor Conde de Vega Mar" (Madrid, 1868).

29. Fermín Rosillo y Alquier, *Noticias de dos ingenios y datos sobre la producción azucarera de la isla de Cuba* (Havana: Imprenta del Gobierno, 1873), describes the work force on España. For Álava, see the 1877 agricultural census in *Revista Económica* 2 (June 7, 1878): 11.

30. The description of Las Cañas as "Cuba's most modern mill" is from *El ingenio*, 1: 250. The figures on the work force are from Rosillo, *Noticias*. Observations on the treatment of the Chinese are from Juan Pérez de la Riva, "Duvergier de Hauranne: un joven francés visita el ingenio Las Cañas en 1865," *Revista de la Biblioteca Nacional José Martí* 56 (October-December 1965): 85–114.

31. On the Chinese in Cuba, see Juan Pérez de la Riva, "Demografía de los culíes chinos en Cuba (1853–1877)" and "La situación legal del culí en Cuba," in his *El barracón y otros ensayos* (Havana: Editorial de Ciencias Sociales, 1975), pp.

469–507, 209–45. See also Denise Helly, *Idéologie et ethnicité: les chinois Macao à Cuba, 1847–1886* (Montreal: Les Presses de l'Université de Montreal, 1979). The question of whether the Chinese should, for the purposes of analysis, be considered wage workers is a difficult one. The extraeconomic coercion to which they were subjected was so great, and so similar to that inflicted on slaves, that I am inclined to doubt the substance of their "freeness." If in Cuba they were seen as particularly suited for work with machinery, this may in part have reflected employers' high expectations of the Chinese relative to their low expectations of slaves. It may also have reflected actual differences in performance, but these differences could have had as much to do with the cultural background of the Chinese and their anticipation of a future freedom as they did with any alleged juridicial freedom while under contract, a freedom often violated.

32. See Albert O. Hirschman, *The Strategy of Economic Development* (New Haven: Yale University Press, 1958), ch. 8.
33. See, for example, the records of slave rentals on the Ingenio Delicias in ANC, Misc. de Libros, núm. 10802, Libro Diario del Ingenio Delicias, 1872–82.
34. Data on the work force at Angelita are from ANC, Misc. de Libros, núm. 11536, Libro Diario del Ingenio "Angelita" de la propiedad de Sr. J. A. Argudín, 1868–71, and ANC, Misc. de Libros, núm. 10789, Libro Diario del Ingenio Angelita Argudín, 1877.
35. Other daybooks and slave lists for the 1870s include Archivo Provincial de Sancti Spíritus, Fondo Valle-Iznaga (hereafter APSS, Valle-Iznaga), leg. 27, Libro con la dotación de esclavos del ingenio La Crisis; ANC, Misc. de Libros, núm. 10802, Libro Diario del Ingenio Delicias; ANC, Misc. de Libros, núm. 10806, Libro Diario al parecer de un ingenio, 1879–81; and ANC, Misc de Libros, núm. 11245, Libro Mayor del Ingenio Nueva Teresa, 1872–85.
36. For a further discussion of the politics of abolition, see Corwin, *Spain and Abolition of Slavery*, and Knight, *Slave Society*.
37. ANC, Misc. de Libros, núm. 10831, Libro Diario del Ingenio Nueva Teresa, 1880–86.
38. Ibid.
39. ANC, Misc. de Libros, núm. 11245, Libro Mayor del Ingenio Nueva Teresa, 1872–85.
40. APSS, Valle-Iznaga, leg. 24, Libro que contiene documentos del estado general de la finca Mapos.
41. For provincial figures on emancipation, see AHN, Ultramar, leg. 4814, exp. 273 and exp. 289; leg. 4926, exp. 144; and Manuel Villanova, *Estadística de la abolición de la esclavitud* (Havana, 1885).
42. For the debate, see AHN, Ultramar, leg. 4818, exp. 84, Sobre pago de contribuciones de las tiendas de los Ingenios.
43. For a more detailed discussion of the operation of the *patronato*, see Rebecca J. Scott, "Gradual Abolition and the Dynamics of Slave Emancipation in Cuba, 1868–86," *Hispanic American Historical Review* 63 (August 1983): 449–77.
44. AHN, Ultramar, leg. 4926, exp. 144, núm. 300, Informe del Consejo de Administración, August 8, 1884.
45. Edo y Llop, *Memoria histórica*, pp. 988–89.
46. ANC, Misc. de Libros, núm. 11245, Libro Mayor del Ingenio Nueva Teresa, 1872–85.

47. ANC, Misc. de Libros, núm. 10831, Libro Diario del Ingenio Nueva Teresa, 1880–86.

48. Ibid.

49. See AHN, Ultramar, leg. 4926, exp. 144, núm. 323, telegram from the Governor General of Cuba to the Minister of Ultramar, Havana, August 12, 1886.

50. For the debates in the Spanish parliament, see Spain, Cortes, 1879–80, *Discursos de la ley de abolición de la esclavitud en Cuba* (Madrid, 1879–80).

51. A good example of the latter would be Francisco Feliciano Ibáñez, who was a major planter, a conservative on abolition, and a proponent of the development of central mills. See Francisco Feliciano Ibáñez, *Observaciones sobre la utilidad y conveniencia del establecimiento en esta isla de grandes ingenios centrales* (Havana: Imprenta y Lit. Obispo 27, 1880).

3. The Development of Capitalism in Cuban Sugar Production, 1860-1900

Fe Iglesias García

Cuba underwent profound social transformations during the second half of the nineteenth century. The key to these transformations was the development of capitalism. We start with the premise that before an analysis of the development of capitalism in Cuba can be undertaken, we must understand the development of the sugar industry, which was the foundation of the Cuban economy.

The development of the sugar industry in Cuba displays notable regional differences. In addition, during the period in question, two important wars of independence fundamentally affected the eastern zone of the island. This chapter therefore considers only the western region. The western region was the center of sugar production for most of the nineteenth century. It includes the old regions of Colón, Cárdenas, and Matanzas, as well as Havana and Pinar del Río, which with their unique characteristics had been growing briskly since the eighteenth century. The region also includes Sagua la Grande, which underwent a later, but equally powerful, productive impulse.

We attempt to study capitalism in depth in the area where the conditions of growth for large industry developed. In the eastern zone sugar developed as an extension of the industry in the west. In a process that culminated only in the twentieth century, sugar moved east in search of free, fertile, and abundant land. Although external factors play an important role in the Cuban case, it is possible to study the internal processes in the phases of the development of capitalism. In this paper we intend to clarify particular aspects of Cuban development that have frequently been explained in terms of analyses of external factors. Our objective is to achieve a solid point of departure that will enable us to understand the beginning of the process and to undertake future studies on the development of capitalism in Cuba.

CHARACTERISTICS OF SUGAR PRODUCTION

Cane sugar production has peculiar characteristics. The raw material is agricultural and must be harvested at a particular season and processed immediately after the harvest. Sugar cane cannot be stored and used according to the need and capacity of the extractive phase. The processing of cane requires a constant input of the raw material, which is voluminous and difficult to transport. Consequently, although the agricultural and industrial sectors are technologically independent, they are nonetheless tightly linked by their rhythms of production.

Sugar production requires more concentrated labor and exploitation of natural resources than the virtuosity of artisan production, which is why manufacturing was able to develop on the basis of slave labor. The labor intensity required by sugar also permitted the development of various adaptive forms that enabled productive relations in Cuba to remain predominantly those of slavery until the end of the manufacturing period of sugar production.

Another peculiarity in the production of cane sugar is that its dependence on the agricultural phase makes it a seasonal production, taking place during the months in which the sugar content of the cane makes its extraction profitable. This had repercussions on the cycle of capital use. The slaveowner had to support his slaves throughout the year, although they could be exploited fully only during the harvest period. These disadvantages could be compensated for by Cuba's exceptional natural conditions, which permitted the slaveowners to reduce slave rations to the minimum.

SUGAR PRODUCTION IN 1860

In 1860, sugar production in Cuba was in a traditional phase, about to move toward industrial production.[1] Production took place in more or less large units (by the standards of the time), and many units had achieved a high level of technical development. Cooperation was the predominant form of labor in the productive process. For an analysis of sugar production in 1860, we use Moreno Fraginals's classification (see table 3.1). While the mechanized mills—the forerunners of the modern industrial mills—represented 4.86 percent of the milling units in 1860, and produced 14.80 percent of the sugar, the semimechanized mills represented 67.45 percent of the mills and produced 76.62 percent of the sugar.

The semimechanized mills were the typical producing units. Although they used a steam engine in the milling process, they used the Jamaican train, which was manually operated in the fundamental processes of alka-

Table 3.1   Sugar Production According to Mill Type, 1860

Mill Type	Number of Mills	Percentage	Total Production (metric tons)	Percentage
Animal traction	359	27.24	41,625	8.08
Water power	6	.45	2,567	0.50
Semimechanized	889	67.45	395,273	76.62
Mechanized	64	4.86	76,276	14.80
Total	1,318	100.00	515,741	100.00

Source: Manuel Moreno Fraginals, El ingenio (Havana: Editorial de Ciencias Sociales, 1978), 1:173.

linization, clarification, and evaporation of the *guarapo*, or sugar cane juice. That is to say, the principal productive activities in the agricultural phase were manual: plowing the land, seeding the cane, cultivating it, harvesting it, and transporting it. In the final phase of production, the crystallization of the massecuite, the purging or separation of molasses, and the pouring into molds were done by hand. All of these manual activities required simple cooperation, which was the organization of labor corresponding to this stage of development. Until 1860, sugar production in Cuba took place in productive units that were at a "manufacturing" stage. Steam engines had not been introduced in 27.7 percent of the mills—and many of these were at the level of simple mercantile production—whose contribution to total production was 8.6 percent. Only 15 percent of the sugar was produced in units whose technological development was at the advanced level of industry; we cannot yet speak of the existence of industrial production.[2]

In the region selected for this study—the most advanced on the island—86.56 percent of the mills were based on steam, whereas 13.43 percent used animal traction. Six percent of the mills were fitted with modern equipment for evaporation and refining, while 94 percent did it with Jamaican trains. The use of steam in the mill did not necessarily imply that improvements had been introduced in the rest of the process. Steam was applied to one sector of the flow of production—replacing animal traction or water power—but manual processes were retained in other sectors. Naturally, the steam engine increased milling capacity—traditionally milling itself had been the bottleneck of the *ingenio*—and this required greater supplies of sugar cane and more manual equipment to process the juice. Thus the semimechanized sugar mills were able to produce more than those based on animal traction.

After the introduction of the steam engine, there began a search for manual solutions, within the constraints of the slave system. In a desperate effort to reduce costs, millowners attempted to use technological advances that were economic and easy to manage. Because black slaves were thought to be of an inferior race, they were not believed capable of operating modern machines. Moreover, the organization of Cuban slave society conspired against the use of machines: thus the use of machines—the "industrial slavery" of which contemporary North American historians speak—demanded the imposition of norms that presuppose a crisis in the institution of slavery. Innumerable applications for patents for appliances were really no more than variants of the existing systems adapted to the routine and simplified work patterns imposed by slavery.

The Cuban landowners were obliged to import their means of production and their labor force—and both represented an investment of constant capital—and the emphasis placed on one or the other depended on market conditions. This disjunction motivated landowners during most of the transition, contributing considerably to the heterogeneity of the producing units.

Thus, as late as 1860, some mills were powered by animal traction, using "common," or Jamaican, evaporation trains, and coexisted with semimechanized mills, and the forerunners of large industry in which complex systems of machinery had been installed. Among this diversity of productive units were mills in which elements of each were superimposed. It is not rare to find manufacturing units in which the Jamaican train was used for the first phase of evaporation, and vacuum evaporators for the final stage of concentration, and in which the production process ended either with centrifuges or by manual purge in hogsheads.

The productive capacities of each type of mill differed considerably. In 1860 the national average for mechanized mills was 1,192 tons of sugar; for semimechanized mills it was 445 tons; and for mills based on animal traction it was only 116 tons.[3] It is clear from Moreno Fraginals's calculations for the different types of units between 1858 and 1860 that those who owned the more developed mills made extraordinary profits. According to his estimates, a mill based on animal traction, using vertical or horizontal *trapiches* of low productive capacity and producing muscovado sugar exclusively, showed yields of 2.5 to 3 percent of sugar from the cane. This meant incomes of 135 to 180 reales (calculated from the average of triennial prices) for each 1,000 *arrobas* of processed cane. The semimechanized mills, using good *trapiches* and Jamaican trains, yielded 2.5 to 3.25 percent (on the same basis), which represented 150 to 195 reales per 1,000 *arrobas* of processed cane. Finally, the mechanized mills, with a yield of sugar of 4.5 to 5.5 percent, obtained 446 to 557 reales for each 1,000 *arrobas* of cane.[4]

This was not a case in which producers in the same business competed for the internal market but rather one of production for external markets, which was characterized by strong protectionist barriers (in Europe for the protection of beet sugar and in the United States for the protection first of Louisiana sugar and later of the interests of sugar refiners). Although sugar prices remained relatively high, the *hacendados* were able to take advantage of exceptional natural conditions (geographic situation, climate, soil fertility, etc.) and the merciless exploitation of slaves. This meant a significant margin of profit, even for the less efficient units, since all the units used slave labor, which prevented the transformation of the technical and social conditions of labor.

Several factors tended to equalize the situation of the different kinds of *hacendados* in determining the labor time that was socially necessary for sugar production in Cuba. Slaves were part of the fixed investment capital. The maintenance of this capital meant a constant expense on subsistence plus an annual depreciation, which the slaveowning *hacendado*, Juan Poey, calculated at 2.5 percent per annum.[5] Subsistence expenses could not be reduced without endangering invested capital. Thus subsistence costs were a fixed annual expense, regardless of the amount of time the labor force could be exploited to the maximum.

In view of these conditions, most Cuban *ingenios* were constantly threatened by labor shortages, especially after the end of the slave trade and most severely after successive epidemics of cholera. The conditions that determined increases in labor productivity were not achieved in a day, especially as the process was fettered by the existence of slavery. Thus slavery was both a drag and a spur to development in sugar production, until the circumstances that would favor superior forms of organization developed. Cuban *hacendados* were constantly adjusting to the laws of supply and demand in the labor market with the available means, always within the confines of slavery.

With steam engines came mechanics, who were mostly foreigners. Before the introduction of steam, the sugarmaster was generally the only free worker on the *ingenio* who was directly involved in the production process. (There were other free laborers, but they worked in the service sector: overseers, administrators, ox drivers, etc.). The number of free workers depended on the size of the *ingenio*, but in general, until the 1860s the free labor force did not vary in its composition. It is clear from the memoirs of foreign mechanics in the Cuban National Archives that most of the *ingenios* employed only one machinist: only the largest producers employed two or three.[6] In a sample of 100 *ingenios* in the zone under consideration, Moreno Fraginals discovered some 50 slaves whose occupations were defined as mechanics. Since in almost every case in which there was a slave mechanic, there was also a salaried mechanic, the former were probably assistants to the latter. This suggests an interest in industrializing with slaves, which failed but which doubtless contributed to the transformation of the workers' quality of life during the transition period.

According to census data from 1862, of the population residing on *ingenios* 79 percent were slaves or "emancipated" slaves, 2 percent were free blacks, and 19 percent were whites and orientals.[7] There are similar proportions in partial registers in various areas of the Matanzas province.[8] These data correspond to the reports by overseers on some of the *ingenios* that we

Table 3.2   *Caballerías* Seeded in Cane, 1860

Caballerías	Percentage of *Ingenios*
1–10	26.09
11–20	33.58
21–30	23.53
31–40	10.43
41–50	4.96
51–60	1.27

Source: Carlos Rebello, *Estados Relativos a la Producción Azucarera de la Isla de Cuba* (Havana: Imprenta del Gobierno, 1860).
Note: 1 *caballería* = 13.42 hectares = 33.162 acres.

have been able to study. The most significant event up to that time was the introduction of the semi–slave labor of Chinese contract laborers. (In Cuba, these were always designated by the generic term *asiáticos*.)

In order to analyze the position of capital, several factors must be kept in mind, since the number of mills owned by an *hacendado* or a company was not by itself a sufficient indicator of the magnitude of capital invested. Among these factors, the extension of lands, and especially the area under cultivation, played an important role. Machinery was not a basic cost of the semimechanized mills. On the other hand, the value of the labor force was an essential investment category, which is why these investments must be considered as constant capital. Slaves were the most important element in the productive process: for the semimechanized mills, their value represented about 40 percent of invested capital, whereas investments in machinery did not even constitute 10 percent.

Asiatics were included in all inventories and economic transactions, as were slaves. But their value was calculated on the basis of the investment in acquiring the contracts and of the estimated value of the forced labor required for the remaining years of the contract. On average, the labor force on a mechanized mill represented some 38 percent of total value, while the machinery represented 18 percent.[9] Obviously, the range of variation in component values among the mechanized *ingenios* was much broader.

The nature of capital corresponded to the level of development attained by production. If we consider the number of *caballerías* seeded in cane, the largest *ingenio* in 1860 was the Alava. In 1860, Cuban sugar production was still dispersed in small *ingenios*, with cultivated lands of 1 to 20 *caballerías* in 60 percent of the cases (table 3.2). Only 1.27 percent of *ingenios* planted 50 to 60 *caballerías*. In the region under study only 1 *ingenio* had over 60 *caballerías* seeded in sugar cane. In this heterogeneous picture there were also regional differences. Whereas in the Colón region the average number of *caballerías* in cane was 27.26, in Pinar del Río it was 9.38.[10] If we consider that the quantity of sugar did not always correspond to the quantity of cane planted, we can understand the varied nature of Cuban sugar production.

Ownership in land was dispersed among many owners. In the region under study only 10 percent owned more than one *ingenio*. The only suggestion of the future concentration in land was present in a few companies, among them the Compania Territorial Cubana, which owned eleven *ingenios*, the largest of which cultivated 60 *caballerías*, and the rest 10 to 45 *caballerías*. Concentration in property was not related to concentration in production. Another company that represented a degree of centralization was La Gran Azucarera, which owned two large *ingenios*, of sixty and forty *caballerías*, respectively. The rest of those owning more than one *ingenio* were individual proprietors or family groups.

Although at the level of bookkeeping there are indications of centralization in the presence of a few shareholding companies, these are anachronistic elements, which developed as a consequence of the speculative crisis of 1857. By 1860 the Compania Territorial Cubana was in financial difficulties, and in general, all of the corporations of the time led ephemeral lives, plagued by financial difficulties, like foreign bodies out of their element.

Foreign capital was not present in the largest companies or among the largest landowners. These were always Cuban-born or Spaniards who had moved to Cuba and whose fortunes had been accumulated in trade. In many cases their commercial activities had included slave trading.

In an effort to obtain sound indexes, we correlated the total number of *caballerías* seeded in cane with the number of *ingenios* and obtained a coefficient of plus 0.971. This suggests that the amount of cane planted depended directly on the number of *ingenios*. We also correlated the *arrobas* of sugar produced in 1860 in each of the regions under consideration, with the number of *caballerías* planted in cane. We obtained a coefficient of plus 0.916. We did this calculation for the twenty-one *ingenios* with the highest productivity in relation to land on the island, which were selected by Ramón de la Sagra.[11] We obtained a coefficient of plus 0.910, which is almost the same as that obtained for the region studied as a whole.

We examined these results by correlating the number of *arrobas* of sugar produced with the index of yield per *caballería* seeded in cane, both for the region as a whole and for the sample of twenty-one *ingenios*, and we obtained fairly low coefficients of plus 0.603 and plus 0.388, respectively. These results show that the volume of production depended more on the number of *caballerías* seeded in cane than on the yield per *caballería*. Thus, in 1860, the sugar production was still directly dependent on the number of *caballerías* planted, and the area that could be planted depended on the number of *ingenios*.

The *ingenios* differed as much in volume of production as they did in other aspects. The giants, of which there were 3 in the whole country, each produced over 2,000 tons; the small ones, of which there were 239, each produced less than 100 tons. Among the latter, only 46 were mechanized, and the rest milled on the basis of animal traction. Most of the island's *ingenios*, 75 percent, produced 100 to 1,000 tons per harvest, while 5.15 percent produced 1,000 to 2,000 tons.[12]

For most of the nineteenth century it is difficult to measure the amount of sugar produced per quantity of processed cane. It is generally necessary to resort to calculating yield per area under cultivation. This tends to distort the yield because agricultural yields depend in turn on the fertility of the land. The average yield of sugar per *caballería* in cane in 1860 was 2,211 *arrobas* for the whole country. The yield of *ingenios* that used vacuum evaporators was 2,815 *arrobas*; those that used Jamaican trains yielded 2,150 *arrobas*. Regionally the yields varied from 769 *arrobas* in the zone of Jaruco to 2,895, in Matanzas.[13]

An essential aspect in the analysis of the development attained in sugar production by 1860 is labor productivity. To study this, we must determine the degree of exploitation of the labor force. In order to achieve any precision in this regard (and keeping in mind, as well, the difficulties presented by the colonial statistical sources), it is necessary to begin with general studies of the population. For the region of Colón in 1859, 89 percent of the labor force were slaves, and each of these slaves produced 157.80 *arrobas* of sugar, for an average gross yield of 247.95 pesos. To achieve this yield, it was necessary to employ 9 men per cultivated *caballería*, with an average of 212 men per *ingenio*. For the sample of twenty-one *ingenios*, the correlation between sugar production and the number of slaves was plus 0.941; for the district of Palmillas, in the same province, it was of plus 0.916, which suggests the close relationship between production and the labor force.[14]

These are the parameters measured to date. Although we believe that they are affected by the flimsiness of the statistical sources of the time, and that our calculations can be refined, they show that the production of sugar in 1860 was at a stage of development in which quantitative elements were most important for increments in production. The marked dependence between the labor force and productivity indexes shows that a qualitative change had not yet taken place in production based on slave labor.

TRANSITIONS AFTER 1860

In the study of socioeconomic formations, and especially of processes of change, it is important to identify the predominant tendencies in development. Periodization in the study of such problems presents great difficulties because of their complexity and because the predominant tendencies never reveal themselves in clearly defined ways. This is why we emphasize phases of development and use chronological milestones simply as markers in time. When we refer to a particular year, we use it as a guide in order to study a particular process. In our view, historical dates are to be used as indicators in the study of processes, and we do not adjust processes to meet the needs of periodization.

Properly speaking, the transition extends from 1860 until 1881, the date in which the public railroads began to move cane for processing in the *ingenios*, thus encouraging the social division of labor and the introduction of mercantile relations in the process of sugar production. The years between 1881 and 1891 are the period of the great transformations.

Since the available sources permit us to establish comparisons on productivity and property between 1860 and 1877, we use the latter date for our analysis. In the case of the province of Matanzas, we can make comparisons between 1860 and 1881. Total sugar production increased until 1879, both in absolute and relative terms, although there were a few fluctuations. General statistics reflect a definite process of concentration, although more detailed studies show that the increase in production took place at the expense of the quality of the sugar produced.[15] The lack of statistical standards in sugar production (the first were established at the international conference at Gratz in 1894) meant that production was expressed in global figures, which included, for example, centrifuged sugar with a Pol of 98 degrees and muscovado sugar with a Pol of 82 degrees.

The decade between 1860 and 1869 was characterized by a tendency to growth. For the first time, a half million tons were produced; by the end of the decade, over 700,000 tons. The years between 1870 and 1879 were characterized by a stagnation in production. With a few oscillations, the high levels achieved during the previous decade were maintained. The largest decreases in production took place at the end of the Ten Years' War, although in 1879, the first year of peace, production reached 775,368 tons, the highest production figure for Cuba for the first 90 years of the century and the greatest attained in the world by an economy based on slave labor.

Regardless of the multiplicity of factors that intervened in the process, from 1875 on, sugar production entered a period of stagnation that cannot be attributed only to the effects of the war. During the 1880s the tendency to stagnation manifested itself in decreases in production. From 1890 on, development trends shifted, and new historical peaks in production were attained, peaks interrupted by the War of Independence (1895–98).

With regard to the number of producing units, a factor of fundamental importance in production on the basis of slave labor, these decreased between 1860 and 1877 in the country as a whole. But the destruction and demolition of *ingenios* affected essentially the eastern zone (the old provinces of Camagüey and Oriente), while in the western zone, new units entered production. This suggests that during this period, growth in sugar production continued to depend on the increase of productive units, since it is known that the west carried the weight of sugar production and that the units that were destroyed or demolished in the east were all small ones (table 3.3).

With regard to capital, what actually took place between 1860 and 1877 was its dispersion. By 1877, either the corporations were bankrupt, like La

Table 3.3   Number of *Ingenios* in Production, by Province, Selected Years

Year	Pinar del Río	La Havana	Matanzas	Las Villas	Camagüey	Oriente	Total
1860	102	126	442	395	101	216	1,382
1877	87	179	517	326	—	81	1,190
1881	77	155	473	347	3	115	1,170

Sources: Carlos Rebello, *Estados Relativos a la Producción Azucarera de la Isla de Cuba* (Havana: Imprenta del Gobierno, 1860); *Revista Económica* 1, no. 8 (1877):60–61; *Boletín Oficial de Hacienda,* 1881, various appendixes.

Gran Azucarera, or they had been dissolved, as had been the Compania Territorial Cubana. By 1877 the *ingenios* that had belonged to the latter either appear under the names of individual owners or are not registered at all, which leads us to suppose that they had been torn down.

Most of the *ingenios* were under individual ownership; only 8.3 percent of owners owned more than one. Capital movements due to the sale, purchase, and mortgage of *ingenios* are characterized by complexities appropriate to a period of crisis. The scarcity of financial capital was reflected in high interest rates, usually 12 percent per annum, and in the structure of the purchases, which were mostly in individual names, with the purchaser remaining in debt to the seller or third parties. There are no records of loans by credit companies, nor do any individuals or companies stand out as centralizing agents for capital.

Until 1865, mortgages were characteristically given as collateral for debts to merchant-lenders or represented a closing of accounts, almost always for debts with a merchant-lender creditor. Many sales took place because of debt, with part of the value of the property going to settle the debt. In other cases the buyer assumed responsibility for the debts of the seller. Beginning in 1865, mortgages to guarantee sales before the harvest became more common, although interest rates remained high. Sales of parts of *ingenios* were common, and some demolished *ingenios* were also sold. Almost all of the mills sold or mortgaged were encumbered by prior liens. These liens were *censos impuestos* on part or on all of the estate's lands in favor of religious institutions, minors, etc. These received 5 percent a year on the money advanced, and the contracts could be in perpetuity or redeemable within a certain time, decided at the time the *censo* was imposed. An *ingenio* could, moreover, be mortgaged with the Royal Hacienda for the payment of back taxes or mortgaged to individuals. A given property could have various liens and mortgages on it, each of which could be the object of fraud or sale.

Clearly this factor delayed the process of change. Property relations under slavery and elements inherited from the Spanish feudal superstructure were responsible for slowing the development of the circulation of currency and of credit institutions. The period until 1880 was characterized by the fore-

Table 3.4   Wage Laborers on the *Ingenio* Jesus Maria, 1866

Worker	Monthly Wage
Ox driver	34 pesos
Second ox driver	25 pesos
Carpenter	50 pesos
Sugar master	100 pesos
Mechanic	116 pesos
Steward	51 pesos
Fire watchman[a]	45 pesos
Overseer	51 pesos
Judicial administrator[b]	200 pesos
(The doctor charged per visit)	

Source: Archivo Histórico Provincial de Matanzas, Ingenios 7/108.
  [a] This position appears almost exclusively among *ingenios* that had been embargoed, were the object of litigation, or where sabotage was feared. It increased with the onset of the Ten Years' War.
  [b] An unusual position, relating to embargoed *ingenios*.

going tendencies, although the circulation of currency had been slow since 1875, and became even slower at the end of the decade. This tendency paralleled the evolution of overall production. There were no cases in which foreign capital appears as a purchaser or mortgager of *ingenios*, nor is there any evidence of a North American presence in Cuban sugar production until 1880.[16]

With regard to technological developments, it appears—on the basis of petitions presented by *hacendados* requesting the restitution of rights— that there were few imports of vacuum evaporation apparatuses. Most of the petitions concerned milling machines and carts for the transportation of cane, etc. Accessories were also imported for the other open-air evaporation systems, from which we conclude that the old systems were maintained, since it was not possible to achieve a broader renewal of production equipment.[17]

The composition of the labor force did not change significantly, either. In the province of Sagua, for example, 73 percent of the resident population in 1862 were slaves, 2 percent were freed blacks, and 25 percent were whites and Asians. These figures are similar to those in the "Contrato para la renta decimal en Quemado de Güines" ("Contract for Tithe-Rents in Quemado de Güines") in the same jurisdiction, according to which 79.39 percent of the labor force of the 21 *ingenios* were slaves, 17.56 percent were Chinese, and 3.04 were white.[18]

The functions of wage laborers had not changed either, as table 3.4 indicates. On that establishment a total of 37 pesos was paid for iron work; 612 pesos for building the sugar kettle; repairs on the molds were settled for 397 pesos, and repairs on the oven, for 306 pesos.[19] These expenses, and similar ones also accounted for, reveal the work in repairs and maintenance that were undertaken by free laborers, working on a contractual basis. The books of the Australia *ingenio* for 1867 also show a contract with some neighboring *colonos* to buy cane for 2 pesos per 100 *arroba* cartload.[20]

These accounts reveal the presence of elements in the social division of labor that had always been present in plantation slavery. But during the seventies the typical *ingenio*, regardless of these manifestations, continued to be a closed unit, based predominantly on the exploitation of slave or semislave labor. In the first years of the seventies were few changes of any importance, although elements in the social division of labor become more frequent.

Until 1877 we found no documentary reference to machinery imports. After this date there is a marked tendency to import apparatuses and accessories for vacuum evaporation and sugar centrifuges. This was a logical consequence of the changes that were taking place in the North American buying market (which was by then dominant in Cuba). There was a significant increase in the demand for centrifuged sugar packed in bags, rather than for the classic *bocoyes* of muscovado. Imports of narrow-gauge railroad cars or portable railroads for the transportation of cane were also frequent. A good part of this equipment came from New York, which indicates that the European suppliers of machinery had been replaced. The equipment was sent to *ingenios* in Matanzas and Sagua; this shows that the expansion of cane to other areas of Cuba had not yet begun.

The crisis that the country was undergoing did not affect everyone equally. An analysis of the machinery import forms reveals that machinery was imported by the owners of the larger *ingenios*, owners of several *ingenios*, or those who, in addition, may have had capital invested in other sectors. Many were merchants who had invested in the sugar industry from approximately 1860 on. But even the largest native slaveowners were strong enough to make a last effort at salvation. Miguel Aldama, for example, got his estates disembargoed (they had been embargoed for political reasons during the Ten Years' War) and the following month began to import machinery.[21]

Efforts to solve labor shortages resulted in a scandalous incident following the prohibition of contracting Oriental labor after the king of Spain and the emperor of China signed a treaty on November 17, 1877. The Company to Import Free Laborers was formed in order to bring in immigrants from the Canary Islands. The immigrants were brought under conditions similar to those under which the Chinese had been brought. They had to sign a contract obliging them to work until they had paid the expenses of their trip, which had been advanced by the contracting intermediary. In order to repay him, the immigrant had to subtract 1 percent from the monthly wage of 8 pesos stipulated by the contract (the average wage for a sugar cane worker at the time was 20 pesos a month). The contract further stipulated that "in the workplace, as well as away from it, the worker remained subject to the order established in the *ingenio*, plantation or establishment." If he were not satisfied, he could leave but not before paying his creditor an additional 12 percent interest.[22]

This was the "free" immigration to which Cuban slaveowners aspired. It is well known that if it is possible to establish the laws of supply and demand with regard to the labor force, it is impossible to depress the wages of free workers. Thus, by means of contracts, they attempted to avoid paying the going wage. The multiplicity of forms of exploitation and means of payment was reflected in an article in the *Revista de Agricultura*:

> Today it can be said that slaves have as a daily wage the value of their food and their clothing, and medical attention in the case of illness. We believe that we do not depart too much from the truth if we calculate this wage at 6 or 7 pesos a month. For the Chinese contract laborer, we calculate 15 gold pesos in cash wages and 5 pesos food and health care. Free Chinese earn 21 gold pesos. Free blacks and whites who can do all work are about the same in their monthly wages as the above, and they cost about 5 pesos for food. Teams of black slaves work in two ways. There are those who have been living on the same establishments for a long time, who would earn over 22 pesos, plus 5 in food, clothing and medical assistance; and there are those whose owners have been clever enough to force the desperate owners of *ingenios* to hire them during the month of November (the beginning of the harvest and the beginning of the agonies), and for the following year until the next November, when a new opportunity for strangulation arises. These cunning fellows rent them for up to 27 gold pesos, plus 5 in food and clothes and 15 sick days, for which they are paid the whole daily wage, even if the slave doesn't work.[23]

Convict labor was also used on the *ingenios*. The contract with the authorities stipulated a wage of 12 pesos a month, of which the prisoner received only one; the rest went to the treasury, except for 2 pesos for the prison's utility fund.[24]

These diverse forms of labor coexisted with slavery and complemented it—as in the work of administration and labor control. Wage labor, contract labor, and the purchase of cane from small agriculturalists were also elements of a more advanced stage of society that was developing at the heart of the earlier stage. It is clear, however, that slavery continued as the predominant element, representing in 1877, 76 percent of sugar production in Pinar del Río, 66.32 percent in Havana, 72.18 percent in the province of Matanzas, and 71.30 percent in the region of Sagua la Grande.[25]

The fundamental difference between free labor and slavery or semislavery is not to be found in its cost alone, but also in its yield, and in the obstacles that it places in the way of increased labor productivity. In spite of an increase in the number of *ingenios* in which technological advances had been introduced, by the end of the seventies there had been no radical change in the organization of labor, because it had been impossible to achieve important increases in productivity.

The development of the internal market was always held back by production for export. For most of the nineteenth century, sugar displaced other crops and came to cost more because of the tendency to export more sugar and to import necessities. On the other hand, the existence of slavery prevented the direct producers from entering the market as consumers. These circumstances slowed the development of mercantile relations.

During the seventies the *ingenio* remained a closed economic unit that included all the phases of sugar production and, at times, subsistence production. Its relations to the internal market were limited almost exclusively to receiving from the merchant-lender the supplies necessary to maintain the slave rations and keep up production. Not even in this case did mercantile relations take place freely. The landowner did not acquire his supplies on the market but rather received them from the merchant-lender under the terms of a contract.

In the transition from production with slave labor to more advanced forms, at first the reproduction of capital on a broad scale translated into more land and more slaves. Without a change in the conditions of production, the *ingenio* reached its limits. At this point, the reproduction of capital translated into more *ingenios*. When the steam engine was applied to the *trapiche*, the *ingenio* was able to grow, but new limits were set by the problems of transporting cane. The *ingenio* could not extend its cultivation beyond the radius that could be covered by ox-drawn carts. And beyond this, there were no quantitative solutions to maintain growth.

From midcentury on, attempts had been made to loosen the bottleneck in cane transportation by means of the portable railway. This was the last effort to achieve increases in productivity by reaching for a new optimum size within the framework of slave labor. But the portable railways presented serious technical difficulties. The internal economic crisis, however, was more important in restraining growth in the units than technical difficulties.

In fact, few landowners were able to make the initial investment entailed in introducing rail transportation for cane and then to absorb the costs of maintaining it throughout the year. Both the technical difficulties and the size of the initial investment increased, the larger the milling capacity of the *ingenio*. And it was precisely the large *ingenios* that most needed a rapid and secure transportation system for their raw material. If we also consider that the cultivation of cane was extensive—and it was not possible to change the agricultural system as long as slavery was in effect—we conclude that the *ingenio*, as an economic unit, had reached the limit for quantitative expansion. In fact, most of the large *ingenios* of the 1860s and 1870s that had installed heavy industrial equipment were producing far below their theoretical capacity and were thus not receiving the benefits of economies of scale.

When, during the 1881–82 harvest, public railroads were introduced for the transportation of cane, and new branches and stations were built, an important step was taken in the social division of labor, which encouraged the organization of production on entirely new bases. In the first place, with public rail transportation of cane, mercantile relations penetrated sugar production. It is from this moment that one can speak of a qualitative change: appropriately, the legal processes for the final abolition of slavery had begun a year earlier.

But the sale of cane transportation to the *ingenios* by the public services had another general characteristic that has been recognized only obliquely. Even after slavery was abolished, one of the great obstacles to growth for the *ingenios* remained the large investments in railroads and—from the turn of the century on—in electric energy. If they were only in use during the short harvest months, these became costly economic deadweights. It was necessary to link productive service for the *ingenio* to public service, and this solution was adopted. A variant of a system developed during the 1890s in which the *ingenio's* railroads and electric plants were put to public use. The first option did not exclude the second.

CHANGES IN SUGAR PRODUCTION, 1860–1881

Although the statistical series that would permit a detailed analysis of the evolution of some parameters of production do not exist, it is possible to study the basic trends. In spite of our conviction that the simple figure obtained by dividing the total tons of sugar produced in a given year by the number of productive units yields a very gross index, it does reflect the situation at a general level. In considering the tremendous regional differences and different types of *ingenios*, it would be ideal if we could do regional analyses and obtain weighted indexes, including variables such as the theoretical productive capacities of the installed equipment and the extension of land planted in cane. But the available statistics of the period do not permit this, and we must reason where we cannot calculate.

If we consider that the national average for the semimechanized *ingenios* of 1860—the only year for which such figures are available—was 445 tons, and that that of the mechanized *ingenios* was 1,192, we may conclude that during the twenty-one intervening years there had been no perceptible increase in productivity. In effect, an extremely high percentage of *ingenios* that disappeared between 1860 and 1881 were based on animal traction, which distorts the figure obtained for the first of these years, 1860 (see table 3.5). We have been able to document the demolition of 136 of these in the jurisdictions of the department of Oriente alone.

The number of *caballerías* is an important index of the level of development reached, since—independently of other agricultural yields—the area under cultivation generally corresponded to the productive capacity of the units. The area in cane depended on the *ingenio's* milling capacity as well as on the means of transportation.

Before production became centralized, the *ingenio's* total area did not

Table 3.5   Index of Annual Production per Unit, National Average for All Types of *Ingenios* in the Country

Year	Number of *Ingenios*	Total Production (metric tons)	Tons per *Ingenio*
1860	1,382	428,769	310
1877	1,190	516,268	433
1881	1,170	580,894	496

Source: See table 3.3.

correspond to the area under cultivation. Several patterns suggest the distinctive uses to which land was put. Large areas were left forested, as fuel reserves, and others were left fallow for new cane plantings when the fields already in cane were exhausted and their agricultural yields began to decline. There were fields planted in food crops and pastures for the *ingenio's* cattle.

As seen, between 1860 and 1877, increases in production *in this province* had taken place at the expense of increases in the number of mills. The agricultural situation seems to have remained stable during the whole period. The variations reflected in table 3.6 are minimal and can be attributed equally to insignificant changes or to statistical errors, typical of the figures of the period.

A significant reduction in sugar yields per unit of cultivated land took place (table 3.7). This may have resulted from the interaction of two separate factors. In the first place, the foregoing figures are based on the areas *planted* in cane but not on the areas actually *harvested*. This means that the area harvested was considerably less than that planted. Although this implies a serious underutilization of resources in land, it was typical of poor harvest periods like the 1881 season. The second factor to consider is the decline in agricultural yields, which began to affect production seriously.

CHANGES IN SUGAR PRODUCTION AFTER 1881

From the technological point of view, Cuban sugar production reached its peak during the 1870s in the most developed regions and units; it included

Table 3.6   Area Planted in Cane by *Ingenios*, Province of Matanzas (Average Size in *Caballerías*)

Region	1860 Average Size	Percentage in Cane	1877 Average Size	Percentage in Cane	1881 Average Size	Percentage in Cane
Matanzas	19.35	48.58	18.44	47.37	21.74	54.87
Cárdenas	18.86	55.49	19.01	42.99	18.66	48.02
Colón	27.26	50.32	26.41	47.23	28.99	48.74

Source: See table 3.3.

Table 3.7   Sugar Yields per Planted *Caballería*, Province of Matanzas

Region	1860 Arrobas/Caballería	1881 Arrobas/Caballería
Cárdenas	2,177	1,612
Colón	2,358	1,887
Matanzas	2,895	2,049

Source: See table 3.3.

many elements that correspond to the stage of large industry. The efficiency of the various units was reflected in their profitability and ability to reproduce themselves on a broad scale. Neither their productivity nor their organization of labor, however, was at an industrial level.

The essence of the changes after the 1880s was of a socioeconomic rather than of a technological order. This is not to say that improvements in machinery and processes were not introduced, but the new machines and changed processes did not imply a technological revolution. The essential machinery for the modernization of the sugar industry had been present on the world market since the 1870s, when double-pressure grinders, the multiple effect, the double-bottomed defecators, the large kettles, the centrifuges, the filters, the green bagasse–burning ovens, and the multiple-control mechanisms became available. All of these had been imported to Cuba as soon as they were produced.

The introduction and installation of modern machinery continued during the 1880s. Numerous double-pressure grinders were installed (the first on record actually began to work in 1879), and hydraulic regulators were installed in 1883. Defiberators and crushers were tried in 1881 and 1882; the multiple effect became common and by 1889 a quadruple effect is spoken of. In spite of the existence of slavery, and the constraints imposed by colonial domination, a radical transformation was taking place in the conditions of production. The stimulus of competition on the world market became stronger because the development of the beet sugar industry led to a sustained lowering of prices. This was the crisis that ruined the slaveowning *hacendados* of Cuba. Those who managed to survive were obliged to alter radically the conditions of production on their *ingenios*.

The transformation of the productive process was not merely a matter of installing new industrial equipment (which was already present on many *ingenios*) but rather a complete renewal at the social, institutional, and productive levels. Slaveowners could not undertake such a renewal and they were condemned to perish together with slavery. The slaveowners created the *patronato*, which was not much more than a veiled slavery in its death throes. The *patronato*, in turn, died as totally new social conditions emerged: the prerequisites for capitalism had matured. The slaveowners kept and maintained their slaves as long as possible. They shackled themselves to the slaves by considering them part of their investment capital, tying themselves to a past destined to die. Perhaps they had no other option. Finally, when slavery as a system of labor had exhausted all its possibilities, the slaveowners clamored for the suppression of the *patronato*. This is to say, they gave up their slaves when the logic of the situation compelled them to do so. During the first year of the *patronato*, 6,333 *patrocinados* obtained their freedom; in the second year, 10,249; in the third, 17,418; and during the fourth, 26,507.

As capitalist means of exploitation came to dominate the sugar industry, it also moved into the agricultural production of cane, as cane became a commodity. At first, this did not imply changes in the relations of property in land but just in its mode of exploitation. The supply of cane to the mill was extended as far as possible by the railroads. Many landowners who could not industrialize abandoned the extractive phase of the *ingenio* and tried to maximize their investments in agricultural infrastructure and the area seeded in cane. They thus became suppliers of cane to the central mills, the centrales. The millowners, for their part, did not need to extend their property in land but rather concentrated their activities on industrial production.

Although the division of agricultural labor entailed by sugar factories introduced improvements in the cultivation of cane, we cannot yet speak of intensive sugar cane planting. What took place was an improved use of the land, without intensification of agricultural practices. Thus the increased productive capacity of the centrales required increased control over the land planted in cane. The conditions for sugar cane latifundia were present.

Improvements in the transportation of cane enabled a constant and secure supply of cane to accelerate the flow of production considerably. Improvements in the extractive phase increased the yields of sugar to cane, thus compensating for the exhaustion of the land. In 1888 the *Revista de Agricultura* estimated that the average yield for Cuba was 35,000 *arrobas* of cane per *caballería* and that some *ingenios* with improved planting practices could achieve 50,000 to 60,000 *arrobas*.[26] These figures are far too low, and they contradict information subsequently published by the same journal. Nonetheless, they reveal a preoccupation with the low agricultural yields that were striking at the industry's development. In 1860 Ramón de la Sagra estimated Cuban agricultural yields at over 80,000 *arrobas* of cane per *caballería*,[27] and during the 1880s experts used 74,649 *arrobas* as a base to calculate the yields of the establishments.[28]

These figures show that the fundamental problem of slave production was not in agriculture, because the natural condition of the land on the island compensated for the forms of extensive cultivation. Unfortunately, few data are available to analyze these questions in detail. It is staggering that there are no agricultural statistics on sugar cane at a national level until 1931. We are able to reach a few conclusions for the final decades of the nineteenth century, however. First, except among a few *ingenios* and iso-

Table 3.8   Cuban Sugar Exports, Percentage of Total Exports in Bags

Year	Percentage
1890	95.89
1891	95.99
1892	96.77
1893	98.60
1894	99.35
1895	99.68

Source: Calculated from the export statistics published by the *Revista de Agricultura*.

lated planters, extensive cultivation of cane predominated. Second, the division between the agricultural and industrial sectors of production transferred the problems of low agricultural yields to the cane growers, since the mills paid for cut, clean cane deposited in the mill's yard or loader, without concerning themselves with the area that had been required to produce it.

At first, the competition for supplies of cane between the centrales favored the small planters (*colonos*, in the lexicon of the Cuban sugar industry). The price paid for cane varied in the different regions of the country, depending on the supply, the demand of the centrales, and transportation facilities. Then, the owners of the central mills began to put a brake on the free play of supply and demand by means of "contracts of *colonato*" and moneylending, which the small planters, in the absence of alternatives, were obliged to accept. These contracts obliged the *colono* to supply cane exclusively to the particular central at stipulated prices and conditions. To protect itself from oscillations in sugar prices, the central occasionally committed itself to pay only for a specified weight of sugar—not in cash but for the sale price the sugar attained on the market—excluding the commission.

In summary, with regard to industrial installations and the means of exploiting the labor force, and social relations in general, by 1890 one can speak of the existence of capitalism in the Cuban sugar industry. Many *ingenios* were still producing muscovado with the use of Jamaican trains, but their weight in overall production was negligible. There was, however, a relatively high per capita consumption of these low-quality sugars.

It is difficult to say precisely when muscovado was no longer produced for export. There are no statistics according to sugar type. The kind of packaging used is not an appropriate indicator because until the 1890s centrifuged sugar with a Pol of 92 degrees or less was packaged in hogsheads. Since muscovado cannot be exported in bags, it is possible that some of the hogsheads of sugar that appear in the Cuban export figures could have been muscovado sugar. In any case, this category slowly disappeared from Cuban exports (table 3.8).

The near predominance of bagged sugar shows that a modern sugar industry was fully established—the only means of producing centrifuged

Table 3.9   Number of *Ingenios* in Production, Province of Matanzas, 1860–1900

Year	Number of *Ingenios*	Percentage of Pervious Year	Index
1860	442	—	100.00
1877	517	116.96	116.96
1881	473	91.48	107.01
1895	99	20.93	22.39
1899[a]	37	37.37	8.37
1900	33	89.19	7.46

Sources: For 1860, 1877, and 1881, see table 3.3. For 1895, Archivo Histórico de la Provincial de Matanzas, Gobierno Provincial, estadísticas 8/9. For 1899 and 1900, Military Government of Cuba, Department of Agriculture, Commerce, and Industry, *Report*, p. 244.

[a] The first year of peace: the end of the War of Independence.

sugar of high polarization. According to the New York company, Willet and Gray, Cuban sugars imported by the United States during the 1890s had an average Pol of 95 degrees.

The installation of a modern sugar industry did not mean an end to the processes of concentration. Until 1895 the less efficient industrial units continued to disappear, as did numerous old manufacturing establishments that had remained in production for local consumption. That process was fairly accelerated up to 1895 (table 3.9).

The process of concentration in land did not take place in the same way. This was not possible in view of the ways in which capital movements had developed. After 1880 the situation was similar to that observed for the two previous decades. A large sample of *ingenios* in the region, including the old jurisdiction of Matanzas, reveals that during the 1880s sales and loans continued as before. The liens on the land continued in effect. By the end of the 1880s there was an increase in the number of *ingenios* auctioned to pay debts, for far lower prices than their tax assessment value. Among those in which investments had been made, the owners had even contracted with the European machinery suppliers on the basis of mortgages. This was a fairly generalized practice.

The landowners clamored for reforms that would increase the available financing for the industry. It is clear that both the types of credit available and the liens were remains of an earlier social formation that fettered the full development of capitalism in the industry. Under these circumstances it was almost impossible to find financing for production. Consequently, since the industry's industrial plant was already in place, the fundamental obstacles to the development of production lay in getting adequate financing. This situation obtained until the end of the century. This was one of the factors that prevented the centralization of property.

At this time, North American capital in sugar production cannot be discerned in landed property. Some North Americans had acquired property in sugar, just as some French, Canadian, and German merchants in Cuba had bought land. However, of the 46 mills operating or being rebuilt in the province of Matanzas in 1900, 93.47 percent represented domestic capital,[29] of which 50 percent was Cuban and 43.47 percent was Spanish. The remaining 6.53 percent represented other nationalities, including North Americans.[30]

Nonetheless, of the four mills that appear to be North American property, two belonged to Spaniards or Cubans who had taken American citizenship. The third belonged to an heir of a North American (a brother of Moses Taylor's who had lived in Cuba since midcentury), and the fourth belonged to the Feliz Sugar Company, incorporated in New York in 1898. But the real owners were the Piedra Perez family and Manuel Ceballos, a Spanish relative, who was a sugar broker and a partner in the company of Rionda, Ceballos and Company.[31]

Although this may be an isolated case, it is probable that during the period of the first intervention, mechanisms of this sort were used to seek protection from the government of the United States. For this reason, even when centrales appear to be the property of Americans, it is important to investigate their origins. Nor was North American capital present in the mills that were torn down.[32] At the end of the century there was no significant foreign capital in the Cuban sugar industry, either in property or in finance.

CONCLUSIONS

These are some of the results of our studies on the formation of capitalism in Cuban sugar production. They will undoubtedly be improved on and complemented by future studies. Among the principal problems requiring special attention in order to increase our understanding of the complex transformations during the second half of the nineteenth century, we suggest the following studies: credit and the circulation of currency; the non-sugar sectors, e.g., tobacco; and the development of infrastructure. We need detailed studies of all the forms that Cuban agriculture assumed in order to increase our understanding of internal factors in the genesis of capitalism. For these reasons we consider this paper as a first step in untangling the broad and complex panorama of Cuba's economic development at the end of the colonial period.

NOTES

This chapter represents a condensed version of the paper presented at the conference. Those wishing to see the fuller version should write to the author. The translation was done by Elizabeth Hansen.

1. For a description of Cuban sugar production up to this date, see Manuel

Moreno Fraginals, *El ingenio: complejo económico social cubano del azúcar*, 3 vols. (Havana: Editorial de Ciencias Sociales, 1978).

2. See table 3.1. See also the calculations in Moreno Fraginals, *El ingenio*, 1:174.
3. See table 3.1.
4. Moreno Fraginals, *El ingenio*, 1:254–55.
5. Juan Poey, *Informe sobre Reformas de Aranceles en Cuba y Puerto Rico* (Havana: Imprenta del Gobierno, 1862), appendix 2, p. 16.
6. Archivo Nacional de Cuba (hereafter, ANC), Fondo: Gobierno Superior Civil, 1285/5026 to 45 and 1115/4142.
7. Calculated from *Noticias Estadísticas de la Isla de Cuba, en 1862* (Havana: Imprenta del Gobierno, 1864).
8. Archivo Histórico Provincial de Matanzas (hereafter AHPM), Gobierno Provincial, Estadísticas.
9. Poey, *Informe sobre Reformas*, appendix 2, pp. 3, 4–7, and 17. These data have been checked against documentary appraisals, and these rough proportions are maintained.
10. Calculated from the data on *caballerías* seeded in cane in Carlos Rebello, *Estados Relativos a la Producción Azucarera de la Isla de Cuba* (Havana: Imprenta del Gobierno, 1860).
11. Ramón de la Sagra, *Cuba: 1860* (Havana: Comisión Cubana de la UNESCO, 1963), p. 145.
12. Moreno Fraginals, *El ingenio*, 1:174.
13. La Sagra, *Cuba*, pp. 136–44.
14. Calculated from Padrón de Fincas Rústicas de la Jurisdicción de Colón para 1859. ANC, Misc. de Expedientes (hereafter ME): 4120/M.
15. Moreno Fraginals, *El ingenio*, 2:174–221.
16. ANC, Fondo: Protocolos, Anotaduría de Hipotecas, Ts. 80-103, 1860–80. Anotaciones: Ingenios.
17. ANC, ME: 1465/N, 1483/D, 1507/K, 1515/Y, 1465/Bj, 1698/Bm, 1910/Ai,P, 2333/af, 2088/Ba, 3230/A, 3288/Ah, 3695/N, 4247/Ao, 4347/B, 4268/All, Am, An, Añ, Ao, 4269/Aa.
18. ANC, ME: 3191C.
19. AHPM, Ingenios 7/108 and 2/18.
20. ANC, ME: 4204/M.
21. ANC, Consejo de Administración, 93/8461.
22. *Revista Económica* 2, No. 40 (1878): 86.
23. *Revista de Agricultura* 1, No. 4, p. 83.
24. ANC, ME: 3947/D.
25. Calculated from data in *Revista Económica* 2, No. 37, appendix.
26. *Revista de Agricultura* 9, No. 34, p. 505.
27. La Sagra, *Cuba*, p. 107.
28. ANC, Escribanía de Montalván, 20/18.
29. According to the term introduced by Oscar Pino Santos, in *El Asalto a Cuba por la Oligarquía Finaciera Yanqui* (Havana: Casa de Las Americas, 1973), p. 38.
30. Calculated from data in the AHPM, Gobierno Provincial, Estadísticas 8/37.
31. Registro Mercantil de la Provincia de Matanzas, Book 127, F. 107.
32. Robert Porter, *Industrial Cuba* (New York: G. P. Putnam's Sons, 1899), pp. 254–55, 305, and 355–58.

Cuba, 1899

Atlantic Ocean

SANTIAGO

Bayamo

Santiago
de Cuba

PUERTO PRÍNCIPE

Puerto
Príncipe

SANTA CLARA

Cienfuegos

MATANZAS

Matanzas

HAVANA

Havana

PINAR DEL RÍO

Caribbean Sea

N

4. Cuba:
Dependence, Plantation Economy, and Social Classes, 1762–1902
Francisco López Segrera

This chapter describes the peculiarities of the nineteenth-century Cuban plantation economy by means of an analysis of social classes. I shall try to explain how and why international capitalism and dependent Cuban capitalism introduced, modified, and then destroyed slavery during the colonial era; how and why the contradictions of international capitalism and dependent Cuban capitalism led to the transition from slave labor to free labor; and, finally, how social classes evolved in the process.

An exposition of my theoretical and methodological ideas on how the subject should be approached is beyond the purposes of this essay; nonetheless, I must briefly state my understanding of the relations between slavery and capitalism in America, and of the process that led to the transition from slavery to free labor on American plantations. My approach to these problems can be summarized as follows:

1. Commercial capital led to the rise and development of social formations based on slave labor in the Americas. The exploitation of this kind of labor was subordinate to, and dependent on, European commercial capital, which directed the processes of accumulation and circulation of capital but without regard for the processes of commodity production on American plantations.
2. Commercial capital created the coexistence and interdependence of free labor and slave labor, which would be destroyed by industrial capitalism. When slave labor ceased to be an engine of growth, it was destroyed by industrial capitalism.
3. The transition from slavery to free labor took place at a point in the

77

history of capitalism when the process of production moved from a subordinate to a hegemonic position in relation to the circulation of capital.

What follows is an attempt to document these three assertions systematically.

CUBAN SOCIETY DURING THE PLANTATION ERA, 1762–1880

Cuba and International Capitalism in Its Industrial Phase

At the end of the eighteenth century, Cuban development accelerated with the establishment of a plantation economy, with tight connections to international capital established after the capture of Havana by the British (1762). The colonial export system developed rapidly and deepened the island's underdevelopment as the sugar sector of the economy grew out of proportion, to the detriment of other sectors of production. The sugar sector became more dependent on factors external to the colony, and wealth was concentrated in fewer hands, thus preventing the development of production for an internal market, the development of technology, and the development of social classes related to the growth of an internal economy. Cuba was ready to be exploited, not by the mercantilist policies of commercial capital but by the free trade policies of industrial powers like England and the United States, nations that protected their own industries with tariff barriers. In addition, Cuba was subject to the mercantile and manufacturing interests of Spain in its trading relations and to the interests of the Spanish Crown and its taxes.

The transition from commercial, mercantile capitalism to industrial, free trade capitalism involved the replacement of regulated commerce by free trade, and according to Karl Marx, "today industrial supremacy implies commercial supremacy," not vice versa, as had been the case in the earlier period.[1] This meant the displacement of Spain, Portugal, and Holland as hegemonic powers by England, the United States, France, and Belgium and also the specialization of colonial areas in a few products, such as sugar, coffee, and tobacco. Thus the colonial exploitation typical of mercantilism—tributary pillage, the search for precious metals, and the establishment of trading houses by means of territorial occupation—was replaced by the methods of exploitation of free trade with the exchange of cheap raw materials for expensive manufactured goods. In order to achieve these ends, the industrial powers used military, political, and economic means.

The beginnings of unequal development also stem from this period, resulting in a sharpening of the contradictions of capitalism, not in the metropolitan areas but principally in the colonies. As the weakest links in the chain of exploitation, the colonies could not, as the metropolis could, export their crises to other countries. In view of the colonial exploitation by the foreign metropolis, and in order to increase their incomes, the capital and metropolitan areas in the colony superexploited, and thus underdeveloped, the interior regions of the country. And the dominant classes, in turn, superexploited the other classes in order to increase their own profits.

Historically, this process coincided with the occupation of Spain by Napoleonic troops, which provided the favorable conjuncture necessary for Latin American independence. Nonetheless, independence meant little more than the passage from Spanish colonial exploitation to English exploitation. Spain had to resort to mercantilist prohibitions to prevent American manufactures from competing with its own manufactures. The English, on the other hand, needed only freedom of trade to destroy Latin American industry with competition from its own, and this without obstructing political independence, for, as Marx pointed out, "the low prices of their goods constituted a heavy artillery, able to destroy all walls."

Because of the expansion of industrial capitalism and its free trade policies, Latin America's economic structures were adapted to the needs of the metropolitan powers: England in the case of independent Latin America, and Spain, England, and the United States in the case of colonial Cuba. Therefore, the transition from commercial capitalism to industrial capitalism did not mean the beneficial opening of the continent to commerce, as traditional historiography maintains. Instead, the transition conditioned and adjusted the region, in intimate harmony with the interests of the Latin American oligarchies that directed the local processes, to the needs of international capitalism and established its character as an exporter of raw materials and importer of manufactured products. This domination assumed a narrower character in the Andean and Central American regions than in the countries on the Atlantic coast. The latter became dynamically linked to England, and once independence had been attained, their agrarian commercial bourgeoisies were able to integrate the various sectors of society under their political domination. This was possible because this bourgeoisie had inherited the productive aparatus of the colonial epoch and also because England's economic activities focused on acquiring raw materials for the metropolitan center, not in capital investments. Because of this, the export sectors of the bourgeoisies in the Atlantic coast countries became rulers of their countries, as well as rulers in their homes.

In contrast, in the Andean and Central American countries, agrarian decline and political chaos developed. Unlike those on the Atlantic coast, these countries were not able to become linked directly and dynamically to the European metropolis until the end of the nineteenth century. Here, in the absence of a bourgeois sector sufficiently strong to impose itself on other classes, a bloody political battle developed between the bourgeoisies and the military *caudillos* who emerged from the wars of independence. The agrarian bourgeoisies were not able to consolidate their power until the end of the nineteenth century, when their links to the international capitalist system and to the world market became based on the exploitation of raw materials controlled by the metropolis—but by then it was already too late.

The exploiting metropoles did not limit themselves to the appropriation of raw materials. In addition, and most importantly, they assumed control of internal productive sectors, by investing in enclaves, forming dynamic sectors characterized by the heavy use of capital and technology and the limited use of labor. This resulted in the interruption, paralysis, and destruction of the development of the internal market, typical of parasitic imperialist investment and its concern with exports and cheap labor instead of the countries' development. In these countries the dependent bourgeoisies could not, therefore, establish a political and economic dominance over society, as did those of the Atlantic coast. Instead, they saw themselves reduced to the role of political representatives of metropolitan interests, and they became a pseudo-bourgeoisie, a lumpen-bourgeoisie, a dependent bourgeoisie.

Cuba belonged to this second group of countries, but still other particulars contributed to its becoming a superexploited economy. First, the failure of the War of 1868 ruined the nationalist and revolutionary sector of the bourgeoisie in the eastern region. Second, between 1840 and 1860 the Cuban sugar bourgeoisie (*sugarocracy*) entered a period of crisis, and control of the sugar industry fell to Spanish commercial capital. Third, between 1860 and 1880 a corporative oligarchical block developed, composed of antinationalist Cuban, Spanish, and North American interests, which hastened the process of adapting the island's economic structure to the needs of the export trade. Fourth, from 1880 on, North American capital, in its imperialist phase, increased its investments in the sugar sector considerably, because of the crisis following the Ten Years' War, with the aim of assuming control of the colony's economy by establishing the enclaves that adapted colonial production to metropolitan needs.

Finally, nineteenth-century Cuba came to be exploited by three mechanisms simultaneously, and not one or two as happened in most of Latin America. These were the Spanish tax; the extraction of raw materials in exchange for manufactured products from Spain, England, the United States, etc.; and North American imperialist exploitation and its system of enclaves. These conditions, which were peculiar to the Cuban economy and which entailed the plunder and removal of tremendous wealth from the colony to the metropolitan areas, resulted in interregional and class exploitation of enormous proportions. Regionally, the west, and especially Havana, exploited the rest of the island, and the western oligarchical section of the bourgeoisie superexploited the other social classes, especially the slaves. Thus, the fact that unlike most Latin American countries, Cuba did not achieve its independence until the turn of the century (for fear of the slaves, among other factors) prevented the crystallization of a national bourgeoisie. This meant that the real power was exercised, once the War of Independence was over and José Martí (the powerful factor who might have prevented this) had disappeared, by the corporative, privileged Cuban-Spanish-North American block. In harmony with the interests of Yankee imperialism, this block used some of the heroic *mambises caudillos* as instruments of political domination.[2] The dependent Cuban bourgeoisie were thus reduced to the role of mere political interpreters of the designs of the metropolis.

The transition from mercantilism (1510–1762) to free trade (1762–1880) in Cuba obeyed three principal factors. Spain was collecting large fiscal revenues with its taxes on the island's trade. Spanish, English, and North American industrial interests needed markets from which to buy cheap raw materials and in which to sell the commodities produced by their industries. And in free trade the Creole oligarchy saw a road to rapid wealth, with no thought given to its dire consequences. At this stage, Cuba was exploited not by the typical monopolies of the mercantilist era but by free trade, partial in 1762 and complete by 1818, with the compliance and approbation of the privileged sector of Creole *hacendados* and Spanish merchants, who enriched themselves at the cost of increasing the country's underdevelopment. Thus, the island paid for imports with the money that it borrowed at high interest rates from the industrializing countries, the United States and England, and it sold to them, at low prices, the raw materials that they required.

The only ones who might have opposed free trade, to the extent that they had been favored by mercantilist regulation, were the Spanish merchants, but they too adapted to free trade. Because of the large capital accumulations they had made on the slave trade, in which the metropolis had supported them, they became merchant lenders to the *ingenios*; in the long run, they came to own the sugar industry. The most powerful sector of the Cuban bourgeoisie, the western sugar *hacendados*, preferred to accept exploitation by the metropolis and the merchant lenders. They enriched themselves by superexploiting interior regions of the country, and the other social classes, and by fighting against the wars of independence, as their peers in the rest of Latin America had done. Among other factors, this was because of their fear that Cuba would become another Haiti, and they would be deprived of their wealth. In the long run, this meant that the bourgeoisie would be destroyed or that the descendants would be assimilated into groups of Spanish or North American foreigners, who forged a corporative, antinationalist, Cuban-Spanish-North American block. Because it lost economic power, the Cuban bourgeoisie became an instrument of political domination in the service of the imperialist international oligarchy.

In view of the foregoing, the restructuring of colonial exports in Cuba during this period cannot, as in earlier periods, be unilaterally attributed to the processes of the international capitalist system. The autonomy of the

Cuban *cabildos*, especially during the land grant period, and the power retained by the Havana consular oligarchy until the captain generalcy of Tacon show that independent of the role of the international capitalist system and Spain in Cuba's formation, dependent export colonial capitalism in Cuba had responded to the interests of the colonial oligarchs since the sixteenth century. In fact, the Havana-Spanish oligarchy of Arango and Don Luis de las Casas (1790) was responsible for fostering the plantation economy, deepening Cuban underdevelopment, and tying the island even more tightly to international capital, to which it had been linked since the sixteenth century, especially after 1762.

At the beginning of the nineteenth century, Cuba's future depended on the struggle between five interest groups. First were foreign slave traders, who also acted as merchant-lenders to the Creole sugar planters. These traders wished to maintain the status quo. They were of recent immigration, and most of their fortunes had been made on the slave trade, as in the cases of Terry, Baro, and Zulueta—and they gradually took over the sugar industry by developing enormous sugar factories with modern equipment. Second was the old oligarchy of Creole sugar planters from the West, who depended on the merchant lenders. Representatives of this group include the Arangos, the Alfonsos, and the Calvos de la Puerta. They aspired to a peaceful change in the political structure so that they could replace the Spanish merchants in exports and in exploitation. But, for fear of a black insurrection, they were systematically opposed to an armed struggle. Third were the Creole landowners from the eastern region of the island—Oriente, Camagüey, and part of Las Villas—who planted sugar, as in Cuenca del Cauto, or who raised cattle, as in Puerto Príncipe. These; the impoverished and downwardly mobile middle sectors composed of professionals, tobacco planters, etc.; and the slaves wanted a political and social revolution. Fourth was Spain, a colonial power in decline, which wanted to keep the status quo on the island for three reasons: to reconquer Latin America, using the "ever faithful island of Cuba" as a base; to continue collecting the large sums that the island provided in taxes, especially taxes on trade; and to continue to export its expensive manufactured products to Cuba and to receive in exchange cheap raw materials. Fifth were England and the United States, both in industrial expansion, which wanted economic, and possibly political, control of the Spanish colony, in which they saw a magnificent market for their manufactured products and a supplier of raw materials. The English foreign minister, Canning, announced in 1824: "Spanish America is free; and if we don't manage our business badly, she is English." Although this was truer of the rest of Latin America than of Cuba, the Cuban market was nonetheless flooded by English products, and Cuban exports to that country were voluminous. The country that most benefited from the establishment of free trade in Cuba, however, was the

United States. In 1823 the American secretary of state, Adams, wrote that it would be indispensable to annex Cuba to the United States.

In sum, the antagonisms were between those who, for one reason or another, supported the status quo, that is, Spain, England, and the United States (which, since it could not take over the island, preferred that it continue under Spanish control); the merchant lenders; the western Creole sugar planters; and those who were opposed to the status quo—the Creole oligarchy from Oriente, Camagüey, and part of Las Villas, the middle sectors, and the lower classes and slaves.

The Metropolis-Colony Contradiction

The development of the plantation economy strengthened the export emphasis of the Cuban economy. The producing and consuming sectors in Cuba were affected by the monopolist policies of the Havana oligarchy. The sugar planters among the Creole bourgeoisie were opposed to monopoly, but the tension between them and the Spanish commercial interests was not of adversaries, for on several occasions the Havana planters associated with the Spanish merchants. There were attempts to break the power of the monopolist merchants, but the dynamic inherent in dependent capitalism's mode of production prevented this. The Creole interests of Puerto Príncipe, who favored the autonomous growth of the country by developing a balanced economy, clamored against the monopolist policies of the merchants and the privileged sectors of Havana.

Two factors in the exploitation of the Cuban colony during this period by metropolitan interests—Spanish, North American, and English—by means of foreign trade deserve special attention. They were the plundering of the colony by metropolitan capitalists and the reduction of Spain to the role of a mere political metropolis as the United States became the new economic metropolis. With regard to the plunder of foreign trade, the protests of the Creole sugar oligarchy were incessant. In 1792 Arango emphasized that only one-tenth of the wealth remained in the hands of the producers, and the rest escaped abroad.[3] Similar were the protests of the Creole producers of Puerto Príncipe. In a brief sent to the royal consulate in 1805, Ignacio Zarragoitía accused the merchant monopolists of impoverishing the rest of Cuban society.[4]

With regard to the second factor, sugar traders had been present in the great North American ports since the 1820s and 1830s: the companies of Moses Taylor and Atkins are famous.[5] Until 1860, Cuban exports were distributed roughly as follows: 62 percent to the United States, 22 percent to Great Britain, 3 percent to Spain, and the remaining 13 percent to other countries. Imports were distributed as follows: Spain, 30 percent; United States, 20 percent; Great Britain, 20 percent; and other countries, 30 percent.[6] Moreover, we can see the development of a tendency inherent to the commerce of underdeveloped countries, a heavy concentration in the structure of export products and a wide dispersal in the structure of imports. While Cuba imported innumerable products for internal consumption and for the sugar industry, its exports revolved around three products—sugar, tobacco, and coffee—but especially around sugar. During the 1860s, sugar provided 80 percent of exports; tobacco, 10 percent; and coffee, 2 percent.[7]

In addition, the growing dependence on the North American market meant that the periodic economic crises in its capitalist economy were exported to the island because of the law of unequal development. This took place in 1847, in 1857, and in 1866, and the Cuban economy suffered great damage because of the declines in the price of sugar. The tendency that was to dominate the Cuban economy until the revolution, the dependence on the changing prices of sugar—latent since the end of the eighteenth century and the beginning of the nineteenth—became definitively fixed in the structure of underdevelopment of the colony. During the crises of 1857 and 1866, as in previous periods of depression, the merchant lenders didn't suffer, but the Cubans did, because "the financial institutions created by the Creoles were dissolved, so that, in the absence of any competition, the Spanish Bank and the North American merchants became the absolute masters of the market."[8] It is also important to recognize that "in general, the fiscal regime weighed more heavily on Creole groups, and others dependent on exports, than on the Spanish merchants, who were favored by their connections to Colonial power."[9] The terrible exploitation represented by this fiscal regime is illustrated by the duties charged in all the island's ports by the Spanish metropolis.[10]

The East-West Contradiction

The plantation economy increased the underdevelopment of Cuban society and resulted in greater regional inequalities. In the nineteenth century there were two major regions: the exploiting western region, which included the provinces of Havana, Matanzas, and part of Las Villas, and the exploited eastern region, consisting of Oriente, Camagüey, and the rest of Las Villas. The French coffee belt of Santiago de Cuba and Guantánamo, although in the eastern zone and exploited by the west, produced in a limited area the typical relations of a western plantation economy, just as the sugar sectors in Las Villas constituted a kind of frontier area between the two regions. In the eastern zone, urban slaves predominated over rural slaves, and slavery retained its patriarchal character. The whip of the overseer was rarely heard, and cowhands watched over the cattle in the fields. In the west, on the other hand, a typical plantation economy was established, in which slaves were exploited to the maximum. This regional difference

Table 4.1　Various Economic Indicators by Region, 1862

	Western Region	Eastern Region
Foreign trade	90 percent	10 percent
Tax collection	87 percent	13 percent
Railroads	87 percent	13 percent
Wealth	$236,000,000	$69,000,000
Annual per capita income	$350	$165

Source: Juan Pérez de la Riva, "Aspectos Demográficos y su Importancia en el Proceso Revolucionario del Siglo XIX," in *Union de Periodistas de Cuba* (Havana, 1968), pp. 30–49.

was fully established by the time of the Havana-Matanzas boom of 179u to 1800. The west surpassed the east in the transportation, warehousing, and sales of sugars and syrups. The growth in manufacturing in the western region increased the number of slaves enormously and included profound technological changes, which did not occur to the same degree in the sugar areas of the eastern region. It is also important to understand that the breach between the two regions was economic and not technological. Because import and export operations were practically monopolized by Havana, the eastern region had difficulty in obtaining slaves and access to markets. These regional differences "became crushing with the advent of the western railroad beginning in 1837. The development of Oriente and Puerto Príncipe was halted, and a new boom was produced in Occidente and Las Villas."[11]

We should not be surprised, therefore, that over 90 percent of Cuban sugar production in the nineteenth century took place in the western areas of Havana, Matanzas, Trinidad, Cienfuegos, and Sagua, while the sugar zones of secondary importance in the eastern regions of Sancti-Spíritus, Puerto Príncipe, Santiago de Cuba, Bayamo, and Holguín produced only 10 percent. In 1860 the western region produced 452,000 tons, and the eastern region 63,000 tons, of which 47,000 tons were produced in Oriente and 15,000 in the province of Camagüey.[12]

This regional inequality, largely the result of the plantation economy, is reflected in a few figures on foreign trade, tax collection, railroads, and the distribution of the national wealth and per capita income in 1862 (see table 4.1). The population of the eastern region, constituting 35 percent of the island's total population, received only 22 percent of the national product, an index of regional underdevelopment. Moreover, the differences in per capita incomes are even greater if we recall the low incomes distributed among the enormous mass of slaves in the west. As pointed out by Pérez de la Riva: "We can get a better idea of what this figure represented at the time, both as an index of the island's wealth and as an index of regional imbalance, if we realize that with the purchasing power of the Cuban peso a century ago, a per capita income of $350 is comparable to the 1955 per capita incomes of Switzerland, Sweden, France or England. The regional imbalance was analogous to that existing two decades ago between the North and South of Italy."[13]

Nevertheless, "the island's wealth" was really the wealth of a small privileged group, especially of the export sector and metropolitan interests. Some writers have been misled by Cuba's enormous exports and have taken these as a symptom of wealth and development, when in fact they were signs of underdevelopment. Thus, the countries that were undergoing underdevelopment, like Cuba and the French Antilles, exported thirty dollars to sixty dollars per capita, respectively, while the developing countries, like the United States and England, exported only twelve dollars and eight dollars per capita, respectively.[14]

The conflict between the interests of national groups favoring diversification and independent development, and those connected to the plantation economy is clearly illustrated in the rivalry between Havana and Puerto Príncipe. As Moreno Fraginals notes: "Puerto Príncipe was the island's only important area totally dominated by Creole capital, without the smallest intrusion by Spanish merchants."[15] In 1774 this city in the Province of Camagüey in the eastern region was the second city of Cuba, with 30,000 inhabitants. In 1883 Bachiller wrote of Puerto Príncipe, "It was once a wealthy town."[16] Puerto Príncipe's wealth derived from sugar and cattle, which were exported abroad thanks to a magnificent network of smugglers. Not only did it supply beef to the plantation economies of the Caribbean, but it also came to produce a significant amount of sugar. In 1729 there were sixty *ingenios* and in 1760 Puerto Príncipe produced 65,960 *arrobas* of sugar.[17] The economy of Puerto Príncipe began to decline and to be exploited by Havana with the free trade measures of 1762. From that point on, Puerto Príncipe began to lose the large incomes produced by smuggling sugar and beef directly to foreign merchants, independently of the decline in smuggling that took place in the first half of the eighteenth century. Thus, with the elimination of export barriers, foreign merchants stopped looking in Puerto Príncipe for these contraband goods that they could freely obtain in Havana. Moreover, with the decline of smuggling, cattle were no longer exported, and the region's cattle began to be consumed by the plantations of the west. In the short run, this allowed the Puerto Príncipe elite to survive on their incomes from cattle, but in the long run, they were completely ruined, as they came into the domain of the western region, which exploited it heavily in order to increase its own gain.

The rivalry between Havana and Puerto Príncipe is further illustrated by a brief written by the *principeño*, Ignacio Zarragoitía y Jauregui, in 1805 to the royal consulate. This document clearly expounds the economic ideas of the revolutionary and nationalist sector of the Cuban bourgeoisie, just as Arango's *Discurso de la Agricultura en la Habana* is the best expression of

Cuba's reactionary and antinational sector. In this letter, Zarragoitía attacks the merchants and writes that "the merchants' interests are absolutely contrary to those of the State."[18] He criticizes the privileged Havana block of Spanish merchants and Creole sugar planters and denies that the apparent development of Cuba brought any benefits at all, "except for the four privileged ones."[19] He clearly establishes the nationalism of this Creole sector and this region and attacks the elite of the west, when he maintains that "the inhabitants of Havana, Trinidad, or Matanzas do not represent, nor are they, the people of the island of Cuba. The people of Cuba include all its inhabitants: they should form one family, and it is among the members of this one family that the assets and liabilities should be distributed, without distinction or privilege."[20]

The conflict between Puerto Príncipe and the western region was not so much a conflict between a sugar-producing region and a non-sugar-producing region as it was a conflict where one region developed at the expense of another. As examples of the conflict between these two regions, we may point to the aggressive response of the royal consulate to the Puerto Príncipe petition to declare Nuevitas a free port, the criticisms leveled by the Havana oligarchy at Aguero when he freed his slaves, the conviction of the captains general that Puerto Príncipe was the primary center of rebellion against the Spanish Crown, and also the struggle of Agramonte, beginning with the Ten Years' War, for the abolition of slavery.

The Contradiction between Slave Labor and Free Labor

Another interesting aspect of the underdevelopment of Cuba during these years lies in the contradiction between free labor and slave labor. The massive introduction of Africans prevented capitalist industrialization, which is incompatible with unskilled labor, and deepened the underdevelopment of the country. The unresolvable contradiction between machines and slave labor provoked the disproportionate growth of the sugar industry. The colonial slave labor regime, an important engine for international capital accumulation, should not confuse us and lead us to speak of a slave regime as some Cuban historians have done, since what really existed was a colonial and dependent capitalist mode of production, in which slave labor was used because it was cheaper than wage labor.[21] Marx, in a magnificent phrase, points to the connection between the slavery of the New World and the slavery of the European proletariat within the system of international capitalism. According to him, "the veiled slavery of the wage-earners in Europe needed, for its pedestal, slavery pure and simple in the New World."[22]

Because of the abundance of land in the Cuban colony, free men were not obliged, as in Europe, to look for wages and to become wage workers in order to secure their subsistence. Thus, while the monthly wage of a daily worker in Cuba at midcentury was twenty or thirty pesos, in Europe at the same time it was two or three pesos, and in the case of skilled labor ten to twelve pesos. In an 1844 report, Vasquez Queipo writes that the annual cost of an agricultural slave, including interest and amortization of capital, was seventy pesos. Because of the enormous cost of free labor compared to slave labor, the sugar oligarchy defended the latter, motivated as it was by a desire for rapid wealth, without regard for the deadly consequences this would have for the country.[23]

La Sagra, writing in 1848, clearly perceived the contradiction between slave labor and economic development:

> It is absolutely impossible to organize an agricultural system and a rural economy founded on scientific principles, as long as the planting is done with slave labor. . . . It is hard to establish on the large cane and coffee plantations worked by slaves, because it is impossible to get the necessary care, intelligence, and love of work from some miserable beings which an absurd system considers to be more useful the stupider they are. If, therefore, brutalization and moral degradation are seen as valuable qualities in the large masses of blacks, because they are thus kept in peace and obedience, does this not deprive agriculture of the most essential elements for prosperity, which are intelligence and application?[24]

From 1844 on, especially after 1860, the sugarocracy became increasingly aware that the contradiction between technology and slavery would lead them to ruin. Thus, the reform deputies stated the following in a document written by Jose A. Echevarria and presented to the *Junta de Información*: "The damage to the moral order occasioned by slavery sprouts with double vigor in the material and economic order, making work sterile and preventing the accumulation of capital."[25]

The eclectic solution by which the sugarocrats sought to combine more skilled labor with African slave labor maintained extraeconomic coercion involving the importation of 140,000 Chinese coolies. According to the contract by which they were recruited, the Chinese had to work in the *ingenios* for eight years. Seventy-five percent of them died over this period, and their lives differed from those of slaves only in that they undertook the specialized industrial tasks, while the Africans did all the heavy labor in the fields and in the mills.[26]

In sum, the massive introduction of slave labor deepened Cuban underdevelopment because it converted the island into a plantation colony, because it delayed the development of nationhood between 1762 and 1868, and because it prevented the Cuban bourgeoisie from taking power, as their counterparts in Latin America had done at the beginning of the nineteenth century. Fear of the "black peril" meant the ultimate ruin of this class and the greater dependence of the country on foreign merchants and international capitalism. The slave trade also had enriched the Spanish slavetraders and merchant-lenders, who, in the long run, replaced the sugarocracy in economic predominance. It created a hierarchy of values that, because it reinforced the devaluation of manual labor inherent in the Spanish ethic, increased vagrancy and made it more difficult to find the free laborers who would undertake productive work; finally, it drastically increased regional and class inequalities, as the privileged western block of merchants and sugarocrats became fabulously rich.

Class Contradictions

The plantation economy greatly increased sugar and coffee production, giving the island an appearance of wealth. But in reality social inequalities became sharper and underdevelopment increased. Only the merchant and planter class in the west benefited from the conjuncture that in 1800 had concentrated all of the island's wealth among five hundred families, making the rich richer and the poor poorer.[27] Increased inequality is evident on the regional level. In 1868 there were 660 *ingenios* powered by steam in the west and only 266 in the eastern region. It is also seen on the social level. This is apparent from an analysis of the division of the national product in 1868 between the various social classes. The upper classes, consisting of a thousand wealthy families of sugar plantation owners and important merchant importers, received 40 to 50 million pesos of a total national product of about 300 million pesos. The upper-middle class, consisting of 50,000 families of professionals, medium and small merchants, cattle-raising landowners, tobacco planters, coffee growers, and owners of small *ingenios*, received 120 million pesos. The lower-middle class, composed of 150,000 families of small farmers, urban artisans, salaried workers, and commercial employees, received 130 to 140 million pesos. The lower class, composed of 100,000 families of slaves, Chinese coolies, and free laborers, many of them without any family nucleus at all, received 25 million pesos. Moreover, while a member of one of the plutocratic families received 5,000 pesos a year, a slave received only 100.[28]

Spanish merchants, as well as others of foreign origin, exploited the landowning sector of the Havana oligarchy. But there was also a tendency among the merchants, once they became wealthy, to buy haciendas. Therefore, landowners and merchants were frequently the same persons. Wealthy merchants bought sugar plantations in search of social prestige and investment opportunities. For the merchants, these were secure investments, although for the Creoles, without any commercial capital, they were ruinous. The merchant turned planter received high dividends, and so he did not have to resort, as did the Creoles, to intermediaries. Because of the capital that he controlled, he was able to supply his hacienda with goods that he purchased directly and stored in his warehouses. In addition, he could sell his harvest through his own commercial channels. James Drake provides a typical example of the merchant-plantationowner, for he was at once the owner of one of the most important commercial establishments—the house of Don Santiago Drake and Company—and one of the wealthiest landowners of the city.[29] Thomas Terry also made his fortune as a merchant banker before becoming a landowner. Upon his arrival from Venezuela, he began his Cuban enterprises with speculative sales of slaves and later on became a merchant-lender. Ely comments: "He did not let sugar production become his principal field of action for very good reasons. The rewards for a merchant-lender were much higher."[30]

The sugarocracy suffered not only from the exactions of Spanish merchants, like Baro and Zulueta, but also from those of South Americans, like Terry; North Americans, like Richardson (Terry's partner); and Englishmen, like James Drake. Moreover, when Louisiana and Florida became American territories and Latin America became independent of Spain, many wealthy Spanish royalists came to Cuba from these countries and established themselves as merchants. We should therefore not be surprised that by 1840 the decadent old Creole aristocracy—the Cardenas, the Herreras, the O'Farrills, the Calvos de la Puerta, the Angrangos, the Inagas—were replaced by immigrants from Spain, Latin America, the United States, and England—Terry, Baro, Zulueta, Aldama, Drake—who had enriched themselves from the slave trade and merchant lending and who, because of this, could buy the *ingenios*, which became profitable in their hands when the necessary technical innovations were introduced. From 1850 on, whether or not he had been a slave trader, the merchant who also owned a plantation was, in a way, the only free landowner, in as much as he supplied himself and did not depend on merchant lenders.

Nevertheless, the contradictions at the heart of the western corporative, oligarchical block, particularly in Havana, between Creole landowners and foreign merchants, should not obscure the fact that with few exceptions the sugar plantation owners of the west preferred to support a status quo that guaranteed their opulent life styles, rather than to fling themselves down the path of armed struggle, freeing the slaves and losing at a stroke the capital invested in this labor force. The contradiction, therefore, between the sugar bourgeoisie of the west and the merchants who sustained the colonial regime was not antagonistic. On the other hand, the Creole bourgeoisie of cattle and sugar from the provinces of Oriente, Camagüey, and part of Las Villas (the eastern region) was the superexploited sector of the bourgeoisie, in as much as their distance from the Havana market precluded access to the commercial operations that had been concentrated in the capital since the advent of free trade.[31] This, together with the facts that of the 370,000 slaves and emancipated blacks counted for 1861, 46.7 percent were to be found in *ingenios* and 90 percent of these were in the western region, helps us understand why the sugar bourgeoisie of the west wished to avoid armed struggle for fear of another Haiti. This fear has been commonly recognized since Concha. His reports of 1850 underscore the profound separatist spirit of the middle class of professionals and public servants and the colored slave population's propensity to conspire for its liberty; in the reports of 1867 he writes that "the fear that freeing more than two thousand negroes at once could produce a serious conflict" was not exaggerated.[32] Foner has pointed out the fears produced by the rebellions of 1832, 1835, 1836, and 1837.[33] According to José Luciano Franco, "In spite of their visible discontent and their inappeasable need for substantial reform, the rich Creole landowners were systematically opposed to any movement for independence because of their fears of slave uprisings."[34]

Thus, while the landowners of the west were reformist, those of the eastern region joined the middle classes and the mass of slaves and led them to make the Cuban nation crystallize by an armed struggle for independence. In Cuba's objective conditions, however, it was impossible to form a nation unless the stratification of the plantation regime were not destroyed. Céspedes, Agramonte, Maceo, Gómez, and Martí understood this during a thirty-year struggle (1868–98) that changed the nature of the war from a war of the bourgeoisie—Céspedes and Agramonte in 1868—to a war of the popular sectors—Martí, Maceo, and Gómes in 1895.[35]

CONCLUSIONS

The transition from colonial dependence on Spain to neocolonial dependence on the United States between 1880 and 1902 increased Cuban underdevelopment. The expansion of underdevelopment is apparent in the destruction of the revolutionary and superexploited sector of the Cuban bourgeoisie from the eastern region; in the ruin of the weakest members of the Creole sugar bourgeoisie of the West; in the expulsion of the Creole owners of small *ingenios* from the industrial sector and their reduction to the agricultural role of *colono* (suppliers of cane); in the conversion of the proletariat into de facto, if not de jure, slaves; in the appropriation of Cuban foreign trade and the internal economy—especially the sugar sector—by North American imperialist interests; and in the exports of raw materials, like tobacco leaves and raw sugar, to the United States when they could have been processed on the island.

This later period saw the transition from colonial dependence in its industrial free trade form, which since 1762 had made Cuba into an important supplier for the industrial nations (the United States, England, etc.) and an important market for their manufactures, to the neocolonial monopolist form of imperialism, which converted the island into a fertile field for the investments of the American financial oligarchy. The transition from colonialism to neocolonialism took place with the support and acquiescence of the western sector of the Creole bourgeoisie in an alliance with the new metropolitan interests and at the expense of the nationalist and revolutionary bourgeoisie of the eastern region. The Cuban economy thus became more tightly linked to the international capitalist system, and in particular to Yankee imperialism, and Cuban underdevelopment was further accentuated. The thirty-year War for Independence (1868–1898) was undoubtedly a step toward the definitive liberation of 1959, but these years also saw transformations in the national and international relations of capitalism. Internationally, the shift in the metropolitan center from Spain to the United States, and on the national level the replacement of Cuban capital by Spanish and especially American capital, all made Cuba more underdeveloped and more dependent.

NOTES

This is a condensed version of the paper presented at the conference. The longer version is available from the author. Translation was done by Elizabeth Hansen.

1. Karl Marx, *Capital* (New York: Modern Library, 1936), p. 826.
2. *Mambises*: Cuban soldiers who fought against Spain in the wars of independence.
3. Francisco de Arango y Parreño, *Obras*, 2 vols. (Havana: Dirección de Cultura, 1952), 1:120.
4. Manuel Moreno Fraginals, *The Sugarmill* (New York: Monthly Review Press, 1976), p. 69.
5. Roland T. Ely, *La Economía Cubana Entre las dos Isabeles 1492–1832* (Havana: Editorial Martí, 1960).
6. Julio Le Riverend, *Historia Económica de Cuba* (Havana, 1965), pp. 186–87.
7. Ramón de la Sagra, *Historia Económica, Política y Estadística de la Isla de Cuba* (Havana: Imprenta de las vivdas de Araza y Soler, 1831), and Jacobo de la Pezuela, *Diccionario Geográfico, Histórico, Estadística de la Isla de Cuba*, 4 vols. (Madrid: J. Bernat 1863-65).
8. Le Riverend, *Historia Económica*, p. 187.
9. *Historia Económica*, p. 196.
10. Richard Madden, *The Island of Cuba* (London: Charles Gilpin, 1849).
11. Manuel Moreno Fraginals, "Desgarramiento Azucarero e Integración Nacional," *Casa de las Americas* 62 (September-October 1970): 11.
12. Moreno Fraginals, *The Sugarmill*, p. 68.
13. Juan Pérez de la Riva, "Aspectos Demográficos y su Importancia en el Proceso Revolucionario del Siglo XIX," in *Union de Periodistas de Cuba* (hereafter *UPEC*) (Havana, 1968), p. 46.
14. La Sagra, *Historia Económica*, p. 336.
15. Moreno Fraginals, *The Sugarmill*, p. 69.

16. Antonio Bachiller y Morales, *Cuba* (Havana: Oficina del Historiador de la Ciudad, 1962), p. 45.
17. Moreno Fraginals, *The Sugarmill*, p. 69.
18. Ibid., pp. 69–70.
19. Ibid., p. 70.
20. Ibid.
21. Eric Williams, *Capitalism and Slavery* (New York: Capricorn Books, 1966).
22. Marx, *Capital*, 1:833.
23. Juan Pérez de la Riva, "La Contradicción Fundamental de la Sociedad Colonia Cubana: Trabajo Esclavo contra Trabajo Libre," in *Economía y Desarrollo* 2 (April-June 1970):144–47.
24. Quoted in Pérez de la Riva, "La Contradicción," p. 149.
25. Raúl Cepero Bonilla, *Obras Históricas* (Havana: Instituto de Historia, 1963), p. 37.
26. Sergio Aguirre, "Las Clases Sociales en el Siglo XIX: Corrientes Políticas e Ideológicas de la Época" in *UPEC* (Havana, 1968), p. 28.
27. Fernando Portuondo, *Historia de Cuba* (Havana: Editorial Nacional de Cuba, 1965), p. 243.
28. Pérez de la Riva, "Aspectos Demográficos," p. 44.
29. Ely, *La Economía Cubana*, p. 114.
30. Ibid., p. 160.
31. Fuerzas Armadas Revolucionarias, *Dirección Política: Historia de Cuba* (Havana, 1967), pp. 151–59.
32. José Gutiérrez de la Concha y de Irigoyen, *Memoria Dirigida al Exmo. Sr. d. Francisco Serrano y Dominguez, Capitán General de la Isla de Cuba* (Madrid: Imprenta de La Reforma, 1867). Carlos de Sedano, *Cuba desde 1856 a 1873* (Madrid: Imprenta Nacional, 1873).
33. Philip Foner, *A History of Cuba and Its Relations with the United States*, 2 vols. (New York: International Publishers, 1962–63), pp. 290–91.
34. José Luciano Franco, "Introducción al 68," in *Diez Años de la Revista Casa de las Americas 1960–1970* (Havana, 1970), p. 95.
35. Jorge Ibarra, *Ideología Mambisa* (Havana: Instituto del Libro, col. Cocuyo, 1967), p. 51.

5. Jamaican Migrants and the Cuban Sugar Industry, 1900–1934

Franklin W. Knight

Migration constitutes one of the most important themes in the historical experience of the Caribbean.[1] As long as its recorded history can be ascertained, the region has been consistently attracting or expelling inhabitants. The Arawaks moved in and dominated the Guanahuatebey. The determined, although unfortunately misnamed, Caribs entered to contest and in some cases expel the Arawaks.[2] The Spanish adventurers and colonists had barely destroyed the indigenous population when they confronted the relentless competition of the French, the English, the Dutch, the Danes, and the Swedes. The inexorable thrust of the westward expansion of Europe and the establishment of the South Atlantic System gave a new dimension to the Caribbean experience. Africans became the largest migrant group. Their entry, primarily under the auspices of the transatlantic slave trade, was perhaps the single most important aspect of the history of the Caribbean, and the African impact remains pervasive and indelible. The insatiable demand of labor brought Chinese, East Indians, and West Africans under terms of contract not far removed from the atrocious earlier forms of outright slavery. Migration and labor requirements created the pluralistic, polyglot, variegated structure of the present Caribbean societies and cultures.[3]

The peoples of the Caribbean have been consistently restless. Throughout the long and complex history of colonialism and imperialism the centrifugal tendencies propelled would-be residents to the Spanish mainland, to the English North Atlantic possessions, or back along the return route to their African and Asian homelands.[4] Migration patterns continued to be heavy, erratic, and varied throughout the twentieth century.

The earlier, larger patterns of migration—especially involving the long-distance travel of American Indians, Europeans, and Africans—have been extensively studied.[5] Even tourism as a form of migration attracts considerable scholarly and popular attention.[6] The Caribbean exodus to the United States, Canada, England, and France remains the dominant theme in examinations of recent migrations.[7] But these should be properly seen as merely one aspect of a general theme.

Far less attention has been given in the standard historical works to the incidences of emigration and intraregional migration during the past century. This was the period when the region as a whole was readjusting to the transition from slave labor to free wage labor, as well as readjusting to an altered economic relationship with external metropolises. The plantation economy, while still alive and well, no longer completely dominated all the local economies. Peasant economies were rapidly developing alongside, and in some cases in competition with, the plantation economy; the expansion of a wage-conscious, independent working class exerted pressures on the local governments.[8] But most important, if colonial governments and their supporting local elites were unwilling or incapable of instituting those conditions that increased economic opportunity, then the masses expressed their opinions by deserting their homelands and traveling to areas perceived as offering those opportunities. Denied a political voice, those masses could still "vote" with their feet.

The study of population movements within the region tends to give priority to the fluctuating waves of workers who left to work on the Panama Canal or left for Costa Rica and other parts of Central America or the United States, Canada, and the United Kingdom. Overshadowed in the process have been the equally important departures of a more local, often more temporary, nature such as the Leeward Islanders moving to Trinidad, Barbados, and Puerto Rico or the Haitians and Jamaicans to Cuba.[9]

In the local general histories of Cuba and Jamaica, this migration fails to attract attention, although it constituted an important connection culturally and economically for both islands. Jamaicans left their island and went to Cuba to work at a time when the local sugar producers were still talking of a labor crisis. These Jamaicans made an important contribution to the expansion of the Cuban sugar industry in the early decades of the twentieth century, when sugar production dominated Cuban politics, economics, and society. Most of the Jamaicans worked for American concerns that were extending the sugar zone eastward from the present provinces of Sancti Spíritus and Ciego de Avila to Holguin, Guantánamo, and Santiago de Cuba.[10]

PATTERNS OF OUTMIGRATION

External migration was a dominant theme in Jamaica after the abolition of slavery, and especially after the crisis of 1865 when the colonial government demonstrated its hostility to the peasants' desires for more land.[11] As the economy stagnated, Jamaicans left their homeland seeking better opportunities elsewhere. This outmigration displayed two patterns: one between 1881 and 1921 and the other after 1921.

In 1881 the Jamaican population was approximately 581,000, a figure that represented a dramatic improvement in the rate of increase during the previous centuries of slavery and coercive control of the free nonwhite population. This rapid expansion continued, pushing the island total to 831,000 in 1911 and 858,000 in 1921.[12] Despite the inflow of some Asian indentured laborers until 1917, Jamaica experienced a continuous net outflow of its inhabitants during the period. This net outflow accounted for a loss of 24,800 individuals between 1881 and 1891, a net loss of 43,900 between 1891 and 1911, and a net loss of 77,100 between 1911 and 1921.[13]

As with all forms of migration, the push-pull factors were complex. In general, as indicated, one strong attraction was the expansion of opportunities to participate in a number of developmental projects abroad at wages above the prevailing rates in Jamaica. The first major exodus was to Panama. The numbers of Jamaicans who went to work with the Panama Canal Company cannot be accurately ascertained, but the earliest went in the 1880s to work with the French company. More than 24,000 Jamaicans went to do seasonal labor in 1883–84 alone. When the Americans took control of the canal company in 1904, they started a new phase of actively recruiting Jamaicans and other West Indians. Between 1904 and 1914 the Canal Zone officially recruited 47 Jamaicans, although the far larger number that departed voluntarily may be indicated by the repatriation figures, which indicate that the Canal Zone sent back 10,500 Jamaicans before 1943.[14] The United Fruit Company's expansion of the banana industry in a number of Central American states also attracted Jamaicans in large numbers. The annual report of the Isthmian Canal Commission, 1913–14, indicated that thousands of former Antillean canal workers had gone to Honduras, Costa Rica, and farther afield.[15] The open immigration quota laws prevailing in the United States until 1921 and regular, convenient, and relatively inexpensive steamboat transportation facilitated the departure of many Jamaicans. Departure by banana boat was a feature of Jamaican emigration before the transportation revolution introduced by the jet plane after the 1960s. With such wide-scale facilities and incentives to move, the magnetic attraction of Cuba was just one among many areas of opportunity.

Domestic conditions in Jamaica contributed to the expulsion of many residents either directly or indirectly. The unimaginative, if not mentally bankrupt, colonial administration considered low wages inevitable and work on the sugar estates a necessity. When workers refused to work for low wages, they interpreted their action to be antagonism to the sugar estates and insisted that local laborers were unavailable; therefore East Indians had to be encouraged to enter the island.[16] What the local elites and administrators never explicitly acknowledged was the depressing effect that imported contract laborers had on wage scales in Jamaica. Such was the calculated effect of sponsored immigration. For it could not be honestly maintained that Jamaicans were averse to manual labor on the sugar estates, when that was precisely the type of labor they did in Cuba and elsewhere. It was undeniable, however, that workers knew the value of wages and eschewed low wage rates. Poor wages, then, became a catalyst for emigration.

None of the octogenarian Jamaicans whom I interviewed in the summer of 1980 could recall how much they were paid for their first job in Cuba. But they all declared that they could not find suitable jobs—or any jobs at all—in Jamaica, and so they decided to take a chance abroad. Prevailing daily wage rates were about 1 shilling and 6 pence, or $0.30 in United States currency equivalent. In 1914, Canal Zone wage rates averaged between $0.80 and $1.04 per day.[17] In 1916 the United Fruit Company was paying $1.40 to $2.00 for daily nonskilled work on its Cuban estates, although the tendency to pay task rates rather than time rates was becoming generalized.[18] Compared with Jamaican wage scales, these wages were attractive enough that potential emigrants willingly deposited the sum of £1 (Jamaican currency) on departure for Panama, and later when the Jamaican government imposed a £3 head tax on adults, a $30 deposit against return passage, and $15 cash in hand, there seemed no apparent diminution of the enthusiasm to leave the island.

Throughout the first third of the twentieth century, Jamaican economic conditions fluctuated between the bad and the atrocious. The sugar industry continued its prolonged period of uncertainty. The banana industry, while expanding rapidly, had not yet attained major stature, and natural disasters plagued peasant production. In 1903 a disastrous hurricane devastated the northeastern parishes of St. Thomas, Portland, and parts of St. Mary. In 1907 a great earthquake virtually destroyed the capital city of Kingston, resulting in approximately 800 fatalities and property damage estimated at approximately £2 million. Powerful hurricanes devastated the western and north-central parishes in 1912, especially Trelawny and St. Ann; extensive damage resulted from the two hurricanes of 1915, that of 1916, and the two of 1917.[19] Three consecutive years of severe hurricane damage disrupted agricultural production and depressed agricultural prices—a situation further aggravated by the great war in Europe. By 1917 banana export had virtually ceased, and the great influenza pandemic of that year exacerbated the general distress of the laboring classes, especially the rural masses.[20] Economic incentives to emigrate, therefore, appeared very strong before 1921.

The economic dislocations affected the peasants and laboring poor with disproportional severity. The cultivation of bananas for export and ground provisions for the internal domestic markets had been the chief remunerative activities in the highland regions, where the sugar estates had abandoned the growing of sugar cane or where the land was simply not suitable. Moreover, these peasant activities were viable on small plots of land with not more sophisticated technology than a simple hoe, machete, and strong arm. But even with supplemental income from wage labor on the sugar estates or the pursuit of skilled and semiskilled crafts, the daily existence of this class did not extend much beyond economic marginality. Three successive years of lost income reduced many to an insuperable penury. Regaining lost ground was difficult without leaving the locale of past failures. The short-term vibrancy of some sectors such as sugar or logwood was too localized and transitory to offset the urgent sense of futility that permeated the predominantly peasant zones of Portland, St. Mary, St. Ann, Manchester, Clarendon, Hanover, and St. James. Nevertheless, it would be a serious error to conclude that the majority of Jamaican emigrants were peasants. Indeed, the available archival data as well as the representative sample of survivors interviewed in 1980 present strong indications to the contrary (table 5.1).[21]

Natural disasters were, of course, beyond the control of colonial administrators. But there is no evidence that English colonialism served Jamaica well during the early years of the twentieth century. The myopic official obsession with the fortunes of the sugar industry precluded the methodical pursuit of ways to alleviate the distress of the laboring classes or to ameliorate the general condition of the majority of the population. In a long and obliquely critical review of the competence of colonial administrators and the dire consequences for the island, *The Daily Gleaner*, the leading newspaper and usually a strong supporter of planter interests, declared in 1921:

> Where does Jamaica stand after 17 years of Crown Colony Government and 37 years of a system of half-representative and half-Crown Colony Government by which the Government since 1899 has maintained a permanent majority in the Legislative Council in which it takes nine out of the Elected Members to give effect to the people's wishes in the matter of expenditure? Pauperism has increased 200 percent during the past 20 years. In many parishes the bulk of the colonial revenues goes to maintain larger poor houses and to make weekly doles to needy persons. During the past 10 to 15 years crime has increased by at least 125 percent. . . . The high rate of emigration has now become a matter of grave concern. Of recent years far more people than the island can spare have been leaving their homes and seeking in other lands the remunerative employment that is denied them here. Last January, in spite of the official and other warnings that industrial conditions in Cuba were anything but hopeful, 4,451 men and women embarked in Kingston for Santiago in search of work, the highest number recorded in any one month since the emigration movement to Cuba was started close upon four years ago.[22]

These statistics from a leading Jamaican newspaper cannot be easily verified. It cannot be accepted without reservations since it is obvious that what

Table 5.1 Occupations of Jamaican Immigrants, 1927

	Number of Immigrants	Percentage of Total
Professional		
Actors	1	
Clergymen	4	
Sculptors	1	
Engineers	4	
Schoolteachers	1	
Doctors	1	
Unspecified	3	
Total professional	15	0.6
Artisan		
Carpenters	44	
Seamstresses	121	
Machinists	1	
Sailors	3	
Mechanics	33	
Bakers	2	
Painters	4	
Tailors	13	
Shoemakers	5	
Unspecified	1	
Total artisan	227	9.7
Varied		
Agents	2	
Bankers	2	
Merchants	50	
Day laborers	861	
Fieldhands	5	
Domestics	856	
Unspecified	3	
Total varied	1,779	75.8
Unskilled, including women, children	327	13.9
Total	2,348	100.0

Source: Cuba, Secretaria de Hacienda, *Inmigración y movimiento de pasajeros en el año de 1927* (Havana: La Propaganda,1928).

the paper calls the emigration movement began well before 1917. But *The Gleaner* represented an influential sector of public opinion, however small, and its statements probably indicated an acknowledgment of the spreading consciousness of social and economic change in Jamaica.

The conditions affecting migration were changing fast not only in Jamaica but also in the wider world, especially within recipient countries. In Cuba, the "dance of the millions" was abruptly ending, creating economic chaos and frustrated hopes among those who wished for jobs, profits, and security.[23] Jamaicans continued to travel to Cuba since conditions still appeared more promising than in their own island, but the cases of economic success proved harder to locate. After 1921 a different phase developed in the pattern of Jamaican migration as legal conditions in the recipient countries changed drastically. Both in 1921 and again in 1924 the Congress of the United States passed laws that virtually closed the door to the legal immigrants from Jamaican and other nonwhite peoples from the Caribbean. The termination or stabilization of the work projects in Central America on the canal in Panama and the banana plantations of Costa Rica followed by the anti–foreign-labor laws of the Gerardo Machado dictatorship in Cuba in the late 1920s greatly constricted the opportunities for continued migration from Jamaica.[24]

The 1920s was the peak period for the outmigration of Jamaicans to Cuba. The principal flow began in late 1912 under the auspices of the United Fruit Company, actively aided and abetted by the opportunistic administration of Cuban president José Miguel Gómez. By 1917 nearly 6,000 Jamaicans went to seek employment in Cuba. The number increased to 7,317 in 1918, to 23,859 in 1919, and to 24,461 in 1920 and decreased to 7,868 in 1921.[25] By 1931 only 52 immigrants arrived from Jamaica, a slight improvement over the years before but a sharp contrast to the 8,469 returnees of that year. The ebb tide of Jamaican immigration had clearly begun. Jamaicans would continue to travel to Cuba to join relatives or to seek employment, but the magnetic attraction of the neighboring island would no longer prevail. At other times greater waves of Jamaican emigrants would go to other places. But law and circumstances combined to diminish the continuation of a relationship that for a short while was of mutual benefit to two sister Caribbean islands.

The Jamaican migrant stream to Cuba comprised a major component of Jamaican emigrants until the early 1920s. Until 1923, Jamaicans accounted for 20 to 30 percent of the total immigrant pool (table 5.2). The only other Caribbean territory to rank consistently above Jamaica as a migrant contributory source was Haiti. Until 1925, Cuba was the preferred destination for more than one-third of all Jamaicans leaving their country (table 5.3). After 1925 more Jamaicans returned from Cuba each year, and the net outmigration was reversed for the British colony. One of the returnees was the political firebrand, Alexander Clark Bustamante (knighted by the British government in 1955), founder of the Jamaica Labor Party and first prime minister of Jamaica.[26]

CHARACTERISTICS OF MIGRANTS

The Jamaican migrant stream exhibited some remarkable characteristics. Males outnumbered females, but by a small percentage[27] (see table 5.4). It continued to expand when the Cuban segment ceased, and the international economic order was enduring the severe crisis of 1929–33. Indeed, would-be Jamaican emigrants appeared to disregard entirely the official

Table 5.2   Jamaicans within the Cuban Immigrant Pool, 1919-31

Year	Total Immigrants	Number of Contributing Countries/Regions	Number of Jamaicans	Percentage of Total Pool
1919	80,488	34	23,859	29.64
1920	174,221	34	24,461	14.04
1921	58,948	33	7,868	13.25
1922	25,993	33	5,016	19.30
1923	75,461	35	5,844	7.74
1924	85,288	27	5,372	6.30
1925	55,904	24	4,925	8.81
1926	32,269	16	2,805	8.70
1927	31,414	46	2,348	7.48
1928	27,314	49	974	3.57
1929	17,179	45	243	1.41
1930	12,219	44	38	0.31
1931	2,796	44	52	1.86
Total	679,494		83,805	12.33

Sources: United Nations, *Sex and Age of International Migrants: Statistics for 1918-1947* (New York: United Nations, 1953), table 23; Cuba, Secretaria de Hacienda, *Inmigración y movimiento de pasajeros en el año de.* . . [1918–1931] (Havana: Imprenta La Propaganda, 1919–1932). Microfilm copies of these publications courtesy of Biblioteca Nacional José Martí, Havana, Cuba.
Note: 1. Variations in the number of Jamaicans from these sources are derived from differences between figures given for ports of departure and nationality. Where possible, nationality figures are used.
2. Figures do not include transients.

Table 5.3   Jamaican Migration, 1919-31

Year	Total Emigrants	To Cuba	Percentage of Total to Cuba	Total Returnees
1919	—	23,859	—	—
1920	—	24,461	—	—
1921	—	7,868	—	—
1922	13,002	5,016	38.58	14,917
1923	17,194	5,844	33.99	12,116
1924	16,008	5,372	33.56	12,460
1925	13,752	4,925	35.81	13,962
1926	17,356	2,805	16.16	20,951
1927	18,388	2,348	12.77	22,334
1928	20,646	974	4.72	26,066
1929	24,456	243	0.99	28,512
1930	30,511	38	0.12	38,118
1931	30,323	52	0.17	42,042

Sources: Compiled from United Nations, *Sex and Age of International Migrants: Statistics for 1918-1947* (New York: United Nations, 1953), table 28, Jamaica; Cuba, Secretaria de Hacienda, *Inmigración y movimiento de pasajeros en el año de.* . . [1918–1931] (Havana: Imprenta La Propaganda, 1919–1932).
Note: These figures vary from those estimated by George Roberts in *The Population of Jamaica* (Millwood, N.Y.: Kraus Reprint, 1979), p. 139, and pp. 339–40.

Table 5.4   Sex of Jamaican Emigrants, 1922–33

	Males		Females		
Year	Number	Percentage	Number	Percentage	Total
1922	7,045	54.18	5,957	45.82	13,002
1923	9,561	55.61	7,633	44.39	17,194
1924	8,762	54.73	7,246	45.27	16,008
1925	7,568	55.00	6,184	45.00	13,752
1926	9,328	53.75	8,028	46.25	17,356
1927	9,496	51.64	8,892	48.36	18,388
1928	10,390	50.32	10,256	49.68	20,646
1929	12,845	52.52	11,611	47.48	24,456
1930	15,554	50.98	14,957	49.02	30,511
1931	16,236	53.54	14,087	46.46	30,323
1932	17,737	50.63	17,293	49.37	35,030
1933	18,920	51.08	18,117	48.92	37,037

Source: United Nations, Sex and Age of International Migrants: Statistics for 1918–1947 (New York: United Nations, 1953), table 28, Jamaica.

economic forecasts and the stern warnings not to leave their country. In the early years it must have been obvious that, as a predominantly black labor pool, their reception in Cuba would not have been enthusiastic. The immigration law of 1906—subsequently violated with impugnity—had explicitly stated that 80 percent of the Cuban resources should be used to subsidize immigrant "families from Europe and the Canary Islands; with the remaining 20 percent for workers from designated places . . . braceros from Sweden, Norway, Denmark, and the Northern Italian provinces."[28]

Race and color concerns obviously did not dissuade the Jamaicans. In 1921 the Jamaican newspapers kept a stream of negative news from Cuba, emphasizing the rapidly deteriorating economic condition and the particular difficulties of West Indians. For example, The Gleaner reported on a front-page story in its edition of Friday, April 1, 1921, that anti-Chinese sentiment was attaining alarming proportions owing to lack of work on the sugar estates. On Wednesday, April 11, the paper had a long story on page 11 entitled "West Indians in the Islands of Cuba," which began:

According to private advices received here from Cuba, not only are the West Indian laborers finding difficulty in obtaining work on the sugar estates in the republic but many of those employed are experiencing difficulty in getting their pay. Up to a year ago, a good laborer could earn as much as five dollars a day cutting canes. Today the rate of pay is between 80 and 90 cents per day, and then the laborer is given a "good" and he has to wait for some time before he can redeem this "good." This is having an effect on the domestic arrangements of many Jamaican laborers. Many of these had been accustomed to send drafts to their families regularly, but owing to the new system of "goods" they are without money and the consequence of this is that their families are suffering. . . . But despite all the drawbacks laborers are flocking to Cuba from different parts as it certainly is the largest field for laborers. The President of Cuba is still insistent in his attitude that the sugar estate owners must replace West Indian laborers by natives of Cuba.[29]

Two reports in June continued the theme. On Saturday, June 25, the paper reported that it had received a letter from a Jamaican in Cuba describing widescale unemployment, starvation, and increasing problems with the police.[30] A subsequent report of Wednesday, June 29, ran, "We are informed by the Colonial Secretary that a telegram has been received from the British Minister at Havana in which he states that natives of the British West Indies in Cuba are in great distress and unemployment and it is important that further emigration to that country should be discouraged for the present."[31]

In the light of such alarmist warnings, the Jamaicans apparently began to reconsider their options. The Cuban outflow dramatically declined. As table 5.3 shows, Cuba attracted only 7,868 emigrants in 1921, compared to 24,461 in 1920. But large numbers of Jamaicans would continue to leave their island for other destinations, indicating the patent failure of the local colonial polity to provide jobs and opportunities commensurate with local expectations. Nevertheless, by 1931 far less than 1 percent of the Jamaicans leaving their island found a refuge in the neighboring island.

According to the study by George Roberts, the external migration from Jamaica was achieved without an accompanying movement to the cities.[32] Every parish of the island lost population between 1911 and 1943, with the economically distressed parishes of Portland, St. Mary, and St. Ann experiencing the greatest loss. In the period of 1911 to 1921, female emigrants from Kingston outnumbered male emigrants, 4,400 to 3,100, while those from St. Catherine outnumbered their male counterparts 900 to 400. The great majority of these emigrants went directly from their rural residences to their foreign destinations, embarking in the ports of Kingston, Port Antonio, Port Maria, Falmouth, or Montego Bay.

By contrast, returning emigrants settled in the cities, rather than return to the rural areas. This concentration in the cities aggravated the political and social problems of the island and contributed to the labor unrest that characterized the island in 1937–38. At the same time, the population of suburban St. Andrew virtually exploded after 1921, gaining some 15,500 net population by the census of 1943.[33] The only other parish to demonstrate extraordinary increase was Manchester, a parish with a long tradition of small-scale landholding.

The most popular port of entry for Jamaican migrants to Cuba was Santiago de Cuba. Of the 12,469 Jamaican migrants and visitors who entered Cuba in 1921, the overwhelming majority disembarked at Santiago: 11,739.[34] Only 726 entered through Havana, and many of those probably came from the United States rather than directly from their homeland. The remaining 4 travelers disembarked at Manzanillo. The maritime communi-

Table 5.5   Comparative Data on Jamaican Immigrants, 1923 (in percentages)

Origin	Number	Male	Age 14–45	Married	Had Job	Paid Own Passage	Literate	With $30	Second Visit
Jamaica	5,844	73.4	89.6	21.6	93.7	100.0	94.5	100.0	34.3
Spain	46,439	83.0	93.7	14.7	85.5	68.9	83.9	81.1	2.8
Haiti	11,088	89.4	98.6	12.2	99.0	86.0	20.9	86.1	35.0
Italy	2,053	93.9	97.9	11.8	94.6	97.8	95.4	92.7	0.5
Poland	1,581	84.5	95.0	19.5	84.6	94.3	89.2	83.7	0.0

Source: Cuba, Secretaria de Hacienda, Inmigración y movimiento de pasajeros en el año 1923 (Havana: La Propaganda, 1924). Inmigrantes clasificados por naturaleza, etc.

Note: 1. The 67,005 migrants from these five sources accounted for 88.79 percent of the 75,461 entrants for 1923. None of the remaining sources yielded as many as a thousand immigrants.

2. Spain includes immigrants from the Canary Islands but not from Puerto Rico.

3. The figures do not include transients.

cation between Jamaica and Cuba was excellent. Steamers advertising themselves as "reliable, comfortable and fast," such as the Remlik, Wanderer, Nemesis, and La Belle Sauvage, made the trip from Kingston to Santiago every Tuesday and Friday.[35] The United Fruit Company and the Atlantic Fruit Company had a regular fleet connecting the two islands to Central America and the United States, and the then waterfront streets of Port Royal Street and Tower Street were dominated by shipping agents' offices such as Lindsay, Swan, Hunter Limited, or R. Eden Bodden Limited.

The Jamaican government admitted that it could not physically prevent its citizens from leaving the country.[36] But it did publicize regularly the rules governing would-be emigrants. Apart from having passports (or permits in the case of unaccompanied minors or unaccompanied married women) each adult had to show a minimum of thirty dollars, and deposit the sum equivalent to the return passage (approximately three pounds); "be fit to work"; and free from all contagious diseases. Males had to be between the ages of twenty-one and fifty, while women had to be between the ages of fourteen and forty-five and be "of good moral character." These precautions seem to have been observed.

All the Jamaican immigrants paid for their own passages in 1923. This compares with 69.0 percent (31,981) of the 46,439 Spanish immigrants and 86.0 percent (9,548) of the 11,088 Haitians (table 5.5). Of the 5,844 Jamaicans, 4,290 were male (73.4 percent); 349 (5.9 percent) were below the age of 14; 259 (4.4 percent) were older than 45 years; 1,268 (21.6 percent) were married; 5,480 (93.7 percent) declared some occupation; 5,527 (94.5 percent) were literate; only 5 had less than the required deposit of $30; and 2,009 (34.3 percent) had been to Cuba before. Interestingly enough, the total of $175,543 deposited by the immigrants averaged almost precisely $30 per adult. Although 1923 was an exceptional year for sexual imbalance—Jamaican migrants tended to be more evenly divided by sex—the breakdown was characteristic of the general profile of arrivals from Jamaica.

Except for the usual and remarkable sexual balance, Jamaicans did not vary much in their statistical profile from other immigrants except the Haitians. Compared with the Spanish and Canary Islanders, the Jamaicans tended more likely to be single, more likely to have a job on arrival, more likely to pay the cost of passage, and more likely to have been to Cuba before. Although slightly less likely to be literate, the Jamaicans appeared to have more cash for display than the Europeans.

Migration might have provided, however inadvertently, an opportunity for improving or changing occupations. In any case, the breakdown of occupations that Jamaicans declared in Cuba appears to be more varied than they declared for their home parishes in Jamaica (see table 5.1).[37] While the correlation is difficult to establish (or refute), the 327 self-declared unskilled, women and children seems surprisingly low for a predominantly rural exodus—especially when 276 were less than fourteen years of age.

However the Jamaicans saw themselves or the Cubans recorded their skills, it is clear that the official view of the Jamaican and British government was far from charitable. The British consul in Cuba reported to the Foreign Office at the end of 1926 that the Jamaican and other English Antillean migrants "were illiterate, and a large number of the criminal class, prone to lawlessness and knavery. It would be difficult to keep them in order anywhere. Here the difficulty is accentuated by their adopting an insolent and often defiant attitude toward the police and the local authorities, and constantly flaunting, much to their irritation and annoyance, the fact that they are British subjects. They have been for many years a constant source of trouble between this Legation and the Cuban government. That they have been at times victims of harsh treatment and much injustice cannot be denied. . . . A strong racial hatred prevails against all negroes [sic], and when times are bad the Cubans regard the Jamaicans as interlopers and the cause of all their poverty and distress."[38]

The Jamaicans had a different view, of course, and the reality was somewhere between both views. Both the Cubans and the Jamaicans interviewed in Cuba in 1980 remarked on the generally exemplary conduct of the Jamaican communities. The English-speaking West Indians tended to form extremely close-knit communities, transplanting and retaining their insular traditions and displaying an exaggerated fidelity to the British Empire. Unlike the Haitians, they displayed a strong sense of protocol and undoubtedly demanded the attention of their consular services.[39] But it is difficult to find substantiation for the accusation of general lawlessness. An exhaustive search through the sections dealing with both police and immigration matters in the provincial archives of Santiago de Cuba turned up only three references of criminal misconduct or breaches of public order involving Jamaicans between 1921 and 1931.[40] Neither the archival sources nor the recollections of the surviving Jamaicans, therefore, support the malicious assertion that this group was "illiterate" or "prone to lawlessness and knavery."

THREE BIOGRAPHIES

The survivors of the Jamaican community of the 1920s form a revealing cross section of the contingent that left their homeland. Scattered across Cuba, their most common characteristics are their remarkable survival and their recollections, altered or reinforced, during the years. The three selected biographies illustrate both the variety and the commonality of backgrounds and individual experience of the Jamaican community.

Cyprian Christon Wells was a latecomer to Cuba.[41] Born in the parish of Hanover, he first arrived in Cuba in 1928, at the age of twenty-six, and never returned to Jamaica. Son of a small farmer and landowner in the parish of Trelawney, Wells could find no employment after he had finished his elementary education at the Rio Bueno, Trelawney, grade school. His only work experience before his arrival in Cuba was that of an occasional sailor. He arrived in Santiago aboard the *Remlik*, with no offer of a job but confident that he would succeed as did the others who had returned to Jamaica earlier.

Within a short time Wells got a job with the American-owned Fidelity Sugar Company in the town of San Germán, Holguin. He still lived there in 1980 under the shadows of the tall chimneys of Central Urbano Noris, as the factory has been rechristened by the Cuban Revolution. For the first six months Wells worked as a cane cutter for $2.50 per day. He then moved into the factory, where he remained employed until his retirement in 1973.

According to his recollection, in 1928 San Germán had a population of about three thousand Jamaicans, in addition to a large contingent of Haitians, Barbadians, and workers from St. Vincent, St. Lucia, Dominica, Trinidad, and Grenada.[42] He played cricket on the San Germán team at home as well as in distant Central Miranda and Cayo Mambí. The Jamaicans also played dominoes a lot and gambled on horse racing. Unlike most of the Jamaicans (and others) who lived on the estates, Wells lived in the town, renting a house all by himself, before his first marriage in 1929 to a fellow Jamaican from Browns Town, St. Ann, who had come to Cuba in 1926 to visit her sister. Together they had eight children who attended private, English-speaking schools. Wells was subsequently to remarry twice—once in 1963 and again in 1969—each time to a Jamaican.[43]

In San Germán in 1928 few Cubans worked in the fields cutting sugar cane. Since there were few Cubans around, not many Jamaicans married Cubans. According to Wells, Haitians and Jamaicans got along well with each other, although a few Jamaicans did think themselves superior to the Haitians. The two major social activities were the Liberty Hall of the Garveyite Universal Negro Improvement Association (which changed its name to the British West Indian Advancement Club after the demise of Marcus Garvey) and the local church built in 1924 as a branch of the African Orthodox Church (which changed to Methodist after 1970). Since migrants did not have the vote, they displayed little interest in Cuban affairs. The lottery, however, was a passion, and Wells recalled some Jamaicans who won the lottery and realized immediately their ambition to return to Jamaica. Some winners, however, used windfall earnings to start businesses, usually bars or small grocery shops.

Looking back on his decision of 1928, Wells claimed that he had no regrets. He had enjoyed a good life in Cuba, had attained a position of respect, and had seen his children attain a quality of life that he could not have envisaged in Jamaica. He, however, would like to visit Jamaica to see his younger brother, with whom he had corresponded for fifty-two years.

The experience of Consey Dwyer of Camagüey was different.[44] Born in Westmoreland Parish, Jamaica, in 1897, she first traveled to Cuba in 1921 to join the future father of her children, who worked at Central Elia in Guaímaro, Camagüey Province. She returned home several times, the last in 1931, when the father of her first children died. On her return in 1931, she settled in Central Macareño (now central Haiti) and never left Cuba again.

As a young woman Ms. Dwyer was extremely attractive; she worked as a domestic in various towns in Cuba.[45] Once she worked for six years with an American family in Havana. Between 1923 and 1938 she had seven children, some of whom were born in Jamaica. Her favorite recollections were of the dances held at the local Liberty Hall of the Universal Negro Improvement Association, where admission was usually free for ladies. Her main regret was that she had not returned to Jamaica in the 1940s or 1950s, a regret perhaps based on the failure to realize the level of material well-being to which she aspired.

In July 1980 Esmeralda Leonora Godden Gourzong de Aurelio Arango was still an astonishingly attractive woman whose grace, poise, intelligence, and wit belied her 80 years.[46] She spoke from a book-lined library in her once-elegant home in Santiago, apologizing for the state of the books, deploring the fact that so many were missing, and serving tea in a style that would have made John Hearne's Karl Brandt comfortable.[47]

With remarkable fidelity to detail, Mrs. Arango related her experiences. Born in the western Jamaican parish of Hanover, she had been sent to Cuba as a nineteen-year-old by her mother after she had failed her decisive third-year Jamaica local examination (probably not for the first time).[48] Like other migrants, she took a boat in Kingston, a sailboat that spent three days to make the crossing to Santiago. On her arrival she had no skills and spoke no

Spanish. She got a job as a babysitter, and later as a nurse-aide to a sick person who spoke English. Her first return trip to Jamaica occurred when both her parents died in 1921 and she was needed to care for a younger sister and a younger brother.

A single young lady of twenty-one could find no job in the Jamaica of 1921, so back to Santiago she went—by steamer. Since she had very little money after the remittances to Jamaica, she had to teach herself Spanish, as well as dressmaking for the Arango family, her first employers in 1919, and the family into which she subsequently married.

From 1921 she remained with the Arango family. Although she had been a Methodist in Jamaica, she converted to Catholicism some time after 1919. The church became her only social activity. She could not recall any other West Indian in her church in all her years. In 1926, when she had been earning about forty-five dollars per month, she sent for her sister, and the following year she sent for her brother to join her in Cuba.

In 1930 she had become the companion of Aurelio Arango, whose brother she had cared for in 1919, and they moved to the elegant home in which she still lives, sometime after 1940. (They were married in 1961.) The following year, 1931, she accompanied Aurelio Arango to self-imposed exile in Jamaica, where they waited out the last days of the Gerardo Machado dictatorship. Life became immeasurably better on their return to Cuba, and she traveled a lot to the United States, Spain, and throughout the Caribbean. Mrs. Arango had attained the immigrant's dream—partially.

Looking back on her prerevolutionary experience, Mrs. Arango voiced regrets over the original decision to go to Cuba in 1919, rather than to the United States. Despite her material acquisitions, she felt that the Cubans of her husband's family and her husband's class did not give Jamaicans like herself due respect. She also resented being away from Jamaica as long as she had, although when she visited Jamaica along with her sister in the 1960s, she hardly recognized anyplace or anyone. Like Mrs. Dwyer and Mr. Wells, the Cuban experience had reinforced—if it had not created—a strong sense of Jamaican self-consciousness.

If a single swallow does not indicate the arrival of spring, then three synoptic life experiences cannot cover the entire spectrum of Jamaican immigrant experiences in Cuba. But the three life stories, especially in their youthful phases before 1931, did follow a pattern. The varied backgrounds did not preclude the common quest for a better opportunity—or just an economic opportunity. Although they never explicitly said that they wanted "to make good" and return home to Jamaica, it was clearly implied in their actions and their words. Absence from Jamaica created a sense of identity, a Jamaicanness still obvious after half a century. But it was a different sort of Jamaican self-consciousness from that which developed concurrently in Jamaica. It was a diaspora self-consciousness, exaggerated and slightly, maybe quaintly, anachronistic. Yet it was delightful, spontaneous, and still discernibly Anglo-West Indian—albeit West Indian of a bygone era. The Jamaican identity aroused in exile was a manifestly colonial identity with its strong allegiance to the English monarchy.

IMPACT OF MIGRATION

Although it is easy to see what migration and alienation did to individual Jamaicans, it is more difficult to ascertain the impact on Cuba and Jamaica. For Cuba it is possible to speculate that the labor force formed an integral component of the economic expansion of the years characterized as the dance of the millions.[49] Jamaicans served in the sugar industry, in domestic service, on ranches and citrus plantations. Many of the Cuban *municipios* corresponding to centrales exist today because Antilleans built the *ingenios* and the villages: Baraguá in Ciego de Avila; Haiti in Camagüey; San Germán and Banés and Mayarí in Holguin; and Níquero, Palma Soriano, Puerto Padre and San Luis in Granma and Santiago de Cuba. Jamaicans maintained these communities and they made them socially and economically viable. Juan Pérez de la Riva has demonstrated the varied and important ways in which the Jamaican migrants dovetailed with the Americans and Cubans in Cuba.[50] The Cuban sugar industry expanded progressively from a production value of 34 million pesos in 1902 to a peak of 411 million in 1923, declining to 41 million in 1932.[51] In its expansive phase it needed the Jamaica workers, but by the crisis years of 1932–33, there was a popular crescendo of anti-Jamaican sentiment. By that time the economic attractiveness of Cuba had diminished considerably for the Jamaicans.

The documents in the Jamaican national archives are still not available to the public to study this period. But the assumption that the island derived tangible benefits from exporting its unemployed and accepting the pecuniary remittances appears reasonable. Indeed the Cuban outlet might even have served to mitigate labor unrest in Jamaica in the years immediately following the First World War. Nevertheless, the returning wave of opportunity seekers intensified urbanization in Jamaica and catalyzed the industrial discontent that got out of control in 1937–38. And because Alexander Bustamante was a "graduate" of the Cuban exodus of earlier years, it may even be assumed that the Cuban experience accelerated the political development of Jamaica in the early 1940s.[52] Much remains to be explored of this brief but fascinating relationship between these two neighboring islands. It can be asserted with considerable confidence, however, that the reciprocal advantages of this migration was of considerably greater importance to the two states in their separate phases of transition than previously acknowledged.

Jamaican migrants to Cuba in the period before 1931 demonstrated many of the characteristics of itinerant target earners: a strong economic lure, an enclave mentality and residential pattern, occupational flexibility or opportunism, an initial endogamous marital pattern, and a large residual population with disappointed aspirations. As a group, the Jamaicans compared favorably with other Cuban immigrant groups of the period, especially the Spanish, Canary Islanders and the Haitians. But they also had some traits that affected their integration in the host society. As a predominately black group, they arrived at a time when the Cuban society was becoming increasingly more conscious of color and race, partly under the auspices of United States hegemony.[33] Nevertheless, their English language skills and their British colonial background facilitated their physical and occupational mobility within those areas most dominated by North American enterprises. More than 90 percent of the Jamaicans remained in the eastern part of Cuba in the newly developed sugar areas of Camagüey and Oriente provinces. Their Anglo-Caribbean cultural background also conditioned a reluctance to absorb Cuban religious, social, and cultural characteristics. Along with their economic and occupational advantages, this created the basis for a type of mutually reinforcing cleavage that not only served to segregate the Jamaican communities but also served to inhibit the eventual integration of the migrants to the mainstream of Cuban society.

NOTES

Research for this project was facilitated by a grant from the Social Science Research Council, New York, in 1980. The author wishes to thank the council as well as the following individuals: Ambassador Winston K. Davis of Jamaica; Julio le Riverend, Josefina García Carranza, and Araceli García of the Biblioteca National José Martí; Fe Iglesias García of the Academy of Sciences, Havana; Miriam Verdecia of the Archivo Nacional de Cuba; Oscar Pino Santos, Manuel Moreno Fraginals, Silvester Spencer, Osvaldo Cárdenas, Margaret Reid, and Mary Gentile in Havana; Miguel Garcia, Domingo Rodriguez, Juan Ramon de la Cruz, Agnes Phillips, Mabel Angel, Cleveland Thompson, and Consey Dwyer in Camagüey; Louis Bascom, Eric Knight Edwards, and Mariano Aquino Iglesias in Ciego de Avila; Giram Pérez, Cyprian Wells, Lina Brown, and Reuben Golding in Holguin; Wendell Gaskin, Esmeralda de Aurelio Arango, Minna de Sarruff, Sarah Watt, Mary Johnson, Pedro Nuñez Aleaga, and Santiago Ramon Guillaume in Santiago de Cuba; Barry Higman in Jamaica; Cathy Duke in the United States; and all the participants in the seminar.

1. See *Sourcebook on the New Immigration*, edited by Roy Simon Bryce-Laporte et al. (Washington: Research Institute on Immigration and Ethnic Studies, 1979); *Female Immigrants to the United States: Caribbean, Latin American and African Experiences*, edited by Delores Mortimer and Roy S. Bryce-Laporte (Washington, D.C.: Smithsonian Institution, 1981); Orlando Patterson, "Migration in Caribbean Societies: Socioeconomic and Symbolic Resource," in *Human Migration: Patterns and Policies*, edited by William H. McNeill and Ruth S. Adams (Bloomington: Indiana University Press, 1978); Dawn I.

Marshall, *The Haitian Problem*. *Illegal Migration to the Bahamas* (Mona, Jamaica: Institute of Social and Economic Research, 1979); "The Caribbean Exodus," *Caribbean Review* 11, No. 1 (Winter 1982). Note also that *Caribbean Quarterly* 22, No. 1 (March 1976) devoted its entire issue to "East Indians in the Caribbean."

2. Pre-European Caribbean history is still relatively unexplored, but see Richard B. Moore, "Caribs, 'Cannibals' and Human Relations," a pamphlet published by Pathway Publishers for the Afro-American Institute of New York in 1972.

3. For a summary see Franklin W. Knight, *The Caribbean: The Genesis of a Fragmented Nationalism* (New York: Oxford University Press, 1978) or J. H. Parry and P. M. Sherlock, *A Short History of the West Indies* (New York: St. Martin's Press, 1968). The best summary of the slave trade is Philip D. Curtin, *The Atlantic Slave Trade: A Census* (Madison: University of Wisconsin Press, 1969).

4. Tom W. Shick, *Behold the Promised Land: A History of Afro-American Settler Society in Nineteenth-Century Liberia* (Baltimore: Johns Hopkins University Press, 1980); Monica Schuler, *"Alas, Alas, Kongo": A Social History of Indentured African Immigration into Jamaica, 1841-1865* (Baltimore: Johns Hopkins University Press, 1980). See also Mary Elizabeth Thomas, *Jamaica and Voluntary Laborers from Africa, 1840-1865* (Gainesville: University Presses of Florida, 1974).

5. See McNeill and Adams, *Human Migration*, especially pp. 48-74, and pp. 85-105.

6. Herbert L. Hiller, "Escapism. Penetration and Response: Industrial Tourism in the Caribbean," *Caribbean Studies* 16 (July 1976): 92-116.

7. G. W. Roberts, *The Population of Jamaica* (Millwood, N.Y.: Kraus Reprint, 1979; first published, 1957); George Cumper, *The Social Structure of Jamaica* (Mona: Extra-Mural Department, n.d.); and Ceri Peach, *West Indian Migration to Britain* (Oxford: Oxford University Press, 1968).

8. See Sidney W. Mintz, "The Jamaica Internal Marketing Pattern," *Social and Economic Studies* 4 (1955): 311-25; Woodville Marshall, "Notes on Peasant Development in the West Indies since 1838," *Social and Economic Studies* 17 (1968): 252-63; Walter Rodney, *A History of the Guyanese Working People 1818-1905* (Baltimore: Johns Hopkins University Press, 1981), pp. 60-119; Michael Louis, "An Equal Right to the Soil: The Rise of a Peasantry in St. Lucia, 1838-1900," unpublished Ph.D. dissertation, Johns Hopkins University, 1981; Bridget Brereton, *A History of Modern Trinidad, 1783-1962* (London: Heinemann, 1981), pp. 76-156.

9. Juan Pérez de la Riva, "Cuba y la migración antillana, 1900-1931," in *Anuario de Estudios Cubanos*, 2. *La Republica neocolonial* (Havana: Editorial de Ciencias Sociales, 1979), pp. 1-76.

10. Alejandro García et al., eds., *United Fruit Company: Un Caso del Dominio Imperialista en Cuba* (Havana: Editorial de Ciencias Sociales, 1976), pp. 245-48.

11. Douglas Hall, *Free Jamaica, 1830-1865* (New Haven: Yale University Press, 1959); Philip D. Curtin, *Two Jamaicas: The Role of Ideas in a Tropical Colony* (Cambridge: Harvard University Press, 1955). See also the works by Thomas and Schuler mentioned in note 4.

12. These figures are taken from Roberts, *Population*, pp. 45–46.
13. Note that Jamaica had no census in 1911.
14. Lancelot S. Lewis, *The West Indian in Panama: Black Labor in Panama, 1850–1914* (Washington, D.C.: University Press of America, 1980), pp. 111–13. See also Trevor Purcell, "Conformity and Dissension: Social Inequality, Values and Mobility among West Indian Migrants in Limon, Costa Rica," unpublished Ph.D. dissertation, Johns Hopkins University, 1982.
15. Cited in Roberts, *Population*, p. 136.
16. The last East Indians arrived in Jamaica in 1917.
17. Lewis, *Panama*, p. 30; Roberts, *Population*, p. 136.
18. Alejandro García, *United Fruit Company*, pp. 241-48.
19. See *The Gleaner Geography and History of Jamaica* (Kingston, Jamaica: Gleaner Co., 1973), pp. 70–75.
20. Roberts, *Population*, p. 138. On the flu epidemic, see Alfred W. Crosby, Jr., *Epidemic and Peace, 1918* (Westport, Conn.: Greenwood Press, 1976).
21. See table 5.1. Assuming that those designated fieldhands and day laborers were peasants, the figure would be 866 of 2,348 migrants in 1927, approximately 37 percent. The sample of those interviewed in 1980 is too small for definitive statistical analysis, but it is interesting to note that none of the respondents acknowledged a peasant background before leaving Jamaica.
22. *The Daily Gleaner*, Wednesday, May 18, 1921, p. 8, col. 3.
23. Francisco López Segrera, "Algunos aspectos de la industria azucarera cubana (1925-1937)," *Anuario de Estudios Cubanos*, 2, pp. 165-288; Cuba, Secretaria de Agricultura, Comercio y Trabajo, *Sinopsis económica de Cuba* (Havana: Hernandez, 1925), pp. 10-1; and Ramiro Guerra y Sánchez, *La industria azucarera de Cuba* (Havana: Cultural, 1940), pp. 21-6.
24. These anti-foreign labor laws were directed mainly at English West Indians and Haitians.
25. These figures are taken from Cuba, Secretaria de Hacienda, *Inmigración y movimiento de pasajeros en el año de . . .* (Havana: La Propaganda, 1919-32). The figures do not always coincide with those of Pérez de la Riva in "Cuba y la migración antillana." In any case, it is not always easy to discern legal immigrants from tourists or transients.
26. George E. Eaton, *Alexander Bustamante and Modern Jamaica* (Kingston, Jamaica: Kingston Publishers, 1975), pp. 158-59.
27. Note that after the Second World War, female migrants would outnumber males for all regional sources of migration.
28. Biblioteca Nacional José Martí. Colección Cubana. *Cuba. Leyes y Decretos* c. 340. mis. v7. n.6. Carta de Pio Guanaurd.
29. *The Daily Gleaner*, Wednesday, April 11, 1921, p. 11, col. 3. A "good" was a token commonly used on Cuban sugar plantations at the beginning of the century.
30. *The Daily Gleaner*, Saturday, June 25, 1921, p. 10, col. 8.
31. *The Daily Gleaner*, Wednesday, June 29, 1921, p. 1, col. 3.
32. Roberts, *Population*, pp. 140-41.
33. Roberts, *Population*, p. 141, table 32.
34. Cuba. *Inmigración*, 1921, p. 21.
35. See *The Daily Gleaner*, Friday, April 1, 1921, p. 4.

36. Jamaica National Archives (Spanish Town), File 1B/5/79 Reference 101. *Annual Reports* (Foreign Office) on Cuba, Panama, and Canal Zone, 1925.

37. For occupations in 1921, see *Population of Jamaica, 1921* (Kingston, Jamaica: Government Printing Office, 1922).

38. Jamaica National Archives (Spanish Town), File 1B/5/79. Reference 101. *Annual Reports*, 1926.

39. Pérez de la Riva, "Cuba y la migración antillana," p. 12.

40. Archivo Histórico Provincial. Santiago de Cuba. Fondo de Govierno Provincial, varios legajos. The author thanks Santiago Guillaume and Pedro Nuñez Aleaga for their assistance in this search.

41. Wells gave two interviews: in Havana, June 20, 1980 and in San Germán, Holguin, July 11, 1980. These three people were selected from eighteen interviewed by the author in 1980.

42. San Germán first appears as a pueblo in the census of 1931, when its population is given as 3,061. See *Memorias inéditas del censo de 1931* (Havana: Editorial de Ciencias Sociales, 1978), p. 184. Note that the municipality of Holguin in which San Germán is located experienced a 37 percent population increase between 1919 and 1931, an increase from 91,267 to 127,443.

43. Wells' marital pattern seems to be common for this community. First- and second-generation marriages seem confined to the English-speaking community, with a high degree of preference for mates from the same island. By the third generation, however, marriage with Cubans appear commonplace. Although the data for this Jamaican community are sparse, the pattern seems established for immigrant communities, as revealed in immigration studies done in New York City and Limon, Costa Rica.

44. Interviewed at her home, Central Haiti, July 8, 1980.

45. Ms. Dwyer had several photographs of herself and her family spanning the years of her stay in Cuba.

46. Interviewed at home, Santiago de Cuba, July 13, 1980.

47. John Hearne, *The Faces of Love* (London: Faber and Faber, 1957); John Hearne, *The Land of the Living* (London: Faber and Faber, 1961).

48. The third-year Jamaica local examinations were taken at about age 17 and enabled the successful candidates to enter training schools for teaching or nursing.

49. On "The Dance of the Millions," see H. Thomas, *Cuba: The Pursuit of Freedom* (New York: Harper & Row, 1971), pp. 544–56. It is extremely difficult to establish a reliable cost accounting of the Jamaican contribution to the Cuban economy. Between 1920 and 1931, more than 76,000 Jamaicans traveled to Cuba and worked at various occupations for varying periods of time. The sharp fluctuations in the Cuban economy, especially in the dominant sugar sector, and the imprecision or absence in listing occupations and wages in the census precludes any totals of earnings. It is possible to argue that the Jamaicans depressed wage rates in Cuba, but since there seemed to be little direct competition between Cubans and Jamaicans for jobs, the impact of this argument remains blunted. No remittance figures were available in Jamaica for expatriates.

50. Pérez de la Riva, "Cuba y la migración antillana."

51. Thomas, *Cuba*, pp. 557-62.
52. See Eaton, *Bustamante*, pp. 58-158; Trevor Munroe, *The Politics of Constitutional Decolonization, 1944-62* (Mona, Jamaica: Institute of Social and Economic Research, 1972), pp. 18-35.
53. Margaret E. Crahan, "Religious Penetration and Nationalism in Cuba: U.S. Methodist Activities, 1898-1958," *Revista/Review Interamericana* 8 (Summer 1978): 204-24; Cathy Duke, "The Idea of Race: The Cultural Impact of American Invervention in Cuba, 1898-1912," unpublished paper presented at the Fourteenth Conference of Caribbean Historians, San Juan, Puerto Rico, April 16-21, 1981.

Part Three
Puerto Rico

Puerto Rico, 1886

Atlantic Ocean

Caribbean Sea

N

AGUADILLA

ARECIBO

Arecibo

Vega Baja

San Juan

BAYAMON

HUMACAO

Humacao

GUAYAMA

PONCE

Ponce

MAYAGÜEZ

Mayagüez

6. About Slavery and the Order of Things: Puerto Rico, 1845–1873

José Curet

> What are you doing, Congo?
>
> Master, don't you see? The history, in brief, of Ponce, your grace.
>
> Is that what you think? And you believe that you have only to pick up a pen to be a historian, or historiographer, as they are now being called? History, Congo, is the most delicate of things, for which one needs the most instruction. More learning and less passion. For a hundred poets and novelists in each century, there is born only one historian. For this type of work there is no middle ground: it's sublime or ridiculous . . .
>
> But, master, if what I'm going to write has nothing to do with what you have described, I'll follow the latest styles and that's all.
>
> "Diálogo Semi-Serio," *El Ponceño,*
> *Periódico Literario Local, Mercantil y de Avisos,*
> November 19, 1852

To say that slavery molded the behavior and the mentality of a considerable part of Puerto Rican society during the last century, and that the slave work force performed the large part of the economic activity concentrated on the sugar estates, would be, perhaps, to state an obvious truth. At the same time, it is this truth that most closely relates the experience of Puerto Rico to that of the other islands of the Caribbean. Puerto Rican historiography, however, not only has repeatedly minimized the importance of slavery on

117

the island but has gone so far as to declare that "the roots of social democracy which have been developed in Puerto Rico, can be found in the historical evolution of black slavery."[1] Suffice it to say, generations of historians using this same source have supported countless observations and judgments—now almost axiomatic—about the peculiarities of slavery in Puerto Rico.[2]

Only in the last several years, following a combing of the sources, many of which had been forgotten or were hard to locate and use, has the veil begun to be raised on the interpretations that had traditionally been woven around Negro slavery and the impact of this institution in Puerto Rico. Although more research remains to be done before a definitive reinterpretation can be presented, analysis of sources as diverse as the *Protocolos Notariales*, *Planillas de Riqueza de los Hacendados*, *Repartos de Subsidio*, and the oral trials in the municipalities has permitted us to see from a new perspective the importance of Negro slavery in the economic sphere, as well as in the relations between masters and slaves. The same sources, however, impose certain limitations on the historian. In Puerto Rico, with rare exceptions, no documents meticulously detail the state of wealth, production, costs, and labor force composition on the estates in all the areas of the island. This type of information exists only for some towns in the municipal documentation: for many other towns, countless natural and human calamities have destroyed parts of these documents. In the case of this particular work, the research has focused on the town of Ponce, on the southern coast of the island. In making this choice, historical factors were considered, as well as more pragmatic concerns with the condition of existing documentation.

In Puerto Rico the slave population was centered almost exclusively on the coast where sugar was produced; by contrast, in the interior, where at the end of the nineteenth century coffee was at its height, slavery played a minimal role.[3] From the end of the eighteenth century and continuing through the greater part of the nineteenth century, the production of sugar was not only the island's principal economic activity in terms of the amount collected from its export; it dominated the population centers and life itself in the coastal regions in which cane was cultivated. It is important to note, as has the historian Luis M. Díaz Soler, that the slave population of the islands was, by the mid-nineteenth century, only one-tenth of the total population. But these general figures hide the fact that by the mid-nineteenth century, in the coastal towns where cane was grown, such as Ponce, slaves represented more than 80 percent of the total work force used on the sugar estates.[4]

The town of Ponce produced and exported more sugar than any other on the island. In it was also concentrated the largest portion of the slave population during the second half of the nineteenth century.[5] The Municipal Archive of Ponce contains an almost complete series of sources such as

Padrones de Riqueza, *Repartos de Subsidio*, and *Censos de Población*, which have made possible the preliminary application of some statistical techniques. In this sense, the conclusions presented in this paper are not representative of what was occurring in other zones of the island—as in the interior, where tenant farming and small proprietorship predominated through the mid-nineteenth century—although they could apply to other sugar-producing towns of the coast.[6] In any case, it is precisely in their specificity that these studies underline a new dimension and reveal where many of the old interpretations begin to unravel.

SLAVES AND DAY LABORERS

Certainly not all of the slaves in Puerto Rico were employed in productive tasks. There were domestic slaves, a small number of slaves who fulfilled their duties in urban centers, slaves who worked on estates and ranches, plus a small number whose masters rented them out as piece workers.[7] In Ponce, for example, by 1857, of a total population of 3,119 slaves of all ages and both sexes, little more than 2,000 were rural slaves.[8] In the past, Puerto Rican historians have made much of the fact that a considerable part of the Puerto Rican slave population was made up of domestic slaves, and from this they have deduced that slaves were not primarily employed in economic activities directly connected to sugar production. But this numbers game, which does not take into account the slave population within the units of production, results only in false conclusions. By the middle of the last century the slave population was of vital importance on the sugar estates, and not merely from the quantitative point of view. This is demonstrated in the statements of the governors, as well as in the attitudes of the planta-tionowners toward the problem presented clearly by the governor, Juan de la Pezuela, at midcentury.

In 1849 a plan was proposed to replace slave labor on estates with a wider use of tenants—peasants attached to the owner's lands who remained regis-tered as day workers. In reality this was a completely new plan. From the first decades of the century a number of regulations had been drawn up pursuing similar ends: to create, through the control of vagrancy, a body of workers who could be put at the disposition of the landholders. None, however, had much success.[9] Nor would the 1849 regulation have much success. What gave it notoriety was, on the one hand, the ardor with which the governor, who had promulgated it, attempted to force compliance and, on the other hand, the quantity of abuses—some of them documented— that were committed, within the law, against the day laborers.[10]

One could think that this regulation was handed down at an appropriate moment, in which the governor foresaw solutions to one of the problems that the estate owners expressed constantly and vehemently: the lack of labor for the estates. And if this solution were based on the availability of free labor (although this was only nominally the case), it would have been offered in conformity with the spirit of the century and for the benefit of civilization. So thought Governor de la Pezuela; and if this "disastrous plague"—as he called slavery—turned out to be more costly and less efficient on the estates than free labor, then a happy union between spiritual ideals and material convenience would have been produced. But this was not yet to be in Puerto Rico.

The regulation proved particularly onerous for the day workers. Each was given a booklet in which was written his name, the name of the landowner who employed him, place of residence, and observations about his behavior. The worker was obligated to carry this booklet at all times, thereby circumscribing his movement from one town to another.[11] After one year Pezuela took a census in which he tried to prove the success his methods had obtained. Of a total of 26,223 tenant farmers who had existed on the island in 1849, only 4,437 remained a year later. In Ponce, for example, there were no tenant farmers left but rather 156 day workers and servants.[12]

But neither the functioning nor the spirit of the regulation survived much beyond the term of its progenitor. A few years later, Governor Norzagaray was forced to reduce realistically some of the requirements that Pezuela had imposed on the tenants so that they would not have to join the ranks of the day workers.[13] A little later, in 1866, with the publication of a report on the effects of the passbook, the mayors were totally divided in their judgments on the economic results of regulating free labor.[14] In 1873 the regulation was totally abolished, and in some municipalities, as in Ponce, little time had passed before some of the town council members asked that the folders and loose pages recording the day workers be burned.[15] Ironically, in spite of the many irregularities committed through the use of the passbooks, and the lack of effect on the economy of the *Regulation on Work*, from the middle of the century the landowners began to use free labor on their estates more intensely than previously. To what then, can we attribute the interest in creating a free labor market that would have "made possible," in the words of Pezuela, "a replacement [of slavery] necessarily imposed on us by the spirit of the century"?[16]

PROFITABILITY OF SLAVE LABOR

If we note some of the observations within the literature of the period, we will find affirmations that the efficiency of slave labor compared poorly with that of day labor. For example, in 1847 in his *Memoria sobre la agricultura en la Isla de Puerto Rico*, Darío de Ormaechea stated, "The work of the peasants, for its greater perfection, ease and rapidity, is preferable to that of Negro slaves."[17]

It is curious to note that these same observations have served as evidence to support countless affirmations over the supposed insistence on the part of

Puerto Rican landholders to employ free workers in place of slaves on the sugar estates.[18] But if this had been the manner in which the estate owners truly judged the situation, then the substitution of slave labor would have accelerated. Nonetheless, up to the decade before abolition, the estate owners defended in writings and in deeds their preference for slave labor. In Humacao, for example, Juan Bautista Bestrer, when asking permission of the governor to introduce more slaves on his estate, declared that "one cannot employ free day laborers in the cultivation of cane because generally they do not like to work, and if they do it's for two or three days; they accomplish little and there are tasks which slaves do and free laborers don't want to do . . . thus I prefer slaves."[19] The periodical *El Ponceño* published numerous articles by landowners in which they argued in favor of the permanency of the institution of slavery and refuted, with examples taken from daily experience, the arguments of the abolitionists.[20] This attitude of the landowners was in no way atavistic and was perfectly understandable in economic terms.

The concept of profitability offers a key that, among countless factors, helps explain the landowners' preference for slaves. At the same time it gives a certain economic logic to the permanency of the institution in Puerto Rico, even though counter to the spirit of the century. The slave employed in agricultural tasks represented an investment of capital in the estates, at the same time that he was part of the labor force.[21] If, for a moment, one considers the purchase of a slave by an estate owner only as a capital investment, one can then ascribe to this investment a series of quantifiable variables, which can give a more precise idea of the productivity of this investment.[22]

But in order to determine the rate of profitability of a slave, we must know the average production of a slave, the quantity of production necessary for the care and maintenance of a slave, the buying price of a slave, and the expected number of years of useful work. The problem is where to find this information. The ideal source would be the estate account books. For the period before the twentieth century, however, only the account books of one estate, La Mercedita, exist. Although these have been researched, they do not provide the necessary information for determining profitability.[23] For example, it is indispensable to know average slave production, separate from what could have been produced by day laborers working on the estates. In effect, one of the peculiar characteristics of the Puerto Rican sugar estates was that they employed free labor as much as slave labor, even at the height of slavery in the mid-nineteenth century.[24] The account books, however, while differentiating between slave laborer and free laborer, did not record details concerning the amount produced by each group. How then can one obtain figures for the amount of slave production?

Fortunately, one source, the *Cuaderno de Riquezas de Ponce* of 1845, one of the most complete censuses of production for the last century, notes an estate employing slave labor exclusively, the estate of José de Torres. Composed of 875 *cuerdas*, of which 28 were seeded with cane, with an iron sugar mill operated by oxen, this estate employed only nine slaves. Another virtue of this census, as in those of later years, is that the costs of estate maintenance are included, from which can be deduced a ratio that fluctuated between 30 and 40 percent of the gross production. It was on the basis of this figure, which almost always appeared in the next-to-last column of the censuses, below the heading of taxable net production, that state and municipal taxes were imposed.[25] One could adduce, as did various governors in the nineteenth century, that this information about production submitted by these same landowners for tax purposes was not very accurate.[26] Nonetheless, for the purposes of determining profitability, this fact only introduces an error ("bias") whose effect would produce a conservative estimate of production, one lower than it would have been in reality. Applying the formula for profitability to the estate of José de Torres, a rate of 17 percent was obtained.[27] This is a surprising result if we consider that it is computed on the basis of figures estimated to be conservative. It indicates that the investment in a slave by an estate owner was profitable. More important, this does not appear to be an isolated case. Applying the formula of profitability to other estates that employed a minimum number of day workers in comparison with the number of slaves, very high rates were obtained. For example, on the estate Unión, owned by Antonio Torruella, in which eighty-three slaves and only two day workers were employed, and where a net production value of 3,590 pesos was reported in 1845, the rate of profitability of the investment in slaves was 22 percent.[28]

For only one other year, 1861, could rates of profitability be computed. Using the figures from the pages of the *Riqueza Agrícola* of that year, we can apply the formula for profitability to some estates that employed primarily slave labor. Here, too, high rates were obtained. On the estate, Unión, now in the hands of Torruella's successors, eighty-three slaves were employed in 1859 (the documents do not indicate the number of free laborers) and an income of 16,601.60 pesos reported for 1861. The resulting rate of profit was 31 percent.[29]

Already by 1861, and particularly during the decade preceding abolition, however, one begins to note that the number of free laborers employed on the estate grew considerably, while the number of slaves remained constant on some estates and declined on others. In effect, this pattern could be corroborated more precisely by applying regression analysis to the figures from the *Cuaderno de Riquezas* of 1845 and the records of 1861. Using a representative sample of the estates of Ponce in 1845, one can trace the variations in production and in the number of slaves and free workers employed in the estates existing in 1861. Tables 6.1 and 6.2 indicate the production and the number of slaves and workers on the selected estates for the sample in 1845 and in 1861. The increased average income per farm, with little change in the number of slaves per plantation, suggests an

Table 6.1 Slaves, Free Workers, and Net Income in 1845 (from a Sample of Plantations in Ponce)

Case	Plantation	Owner	Slaves	Free Workers	Net Income (in pesos)
1	Concepción	Petrona Villar Molina	45	4	700
2	La Flaca	Dede y Overman	90	30	2,984
3	Las Bayas	Juan Prats	80	20	8,984
4	Bucaná	José Ortiz Renta	130	12	20,555
5	Cintrona	José Archibald	22	20	670
6	Teresa	S. Serrallés	9	14	743
7	Unión	A. Torruella	83	2	3,590
8	Rita	Antonio Albizu	22	16	700
9	Ana María	J. B. Roubert	28	27	1,275
10	—	Rivá y Miralls	100	0	12,975
11	Encarnación	F. Thillet	10	0	250
12	Catalina	J. Van Rhyn	28	12	2,800
	Average		53.9	13.8	4,625.50

Source: Archivo Municipal de Ponce, Cuaderno de la Riqueza, 1845.

Table 6.2 Slaves, Free Workers, and Net Income in 1861 (from a Sample of Plantations in Ponce)

Case[a]	Slaves	Free Workers[b]	Net Income[c]
1	27	23	602.40
2	66	40	11,321.70
3(i)	70	40	10,017.30
3(ii)[d]	40	40	9,409.10
4	85	12	9,527.10
5	10	—	685.80
6	50	—	7,975.80
7	83	—	16,601.60
8(i)[e]	80	—	14,993.10
8(ii)	10	—	4,529.90
9	42	—	7,419.40
12	48	—	5,195.40
Average	50.9	31.0	8,189.90

Sources: Archivo Municipal de Ponce, Gremio de Hacendados, Planillas que han Presentado, 1861; Archivo General de Puerto Rico, Fondo de los Gobernadores, Asuntos Políticos y Civiles, Esclavos, 1860.

[a] The number of cases corresponds to the number of plantations that appeared in table 6.1.

[b] The numbers used for free laborers were taken from an 1859 census because those figures rarely appeared in the *planillas* of 1861.

[c] These figures are an approximation of net income. In the *planillas* the gross production and the price for which it was sold appeared; to obtain net income 40 percent was subtracted from the total. In 1852, in Archivo Municipal de Ponce, Reparto de Subsidio, the cost of maintenance (35 percent to 40 percent) was discounted from gross production.

[d] Juan Prats is listed as administrator of the plantation Caño Verde of Da. Isabel Alfonso.

[e] Antonio Albizu now appears as owner of two estates, Rita and Bucaná.

increase in the income produced per free worker. Regressions of net income per plantation on the number of slaves and the number of free workers, for 1845 and for 1861, indicate that the income per free worker increased dramatically between the two years and in 1861 was greater than was the income per slave.

Unfortunately, sources that would permit similar calculations for the decade immediately preceding abolition (1873) could not be found. Still, these results are dramatic and confirm the fact that during the second half of the century the increased production of the estates was affected through the greater use of free labor in spite of the profits that would have resulted from acquiring slaves. To what can this pattern in the sugar estates of Ponce be attributed?

In the first place, as documented by the literature of the period and corroborated through an analysis of the population censuses, by the middle of the nineteenth century the forced immigration of Africans to the island had practically ceased.[30] While the slave population of the island had grown at an annual rate of nearly 3 percent during the first decades of the century, in the second half of the century an annual growth rate of only 1.1 percent was recorded.[31] In Ponce, for example, while slaves of African origin represented 46 percent of the total slave population in 1840, in 1850 they had fallen to 36 percent and by 1872, slaves of African origin were only 18 percent of the slave population of the town.[32] Clearly this cannot be attributed to a triumph of the antislavery campaign, led at this time by members of the English parliament, nor as a result of the accords reached between England and Spain against the slave trade.

The cessation of slave importations into Puerto Rico was simply a response to the constant economic constraint suffered by the island's planters. They could not compete with Cuban slave purchasers who could pay three times the price that Puerto Rican buyers could pay to acquire African slaves in the international market.[33] The effect of this in Puerto Rico, in addition to a situation that produced greater "creolization" among the slave population of the island, was to place limits on the sale of slave labor to the sugar estates. In fact, according to the planters, one of the problems, throughout the nineteenth century but with greater persistence during the second half, was the lack of abundant labor for their estates. The effect of the stoppage of waves of African importations can be judged by the numerous projects for the immigration of Chinese, Indians, and Canary Islanders that began to be proposed and by the vehement petitions seeking to import contract laborers that the estate owners began to send to Spain in the second half of the nineteenth century.[34] Suffice it to say, many of these petitions received no attention from the metropolitan government, leaving to the owners the attempt to find solutions to the labor shortage problem within the local economy.

For these reasons it is questionable to attribute the greater use of day laborers on the sugar plantations at midcentury to a voluntary decision reached by owners confronted with the inefficiency of slave labor, as Díaz Soler has stated.[35] Although the available information has not permitted a calculation of how much more productive and less costly slave labor was than free labor (if it is true, as has been maintained), one can affirm that in Puerto Rico, at least until 1861, slave labor on the estates was highly profitable. In addition to the proof offered by the high rates of profitability of plantation slaves (17 percent in 1845, more than 30 percent in 1861), the high demand for slave labor demonstrated by the sale of slaves in the market at Ponce can be cited as additional support.

An examination of slave sales in Ponce, registered in the *Protocolos Notariales* of Rafael León y Paz, one of the three notaries of the town of Ponce and the only one whose *Protocolos* were accessible to this investigation, reveals that high prices for agricultural slaves were sustained until 1860. From this date until abolition, the prices and the volume of slave sales fell (see figure 6.1). This decline can be attributed to countless factors.

Figure 6.1 Sale Price of Field Slaves in Ponce, 1845–1872 (in Pesos)

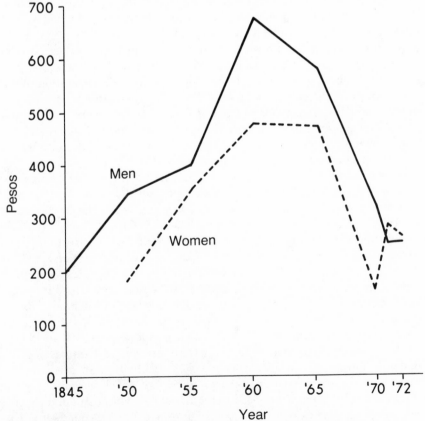

Source: Archivo General de Puerto Rico, Rafael de León, Protocolos Notariales.

One that cannot be dismissed was the political factor, especially the defeat of the proslavery forces in the U.S. Civil War.[36]

For purposes of analysis, we have attempted to determine the quantitative effect of a fall in slave prices or a fall in sugar prices in altering the rate of profit on the investment in the sale and purchase of slaves. A fall in the purchase price of a slave, leaving constant the slave's net production, raised the profit rate. For example, a decline in a slave's purchase price from six hundred to two hundred pesos increased the profit margin more than four times. A fall in the sale price of sugar, on the other hand, produced a decline in the profit rate, unless it affected the price of slaves. If each changed alone, variations in the price of slaves and in the price of sugar had differing impacts on the rate of profit.

If one tries to determine which of these two effects played a determining role in altering the rate of profit on slave investment in the decade before abolition, it can be seen that this is an eminently quantitative question, for which we do not yet possess all of the information that would permit an adequate answer. For example, although the quotations on sugar prices in the international markets exist for the nineteenth century, these were not the prices paid in local markets. The few records that contain this type of information indicate that these prices were half of those paid in New York. Between the processing of muscovado sugar, the only kind produced on the island, and its sale in international markets existed a total and complex structure, beginning with the shipment of sugar from the plantation to the shipping port—the costs of which were born by the planters, causing frequent complaint among them—going from the consignees to the markets.[37] The existence of these various stages in the export of sugar, and the complex tangle of credit lines existing on the island, had no other effect than to eat up part of the plantation earnings.

Even nature itself, such as droughts, or international events outside the control of the local planters could frequently alter the production or earnings of the sugar plantations. The latter, in effect, was what happened in the last decade of slavery on the island. The U.S. Civil War was a double-edged sword for the sugar economy in Puerto Rico. The destruction of the sugar plantations in the South, especially in Louisiana, created a great demand among North American sugar refineries for the island's sugar.[38] But this boom didn't last long. With the imposition of protectionist sugar tariffs in the United States, and with the recuperation of the production of the southern plantations, the island's planters encountered a difficult situation.[39] Even though more sugar was being produced in 1865 than in previous years, this was not being translated into more earnings for the planters. Quite the contrary, earnings were being lost. In his study on Puerto Rico in the nineteenth century, Lidio Cruz Monclova stated: "Sugar production, for its part, increased to the figure 123,414,862 pounds, which represented an increase of 2,000,000 pounds over 1865. Nonetheless, this did not translate into earnings. This rise, contrary to that of 1865, corresponded to a decrease in value, caused by the growth of beet sugar production in Europe and the increase in U.S. tariff rates, and as such, its earnings were insufficient to offset the growing losses experienced by the sugar industry, which due to the effects of the 1866 hurricane, had seen the quantity of production drop to 111,358,765 pounds."[40]

Also, Cruz Monclova recorded that some years later the situation of the landowners improved as sugar prices stabilized in the North American market.[41] At the same time, a direct correlation does not appear to have existed between fluctuations in the North American market and local market prices, which, in the final instance, was what the planters received for their product.[42] Neither are these local market quotations a precise guide for what planters were paid for their products, for when droughts occurred, or owners were forced to sell rapidly, they sold at much lower prices. *El Avisador*, the business periodical of Ponce, carried the following notice in its edition of April 11, 1874: "The absence of rain and the prevalence of the north wind continue their considerable punishment of the sugar plantations, for which reasons the estate owners are being pressured to hurry the processing to increase the yields which augments the stock; this being one aspect of the tension, the other, the disquieting signs from the consumer markets, makes them [the owners] see the need to relinquish their crops at reduced prices to meet their obligations."[43]

The decade in which abolition was decreed was, then, a difficult period for the plantation owners—one in which they discovered the vulnerability of the sugar economy, as well as the vulnerability of the slave system that sustained many of the sugar plantations until the very eve of abolition. On one side, the extensive form in which the sugar economy had developed on the island offered only reduced possibilities to increase production to ward off losses in difficult times.[44] The most viable alternative for the owners continued to be increasing productive factors: more manhours, more land in cultivation. This extensive form for increasing production continued to encounter a contradiction. As Manuel Moreno Fraginals has shown, this process increased the total volume of production but decreased the production per worker, so that the gain was marginal.[45]

On the other hand, besides these economic factors, international political events, such as the defeat of the proslavery cause in the United States, not only led to a fall in the sale price of slaves in the local market but also made the planters aware that the Spanish government, too, could precipitously declare abolition. A British consul on the island reported in 1866:

> Since the emancipation of the negroes in the United States of America, slaves have greatly lost in value here, and more so yet since the termination of the American War. So much so, that, at the present moment, the price of plantation slaves must be called entirely nominal. . . .

There seems to prevail a general feeling here that slavery is doomed and that it is the best policy to be prepared for emancipation. The opinion, even of the Spaniards themselves, is that Spain will be either morally obliged to abolish slavery in these islands or will be forced to do so by foreign intervention.[46]

Given such statements, it would be academic to determine hypothetically how much the rate of profitability of slaves should have fallen in Puerto Rico on the eve of abolition. It would be feasible to suppose not only that profitability fell in these years but that the entire system of sugar estates, which had been based on slave labor, began to crumble at this point. In Ponce, of the eighty-six estates operating in 1845, eighty remained in 1861 but only twenty-two remained in 1886; complaints about planter indebtedness and repossession of estates remained constant; the introduction of technical innovations was extremely slow; and on those estates where some technical reforms had been introduced, slave labor was never supplanted, because the incipient free labor market was never able to satisfy totally the manpower needs of the sugar plantations.[47] This last fact, as Antonio Alfau y Baralt, the representative of the Planters' Guild, stated in 1879, explained in great part the problems that had to be confronted by the planters before and after abolition.[48] But this review of the plantation economy would be incomplete without discussing the human presence of masters and slaves and the relations between them.

CONDITIONS OF SLAVE LIFE

For those human beings who were arriving directly from Africa throughout the centuries, to find themselves reduced to slaves, to *bozales*, to exiles separated by force from their lands and their customs, had to have been a heart-rending experience. Even before arriving on the island, rebellions or other more subtle forms of protest—such as obsessive melancholia, which led in many cases to undernourishment and death—occurred on the slave ships.[49] Of those survivors, who once landed were sold as *bozales* and put to work on the plantations as slaves, not all were disposed to adapt to the rigor of this new life. This is demonstrated by the fact that in the slave conspiracies that are known—a total of nineteen between 1790 and 1845, which have been studied by the historian Guillermo A. Baralt—one or more *bozales* invariably figure in the leadership.[50] However, from the middle of the nineteenth century—when immigration of Africans to the island had ceased—until the decree of abolition in 1873, no slave conspiracies are reported. Nonetheless, this does not mean that a part of the slave population no longer resisted the system.

The flight of individual slaves from the estates, a less dangerous tactic than conspiracy, in which there was always the risk of betrayal, was one of the preferred forms to obtain their freedom. Although this alternative was always present and available to slaves, there were periods in which a greater incidence of flights were reported. In Ponce, for example, in the *Book of Slave Fugitives, Orphans and Notable Occurrences, 1853-1865,* no runaway slaves are listed in the 1850s, but from 1868 to 1871 slave masters informed the authorities of at least ten cases of flight.[51] During these same years, the Audiencia mandated the preparation of a report to explain why there had been an increase in slave criminal cases and incidents that, according to the report, "[were] previously very rare in this area."[52] These facts can be explained not as the fruit of the slaves' imagination, in which, according to the mayor of Arecibo, "the idea of emancipation stirred with greater force than ever," but more as the result of a series of economic factors that had made the plantation work routine a true hell for the slaves.[53]

In describing the life of the slaves on the sugar estates of Cuba, Moreno Fraginals has compared their work to prison regimes.[54] In Puerto Rico the same comparison could be applied. In a report on the courts and legislation in Puerto Rico, published in 1850, Florencio de Ormaechea pointed out, "We have already indicated that life in the sugar mills is hard, much more laborious than that of the penitentiaries." He proposed, as a remedy to prevent "criminal occurrences, [and] for the punishment and precaution of the African race in Puerto Rico . . . and to prevent the demoralization produced in our jails . . . requiring in the first instance, no punishment greater than six years of work, in a sugar plantation designated by the court in its finding, with proper security, as is the custom at the mills."[55] In addition, Ormaechea cynically recommended that "with respect to the deficiencies . . . it would be conducive, in reference to slaves, that the legislation not treat the whip or the lash as corporal punishment, and that the judges, as a result, be empowered to impose up to 200 lashes in different turns or at different times."[56]

As such, the daily life of the slaves on the sugar estates during the nineteenth century was formed by countless experiences, with much that was dehumanizing. Cases can be cited in which the whip was applied, not only to those slaves who committed offenses, but also to pregnant slaves, who due to their condition refused to work;[57] young slaves' eyelashes were cut so that they wouldn't sleep during the nights of the cane cutting;[58] a slave was punished, with the consent of the judges, for the single crime of having spoken to the foreman using the familiar *tú* instead of the formal *usted.*[59]

But, on the other hand, cases can be cited of some masters who graciously gave freedom to their slaves, or of owners, such as Doña María Laporte who specified in their wills not only the manumission or the bequest of some property for their slaves but also instructions to the executors on the education that they should arrange for the slaves.[60] One could also mention the slaves' right to purchase their freedom gradually through *coartación* and also the slaves' right to present complaints in the courts of justice through their representative, the protector of slaves.[61] Clearly these mechanisms were not effectively or frequently used by slaves. There were cases in which these same representatives who had dared accuse owners in the courts, were themselves later called on by the masters and had to appear in court accused of preventing justice.[62]

Although one could point to some instances in which the institution would have functioned effectively for the well-being of the island's slaves—as George Flinter's work purported to show in 1832—such reasoning, trying to distinguish the cases of dehumanization from those where the slaves were granted juridical personality (to use Frank Tannenbaum's phrase), would probably lead to a deadend, in which the arguments become circular.[63] If, however, the relations between masters and slaves are framed within the transitions of the plantation economy, then the behavior of the masters, as well as the slaves, can be seen as less erratic because there were periods, as Sidney Mintz maintains, in which the doctrine of the moral personality of the slave was conveniently forgotten while the plantations expanded.[64]

From the middle of the century until abolition, the sugar economy in Puerto Rico went through two clearly demarcated periods in terms of the intensity with which slave labor was employed. The first period can be fixed from before midcentury to a little beyond 1860. During this time, both the demand and the price of slaves in the local market remained constant. The value of land increased as well, and there was no notable decline in the number of plantations in operation.

In contrast with this situation, during the second period, more specifically between 1865 and 1873, not only did the sale price of slaves fall (see figure 6.1), but there appears to have been a tendency on the part of the owners with large numbers of slaves (50 or more) not to acquire more slaves (figure 6.2). The estates have been divided into three groups according to number of slaves: small, 0 to 24; medium, 25 to 49; and large, more than 50. In Puerto Rico, unlike Cuba, plantations with more than 100 or 125 slaves were rare exceptions. A frequency distribution has been done for the years when *Cuadernos de Riqueza* or censuses that specified the number of plantation slaves could be found, grouping the owners in accordance with the number of agricultural slaves possessed.[65] There was a sharp decline in the number of slaves on the larger estates.

These changes, however, did not alter fundamentally the dependence on slavery nor the extensive form in which the sugar plantations developed throughout the nineteenth century. Although some estates reduced the number of slaves, this does not imply that there was less need for slave labor. Despite a decline in the number of slaves in the last years of slavery on some estates at the same time the number of free laborers employed increased, those estates functioning in 1861 maintained, on the average, the same number of slaves as in 1845, and a similar point holds for those continuing to function in 1872 (see comparison of tables 6.1 and 6.2). As the historian Andrés Ramos Mattei has demonstrated for the plantation Mercedita of Ponce, "Until the abolition of slavery in 1873, Mercedita used a mixed labor force of free laborers and slaves. . . . Nonetheless, it appears that until 1873, the base of the labor system on this particular estate was slave labor."[66]

Pressured to produce more, in order to recuperate their capital investment as quickly as possible, or to compensate for losses due to droughts or increased tariff duties, the planters had no recourse but to stretch the length of the workday. This appears to have been a general response on many estates on the eve of abolition. The reports on the increase in criminal incidents that the local councilmen sent to the state council of the island alluded to the severity with which many masters treated their slaves: "by the excessive work and little rest they are given."[67]

At the same time, the planters were confronted with another serious problem when they tried to acquire more workers for the estates. The quantitative increase in the number of day workers employed is perhaps not

Figure 6.2 Number of Field Slaves by Plantation Size, Ponce, 1845, 1861, and 1872

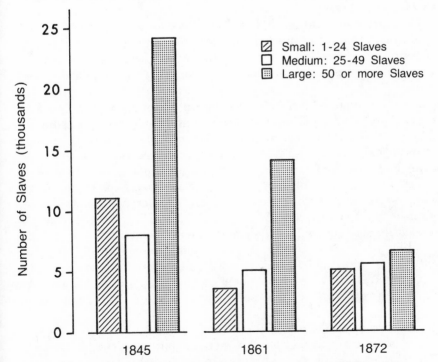

Source: Archivo Municipal de Ponce, Cuaderno de la Riqueza Agrícola, 1845; Planillas, 1861, Archivo General de Puerto Rico, Records of Spanish Governors of Puerto Rico, Political and Civil Affairs, Box 84, Registro de Esclavos, 1972.

the best measure to gauge the many failures encountered by the planters and governors in their efforts to create a market of free laborers on the island. The Regulation of Pezuela is perhaps the clearest example. These extraeconomic measures never managed to achieve their aims completely. On the one hand, they tried to destroy the small holdings (of less than two *cuerdas*) that were rented by tenants and to eliminate the old arrangements between owners and tenant farmers. It was thought that in this way tenants could be forced into the labor market as day workers.[68] On the other hand, the small holdings continued to multiply, making the creation of a labor market more difficult.[69] The planters' complaints about their difficulty in acquiring workers for the estates throughout the century, and the many proposals on the regulation of free labor that the planters submitted to the metropolitan government and that many times were rejected—for example, the proposal of a group of fifty planters in 1876—are perhaps the best indication of what must have been one of the most serious problems that afflicted the sugar industry once slavery was abolished.[70] Don Antonio Alfau y Baralt, the representative of the Agricultural Society of Ponce, expressed it in this way: "The prime cause of the momentary disturbance in Puerto Rican agriculture was a measure that all inhabitants, and the growers themselves, applauded with enthusiasm . . . this being the law of abolition in the Lesser Antille."[71]

He went on to plead for "a just, legal and equitable regulation of free labor, that makes plain, fixes and assures completely the obligations and rights of the planter and workers . . . that prudentially curbs vagrancy as the origin of vices and disturbances that jeopardize the social and public order."[72]

But this had not been the tone nor the attitude of many planters before the abolition of slavery. The United States consul on the island remarked in February 1876 that "strange to say, the enemies of abolition [sic] of slavery in this island are not, with few exceptions, slave holders."[73] In Ponce, for example, Guillermo Cabrera, a rich planter and the most important slave owner, wrote to José Julián Acosta, one of the leaders of Puerto Rican abolition in the Spanish Cortes, "We have done everything possible to dissipate the fear that you [Acosta] inspire . . . They fear that you ask immediate abolition without indemnification."[74] Once slavery was abolished by the Cortes of the first Spanish republic on March 22, 1873, the governor of the island, Primo de Rivera, said that the news had been received in Puerto Rico with jubilation "not only [by] the lovers of reform, but that a major part of the conservatives had participated with equal joy."[75]

This attitude on the part of the old masters led historians to judge the abolition process as an example of democratic spirit or of racial harmony.[76] But if it is questionable that either exists in Puerto Rico today, it is definitely inadmissible to claim that the origins of these attributes can be derived from the form in which the planters' attitudes toward the abolition of slavery on the island evolved. There is nothing mystical in the behavior of the old planters, but rather much economic opportunism. With the offer of abolition with indemnity, the Spanish government agreed to pay the owners two hundred pesos for each slave. This price closely approximated the current price in the local market for a field slave of productive age. In any case, this sum represented no loss of investment to the owners. On the contrary, as a price for all slaves, without consideration of age or condition, the result was favorable for planters with slaves whose value had depreciated.[77] In addition, with the offer of this sum, many planters planned to capitalize or invest in the acquisition of better technology for their estates. But the indemnity was a promise, which like so many others made by the metropolis to the colony, materialized late. The indemnity process was completed in 1890.[78] Neither had the Spanish government foreseen other more immediate problems that were encountered in the attempt to regulate contracts between freed slaves and landowners after abolition.[79]

What remained constant in the years preceding and following abolition in Puerto Rico was the planters' need to have at their disposal more workers, slave or free. And although some planters, like Santiago MacKormick, administrator of the first central established on the island in 1874, pleaded for more capital to transform the old plantations, others continued to insist on imposing new regulations on the workers, atavistic reminders of an institution that many on the island had resisted to consider dead.[80] But once abolition was decreed, Puerto Rico entered one of its worst economic crises. Although this crisis was not caused solely by the abolition of slavery, it did aggravate the difficulty, already bemoaned by the planters, of acquiring labor for their estates. Little time passed after abolition before the old plantations were in ruins.

NOTES

I would like to express my appreciation to José Antonio Herrero for his indispensable help in analyzing the economy of this period and to Jorge Aguilar Mora for his help in revising the text. The translation, from the longer paper presented at the conference, was done by Judith Evans.

   1. Luis M. Díaz Soler, *Historia de la esclavitud negra en Puerto Rico* (Rio Piedras: Editorial Universitaria, 1970), p. 373. This work represents the most fundamental contribution for the study of Negro slavery in Puerto Rico. It was for many years the only study on slavery. The field was greatly enriched with the publication of the collection of documents by the Centro de Investigaciones Históricas de la Universidad de Puerto Rico, *El proceso abolicionista en Puerto Rico: Documentos para su estudio*, 2 vols. (San Juan: Centro de Investigaciones Históricas e Instituto de Cultura Puertorriqueña, 1974, 1979) and the investigations of Arturo Morales Carrión, *Auge y decadencia de la trata negrera en Puerto Rico, 1820-1860* (San Juan: Centro de Estudios Avanzados de Puerto

Rico y el Caribe e Instituto de Cultura Puertorriqueña, 1978). The work of Díaz Soler is solidly grounded; however, the administrative and legal aspects are emphasized more than the economic aspects, although these do not escape the attention of the author. In addition, the work covers a vast period, from the beginnings of colonization until 1890. For this reason it appears at times to be a bit encyclopedic.

2. See, for example, the statements by Eric Williams, *From Columbus to Castro: The History of the Caribbean, 1492–1969* (New York: Harper & Row, 1970), p. 291: "The Puerto Rico situation was unique in the Caribbean, in that not only did the white population outnumber the people of color, but the slaves constituted an infinitesimal part of the total population and free labor predominated during the regime of slavery." Similar statements can be found in the study of abolition in Cuba and Puerto Rico by Arthur Corwin, *Spain and the Abolition of Slavery in Cuba: 1817–1886* (Austin: University of Texas Press, 1967), ch. 9–11.

3. This was maintained by Pedro Tomás de Córdova in his study of the island's economy during the first decades of the last century. *Memorias geográficas, históricas y económicas de la Isla de Puerto Rico*, 2nd. ed., 6 vols. (San Juan: Instituto de Cultura Puertorriqueña, 1968), 4: 412.

4. Díaz Soler, *Historia de la esclavitud negra*, pp. 259, 375. Díaz Soler based his figures for the slave population not on the official figures of the government, but on those from a publication of the abolitionist Rafael M. de Labra, whose figures, Díaz Soler himself pointed out in a footnote (p. 256), are inexact. In contrast, the figures of the Archivo Municipal de Ponce (hereafter AMP), *Cuaderno de la Riqueza Agrícola y Urbana, 1845*, on free and slave labor employed in Ponce, were collected from the estate owners and could be more reliable than those of Labra.

5. The export figures for all ports of the island during the nineteenth century appear in the *Balanza Mercantil*. During the second half of the century Ponce exported about 22 percent of all the sugar exported from the island. See, for example, the summaries of the population censuses in Archivo Histórico Nacional (hereafter AHN), U, leg. 5115, exp. 153, "Censo 1867" [microfiche Centro de Investigaciones Históricas, Universidad de Puerto Rico (hereafter CIH)].

6. For a truly beautiful study of the sharecroppers and day workers in a coffee-growing village of Puerto Rico, see Fernando Picó's book, *Libertad y servidumbre en el Puerto Rico del siglo XIX: Los journaleros utuadeños en vísperas del auge del café* (Río Piedras: Editorial Huracán, 1979). In this book the relatively minor importance of slaves in the coffee economy is noted. In the research that we have recently done on the formation of the labor market in Puerto Rico in the nineteenth century in other sugar towns, preliminary findings are that there was a concentration of slaves on the plantations, while similarities with the estates of Ponce in regard to the proportion of *cuerdas* seeded in cane to the total area of the estate were found.

7. In AHN, U, leg. 5072, exp. 37, "Expediente sobre salarios, 1851" (microfilm CIH) appears a report from the governor on the number and the working conditions of urban slaves on the island.

8. Archivo General de Puerto Rico (hereafter AGPR), Records of Spanish Governors of Puerto Rico (hereafter RSGPR), Political and Civil Affairs, "Censo y Riqueza," box 16.

9. Labor Gómez Acevedo, *Organización y reglamentación del trabajo en el Puerto Rico del siglo XIX* (San Juan: Instituto de Cultura Puertorriqueña, 1970), offers a complete account of the implementation and effects of these measures in the island.

10. In AGPR, RSGPR, Municipalities, Ponce, 1860, box 532, appears a report on the abuses committed by the owners in delivering advance payments to the day workers. See also the comments of Salvador Brau, "Las clases jornaleras de Puerto Rico, (1882)," in his *Ensayos* (Río Piedras: Editorial Edil, 1971), pp. 9–73.

11. AMP, "Policía Jornaleros," exp. 10. See also Gómez Acevedo, *Organización y reglamentación*, pp. 97–116.

12. AHN, U. leg. 5072, exp. 39, "Estado que manifiesta los resultados que ha producido el Reglamento de Jornaleros, mandado observar por disposicion de este Gobierno y Capitanía General" (microfilm CIH).

13. Lidio Cruz Monclova, *Historia de Puerto Rico, Siglo XIX*, 3 vols. (Río Piedras: Editorial Universitaria, 1970), 1: 303.

14. See the analysis of the reports given by Gómez Acevedo, *Organización y reglamentación*, pp. 333–410.

15. AMP, "Actas del Ayuntamiento de Ponce," 1874, fol. 358v.

16. AHN, U, leg. 5072, exp. 39 (microfilm CIH).

17. "Memoria acerca de la agricultura, Comercio y las Rentas Internas de la Isla de Puerto Rico, 1847," in Cayetano Coll y Toste, *Boletín Histórico de Puerto Rico* (hereafter *BHPR*), 14 vols. (San Juan: Tipografía Cantero, Fernández & Co., 1914–1927), 2: 253.

18. See, for example, the similar statements made in 1867 by abolitionist leaders, such as Segundo Ruiz Belvis, José Julián Acosta, and Francisco Mariano Quiñones, in "Informe sobre la Abolición Immediata de la Esclavitud en Puerto Rico," in Cayetano Coll y Toste, *Historia de la esclavitud en Puerto Rico* (San Juan: Sociedad de Autores Puertorriqueños, 1972), pp. 11–92. See also Rafael M. Labra y Cadrana, *La abolición de la esclavitud en el orden económico* (Madrid: Noguera, 1873).

19. AGPR, Fondo de los Gobernadores, Asuntos Políticos y Civiles, "Esclavos, 1847." I owe this reference to Professor Guillermo A. Baralt.

20. See, for example, the article by the planter from Guayama that appeared in the edition of November 2, 1852, and other articles on the same theme that appeared in 1853 in numbers 76 and 77 of *El Ponceño*.

21. Karl Marx, *Capital* (New York: Modern Library, 1936), 1: 241, 292: "The essential difference between the various economic forms of society, between, for instance, a society based on slave labour, and one based on wage labour, lies only on the mode in which this surplus-labour is in each case extracted from the actual producer, the labourer. . . . The slave-owner buys his labourer as he buys his horse. If he loses his slave, he loses capital that can only be restored by new outlay in the slave-mart." Manuel Moreno Fraginals, *El ingenio*, 3 vols. (Havana: Editorial de Ciencias Sociales, 1978), 2: 14, adds with his unequaled

power of synthesis: "By insoluble contradiction, the slave participated in a double contradiction acting both as labor force and as means of production. . . . In his role as means of production he was tied permanently to the sphere of production and transferred value to the product in the same proportion in which he lost his own as use value, and concurrently his own exchange value."

22. Several studies in the "New Economic History" took the analysis of a slave as capital to the limits of quantification. See, for example, the essay of Alfred H. Conrad and John R. Meyer, "The Economics of Slavery in the Ante-Bellum South," and that of Yasukichi Yasuba, "The Profitability and Viability of Plantation Slavery in the United States," in Robert W. Fogel and Stanley Engerman, eds., *The Reinterpretation of American Economic History* (New York: Harper & Row, 1971), pp. 342–368; also Robert William Fogel and Stanley L. Engerman, *Time on the Cross, The Economics of American Negro Slavery* (Boston: Little, Brown & Company, 1974).

23. Andrés Ramos Mattei, *Los libros de cuentas de la Hacienda Mercedita, 1861–1900, Apuntes para el estudio de la transición hacia el sistema de centrales en la industria azucarera* (San Juan: CEREP, 1975).

24. David Turnbull, *Travels in the West. Cuba; with Notices of Porto Rico and the Slave Trade* (London: Longman, Orme, Brown, Greene, and Longman, 1840), p. 559. "The most remarkable fact connected with the history and present state of Puerto Rico is that the fields are cultivated and sugar manufactured by the hands of white men under a tropical sun."

25. On some plantations, such as El Bronce of Buenaventura Foces, where we could obtain the gross production and the taxable liquid product, there was a difference of 36 percent between the figures. From 1873 the net income of the plantations was computed on the base of a fixed rate of 35 percent of the gross product; see the Circular of 1873 of the Administración Económica of the island. (There is a copy in AGPR, Municipal de Lares.) See also Félix Mejías, *Apuntes de historia económica* (Río Piedras: Editorial Edil, 1974).

26. AMP, "Padrón de Terrenos, 1848." A note signed by the governor reads, "The censuses do not appear to have been done with the scrupulousness required."

27. The formula used to obtain the rate of profit was the following:

$$P_e = \sum_{n=1}^{m} \frac{In - Cn}{(1 + i)^n} + \frac{VR}{(1 + i)^m}$$

in which, P_e = price in the market of a field slave at the start of his productive years (age fifteen to fifty-five); I_n = gross income produced by a slave each year; C_n = cost of maintenance of a slave for one year; VR = price of an old slave (55 years); m = productive life of a slave; i = rate of interest or profit.

AMP, "Cuaderno, 1845," gives 200 pesos as the value of the slaves on the plantations. As neither the Cuaderno nor the account books give the costs of slave maintenance, the net reported income was divided by the number of slaves (9), with the outcome being $I - C$. The net income that was reported deducted the costs of maintenance. A circular from 1873 (in AGPR, Municipal de Lares) fixed the deductions for maintenance at 35 percent of the net income of the planters. In the case of the plantation of José de Torres, $I - C = 33.33$ pesos. The price of a fifty-five-year-old-slave was around 75 pesos; m

was assumed to be forty years. On substituting these terms in the equation, one obtains

$$200 = \sum_{n=1}^{40} \frac{33.33}{(1 + i)^n} + \frac{75}{(1 + i)^{40}}$$

The calculated value of i is 17 percent.

28. In 1845 the net income reported by the Hacienda Unión of Antonio Torruella was 3,590 pesos, or 43.3 pesos per slave. All other values were the same as in note 27. The calculated profit rate (22 percent) should have been a little lower, given that two day workers were employed on the estate. However, since the number of slaves on this plantation (eighty-three) was much greater than the number of day workers, this decrease in the rate of profit would be slight.

29. In 1861 the average price for a field slave was approximately 650 pesos, the net income per slave was 119.50 pesos, and the price of a fifty-five-year-old slave was approximately 115 pesos. A productive life of forty years was utilized.

30. Díaz Soler, *Historia de la esclavitud negra,* pp. 121–22; see also Ministerio de Asuntos Exteriores, Madrid (hereafter MAE), U, II E, leg. 2969, exp. 4, "Memorandum on the Slave Trade in Puerto Rico, 1865" (microfilm CIH). The English consul said, "As regards slave trade in Puerto Rico, the subject may at once be dismissed by statistics (sic), that none has occurred or been attempted for many years. . . . Consequently, the slaves which only amount to 7 percent of the whole population are all creoles."

31. The figures on the slave population of the island from the end of the eighteenth century to the middle of the nineteenth century appear in Díaz Soler, *Historia de la esclavitud negra,* p. 117. We computed the population growth during the second half of the century on the basis of official figures that appeared in AGPR, RSGPR, Municipalities, Ponce, 1860, entrada 290, box 532, "Estadística de los nacimientos y defunciones, 1863, 1864." Around the year 1864 the slave population of Ponce was 4,667; a gross rate for mortality obtained was 32 per 1,000 and the gross birth rate was 43 per 1,000. Births and deaths were registered only for the first seven months of that year. For a conservative estimate, the number of births per month was calculated as 200. The rate obtained was very high and compares favorably with the birth rates for preindustrial societies. See E. A. Wrigley, *Population and History* (New York: McGraw-Hill, 1969), ch. 3 and 5, for a study of birth rates in pre-industrial societies.

32. AMP, "Censo de Almas, 1840, 1850;" AGPR, "Registro de Esclavos, 1872," reg. 186, box 84. These percentages were obtained using random samples. For 1840 and 1850 samples were taken from all areas of Ponce (1840, $N = 899$; 1850, $N = 385$; 1872, $N = 108$).

33. Díaz Soler, *Historia de la esclavitud negra,* pp. 117, 118, passim. See also the study by Rubén Carbonell Fernández on slave sales and purchases in San Juan, "Las compra-ventas de esclavos en San Juan, 1818–1873," *Anales de Investigación Histórica* 3, No. 1 (1976). The small impact of the first treaty prohibiting the slave trade on altering the volume or price of slaves sold in San Juan is mentioned.

34. AHN, U, leg. 5080, exp. 1, "Es Instruida la Reina del Expediente de varios

hacendados, 1859" (microfilm CIH). See also Junta Informativa de Ultramar, "Interrogatorio sobre la manera de Reglamentar el Trabajo de la Población de Color y Asiática y Los Medios de Facilitar la Inmigración que sea mas conveniente en las Provincias de Cuba y Puerto Rico, 1866," edited in CIH, *El proceso abolicionista*, 1: 55–63.

35. Díaz Soler, *Historia de la esclavitud negra*, p. 154. "The slave works slowly; a free worker does double the work of a slave. . . . When the Puerto Rican planter perceived this reality, he *insisted* on the use of free labor, so that in the nineteenth century there was not one estate cultivated exclusively by enslaved Negro workers." (Emphasis added.)

36. See, for example, the commentaries of the vice-consul Leopold Krug in 1866, in CIH, *El proceso abolicionista*, 1: 48–51; or MAE, II E, leg. 2969, exp. 4, "Memorandum on the Slave Trade in Puerto Rico, 1865" (microfilm CIH).

37. For an account of the problems that planters encountered when they contracted with sugar merchants and shippers, see AHN, U, leg. 5080, exp. 21 (microfiche CIH).

38. Cruz Monclova, *Historia*, 1: 476.

39. F. W. Taussig, *The Tariff History of the United States* (New York: Capricorn Books, 1964), pp. 174, 175.

40. Cruz Monclova, *Historia*, 1: 476.

41. Cruz Monclova, *Historia*, 2: 117–19.

42. Arthur Cole, *Wholesale Commodity Prices in the United States* (Cambridge: Harvard University Press, 1938), gives the prices paid for muscovado sugar in the Philadelphia market from 1801 to 1861. When one compares the variations in these prices with a few quotations from the local market (AGPR, Fondo de los Gobernadores, Agencias Gubernamentales, Fomento y Comercio, entrada 21, box 323), one can appreciate that there was apparently no correlation between the variations in the two sets of quotations.

43. *El Avisador* (Ponce), April 11, 1874.

44. Ramos Mattei, *Libros de cuenta*, pp. 15–18. In a previous work, *De la esclavitud a la abolición*, Cuadernos 7 (San Juan: CEREP, 1979) I point out the form in which the sugar plantations of Ponce developed.

45. Moreno Fraginals, *El ingenio*, 2: 28–29.

46. "Slave Trade Report," in CIH, *El proceso abolicionista*, 1: 48.

47. For an account of some of the problems faced by the sugar industry in Puerto Rico, see [Hacendados de Caña], "Exposición Pidiendo Franquicia para el Azúcar que se Envia a la Península, 1876," in Coll y Toste, *BHPR*, 11: 373–80.

48. AHN, U, leg. 5115, exp. 52, "Don Antonio Alfau y Baralt, representante de la Sociedad de Agricultores de Ponce, solicita reglamentación del trabajo libre en dicha Isla, 1879" (microfilm CIH).

49. Daniel P. Mannix and Malcolm Cowley, *Black Cargoes* (New York: Viking Press, 1962), pp. 157–58. This book relates some of the violent incidents on board ships destined specifically for Puerto Rico.

50. Guillermo A. Baralt, "Conspiraciones, Sublevaciones y Revueltas de Esclavos en Puerto Rico, 1796–1848" (San Juan: paper presented before the Sixth Annual Conference of Caribbean Historians, 1974, mimeograph).

51. AGPR, Fondo de los Gobernadores, Municipios, Ponce, 1860. box 532.

52. This document appears in the CIH collection, *El proceso abolicionista*, 1: 181–205.
53. Ibid., p. 193.
54. Manuel Moreno Fraginals, "Aportes Culturales y Deculturación," in Manual Moreno Fraginals, ed., *Africa en América Latina* (Mexico City: Siglo XXI y UNESCO, 1977), pp. 13–33.
55. Florencio de Ormaechea, *Memoria sobre los tribunales y la legislación de la Isla de Puerto Rico* (Madrid: Establecimento Tipográfico de D. S. Saungque, 1850), pp. 22, 23.
56. Ibid.
57. See the *juicio verbal* [oral trial] held at the request of the slave, Ana, of the settlement at the Hacienda Bronce, AMP, "Juicios Verbales," May 23, 1845.
58. Díaz Soler, *Historia de la esclavitud negra*, p. 185.
59. This case, which was brought before the mayor of Manatí on December 13, 1862, appears transcribed in Benjamín Nistal, "Catorce querellas de esclavos, Manatí, 1868–1873," in *Sin Nombre* 4, no. 2 (1973): 92–93.
60. AGPR, Rafael de León, Protocolos Notariales, 1851, fol. 297, "Codicilo de Doña María Laporte."
61. Díaz Soler, *Historia de la esclavitud negra*, pp. 194–98.
62. See the case in Arecibo in 1868, when the slave Fernando of the Monte Grande estate died after being beaten by the foreman. The *promotor fiscal* and lawyer, Luis Ealo Domingo, after arguing the case against the owner of the plantation, Antonio Goicuría, and against Andrés Tejada, was accused by thirty-eight residents of Arecibo. "Accusación fiscal contra el Amo y Mayordomo de Ingenio Monte Grande de Arecibo, por muerte de un esclavo," in Coll y Toste, *Historia de la esclavitud en Puerto Rico*, pp. 217–24.
63. George D. Flinter, *Examen del estado actual de los esclavos de la Isla de Puerto Rico* (1832, ed. facsímile, San Juan: Instituto de Cultura Puertorriqueña, 1976). Recently John V. Lombardi, in "Comparative Slave Systems in the Americas: A Critical Review," synthesized the debate growing out of the comparative studies, pointing out the "circularity" in many of the arguments they employ. In Richard Graham and Peter H. Smith, eds., *Approaches to Latin American History* (Austin: University of Texas Press, 1974), pp. 156–74.
64. Sidney W. Mintz, "Slavery and Emergent Capitalism," in Laura Foner and Eugene Genovese, eds., *Slavery in the New World* (Englewood Cliffs, N.J.: Prentice-Hall, 1969), pp. 27–37.
65. For 1845 the "Cuaderno de Riquezas" of Ponce was used; for 1861, the *Planillas de Riqueza*, in which only planters, and not ranchers, appeared. However, the number of slaves on the ranches was very small in comparison to the plantation settlements. For 1872 the "Registro de esclavos" was used, in which only the field slaves employed as laborers or in specialized jobs on the plantations appear listed.
66. Ramos Mattei, *Libros de cuentas*, p. 15.
67. CIH, *El proceso abolicionista*, 1: 184.
68. AMP, *Policía Jornaleros*, exp. 10, box 63.1, Juan de la Pezuela, Circular 67, 1850.
69. In Ponce, for example, in 1845 there were seven plantations and twenty-three

owners of small farms in the Machuelo Abajo area. But by 1862, instead of small proprietorships being reduced, they were increasing; at that point there were eight plantations and more than a hundred proprietors of small farms (from ¹/₂ of a *cuerda* to twenty-five *cuerdas*). AMP, "Cuaderno de Riquezas, 1845"; "Padrón de Terrenos, 1862."

70. AHN, U, leg. 5112, exp. 64, "Remitiendo Proyecto para Reglamentar Trabajo, 1876" (microfiche CIH).

71. AHN, U, leg. 5115, exp. 52 (microfilm CIH).

72. Ibid.

73. Edward Conroy to C. I. Bancroft Davis, San Juan, February 11, 1873. This document appears in CIH, *El proceso abolicionista*, 2 : 286.

74. Cited in Díaz Soler, *Historia de la esclavitud negra*, p. 291.

75. AHN, U, leg. 5112, exp. 42. Primo de Rivera, Carta Oficial 48, April 13, 1873 (microfiche CIH).

76. These are some of the conclusions that Díaz Soler expressed in *Historia de la esclavitud negra*, pp. 373-75.

77. Some of the problems and accords related to compensation appear in AHN, U, leg. 5112, exps. 51, 52, 57, and also 60; "Sanz al Ministro de Ultramar, Sobre motivos y hechos para tasar a los esclavos a un mismo precio."

78. Díaz Soler, *Historia de la esclavitud negra*, pp. 347-91.

79. AHN, U, leg. 5112, exp. 50, May 19, 1874: "Following what up to now has been the practice, the contracts were illusory, in that a large number of the freed entered into 4 or 5 in the same day, causing the contracts to fall into disgrace."

80. Santiago MacCormick, *Informe dado a la Excma. Diputación Provincial sobre el sistema de las factoriás centrales para la elaboración de la azúcar de caña en la Isla de Puerto Rico* (San Juan: Imprenta del Boletín Mercantil, 1880). The governor's report appears with the proposals of a group of the most influential planters for the regulation of work, AHN, U, leg. 5112, exp. 64 (microfilm CIH).

7. Problems in the Social Structure of Slavery in Puerto Rico during the Process of Abolition, 1872

Benjamín Nistal-Moret

The abolition of slavery in Puerto Rico cannot be isolated from the social context in which it took place because it was not an isolated event, nor did it have a single cause. Slavery was a complex social reality: economic explanations are incomplete and somewhat inaccurate, as are purely political or cultural explanations. The abolition (1873) took place in the context of complex changes in the socioeconomic, political, and technological structures in Puerto Rico; its final repercussions became apparent only in the 1880s. In general, the transformations began between 1820 and 1840, intensified between 1850 and 1870, and finally took on a social form during the last ten to twenty years of the century. At first sight, the most dramatic transformation was the increasing dependence of Puerto Rico on foreign industrial markets. This dependence was shaped by the staggering volume of imported goods (luxury, as well as basic consumer items); steam engine technology, primarily for agricultural use; and high-energy-yield fuel.

The connection established between imports—of consumer goods, steam engine technology, and high-energy-yield fuel—and the numerical decline of slavery can be seen by comparing tables 7.1 and 7.2 with figure 7.1. On the basis of these data we can ask a series of questions aimed at understanding the foundations of slavery. For example, was the late introduction of large-scale slavery in the colony from 1820 to 40—late in relation to the rest of the Caribbean—a necessary prologue to the introduction of steam engines on the haciendas? Was slavery used initially to prepare the way for, and later as a means of stabilizing, a semimechanized regime in which slave labor was used intensively in the cutting, carrying, and transporting of cane? Was slavery ever directly connected to mechanical and technical proc-

Table 7.1 Imports of Agricultural Machinery and Steam Engine Technology, Puerto Rico, 1840–97

Year	Casks, Boiler and Evaporation Pans (Kgs.)	Tools/Farming Equipment Value (pesos)	Agricultural Tools Value (pesos)	Number of Steam Engines	Number of Mills
1840	—	130,627	—	—	—
1841	—	115,555	—	—	—
1842	—	69,243	—	—	—
1843	—	—	24,100	4	1
1844	—	—	39,421	13	1
1845	58,000	—	46,534	18	4
1846	60,000	—	41,670	25	2
1847	136,129	—	59,367	19	1
1848	56,000	—	22,174	18	1
1849	163,860	—	22,781	17	5
1850	142,000	—	23,582	42	—
1853	86,407	—	—	—	7
1858	—	—	—	—	—
1863	113,045	—	—	14	—
1868	98,663	—	—	15	—
1873	446,738	—	—	29	—
1878	39,666	—	—	19	—
1883	Imported 2,608,432 Kgs. of machines with motors				
1893	Imported 507,680 Kgs. of machines and apparatus for production of sugar and cane liquor.				
1897	Imported 863,491 Kgs. of machines and apparatus for production of sugar and cane liquor.				

Source: Balanza Mercantil de Puerto Rico (various years).

Table 7.2 Fossil Fuel Imports, Puerto Rico, 1843–97

Year	Kgs.
1843	123,550
1848	153,660
1853	1,575,525
1858	3,863,455
1863	7,081,510
1868	5,498,818
1873	9,500,259
1883	12,611,113
1888	16,448,943
1893	17,512,927
1897	30,517,771

Source: Balanza Mercantil de Puerto Rico (various years).

Figure 7.1 Slave Population of Puerto Rico, 1775–1873

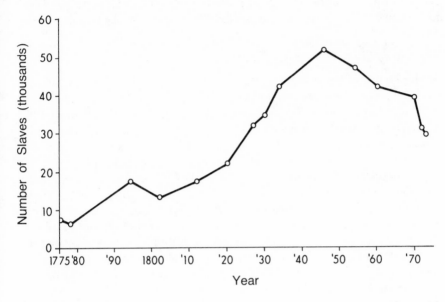

Source: See text.

esses? Is it possible to establish a relation between the costs and investments in mechanization and the costs of purchase and maintenance of slaves? That is, did one process influence the other to the point that the first eliminated the second? How could this relate to the general retention of slavery in the haciendas beginning in the 1850s, with the accelerated acquisition of steam technology imported from Europe and North America? Did the international financial sources that had developed African slave markets during the previous century play an important role in closing the slave trade? In other words, were England and the United States interested in the abolition of slavery and the closing of slave markets and ending of the slave trade because they were the main exporters of technology and fuel and the buyers of muscovado sugar? Was Puerto Rico, which arrived late to the reality of slave-produced sugar, forced to reorganize its economic regime in less than a generation so as to maintain a precarious mode of operation? Did it need to assume a stance of dependence simply in order to survive? Was Puerto Rico undergoing a contracted process of colonial socioeconomic withdrawal? These questions lead to the final questions: Who worked for the abolition of slavery on the island and why? When and where did the efforts begin?

We cannot explore these problems in detail in this essay. But we must have a general idea of the social composition of slavery in Puerto Rico at the moment of abolition in order to answer these questions later. In this paper we do not develop generalizations on the foregoing issues. Rather, we provide a broad and inclusive description of the slave population, based on quantitative evidence and, where possible, interrelated to the broader questions.

ANALYSIS OF SLAVE POPULATION, 1872

For this essay, for the first time in Puerto Rican historiography, an analysis of this magnitude has been completed with a computer. A number equal to at least one-third of the Puerto Rican slave population has been submitted to computer analysis. The slave census of 1872 provided the data base. This census served as a numerical base for the administrative and judicial decisions of 1873 and affected the organization and existence of slavery.

The census of 1872 in the Archivo General of Puerto Rico is incomplete. The one lost volume was found by the writer in the Library of Congress (Washington, D.C.) and microfilmed during the summer of 1975. The census, which was collected in several bound and previously printed folios, includes the names of the owners located according to towns and barrios, the slaves' names, origins, *coartación* status, place of registry, names of parents, number of children (including names), civil status, employment, and marital status. The slaves' sex was identified by their given names. By means of familiar methods, the information was transferred to computer cards, and by using SPSS (Statistical Package for the Social Sciences), the data were submitted to analysis.

An estimate of the total slave population on the island in 1872 was derived on the basis of the censuses between 1870 and 1873, which present inconsistent figures. The estimates follow:

1870 census	39,069 slaves
1872 census	31,042 slaves
1873 census (January)	31,000 slaves
1873 census (March)	29,335 slaves
1873 census (August, during the *contratación*)	29,335 slaves

Taking into consideration the possible margins of error and the effects of the Law of Partial Abolition (Moret Law of 1870) and the Abolition Decree of 1873, we estimated that the approximate population for 1872 was some 30,500 slaves. We analyzed a sample consisting of 12,512 slaves, representing 41 percent of the estimated population. The sample is distributed among the coastal villages of San Juan, Arecibo, Mayagüez, San Germán, Ponce, Guayama, and Fajardo. Areas in the interior are represented by Trujillo Bajo, Trujillo Alto, Aguas Buenas, Naranjito, Morovis, Ciales, Adjuntas, and Utuado. Although we had originally planned to include them, the areas of Añasco and Arroyo-Humacao-Yabucoa were omitted for reasons of cost and time.

Table 7.3 Slaves by Village, 1872

Village	Number of Slaves	Percentage of Sample[a]
San Juan	891	7.1
Arecibo	1,347	10.8
Mayagüez	2,570	20.5
San Germán	1,949	15.6
Ponce	3,251	26.0
Guayama	1,599	12.8
Fajardo	400	3.2
Trujillo Bajo	55	0.4
Trujillo Alto	47	0.4
Aguas Buenas	71	0.6
Naranjito	25	0.2
Morovis	32	0.3
Ciales	38	0.3
Adjuntas	58	0.5
Utuado	179	1.4
Total	12,512	100.1

[a] To get the ratio of the number of slaves in each village to the total slave population of the island, multiply each number in the column by .4102.

As a first step, we studied frequencies so as to identify general tendencies or patterns of distribution. The most useful frequencies at this stage of analysis are presented next. Slavery was primarily a coastal phenomenon, with the highest concentration of slaves in the south, southeast, and west of the colony (table 7.3). This is clearly related to another fact of slavery, namely, that the big haciendas were found in the coastal areas. These represented the best examples of steam engine technology and sugar production, together with some smaller units producing muscovado sugar. Thus, Mayagüez, San Germán, and Ponce had 62 percent of the sample, about one-quarter of the estimated slave population of 1872. The southern sector, in a line from Mayagüez to Fajardo, was the area of greatest slave concentration, as compared with the north. The central regions of the colony, in the mountain areas, were not regions of intense slave activity. The only exception was Utuado because it had a few valleys situated for sugar cane cultivation.

Analysis by age group reveals some surprising figures (table 7.4). The evidence indicates that the assumption that the slaves were old, which is so often accepted as a possible explanation for the abolitionist movement (i.e., because the slaves were old, they were therefore useless) is incorrect. Approximately 60 percent of the sample were ten to thirty-four years old, with most in the group twenty to twenty-nine years of age. We were not able to determine the life expectancy of slaves, much less their real physical condition, so it is not easy to clarify the status of their health. The nucleus of

Table 7.4 Slaves by Age, 1872

Age Group	Number of Slaves	Percentage of Sample
1–4	389	3.1
5–9	1,587	12.7
10–14	1,487	11.9
15–19	1,380	11.0
20–24	1,502	12.0
25–29	1,617	12.9
30–34	1,430	11.4
35–39	799	6.4
40–44	1,010	8.1
45–49	547	4.4
50–54	537	4.2
55–59	208	1.7
60+	6	0.0
Undetermined	13	0.1
Total	12,512	99.9

slavery, however, comprised a relatively youthful population. This statement becomes more important when considered together with additional evidence.

Data on sex show a relative numerical balance between men and women (table 7.5). There is an overwhelming absence of state and church sanctions for marriage (table 7.6). The sample demonstrates that 98 percent of the slaves in the sample were considered single, only 1 percent were recorded as married. This attests to the social abandonment in which slaves found themselves with regard to the legal recognition of permanent matrimonial

Table 7.5 Slaves by Sex, 1872

Sex	Number of Slaves	Percentage of Sample
Male	6,273	50.1
Female	6,224	49.7
Not classified	15	0.1
Total	12,512	99.9

Table 7.6 Slaves by Marital Status, 1872

Marital Status	Number of Slaves	Percentage of Sample
Single	12,273	98.1
Married	125	1.0
Widowed	14	0.1
Not classified	100	0.8
Total	12,512	100.0

and family ties. The argument is strengthened in table 7.7. In the sample, 63.2 percent of the slaves were recorded as black, whereas 35 percent were mulatto or mestizo. This percentage proves the existence of generalized cohabitation between free white men and slave women, whose children, according to law, remained slaves. ("Any child of a slave woman is a slave.")

In considering origin, the principal group was Creoles, born in Puerto Rico (table 7.8). These represented 88.8 percent of the sample, whereas only 10 percent were Africans. The rest were mostly slaves from the neighboring Antilles. These figures are extremely important because they allow us to argue that the largest group of slaves was already undergoing a process of aculturation or cultural synthesis. We suspect that the mestizo group could well have belonged to the large Creole group. In addition, because they were native-born and mulatto, we can assume that mestizos were among the younger slaves. In contrast, the 10 percent of Africans would be in the black group, as well as among the oldest. This is especially important in terms of understanding slave markets and the slave trade.

Over 17 percent of the sample appear to have had no occupations, which could be attributed to their age; 63.2 percent were counted as laborers, whose principal activity was working the land (table 7.9). An unexpectedly large number were counted as being domestics, approximately 17 percent of the sample. On the other hand, only 2.3 percent were occupied in industrial activities related to any of the stages in the production of sugar.

As pointed out, we looked at frequencies in order to identify possible general patterns of behavior that would allow observations on the social

Table 7.7   Slaves by Color, 1872

Color	Number of Slaves	Percentage of Sample
Black	7,913	63.2
Mulatto	4,374	35.0
"White"	187	1.5
Not classified	38	0.3
Total	12,512	100.0

Table 7.8   Slaves by Origin, 1872

Origin	Number of Slaves	Percentage of Sample
Puerto Rico	11,106	88.8
Africa	1,201	9.6
Other	195	1.6
Not classified	10	0.1
Total	12,512	100.1

Table 7.9   Slaves by Occupation, 1872

Occupation	Number of Slaves	Percentage of Sample
Without occupation	2,179	17.4
Laborer	7,904	63.2
Domestic	2,106	16.8
Industrial	289	2.3
Not classified	34	0.3
Total	12,512	100.0

status of slavery. The slaves' inability to purchase their freedom is reaffirmed (table 7.10). Only 3 percent of the slaves were listed as *coartaciónes*, while 97 percent of the slaves were not manumitted. The data on frequency demonstrate that manumission was not a viable instrument guaranteed by law for the achievement of freedom and integration into society.

The slaves' knowledge and maintenance of family ties with regard to formal maternal, paternal, and filial bonds are very different from what has been accepted (table 7.11). The great majority of slaves did not know their families. A suspicion raised earlier is thus confirmed. Most of the slaves (79.5 percent) knew their mothers, for the mother had transmitted the condition of slavery. Only 17.9 percent listed their fathers, while 81.8 percent did not do so. Therefore the reference point for any individual identification was the slave mother. Neither family nor traditional society

Table 7.10   Slaves by Legal Status, 1872

	Number of Slaves	Percentage of Sample
Coartaciónes	372	3.0
Others	12,140	97.0
Total	12,512	100.0

Table 7.11   Slaves by Information on Parents, 1872

	Number of Slaves	Percentage of Sample
[Both] parents known	2,144	17.1
Mother known Father unknown	7,809	62.4
Father known Mother unknown	97	0.8
[Both] parents unknown	2,422	19.4
Not classified	40	0.3
Total	12,512	100.0

Table 7.12 Slave Children by Sex, 1872[a]

Children	Number of Slaves	Percentage of Sample
Male	2,628	52.0
Female	2,345	46.3
Not classified	90	1.7
Total	5,063	100.0
Number of mothers	2,163	

[a] The sex of the slave is determined by the gender of the baptismal name.

apparently served the slave well. Moreover, almost 20 percent did not list their mothers, which further accentuates the condition described. All this amounts to saying that in 1872 slaves in Puerto Rico were social orphans, in colonial situations in which the simple fact of being a slave was a grave enough sin. Well may we ask about the role played by the church and the state in the maintenance of family, religious, cultural, and ethical ties, which by law they were obliged to implement and maintain. All of this is further indicated by the analysis of table 7.12. This table demonstrates that 2,163 slave women were the mothers of 5,063 children, although in the entire sample, only 125 slave women were married.

In general, these tables suggest a moderately defined pattern for the social identity of the mass of slaves: they seem to have been a fundamentally rural and agricultural group, concentrated on the coastal areas. They were relatively young, single, Puerto Rican–born, black—although with important traces of interbreeding with whites—and without sociofamilial ties sanctioned by church or state. There is not a trace of evidence that they were in a process of acquiring their freedom, although they appear to have been undergoing a process of cultural synthesis.

Because this information comes from official sources, it is not wise to make strong generalizations; extralegal arrangements were made at the edge of legal certifications and sanctions in nineteenth-century colonial Puerto Rico. The margin of error, false information, and fraud must be considered. In any case, and in spite of the foregoing reservations, the data are useful in so far as our aim to challenge generally accepted propositions. Thus, more questions, similar to the preceding ones, may be posed.

The average age of slaves, both of men and of women, was about twenty-five years (table 7.13); this finding is misleading if it is not linked to the origin of the slaves. For the Puerto Rican-born female slaves the average age was twenty-three years, while for the Creole males it was twenty-two. The average age for African female slaves was forty-seven years, and for African men, forty-six. The average Creole slave was born during the 1840s, while the typical African had been born during the 1820s. When we examine the origin of the slaves brought from the neighboring islands, the pattern repeats itself, as in Venezuela and Curaçao. This clearly reflects the closing

Table 7.13   Slave Population According to Average Age, Sex, and Origin, 1872

	Male Slaves		Female Slaves	
Origin	Number	Average Age	Number	Average Age
Unknown	4	30.5	3	35.7
Puerto Rico	5,465	22.4	5,639	23.2
Africa	710	45.9	489	47.6
San Tomás	7	43.4	9	36.5
Martinica	2	54.0	2	55.5
Curaçao	49	46.9	46	45.5
Cuba	4	23.8	4	43.5
Venezuela	8	48.5	12	48.7
Santo Domingo	1	8.0	2	50.0
Guadeloupe	3	50.6	1	51.0
Islas Inglesas	8	15.1	4	40.5
S. Bartolomé	2	33.5	4	47.0
Francia	—	—	1	44.0
Santa Cruz	2	36.0	—	—
Las Antillas	1	53.0	3	47.7
San Martín	1	54.0	—	—
Other	4	44.7	1	1.0
Total	6,271		6,220	

of the African markets and the abolition of the slave trade in the early nineteenth century. In other words, Puerto Rico stopped importing slaves legally at about the end of the 1840s. But Puerto Rico started producing sugar with African slave labor rather late. The repercussions of the late entry on the preexisting slave society were multiple and complex. For example, there might have been a greater pressure on Creole slaves to generate more labor power—numerically speaking—to replace the generational lag between the numbers and age groups of Africans and Creoles. Even without going further, in the central towns of the colony, the slaves tended to be considerably younger than those on the coastal litoral (table 7.14). The average age of the male slaves of Trujillo Bajo, Aguas Buenas, Naranjito, and Adjuntas was below twenty years, although Adjuntas did have the highest average age for women, a fact not yet clarified. It might be attributable to the coffee production centered in that area, which gave rise to a new dominant class that was able to use older slave women in a given productive process or, more probably, in domestic service. The coastal villages tended to maintain a certain balance between the age groups, although this equilibrium did not always extend to other categories.

Our earlier statement on age becomes even more meaningful with table 7.15. The youthfulness of the slave population is corroborated, for the bulk of it was composed of a great number of men and women between the ages of ten and thirty years. This assessment is slightly modified in the data of tables 7.16, 7.17, and 7.18, showing ages of slaves by sex and by origins (African and non-African). The data on the African slaves establish that

Table 7.14   Slave Population According to Average Age, Sex, and Village, 1872

Village	Male Slaves Number	Male Slaves Average Age	Female Slaves Number	Female Slaves Average Age
San Juan	386	23.7	503	27.1
Arecibo	687	25.8	655	25.5
Mayagüez	1,249	25.4	1,311	26.0
San Germán	1,001	24.4	948	24.9
Ponce	1,676	26.3	1,571	24.9
Guayama	784	27.2	814	26.5
Fajardo	224	24.5	176	24.8
Trujillo Bajo	28	19.9	27	18.7
Trujillo Alto	25	23.6	22	23.4
Aguas Buenas	40	14.0	31	22.0
Naranjito	14	18.2	11	21.1
Morovis	11	20.5	21	20.4
Ciales	20	23.8	18	22.7
Adjuntas	33	16.0	25	28.6
Utuado	92	20.6	87	19.2
Total	6,270		6,220	

Table 7.15   Slave Population According to Age and Sex, 1872

Age Group	Number of Male Slaves	Number of Female Slaves
1–4	195	192
5–9	821	765
10–14	759	727
15–19	705	675
20–24	748	753
25–29	758	858
30–34	693	737
35–39	398	401
40–44	520	490
45–49	270	277
50–54	288	249
55–59	113	95
60–64	—	1
65–69	—	2
70+	3	—
Total	6,271	6,222

Table 7.16   Slave Population According to Average Age, Sex, and Origin, 1872

Origin	Male Slaves Number	Male Slaves Average Age	Female Slaves Number	Female Slaves Average Age
Africa	710	45.9	489	47.6
Non-African	5,557	22.7	5,730	23.5
Total	6,267		6,219	

Table 7.17   Male Slave Population According to Age and Origin, 1872

Age Group	Number of Africans	Number of Non-Africans
1–4	—	194
5–9	—	820
10–14	—	759
15–19	—	705
20–24	8	740
25–29	15	743
30–34	46	646
35–39	72	326
40–44	195	325
45–49	139	131
50–54	179	109
55–59	56	57
70+	—	2
Total	710	5,557

they were not among the younger age groups, generally being over twenty-four years. More than half of the non-African male population was under twenty-four years; the figure for all male slaves was 58 percent. In the age groups between twenty-five to thirty-nine years, the African male population increased in numbers but totaled only about 20 percent of all African males, whereas for the non-Africans the share was 31 percent. Thus, while the African slaves had one-fifth of their population in the age group below thirty-nine, the Creole slaves had 89 percent of their population in this bracket. In the age group over forty, the pattern changes radically: the share of the male African population reaches 80 percent, whereas the non-African population has only 11 percent.

Table 7.18   Female Slave Population According to Age and Origin, 1872

Age Group	Number of Africans	Number of Non-Africans
1–4	1	190
5–9	—	765
10–14	2	725
15–19	—	675
20–24	2	751
25–29	4	854
30–34	12	725
35–39	37	364
40–44	129	360
45–49	109	168
50–54	138	111
55–59	52	42
60–64	1	—
65–69	2	—
70+	—	—
Total	489	5,730

A similar analysis was made of the female population. Between the ages of zero and twenty-four years, there are no Africans, while 54 percent of the non-African women were in this age bracket. In the ages between twenty-five and thirty-nine years were almost 11 percent of the Africans, but 34 percent of the non-Africans. As for the males, in the group between forty and fifty-nine years, the African share reached 37 percent and that of the Creole 12 percent.

To all appearances, the African group was much older than the Creole. Among the African group, moreover, the women tended to be older than the males, who did outnumber the women. This difference in average ages was also the case among the non-Africans, where the numbers were more or less balanced between the sexes.

Without going beyond these figures, we can ascertain that African slavery had no possibilities of further development. That is, the advanced age of the African population precluded the possibility of reproduction. Among the Creoles there was a sharp numerical gap between the age groups of zero to four and five to nine years, which meant possibly that reproduction was precluded. This gap was not an intrinsic outcome of slavery due to some internal failure or social dislocation but rather the consequence of an administrative legal action taken in 1870, when the legal abolition of slavery began with the Moret Law, or the Law of Partial Abolition. This cut off any possible expectation of a numerical increase of slaves by strangling the expansive capacity of the most youthful group, which could have reproduced for ten or fifteen years after 1870.

As a result of the Moret Law, those born between 1868 and 1870 were acquired by the state by means of an indemnification to the owner, and those over sixty were also declared free. This affected the Creole slaves in particular but also the Africans. According to the slave censuses, around ten thousand slaves were manumitted between 1868 and 1871–72. This figure does not include large numbers of children between the ages of zero and ten or slaves over sixty years of age. The Moret Law administered a *coup de grace* to the tendency to sustain a relatively stable group of slaves on the haciendas. It is thus reasonable to ask if that law were the product of circumstances arising from slavery or whether it was an imposition of a political nature.

The accessibility of slaves to the mechanisms of buying their own freedom was nil. The owners were not disposed to allow slaves between the ages of twenty to thirty years to try to acquire their liberty (table 7.19). The slaves who were *coartados* at 100, 200, 250, 300, 350, and 400 pesos were mostly thirty-five years old or older. In other words, the men and women who were born into slavery during the 1840s did not take part in the process of *coartación*. It is also significant that twice the number of slave women were *coartadas* as were men.

With regard to table 7.20, several of the propositions are confirmed. In the first place, it establishes the existence of an unproductive group of slaves

Table 7.19   Slave Population According to Average Age, Sex, and *Coartación* Price, 1872 [a]

Coartación Price (Pesos)	Male Slaves		Female Slaves	
	Number	Average Age	Number	Average Age
25	2	16.5	—	—
50	—	—	1	43.0
75	1	58.0	2	27.0
100	12	28.9	14	30.4
125	1	59.0	1	43.0
150	4	21.8	6	32.2
175	2	49.0	3	28.7
200	22	31.6	52	33.9
225	—	—	2	49.0
250	11	34.4	19	34.7
275	4	44.8	3	42.7
300	8	39.5	27	41.3
325	—	—	2	46.5
350	3	49.0	13	37.8
375	—	—	1	33.0
400	12	36.4	17	38.6
425	—	—	2	25.5
450	—	—	5	39.8
475	—	—	—	—
500	5	41.0	7	33.3
525	—	—	—	—
550	—	—	3	40.0
575	—	—	—	—
600	1	26.0	5	40.4
625	—	—	—	—
650	1	50.0	1	36.0
675	—	—	—	—
700	—	—	1	42.0
725	—	—	—	—
750	—	—	—	—
775	—	—	—	—
800	—	—	2	39.5

[a] Only those slaves manumitted for prices that are a multiple of 25 pesos are included in this table. This accounts for 89 of the total of 121 males manumitted, and 189 of the 246 females manumitted.

numbering over two thousand, with an average age of eight years. In the second place, 55 percent of the slave women were field laborers, as were 70 percent of the men. Curiously, the average age of both groups was twenty-nine years. This fact deserves clarification. To compare this average age with that of other occupations, one might think that among its ranks was a fairly large group of African slaves whose average age was considerably higher than that of the Creoles. On the other hand, the domestic slaves were younger than the laborers, which gives rise to the speculation that these servants could well have been Creole. Of all male slaves, only 5 percent were

Table 7.20   Slave Population According to Average Age, Sex, and Occupation, 1872

Occupation	Male Slaves		Female Slaves	
	Number	Average Age	Number	Average Age
Without occupation	1,085	8.1	1,076	8.6
Undetermined	6	—	—	—
Farmhand	4,425	29.3	3,397	29.0
Sugar worker	7	34.4	—	—
Cart driver	7	26.8	—	—
Distiller	2	50.0	—	—
Machinist	2	35.0	—	—
Overseer	5	45.4	—	—
Cooper	41	39.1	2	31.0
Herdsman	7	30.4	1	69.0
Workshop	1	19.0	—	—
Tanner	2	38.0	—	—
Domestic	335	21.3	923	25.1
Cook	59	30.6	480	35.3
Washer	2	33.5	222	33.0
Coachman	3	60.0	—	—
Servant	29	20.0	48	21.6
Groom	1	51.0	—	—
Housekeeper	—	—	2	36.0
Industrial	2	33.0	—	—
Mason	40	33.2	—	—
Carpenter	27	37.2	—	—
Shoemaker	19	29.0	—	—
Goldsmith	1	14.0	—	—
Tailor	5	25.4	23	23.6
Baker	67	34.1	7	44.3
Apprentice	14	14.5	2	10.5
Seller	1	43.0	2	46.5
Potter	7	29.9	—	—
Journeyman	32	29.6	3	40.7
Tobacconist	14	36.7	—	—
Coffeemaker	1	29.0	—	—
Fisherman	1	43.0	—	—
Beltmaker	6	26.5	2	37.5
Blacksmith	6	35.2	—	—
Painter	1	29.0	—	—
Not classified	7	20.0	31	20.0
Total	6,270	25.4	6,221	25.4

domestics, whereas 15 percent of the females were domestics. In the occupations that can be classified as specialized or related to some type of skill, slave participation was minimal; where this participation existed, it was generally associated with slaves of relatively advanced age. This table confirms one of the most important propositions made in the first part of this discussion: the vast majority of slaves was tightly linked to primary agricultural processes, like cutting, lifting, and transporting cane, and not with those related to the technology of production based on the use of steam.

THE TRANSITION TO FREE LABOR

What do these pieces of evidence indicate with regard to the transition from slave labor to free labor? A question of major importance at some point must be carefully analyzed; this refers to the position assumed by the large landowning class that owned great concentrations of slaves before the Moret Law of 1870, the Abolition Law of 1873, and the *Régimen de Contratación* of 1873 to 1874. Moreover, it is important to understand the interweaving of their links with post-1868 liberalizing policies and their interests as a slaveowning class. It is also essential to be clear about the national origins of that class and their possible direct socioeconomic and cultural dependencies abroad, with Spain in particular, as well as their relations with the large mercantile class of the colony. From these questions others follow, concerning, for example, their relations with English, French, and North American technological and financial centers. Finally, answers to these questions would allow us to establish correlations between the large Creole class of hacienda owners and the development of the national social classes. We may ask, however, why it is necessary to establish all of these relations before providing an approximate explanation of the phenomena under examination.

Because the 1872 census registered the names of the large slaveowners, it raised some important issues. Among these is the relationship that was clearly established by the author between the slaveowning *hacendados* belonging to the Conservative Party and their connections to the commercial interests and anti-abolitionism promulgated by the conservatives. There is no doubt that this was the case in Manatí. Among the important findings was that the great slaveowning *hacendado* class of Manatí belonged to the Conservative Party. They were proslavery, controlled the greater part of commerce, and occupied the most important public and judicial positions in the municipality. Significantly, many of their members were Spanish Catalans. If it were possible to confirm this hypothesis at the level of the colony, the abolition and the transition from one form of labor to another would have important political, as well as socioeconomic and cultural, implications.

In leaving these issues aside, and in light of the foregoing discussion, slavery in Puerto Rico could have been economically profitable at the time of its abolition—but only if by this we understand that it performed an agricultural function that was very important, within specified limits. As demonstrated, the great slaveowning class of Manatí did its utmost to avoid freeing its slaves. Moreover, it undertook legal and illegal measures to prevent the dissolution of the owner-slave ties during the period of the *Contratación* and the period immediately after, when the slaves were presumably free. These measures required the personal intervention of the colonial governor.

The question may seem academic, but why did the owners not wish to free their slaves? Why did they attempt to tie the freedman to the lands where for years before they had been slaves? Was it economically and socially possible for the slaveowners to allow the slaves to leave their haciendas and radically alter the control and disposition of a labor force that had allowed them to be what they were, without threatening the essence of their class position?

Finally, the transition from slave labor to free labor in the nineteenth-century colonial world of Puerto Rico must be analyzed from a broader perspective than a limited demographic, economic, social, or political framework. This paper restricts itself to pointing out some of the social realities and component elements of slavery that, intertwined with data of a different nature, must be examined in order to achieve a better understanding of the liberal abolitionist movement.

NOTES

This essay is based upon collective research undertaken by Raquel Brailowsky, Evelyn Foundos, Juan González, Eric Hellerman, Eliseo Meléndez, Javier Meléndez, Jaime XX, and Héctor Sánchez, graduate students of the City University of New York at Stony Brook, 1975–76; and Lucila Acevedo, Marlene Anastasia, John Belardo, José Colón, Carmen López, Aida Pacheco, Miguel Rivera, Noemí Rodríguez, Miguel Román, Servando Sánchez, Carlos Smith, Ramón Soto, Rubén Soto, and Myrna Troche, undergraduate students of the City University of New York at Brooklyn, 1978–79, under the direction of Benjamín Nistal-Moret. For many different reasons the author wishes to express his gratitude to Joel Rosenthal, Nathan Schmukler, Herbert S. Klein, Manuel Moreno Fraginals, Carmen I. Raffucci, George Reid Andrews, and Frank Moya Pons.

This chapter has been condensed severely from the version presented at the conference. The original paper had more information and analysis of Puerto Rican slavery. For further details see the author's doctoral dissertation, *El Pueblo de Nuestra Señora de la Candelaria of del Apóstol, San Matías de Manatí, 1800-1850: Its Ruling Classes and the Institution of Black Slavery* (State University of New York at Stony Brook, 1977). The translation was done by Elizabeth Hansen and edited by Tom W. Bartelt.

8. Technical Innovations and Social Change in the Sugar Industry of Puerto Rico, 1870–1880

Andrés A. Ramos Mattei

During the last third of the nineteenth century, the Puerto Rican sugar industry underwent one of its most critical stages and greatest changes since its growth in 1815. Many internal and external factors directly and fundamentally affected the way in which sugar was produced, and the specific problems that emerged required new solutions.

The hacienda was the unit of production that had fueled the growth of sugar in the island since the beginning of the nineteenth century. By 1870 there were 550 sugar-producing units spread around the island's coastline. That year they produced almost 100,000 tons of muscovado sugar for export. That was the highest production figure, unequaled during the rest of the century.[1]

The haciendas were the basis of a socioeconomic system of production predicated on the capitalist mode of production for the international market. The units were privately owned and had enough land for the cultivation of cane and a factory or mill, in which the cane was processed. The haciendas produced a crude or unrefined sugar, which they exported abroad. This sugar was the basis for the refining industries that had long been established in the industrial countries. In the Puerto Rican case, most of the muscovado, or unrefined sugar, was purchased by North American refineries.

The ties to the market created by the production of sugar on haciendas was one of the most important factors in the growth of the sugar industry. Sugar was subject to the whims of supply and demand, with oscillations in price, competition from other areas, tariff policies in the purchasing countries, etc. These circumstances were beyond the control of the sugar producers in Puerto Rico. The prices of different grades of sugar, for example, were fixed in the principal buying centers abroad, particularly New York and London. Some countries' tariff policies caused major difficulties on the island. Also Puerto Rico was still a Spanish colony. Spain was the metropolis that was to negotiate any tariff benefits from the sugar-buying countries. To the despair of the *hacendados* in Puerto Rico, Spain procrastinated during the last third of the nineteenth century and did not formulate a firm and clear policy in response to the protectionist measures in the North American market. The Spanish metropolis kept the Puerto Rican *hacendados* on tenterhooks for almost twenty years regarding whether Spain would accept crude Puerto Rican sugar, free of duties, in the Iberian market or whether it would reach a commercial accord with the United States.

The hacienda was also a complex social organization whose ramifications went beyond the geographic limits of the unit of production. It sustained the position of the most important social sector in Puerto Rican society during the nineteenth century: the *hacendados*. Not all of them, however, were simply direct producers; some were also merchants. Merchants controlled local credit and in the absence of a banking system acted as financial agents until the end of the century. They bought the sugar harvest at the beginning of each harvest in exchange for advances in cash and supplies. Many haciendas fell into their hands when their original owners could not pay their debts promptly.

Until about 1870, the hacienda's labor force was composed of slaves and free workers. All slaves were legally free in March 1873. They were, however, legally obliged to work under contract for three additional years. The free workers were compelled to work by the notorious Law of the *Libreta*, which had been decreed in 1849. This law declared that all those with no means of subsistence, even if they owned land, had to work as day laborers. To demonstrate their compliance, individuals had to carry a booklet issued by the municipal authorities, in which their names and the names of the landowner for whom they worked were noted. In addition, the regularity of work was noted in the booklet. Thus, until about 1870, relations between workers and landowners were based on legal coercion of a clearly precapitalist sort. In other words, they were not based on labor's ability to sell its labor power for a wage. To the contrary, laborers were forced to work on the haciendas against their will by measures sanctioned by law.

THE COLLAPSE OF THE HACIENDA SYSTEM

In about 1870, unequivocal signs presaging fundamental changes in the production of sugar began to appear. These fissures could at first remain unnoticed but, seen together and in historical perspective, led to the eventual collapse of the whole hacienda system.

The data for this decade leave no doubt whatsoever as to the crisis experienced by the sugar industry. In 1870 the haciendas produced 95,824 tons of muscovado sugar for export. By 1880 exports had decreased to 50,282 tons.[2] In 1870 there were about 550 haciendas in operation, but ten years later there were only 325. The disappearance of haciendas was even more dramatic in some sugar provinces of great importance, such as Guayama. There, where there had been 44 haciendas in 1870, by the end of the decade barely a third were still standing.[3]

How can we explain the structural collapse of the hacienda system in such a short period? First, we must consider changes on the international market. This is where some of the major factors that contributed to the destruction of the traditional modus operandi of the Puerto Rican sugar industry are to be found. They turned the hacienda system into a useless vehicle that could no longer sustain growth in sugar production on the island. For many years, European countries had been developing domestic sugar industries using beet root as their raw material. By the 1870s countries like France, Austria, and Germany were about to become self-sufficient. At the same time England opened her gates for the free entry of foreign sugar. This was a stimulus to Europe's beet sugar industry. France, Austria, and Germany took advantage of this change to export crude beet sugar to England. The Puerto Rican sugar industry—and that of the whole Caribbean—was affected by the entry of beet sugar in very large quantities into the English market. Although, as noted, the United States was the island's principal buyer, England was the next largest buyer. By the end of the nineteenth century England's free trade policy had completely eliminated Puerto Rican sugar.

The increased output of beet sugar had led to a precipitous decline in cane sugar prices. The *hacendados* on the island insisted that it cost them 2 or 3 cents to produce a pound of sugar. Until 1870, the prices of sugar for export fluctuated between 4 and 5 cents, depending on its quality. By the mid-1870s, prices were around 3.4 to 3.8 cents a pound. Ten years later, the situation was devastating; by then the prices had fallen to between 2.1 and 2.3 cents a pound.[4]

Beet sugar represented a major threat to cane sugar not only because of the falling prices but also because of its improved quality. The relatively low saccharine content of beets forced European producers to look for technical innovations to increase their yields. This was achieved by building completely mechanized factories, which not only increased production but produced a crude sugar of excellent quality for refining.

The production of high-quality sugar in Europe was the death knell for the complex of sugar-producing haciendas in Puerto Rico and the rest of the Caribbean. To begin with, most of the haciendas had mills in which the technical improvements of the time were notably absent. To grind the cane, they used mills powered by animals. Very few used water or wind as a motive force. These mills could extract up to 40 percent of the juice from the cane. The *guarapo*, or cane juice, was evaporated and concentrated in open pans over fires, in the (misnamed) Jamaican trains. The separation of sugar crystals from the syrup was done in the same containers in which the product was sent to market. With this basic scheme of production, the haciendas achieved an average yield of 6 percent, whereas the saccharine content of cane could be 18 percent.

The sugar *hacendados* were not completely ignorant of the technical improvements available on the market. By 1870, 20 percent of the units had replaced animal traction in the mills with steam engines, and they had acquired the more modern milling equipment produced in Europe and in the United States. Vacuum evaporators and centrifuges produced by De-rosne and Cail in Paris, had been introduced as early as 1840. These improvements had not spread throughout the island because there had been no pressing need to improve production techniques. Some haciendas at that time could produce harvests of 500 tons with an animal-powered mill. Since most could not reach this figure, it is logical to suppose that they did not require this machinery. When they did increase their output, as demonstrated in *municipios* such as Ponce, Guayama, and Fajardo, the owners could either acquire another unit or buy a steam-operated mill. These adaptations could be undertaken as long as the market didn't demand a better quality product for refining. But beet sugar replaced muscovado in the market for unrefined sugar because of its superior quality, and muscovado completely disappeared by the beginning of the twentieth century.

The situation provoked by the high quality of beet sugar posed a dilemma for the haciendas. To continue producing muscovado sugar meant turning their backs on the future, retreating, and giving free rein to beet sugar. On the other hand, complete mechanization would be the death of the hacienda system because it would radically alter the way of producing sugar on the island. This crisis, brought about by the changes in the market, made it essential to confront the need to reorganize the labor system on the haciendas; the units had used a mixed labor force composed of free laborers and slaves.

Slavery had its heyday in the early period of growth of the sugar industry, until about 1840. Various factors had made the growth of sugar production depend on increases in the number of slaves. The slave trade, however, was legally forbidden since 1820, and this made a massive infusion of slaves difficult. Although a resort to imports of contract labor under conditions of veiled slavery with Chinese or Indian coolies was considered, as in Cuba, Peru, and the British Antilles, the final solution was to establish a regime of forced labor sanctioned by law, popularly known as *la libreta*.

Needless to say, this did not mean that the haciendas abandoned the use of slave labor. To the contrary, the most important units in some municipalities counted on a significant number of slaves until 1870. By buying slaves on the local market and by depending on their natural increase, some proprietors managed to obtain many slaves. Moreover, the use of rented slaves may have been more widespread than supposed. In any event, isolated examples of this practice have been found in various places on the island like Ponce and Vega Baja.

The *hacendados* valued the slaves because slaves provided regular work on the productive units. Free laborers worked irregularly; it was normal that they would not work the whole week. Owners were constantly complaining about the free laborer's "lack of application." At most they worked three days a week, almost never on Mondays, and they quit work in the afternoon for any reason. Moreover, free laborers refused to enter the factories and work when sugar was being produced at night, since they considered the mills a true hell of heat and deafening noise.

The free laborers had the luxury of practically dictating the terms under which they would work, because, as the owners recognized, once they had earned enough to cover their basic needs, they would not return to work. The free laborers had no need to support themselves exclusively on wages from regular work. They could, for example, meet part of their needs from subsistence agriculture and by raising domestic animals near the small buildings that they occupied or owned at the edges of the cane fields. It is no coincidence that as cane spread in the coastal areas, displacing small and medium owners, small properties increased in the mountainous regions of these municipalities. Until the twentieth century the mountains were an impenetrable barrier to cane. They made it difficult for the *Libreta* regime to use wages to tie the free laborer to the haciendas in any regular or systematic manner.

During the last third of the nineteenth century, the signs of crisis in the sugar hacienda system increased. The few newspapers published in the country were filled with a debate, which extended through the end of the century, on whether to build centrales. In 1870 a proposal to establish five centrales around the island was published by a certain M. Esmein. He argued that *hacendados* could not continue to grow cane and make sugar at the same time. The margin between costs and revenues was constantly shrinking. Therefore, it would be better to establish a different division of labor, separating the agricultural phase of production from the industrial phase. That is, the *hacendados* should concentrate on growing cane and close their mills. Sugar would be made in completely mechanized factories that because of their large capacities, would absorb all the cane planted by the landowners of a given region.

This was the beginning of the new system of production, still known as the central system. It was an infallible sign of the immanent disappearance of a decrepit and obsolete system that had been holding back the growth of the industry. The *hacendados* found themselves increasingly pushed against the wall. They would no longer be the most important sector of Puerto Rican society. Their incomes would rapidly evaporate, undermining the base of their social importance. Nonetheless, their prestige was not to disappear overnight. For many years it would be one of the few things left to allow them to look back and delight in their exotic names, in their no longer smoking smokestacks, and in a life style that their ancestors probably never enjoyed.

We should not be surprised that the labor system was also in crisis at this time. Slavery was strongly attacked by the Puerto Rican representatives to the *Junta de Información* in 1866. In 1870 the partial abolition of slavery was declared in Puerto Rico. Freedom was declared for all the newly born and all of those over sixty years of age on or after September 1868. Three years later—on March 22, 1873—slavery was completely abolished.

It is curious that the abolition of the *Libreta* system, which occurred shortly after slavery was outlawed, has received so little attention. This took place in June 1873. The timing does not seem to be a coincidence. Efforts to increase production and improve the product required a concomitant increase in the labor force. It was therefore necessary to end the constraints that bound geographically immobilized workers. First, slavery clearly had to be eliminated; then the legal obligations to work for a whole year for a single owner had to be eliminated. The landowners knew full well that they needed a large number of workers only during the harvest. This lasted at most for some five months a year. Theoretically, a market of free laborers was preferable to laborers who could be used only for a short time but for whom the landowners were responsible for the entire year.

THE RESPONSE OF THE *HACENDADOS*

It should not be thought that the *hacendados* crossed their arms and calmly waited for bankruptcy and ruin. The crisis affecting the sugar industry generated a feverish activity to avoid its worst effects. Beginning in 1870, one can clearly perceive a dynamic of change, but it exhausted itself by the end of the decade. It was characterized by an effort to find alternatives to the total mechanization that could destroy the traditional way of producing muscovado sugar under the hacienda system.

The *hacendados* displayed an excessive confidence in the success of partial mechanization of their units. One of the most important objectives was the acquisition of modern mills powered by steam engines. Orders for these machines abound by the hundreds in the books of European and American manufacturers. Almost 300 steam-powered mills were installed during the 1870s. This means that almost all of the units in operation in 1880—325— had semimechanized mills.

There is no doubt that steam engines offered several advantages. Steam allowed the oxen that had powered the old mills to work in the fields. It economized on the labor necessary for this phase of the operation. By attaching a cane conveyor to the mill, not only was the task of introducing cane to the grinder simplified, but the number of accidents suffered by the workers was reduced. But the fundamental advantage of steam-powered mills lay in their ability to extract up to 70 percent of the cane juice and to crush more cane in less time. Moreover, steam-powered mills did not necessitate alterations in the rest of the equipment in the factories. The other phases of sugar production could continue using traditional methods and instruments.

The increase in cane juice, however, led to a need to install additional equipment, similar to that already present. There is abundant evidence— although it is difficult to quantify adequately at this time—that haciendas added more Jamaican trains. In this way they tried to solve the problem posed by the increase in cane juice obtained from steam-powered mills. Some haciendas resorted to other partial technical solutions. They ordered machines called *monte ius*, which preheated the cane juice before it was transferred to the Jamaican trains. The *monte ius* used the steam generated by the boilers to activate the mills.[5] There were also haciendas that acquired sets of open containers called *clarifiers*. This was for use in the first stage of cane juice evaporation. The juice was decanted with lime. This separated the impurities from the cane juice, which would later be evaporated until it became molasses in the Jamaican train.

Various documents suggest that there was an intent to replace the Jamaican train with an innovation known as the *Wetzel evaporator*, or simply *evaporator*, as it was called in Puerto Rico. This was rectangular and made of iron. A series of copper tubes fitted in circles constantly revolved over the box, reaching the bottom, where the *guarapo* was poured. A boiler-generated steam circulated through the tubes, both stirring and heating the juice. We know of at least one hacienda, Mercedita in Ponce, which complemented the Wetzel evaporator with another machine, known as a *steam boiler*. Its very name indicates that its function lay in concentrating the molasses to the point of crystallization. These steam boilers were rectangular and mounted on a wagon that moved on rails. There were copper tubes inside, through which steam circulated. They thus heated the cane juice poured over them. Underneath was a sluice to empty the syrup and the sugar crystals. The mobility of these boiling pans made it easy to transport the cooked molasses to where it was purged, or where the sugar crystals were separated from the syrup. In 1876, two centrifuges imported from Scotland were introduced at this hacienda. These machines mechanized the purge. They were cylindrical with a metal mesh basket with innumerable and small perforations. When spun at high velocity, the syrup was expelled, and the sugar crystals remained inside.

With these and other innovations, many haciendas were able to increase production. But it is significant that those haciendas that made only partial technical improvements in their mills continued to produce muscovado sugar. They could not change the quality of their final product, although they did increase production. A small group of *hacendados*, mostly on the east coast and in Vieques, installed a machine known as the *Fryer concentrator* in their factories. This machine hardened the syrup and sugar crystals that came out of the Jamaican trains and shaped them into blocks for greater ease in transportation and loading. But like the other machines mentioned, it did not improve the quality of the product one whit.[6]

Some owners did not even have the chance to introduce partial technical improvements in their units. These had reached, or were about to reach, their maximum limits of growth by 1870. They could not justify the acquisition of machinery to increase their production. Increasing the amount of sugar produced meant, among other things, acquiring enough land available for planting cane. An examination of the haciendas in Guayama or Fajardo, for example, shows that the units that had most, if not all, of their land planted in cane disappeared during the 1870s.[7]

It has also been argued that in many cases the main reason for the failure lay in the lack of adequate amounts of capital. The monetary system of the time was a disaster. In the absence of enough Spanish currency, the use of foreign currency was permitted. Taxes on land and taxes on the products of the land and commerce in minerals had to be paid. The colonial administration also required taxes on imports and exports to be paid in currency. Since there were no banks on the island, the merchants acted as the sources of finance for the sugar *hacendados*. They advanced money or provided credit for daily operations, to purchase machinery or to make improvements, and even to pay municipal taxes. In return, they received the harvests as repayments.

The availability of capital from the merchants had its limits. They, too, had limited reserves. It is possible to see how limited the economy was by an examination of the wage records of the landowners. Needless to say, the slaves were not paid in cash. But there was no more than a nominal contractual wage relation with the free laborers. They received their subsistence and primary needs in exchange for their labor. The nature of the sugar business ensured that all but the craftiest of workers would be indebted. Since sugar was a seasonal industry, it required large numbers of workers only during the harvests from January to May. For the rest of the months, many had no work. They resorted to the sugar owner for advances of food, clothes, shoes, etc., with the promise to pay with their labor once the new cycle of sugar production began. With the increase of production, because of technical improvements, the debility of the monetary economy became obvious.

Parallel with the growth of output on the haciendas, a further need to increase the supply of cane developed. The *hacendados* tried to resolve this need by buying cane from third parties. This presaged the process of differentiation in the composition of the propertied class connected to sugar, which culminated with the development of the central system: the *colonato* and sharecropping. But even at this level, difficulties were occasioned by the lack of liquid capital. Money had to be advanced for the plowing, planting, and harvesting of cane. This meant additional expenses in transportation, i.e., ox-carts to bring the cane to the mills. In some haciendas a system of portable railroads was introduced to solve the problem. The need for liquid capital led to the intensification of another latent aspect of the Puerto Rican sugar industry: direct control of production by foreigners.

All these problems could not be separated from the difficult situation posed by the reduction of demand in the traditional markets with the fall in prices and the appearance on the market of a higher quality product. Whatever the particular ways in which specific owners were ruined, in the final analysis their ruin was in response to the growing crisis on the international market.[8]

As mentioned, people thought of the central as the basis of a new division of labor. It was expected that the planters would stop producing sugar and would send their cane to be ground in a mechanized factory, which would centralize the production of sugar for a given region. All of the plans in circulation during the 1870s, and later, assumed that the planters themselves would be the owners of the sugar-producing establishments.[9]

When the new system was established, however, it did not take place in the way that these cooperative plans had anticipated. From 1873 on, mechanized units were established on the basis of individual initiatives. The neighboring haciendas came under the influence of these enterprises, which came to control them directly or indirectly. The destruction of the *hacendados* was much more painful in some regions because it took place against their wills. With the new productive scheme, they had to submit to being relegated to dependent and secondary roles relative to the owners of the emerging centrales.[10]

SLAVES AND FREE LABORERS

We have seen how the efforts to mechanize sugar production in Puerto Rico during the 1870s took place at various levels, ranging from combining a steam-powered mill with traditional equipment to establishing a new system of centrales with completely mechanized factories. The crisis of low prices and the demand for better-quality sugar unleashed this innovative fever, which in most cases was no more than a failed attempt to preserve the traditional hacienda system.

Fundamental changes within the class of sugar proprietors took place as a result of this process. Small and medium-sized producers disappeared. Many of those who survived as *hacendados* until 1880 carried heavy debts, which in time would force them to go under. Others, however, were able to continue within the sugar economy by converting their haciendas into suppliers of cane, either for the centrales that were being built or for other haciendas that survived. Still others joined the *hacendado* class by establishing haciendas in the belief that circumstances favored them at the time. Others made sharecropping contracts or began to plant and send cane to the haciendas or centrales nearest their small properties.

As these changes took place within the landed class, similar changes were taking place within the laboring class in the sugar economy. There were fundamental changes in the composition of, and extent of differentiation within, the labor force. The development of a market for free laborers to meet the needs of the sugar factories was one of the dearest ambitions of the sugar owners, but also one of their gravest problems.

The 1870s began with clear portents of the eventual disappearance of slavery in Puerto Rico. In mid-1870, the metropolis approved the Moret Law. This freed all the slaves born after September 1868 and all those who had reached sixty years of age or more at that date. The Moret Law was made public on the island some months later. In the interim the authorities tried to convince the owners to grant their slaves freedom spontaneously. Some agreed, but the government received much opposition to this suggestion. The sugar planters were especially concerned that the authorities would declare a complete abolition without indemnification by using the Moret Law as a precedent to free all the slaves. As we have seen, at about this time the planters began to order machinery. Although they did not have much liquid capital, they were counting on using the expected indemnification for their slaves to pay for at least part of the cost of the machinery.

The government was forced to promulgate the Moret Law in Puerto Rico, not only because of the owners' refusal to free their slaves on their own volition but also because of fear of rebellions in the slave quarters, in reaction to various rumors on the extent of the Moret Law. The slaves themselves began to spread the news that they had been freed but that the decree of abolition was not being published in Puerto Rico.[11] The mayor of Ponce informed the governor, for example, that on September 29, 1870, he had to go to the hacienda Amelia in the municipality of Juana Díaz, where her 165 slaves refused to work. One of them, José, claimed that they were already free and that the truth was being deliberately withheld from them. He had convinced the others not to work on the hacienda until their freedom was recognized. The mayor decreed that José was to receive five whiplashes and to apologize to his owners in front of all the slaves for the disturbance he had caused. Later he explained to the slaves that only the elderly and the children were to be freed, and that by their owners' volition.[12]

Slavery was abolished on March 22, 1873. The Moret Law was responsible for the freedom of some 10,000 slaves. The abolition ended the servitude of

31,000 other slaves on the island.[13] The abolition law decreed a maximum indemnification of 7 million pesos and the compulsory labor of the *libertos*, or freed slaves, for three more years with their owners.

At the time that the slave regime was dissolving, there is strong evidence that contract laborers were being brought from the neighboring British islands. Large numbers of such immigrants had been working on the small island of Vieques, a few miles off the east coast of Puerto Rico, since at least the previous decade.[14] It is impossible to quantify the size of this immigration. It was connected to the sugar industry in municipalities like Ponce, Humacao, Loiza, and Carolina. The workers came under an annual contract; they had to live on the hacienda estate; and they received a daily wage that varied according to their age and sex. Most were concentrated in single haciendas, rather than spread among the haciendas within a given region. Their owners came to consider these workers so important that they sent agents to the neighboring islands to contract for them. They redoubled their efforts to attract them to Puerto Rico until 1873, when the final abolition of slavery was declared. The British consul in San Juan commented, for example, on how a certain John Archibald had contracted with some 100 workers in Antigua to work on the haciendas in Loiza.[15]

British West Indian contract laborers were important assets on the haciendas where they worked. Some of the establishment in Vieques, like Playa Grande or Campo Asilo, came to operate almost exclusively with British West Indian contract laborers. They, like the slaves until 1873 and later like the freedmen, were another group who provided regularity in working on the various tasks on the haciendas. Since they came with the idea of returning to their countries of origin, they arrived on the island with the intention of saving the maximum and spending as little as possible. They lived on the haciendas and were available to the owners at all times.

The owners, however, began to have serious difficulties with their contract laborers. Since the contracts were written in Spanish, they tried to take advantage of the fact that their workers did not understand the language. Some demanded that they work in the factories at night. Others tried to force them to work on Sunday. The contracts stipulated that they would have to be paid extra for additional work in either case. The owners, of course, claimed that their demands were included as part of their work. In some cases the owners probably got away with this. Many of them had the public authorities at their beck and call.

There is no reason to conclude that a large number of contract laborers came to the island. Efforts to bring them in increased after 1873. The transition from slave to free labor required the establishment of regularity and discipline in the labor force on the haciendas. But the British West Indian contract laborer proved difficult for some owners to control. In early 1874, 150 immigrant contract laborers on the hacienda Playa Grande challenged the authority of the police. The guards reacted by killing a person from Nevis, wounding 2 companions from Nevis and St. Kitts and arresting 37 others.[16] A little later the 164 workers from Campo Asilo set fire to the cane fields of the hacienda and, entrenched in their houses, prevented the authorities from putting out the fire with a hail of sticks and stones.[17] These incidents provoked intervention and pressure on the part of British representatives that British nationals should receive better treatment on the island. The colonial authority received the consul's efforts with displeasure and even considered them an unwarranted interference in domestic colonial affairs and a veiled affront to Spanish authority on the island.[18]

In any event, immigration slowly declined after 1878. This coincided with the crisis then generalized throughout the island's sugar industry. As many haciendas disappeared, the demand for workers decreased and contributed to the loss of interest in attracting contract laborers from abroad.

The crisis had, in fact, led to an oversupply of labor on the domestic labor market. Those who could no longer find work on the estates that had failed had to look for work on those still operating. The number of Puerto Rican laborers immigrating abroad in the early 1880s is an index of the changes. Most went to the Dominican Republic, where a sugar industry based on centrales was developing in the area of San Pedro de Macorís, under the auspices of foreign owners.[19] Others went to work in the Cuban sugar industry, and some went to Panama and the United States.[20]

Theoretically, the forced labor of the freedmen had assured the landowners a contingent of regular and disciplined workers on the haciendas for at least three years. The abolition decree had left it to the local authorities to draft a regulation to implement the contracting of the *libertos*, or freedmen. The regulation was approved by the overseas minister in Madrid on March 26, 1873, and published in Puerto Rico a month later.[21] The regulation on freedmen directed, among other things, that they were to contract with their old owners, or with any one else; that they could not demand higher wages than those prevailing; and that when employers supplied food or clothing, these would be deducted from their wages. The authorities would keep a register of freedmen, and they were responsible for approving the contracts to guarantee their legality.[22]

Toward the end of 1873 the government published a statistical summary of the results of the *contratación*, or the compulsory labor of the freed slaves (table 8.1). According to this, some 21,594 freedmen were working under contract. The balance of the 31,000 ex-slaves were classified as over sixty or younger than twelve years of age. Nonetheless, the government admitted that it did not know the whereabouts of some 818 freedmen who had not contracted themselves.

Innumerable contemporary observers assure us that the transition from slavery to freedom took place in an orderly manner, with no disturbances or interruptions of work on the haciendas, and with the support of most of the landowners except for a small group addicted to the Spanish cause. None-

Table 8.1   Work Patterns of Contracted Freedmen, 1873

Work Patterns	Sex	Rural	Urban
Remaining with Previous Owners			
	Males	5,720	535
	Females	3,364	2,051
	Total	9,084	2,586
Working for others			
	Males	4,105	1,104
	Females	2,081	2,624
	Total	6,286	3,638

Source: *La Gaceta de Puerto Rico,* December 6, 1873.

theless, *hacendados* did experience serious difficulties immediately after abolition. Many freedmen in Guayama, for example, abandoned their jobs when they learned of the decree of abolition. They refused to return to the haciendas unless the owners paid them an agreed daily wage in cash. The planters appealed to the government to force the freedmen to return to work. The governor did not support them. To the contrary, he sent a telegram to the justice of the peace in Guayama, asserting that the freedmen had the right to negotiate any contract as long as it was recorded in the register of contractual regulations.[23] Under these circumstances, the planters in Guayama had to acceed to the demands of the freedmen. Since they were in midharvest, they could not afford the luxury of interrupting sugar production too long.[24]

There is no doubt that the transition to free labor affected many owners in Guayama adversely. The bitterest complaints on the effects of the loss of slaves comes from the owners in this municipality. Eduardo Lind, who owned one of the most important haciendas of the region, attributed his poor economic situation directly to abolition.[25] Simon Moret, another landowner of French origins, wrote in his personal diary that "the year of 1873 was deadly for me because of the bad dealings with Mr. McCormick (another landowner), the emancipation of the blacks, and an especially dreadful drought . . ."[26]

In general, the planters vehemently denounced the difficulties they experienced, because abolition was declared in the middle of the sugar harvest. This placed the freedmen in very favorable positions to negotiate contracts. An eloquent index of this situation is to be found in the diversity of contracts with freedmen in various sugar producing areas.[27]

Shortly after the general contracting of freedmen, the country's newspapers began to write about the sugarowner's dissatisfaction with the situation. Some alleged that in order not to interrupt the harvest, they had to pay wages that were too high; that in two or three days the freedmen earned enough for their subsistence; and that as a result they refused to work the rest of the week. The *Boletín Mercantil* denounced the contract mechanism because the contracts did not tie the workers to a single owner for three years. This newspaper argued that competition for work meant that the freedmen were constantly changing employers when they were offered better working conditions or higher wages.[28]

Beginning with the cane harvest of 1874, it was obvious to the landowners that the contracting of freedmen under the current regulations did not provide them with the regular and disciplined labor required by the sugar factories. The lack of ready cash to pay the freedmen was another obstacle in stabilizing the relations between workers and owners and trying to secure a regular work force for the haciendas. In March 1874 a newspaper from Guayama wrote that many units had been forcibly abandoned by their owners. The lack of ready cash was such that not even the merchants themselves could meet the demand.[29] The same was said in Ponce, where the British vice-consul bemoaned the ruin of plantation owners because of their lack of cash with which to pay their workers.[30]

The situation was precarious for the *hacendados*. Most of them had introduced technical improvements. Although those did not affect the quality of the sugar, they did require a greater supply of cane to justify the investments made in them. It was difficult to increase productivity without a concomitant increase in the labor force, and impossible if one could not get regular workers, week after week, especially during the harvests. The absence of ready cash restrained the structural transformation of the industry, because the machinery had to be paid for and because there was a clear need to develop a cash wage system in order to stabilize the demand for workers.

At this point, the *hacendados* were pleased with the arrival of a new colonial governor as a result of political changes in the Spanish metropolis. In April 1874 a decree ordering a recontracting of freedmen was published. The new contracts were to be for the rest of the period of compulsory work, that is to say, until April 1876. The contracts could not be broken without the employer's consent. It obliged the freedmen to live on the estates on which the worked, and they could not move without the owner's consent. The law also specified that in the event food and clothing were provided, they would be deducted from the freedmen's wages.[31] The new contracts made a group of workers available to the *hacendados*, which partially resolved—in the short run, at least—the need to expand the productive units. The owners took every advantage of the new ruling, as the 1874 contracts in Carolina demonstrate. There 303 contracts were registered. The freedmen had to work from sunup to sundown; that is, from six in the morning to six in the evening, Monday through Saturday. They received an average daily wage of 62.5 cents for males and 50 cents for women. They did not receive food, clothing, or medicine.[32]

It was important to tie the freedmen to the haciendas, in part because they were almost indispensable to the tasks of producing sugar. Under slavery they had made up the major share of workers in the haciendas' factories. The free laborers had refused to work there because of the intense heat and noise generated by the machines. After abolition the newly freed slaves were a group of incalculable value for the haciendas. They were knowledgeable and experienced in clearing impurities from the *guarapo* as it was heated, in decanting it from pan to pan during the evaporation process, etc. There are even isolated instances of freedmen entrusted with the operation of the steam engines that powered the mills.[33] These peculiar circumstances gave rise to a singular situation. One sector of the freedmen were placed in a superior position in the labor hierarchy in the sugar factories. As the British consul wrote in 1874: "The 'liberto' is appreciated not only on account of his superior ability for the work, but also because he is available at all times. . . . In fact, in the process of sugar making, the more skilled 'liberto' is generally employed within the boiling house while the free laborer does the rougher task of cutting and carrying the cane."[34]

This and the presence of *libertos* with artisan skills, like carpentry, rope-making, and toolmaking, led to a redistribution of tasks in which conventional racial criteria had no place. The study of an hacienda in the southern zone of the island confirms this. Its author, Sidney W. Mintz, suggests that there the jobs of making sugar were undertaken by old slaves until the 1880s. In fact, Mintz found that blacks, mulattoes, and whites did not live in segregated housing.[35] The freedmen alone, however, could not resolve the long-term problems of labor in sugar production. In spite of their contributions, there were not enough of them.

Just after emancipation there was the greatest interest in attracting workers contracted abroad to the Puerto Rican sugar industry. The planters wanted them in order to decrease wages by increasing the labor supply, as well as to acquire another nucleus of workers over whom they could exercise direct control.[36] We have already discussed the efforts, which were redoubled after 1873, to bring contracted workers from the British islands in the Caribbean. The *Sociedad de Agricultura* of Ponce had long discussions over the best way to increase the labor force. In mid-1875 a majority decided to petition the government for permission to introduce Chinese coolies to the island.[37] Nevertheless, the authorities ignored the petition, possibly because they were aware of the political and social problems provoked by the imports of coolies to Cuba after 1844.[38]

The interest in legally tying labor to the hacienda also played a role in abolishing the *libreta* system in June of 1873. It was also impossible to attract free day laborers to the haciendas without legal coercion or payment in script and in food and clothing. For this reason, in 1874 the colonial government petitioned for the revival of an earlier, previously annulled ordinance that would permit them to coerce the freedmen to work. The metropolitan authorities refused, pointing to the possible protests that would follow such a drastic measure.[39]

As the expiration date for the freedmen's contracts approached, the need to control labor returned to public discussion. In its editorials the *Boletín Mercantil* was inclined toward the introduction of another law of the *libreta*. The *Sociedad de Agricultura* in Ponce returned to the fray asking for regulation of day laborers beginning in 1876. Even the planters identified with the Liberal party favored new contracts for the freedmen, with legal sanctions in the case of noncompliance. Manuel I. Saldaña, for example, recommended obligatory contracts, but just for the harvest period. Saldaña recognized the need for regular labor during the harvests, when the largest number of workers were required.[40] In response to pressure from the planters the governor requested permission from Madrid to revive the day laborer ordinance. The metropolitan authorities again refused to establish a system of forced labor for the freedmen on the island.[41]

Although sparse, there is evidence that some larger units were successful in attracting and retaining labor. The central San Vicente paid a significant proportion, if not all, of the workers' wages in cash. A Dr. Rafael Romeu has left us a description of a typical harvest day after a visit to the central in 1877. Romeu witnessed the grinding of some 25,000 tons of cane, which produced almost 20 tons of centrifuged sugar and 524 gallons of molasses. Seventy-three day laborers cut all the cane in the field, 69 transported it to the mill, and 136 worked in the sugar-making phase in the factory, totaling 238 workers for that day. But Romeu writes that at particular times San Vicente could have up to 700 workers available during the harvest. The central had built living quarters to lodge the workers who came from distant regions to find employment.[42]

Clearly this entire labor force could not house itself in individual houses near the central, nor could the central employ it during the whole year. Thus it would hardly have made sense to extend the traditional mechanisms like provision of foodstuffs to tie the whole labor force to San Vicente. A clue to the fact that cash wages were the tie between owner and workers is provided by Leonardo Igaravidez. When he complained about the rundown condition of San Vicente, Igaravidez said, among other things, that after his arrest the court-appointed administrator had begun paying the workers in kind with rice and dried cod (and of the worst quality), "thus exploiting their needs and their miseries."[43]

The hacienda Mercedita in Ponce, constantly growing and making technical improvements, resolved its need for labor in a different way. Its account books indicate that housing was built for the unit's labor force on land next to the estate. The labor force was kept on the estate by means of debts with Mercedita's company store for food and other basic necessities. It was, however, a temporary arrangement, because in order to continue growing, Mercedita later had to hire workers just for the harvest, when the highest number of workers was needed.

In general, after 1876 the planters could count on freedmen and some British West Indian contract laborers. Many concessions were granted to the freedmen in order to keep them on the haciendas. The owners provided them with housing and the use of small plots to plant foodstuffs and raise domestic animals. Sidney Mintz found that the residents of hacienda Vieja pastured their cattle on the estate's lands, got bananas from a common plot, and collected wood for cooking from a section of the forest. A cane field, called the cane of the poor, was ground every year at Christmas. The resulting sugar (muscovado), molasses, and rum were shared among the poor of the barrio. At another level, the specific relations of paternalism by way of *compadrazgo* between the owner and his workers was no more than the reflection of the pressing need to motivate the freedmen to remain on the estates.[44]

In 1880 the planters developed at their own initiative a novel monetary system: the coining of chips in various denominations bearing the seal of each establishment. It was an ingenious attempt to regularize relations with the labor force, which the currency-starved economy of the time had rendered impossible. When this practice became general is significant; it coincided with the structural collapse of the hacienda system. The workers of the ruined units were surely looking for work in those in which operations continued. The chips were a new sign of the wish to stabilize the relations between owners and workers by a wage and not by concessions. In this way they hoped to resolve the problem of increasing the labor force during the harvest, while reducing it between harvests without further responsibility on the part of the landowner. In the long run, however, the chips failed to achieve this objective. They were not accepted as legal tender even by other haciendas. They could be redeemed at the company store that had issued them, but only to purchase food and basic necessities. Thus the company store became the main link that chained together planters and workers; concessions of land and subsistence were relegated to a secondary plane.

CONCLUSIONS

By the beginning of the 1880s the effort to transform the sugar industry had exhausted itself. Hundreds of haciendas had disappeared. Of the few centrales that had been built, some were ruined, and others seemed destined to succumb shortly. Almost all of the central workers had been eliminated from the class that included the ruling sector of the industry. Sugar production had collapsed. Thousands and thousands of pesos had been invested in machinery for haciendas that were now moldering.

The initial effort to transform the industry and survive had left profound marks on the society. It had a strong effect on the landowning class and altered its composition. Many were ruined, and others barely survived. Where centrales had been built, or where the haciendas with more advanced technology survived, they displayed a voracious appetite for land. This is where the most intense *colonato* appeared. In the few cases we have been able to study, the *colonato* developed as a side effect of the voluntary division of labor on the part of the sugar entrepreneurs. The bigger units—especially the centrales—exercised domination over the neighboring haciendas. They tended to concentrate land and thus eliminate medium and small owners in various sugar areas of the island.

The structural collapse of the sugar industry destroyed the old landowning sector, many of them the descendants of immigrants to Puerto Rico in the early part of the nineteenth century. In some regions of the island, such as Fajardo, Carolina, and Guayama, the first or second generation of Creoles of foreign descent were replaced by merchants, some of whom were already operating haciendas in the 1870s.

The efforts to transform the industry also had repercussions on the composition of the labor force working in sugar. The technical innovations required an increase in the number of workers during the harvest. The sugar landowners failed to develop a free market for wage workers. The unavoidable need for labor in the centrales and more advanced units, however, led to the development of extralegal mechanisms that made it easier to count on an appropriate labor force during the harvests. Concessions in housing, land, and other privileges reflected the landowners' interest in keeping a nucleus of workers on their estates. Imports of contract labor had the same end. The construction of living quarters to lodge workers from distant areas during the harvest clearly reflected fundamental changes in the owner-worker relation. It partially explains the need to see in a wage the tie that would bind both parties. In the absence of circulating currency, chips were coined for payment, but they were redeemable only in the hacienda or central store. The lack of a monetary system on the island paved the way in decades to come for the intensive exploitation of the unwary laborer by way of the chip-company store system, a system that persisted into the first four decades of the twentieth century.

NOTES

This chapter represents a condensed version of the paper presented at the conference. Those wishing to see the fuller version, which includes considerable detail on individual units and detailed citations to the archives, should write to the author. The translation was done by Elizabeth Hansen. For a fuller discussion of the Puerto Rican sugar economy, see also my book, *La Hacienda Azucarera: Su*

crecimiento y crisis en Puerto Rico (Siglo XIX) (San Juan: Centro de Estudios de la
Realidad Puertorriqueña, 1981).

1. *Estadística general de comercio exterior de la isla de Puerto Rico* (microfilm in
   Centro de Investigaciones Históricas [hereafter CIH]).
2. *La Gaceta de Puerto Rico*, October 23, 1880.
3. *Estadística general del comercio exterior.*
4. These prices are for sugar sold to local merchants, who subsequently shipped it
   abroad. They are the average of prices in the San Juan market, which were
   published every two weeks by *El Boletín Mercantil.*
5. Many of the orders for this machine, like others that follow, were made from
   the Scottish company Mirrlees Watson. This company donated its documents
   related to the nineteenth century to the archives of the University of Glasgow.
   There one may find mechanical sketches of the orders made by Puerto Rican
   planters.
6. The company of Manlove Alliot from England manufactured this machine.
   Juan Serrallés was responsible for introducing one into the Dominican
   Republic. It was installed on his hacienda Puerto Rico, founded in San Pedro
   de Macorís in 1883. See Juan J. Sánchez, *La caña en Santo Domingo* (Santo
   Domingo: Imprenta García Hermanos, 1893) and Andrés Ramos Mattei,
   *Libros de cuentas de la Hacienda Mercedita, 1881-1900, Apuntes para el
   estudio de la transición hacia el sistema de centrales en la industria azucarera*
   (San Juan: CEREP, 1975).
7. This discussion is based on the experience of the hacienda Victoria of Hermaan,
   Emilio, and Joseph Rothschild, and the hacienda Aurora, of Manuel Isidoro
   Saldaña. Both plantations were lost due to debt, Victoria in 1873 and Aurora in
   1880. This material is in Archivo General de Puerto Rico (hereafter AGPR).
8. This discussion is based on the cases of José Suárez of Carolina and José María
   Justo Skerret of Vega Alta, both of whom lost their haciendas to creditors.
   Merchants such as Frederick Huth of London; George I. Finlay, originally of
   Scotland, and Andrés Crosas, originally of North America, entered the
   hacendado class by foreclosing on haciendas. The shortage of liquid capital also
   caused the bankruptcy of semimechanized haciendas such as the hacienda
   Luiza owned by Luis de Boyrie of Maunabo. This material is in AGPR. The
   papers of Frederick Huth and Company, Guildhall Library (London) were also
   used.
9. As an example, refer to the plan proposed by Wenceslao Borda and published
   in *El Boletín Mercantil*, July 6, 1873. Borda proposed to establish eighteen
   centrales around the whole island, using machinery from Cail and Company.
   The financing was to be provided by Moitessier Neveu from Paris, in exchange
   for which the landowners would deliver the certificates of indemnification as
   guarantees. Moreover, Moitessier was to lend up to a million and one-half pesos
   to the *hacendados* as working capital during the harvests.
10. This discussion is based on the experience of the five centrales operating on the
    island by 1880—Luisa, San Francisco, Coloso, Canóvanas, and San
    Vicente—particularly the latter owned by Leonardo Igaravidez. The material is
    in *La Razón* (1873) and AGPR, "San Juan, Protocolos de Demetrio Gimenez
    Moreno and Juan Ramón de Torres."

11. The British consul wrote that in 1870 "already bands of Negroes have seized horses, and riding madly over the country have proclaimed that all the slaves are free; whilst others have peacefully collected, and going in a body to the Alcaldes, have demanded the promulgation of the Law. . . ." See Public Record Office (hereafter PRO), FO 84/1321, Consul Cowper to Earl of Granville, September 26, 1870.

12. AGPR, Records of the Spanish Governors of Puerto Rico (hereafter RSGPR), entry 290, Municipalities, Ponce, box 534.

13. Luis M. Díaz Soler, *Historia de la esclavitud negra en Puerto Rico* (Río Piedras: Editorial Universitaria, 1970), pp. 317, 336.

14. For more information on this migration, see Andrés A. Ramos Mattei, "La importación de trabajadores contratados para la industria azucarera puertorriqueña, 1860–1880," in Francisco A. Scarano, ed., *Immagración y clases sociales en el Puerto Rico del siglo XIX* (Río Piedras: Ediciones Huracán, 1981).

15. PRO:FO 84/1506, Consul Bidwell to Third Marques of Salisbury, February 27, 1878.

16. PRO:FO 72/1381, Consul Cowper to Earl of Derby, March 21, 1874.

17. PRO:FO 72/1381, Consul Cowper to Earl of Derby, March 21, 1874.

18. See the correspondence of the Colonial Governor of the time in Archivo Histórico Nacional (hereafter AHN), Manuscritos Asuntos de Estado, U/2969, 128, April 11, 1874.

19. One of the most important landowners in San Pedro de Macorís was Juan Serrallés from Ponce, Puerto Rico, who was the owner of the hacienda Mercedita. He founded the Ingenio Puerto Rico in San Pedro in the beginning of 1880. Some day laborers from Ponce requested permission to emigrate to Macorís at about this time. See Sánchez, *La caña en Santo Domingo*, pp. 47–48, and AGPR, RSGPR, entry 290, Municipalities, Ponce, box 535.

20. Lidio Cruz Monclova, *Historia de Puerto Rico*, 3 vols. (Río Piedras: Editorial Universitaria, 1971), 3:359–67.

21. Cruz Monclova, *Historia de Puerto Rico*, 2:357, and *La Gaceta de Puerto Rico*, April 24, 1873.

22. Díaz Soler, *Historia de la esclavitud negra*, p. 353.

23. AGPR, RSGPR, Entry 23, Asuntos Políticos, Esclavos: 1860–74, box 69.

24. See a more detailed version of this incident in PRO:FO 84/1410, Vice-Consul Gibbons to Consul Cowper, 30 April 1875.

25. See C. T. Overman, "The Henrietta Estate," mimeographed and deposited in the Colleción Puertorriqueña, Biblioteca General, University of Puerto Rico.

26. "Notas de Simon Moret." I thank Professor Fernando Picó for having made this unpublished diary, in possession of Simon Moret's descendants, available to me.

27. This discussion is based on the experience of several estates in Ponce. The material is in AGPR, RSGPR.

28. *El Boletín Mercantil*, July 4, 1873. See also PRO:FO 84/1368, Consul Cowper to Earl of Granville, April 6, 1873.

29. Article published in *El Martillo* and reprinted in *El Boletín Mercantil*, May 13, 1874.

30. Parliamentary Papers (hereafter PP), *Abstracts*, vol. 76, Report by Vice Consul Basanta on the Trade and Commerce of Ponce for the year 1874, p. 809.
31. *La Gaceta de Puerto Rico*, April 11, 1874.
32. AGPR, Carolina, Expediente 1, 1875, box QQ.
33. AGPR, Carolina, Expediente 1, 1875, box QQ. The merchant planter Ignacio Arzuaga contracted a freedman as a "steam engine machinist" for his hacienda Buena Vista in Carolina.
34. PRO:FO 84/1410, Consul Pauli to Earl of Derby, May 12, 1875.
35. Sidney W. Mintz, "The Culture History of a Puerto Rico Sugar Cane Plantation: 1876–1949," *Hispanic American Historical Review* 33 (1953): 224–51.
36. See, for example, PP, *Abstracts*, vol. 76, Report by Consul Pauli on the Trade and Commerce of Porto Rico for the Year of 1874, p. 804.
37. The news was published in *El Boletín Mercantil*, July 28, 1876.
38. See Pedro Deschamps Chapeaux and Juan Pérez de la Riva, *Contribución a la historia de la gente sin historia* (Havana: Editorial de Ciencias Sociales, 1974).
39. *Boletín Histórico de Puerto Rico*, vol. 12, "Orden manifestando que no debe reglamentarse el trabajo," October 27, 1874, pp. 234–35.
40. *El Boletín Mercantil*, February 6, 1876.
41. AHN, U/5112, 64, 1876.
42. *El Boletín Mercantil*, May 20, 1877.
43. AGPR, Audiencia Territorial de Puerto Rico, Juzgado de San Francisco, Sección de lo Criminal, Sobreseimiento por fraude a Don Leonardo Iagaravidez y sus acreedores, 1884, box 448.
44. Sidney W. Mintz, "The Culture History," pp. 238–39.

Part Four
Dominican Republic

Dominican Republic, 1911

9. The Land Question in Haiti and Santo Domingo: The Sociopolitical Context of the Transition from Slavery to Free Labor, 1801–1843

Frank Moya Pons

It was the conviction of Toussaint L'Ouvertue and the other black leaders who carried out the Haitian revolution and independence from France that the plantation system should remain the fundamental base of the Haitian economy. To this end they concentrated their efforts; they were convinced that only by recovery of the earlier levels of production, which had made Saint Domingue the richest colony of France, could they bring prosperity to the ex-slaves. These had been emancipated but converted into a dependent labor force bound to the plantations by the agricultural policies established by Toussaint in the constitution of 1801. These policies—which provided the plantations with a stable labor force—achieved some success at the expense of the ex-slaves whose previous condition was modified only in that they now received a salary and had the option of enlisting in the army. Working on the plantations was an obligation for the ex-slaves, who were recruited by the planters under a system of strict contracts supervised by a rural police.[1]

Following the capture of Toussaint and the defeat of the French troops in 1803, Dessalines proceeded to strengthen the plantation economy. In April 1804 he canceled all transactions pertaining to sale and donation of lands that had been made to mulattoes and to many army officers during the revolution before 1803. By this measure he attempted to concentrate in the hands of the state the bulk of Haitian landed property and to make the plantation system the country's sole economic reality. This measure was unpopular not only because of its immediate significance but also because of its implications. It indicated that the system of servitude, into which the former slaves had fallen after their independence, would be indefinitely maintained under the absolute control of the military chiefs who now possessed total control of the political and economic life of Haiti. That unpopularity cost Dessalines his life. He was assassinated in October 1806 by his enemies, who threw his corpse into the streets, where it was destroyed by mobs. But in those two years the confiscations had been so effective that at the time of his death Dessalines had been able to transfer to the state between two-thirds and nine-tenths of the land, keeping the laborers permanently attached to the plantations, unable to leave them without permission.[2]

FROM 1807 TO 1818

After 1807, Haiti was divided into two politically antagonistic and independent units. In the north, Dessalines' successor, Christophe—himself molded under Toussaint's leadership—pursued the policy of his predecessors in preserving the plantations intact. He introduced new measures that not only tended to increase productivity but permitted an expansion of the political base of his regime and the increase of the wealth of the state. His solution was to permit the most important men of the kingdom, i.e., the wealthy and the military chiefs, to lease or administer the plantations as long as they kept them in production, paid to the state a tax of a quarter of the annual production, and provided another quarter as payment to the workers. The remaining fifty percent was to be the income of the administrators of the plantation, who usually acquired noble titles within the social and political hierarchy of northern Haiti. In this way Christophe assured the revival of traditional exports, tied the majority of the population to agricultural work, kept the army occupied with the supervision of agricultural workers so that the latter would not spend their time in unproductive idleness, and maintained an enriched military elite who would do anything to prevent a change in the status quo.[3]

In the south of Haiti, however, the status quo was changing under the presidency of General Petión. In this region, politics differed radically from those in the north. After the death of Dessalines, the mulattoes, far from accepting the government of Christophe, which would have meant the perpetuation of the previous tyranny, preferred to employ the armed forces loyal to Petión against Christophe, who endeavored to unify Haiti under his rule. In this struggle there were neither victors nor vanquished, and Christophe was forced to remain in the north. In the south, the mulattoes used all their influence to proclaim a republic, naming Petión as its president. Their major problem was to defend themselves against Christophe, and

Petión's solution was to use the land. As salaries were owed to the soldiers and there was no money to pay them, Petión proceeded to distribute among them, from the most lowly ranked soldier to the highest official, parcels of land in proportion to the sums owed. With this simple measure, he made all the members of the army proprietors and automatically won their loyalty. Since 1807, Petión had been restoring to their former owners the great plantations of the mulattoes, confiscated in the times of Dessalines, thereby guaranteeing the support of this class that had brought him to power and needed the army to defend their properties in the event of an invasion from the north.

The underlying theory in this distribution of land among the greater part of the southern population was, according to Petión, that it was much easier to maintain peace where the majority of the population was free and had a stake in the land than where the population was subject to servitude.[4] Hence, apart from the army and the great proprietors, almost the entire population of former plantation workers received parcels on which they could devote themselves to cultivating whatever they wished as free farmers without having to be supervised by the former "inspectors of agriculture" of the Dessalines era. In seven years, by 1814, the majority of the land in the south of Haiti had been restored to private ownership and the economy of the region rested on two different forms of holding and exploitation of the land: the large latifundia and the minifundia (*la grande et la petite cultures*).

The immediate result of this policy of general parceling of land was that the majority of the new owners of small plots began to replace production for export with subsistence cultivation, since they preferred the harvest of foodstuffs for their own use to the cultivation for export of sugar cane, cotton, coffee, or cacao. These required complex processes of preparation and commercialization. As a consequence, export production to yield foreign currency to the state began to decline gradually, while the old plantations gave way to small plots where family need was the determinant of food production or where nothing at all was cultivated since, whether by law or negligence, no one was forced to work his own land. Another outcome was the shortage of manual labor to work on the great plantations. Since proprietorship was now general, it was difficult for large landowners—who indeed would have liked to keep sufficiently large units cultivated in sugar, coffee, cotton, or cacao—to recruit peons. Of all these products, sugar's output declined the most. By 1818, the year of Petión's death, production had fallen to a little less than two million pounds as compared to some sixty million in the times of Toussaint. Indigo, which required much manual labor, ceased to be cultivated entirely, and cotton output declined to about five percent of the earlier production, which had reached five million pounds. In the process of decline, coffee managed to stave off total ruin for the country, for the decline of production was much slower, and even in 1818 one-third of the earlier output was still being produced.[5]

BOYER AND HIS POLICIES, 1818–23

Such was the general situation in 1818 when Petión died, to be succeeded by his secretary and minister, Jean Pierre Boyer, who enjoyed a reputation for meticulousness and philanthropy. The situation did not change until mid-1820, when Christophe suffered a stroke while attending church on August 6, and his illness gave encouragement to a conspiracy among his followers. The ailing king, on discovering the plot, considered himself betrayed and took his own life on October 8, with a pistol-shot through his heart. An uprising immediately followed, and the rebels, by now weary of the rigid system of exploitation to which Christophe had subjected them for thirteen years, called upon Boyer, who quickly put his army on the march and occupied the city of Cap Haitien (Cap Henri) at the end of October 1820.

The clearest proof of the differences in production between the economic regimes of the north and of the south could be seen when Boyer occupied the residence of Christophe, la Citadelle. He found accumulated in gold some 150 million francs (45 million gourdes). But those differences in production also meant differences in degree of control. The former slaves preferred the simple liberty that Petión had granted to the inhabitants of the south to the enrichment of the state, to which Christophe had always pointed to foreign visitors. As with Dessalines, Christophe died unpopular with the blacks, his own race, and the mulattoes, his traditional enemies. When Boyer united Haiti, there had been for some years an intense migration of workers from the north, who were fleeing to Petión's republic in search of land and liberty, which they could not find in the north. It is not surprising, therefore, that when Petión died, thousands of people, Negroes and mulattoes, wept inconsolably before his body, declaring that they had lost their "petit pere"; or that Boyer, who had worked with him so closely as secretary and minister, was looked to by the masses of the north as a savior who would give them land and remove them from the regime of semislavery to which they had been subjected from the time of French rule. Boyer appeared to the Haitians as the benefactor, as well as the unifier.[6]

Boyer wanted to maintain, at all cost, the image of a man of good for his people. Boyer did for the former subjects of Christophe what Petión had done in the south, dividing plantations in proportional lots among members of the army, government servants, and workers. This provoked great waves of sympathy among the new citizens of the republic. The results were the same, and by 1823 nothing remained of the golden treasure that had been found in Christophe's palace. But while Boyer carried out his plan of parceling land in the north of Haiti, in the eastern part of the island were events in which he would also come to play a critical role.

Indeed, the intrigues hatched by some adventurers who tried to revive the interest of the French government in the reconquest of the island (both the Spanish and the Haitian sides) kept the government of Haiti in a state of nervousness for several months, especially when the rumors circulated among the people of Santo Domingo.[7] Those rumors were alarming, for the two attempts of the French government to take possession of Haiti, in 1814 and in 1816, although discovered in time, were still fresh in the memory of Haitians.[8] These invasions impressed on the Haitians that the interest of the former French planters were continuing to play an important role in the external policy of the French government. Those rumors gained in intensity in 1820, and once more put Boyer on the alert. The news was that some French ships had arrived in Martinique and would be used to further the cause of an invasion that certain adventurers would launch against the Spanish part of the island. The invasion was to be followed by the dispatch of French troops, who would simulate a military operation and receive the province from the adventurers.[9] Everything indicated that the weak link of Haitian independence was the eastern part of the island, either because the garrison at Santo Domingo would not be strong enough to resist an attack from outside or because it continued to be a Spanish possession. In 1820 France and Spain had entered into an offensive and defensive alliance, which continued to generate the suspicion that there would be assistance from the Spanish government for a French effort to recover her lost colony.

Boyer's reaction to the news of the preparation for a French invasion of Santo Domingo was to prepare militarily for its repulsion. At the same time he tried to induce the inhabitants of the eastern part of the island to rise against Spanish rule and to incorporate themselves into the republic of Haiti. This was, in part, with the aim of establishing the republic's natural frontiers to make the island strategically a more defensible unit against naval attack.[10]

Through his agents, Boyer finally managed to create, among some colored groups in the Spanish part of the island who had been connected with Haiti in the border areas and who earned a living by selling cattle to the Haitians, a climate against Spanish rule and favorable to a political union with Haiti. This he did at a time when there was considerable ferment in favor of the emancipation of the Spanish colony among the white Creole groups in the city of Santo Domingo, who had been in contact with revolutionaries of South America, particularly with those in Caracas.[11] After more than a year of preparations, both parties, working independently of each other, developed plans that culminated in a declaration of independence in November 1821 by the pro-Haitian group. As a reaction to it, in early December of that same year, the Creole elite of Santo Domingo staged a coup d'etat, expelling from the island the Spanish authorities and proclaiming a so-called independent state of Haiti, which was designed to become eventually a member of Simon Bolivar's Confederación de la Gran Colombia.[12]

This unexpected outcome created, in the eyes of Boyer, a dangerous political vacuum in the eastern part of the island which could rapidly accelerate the French invasion under preparation in Martinique. The new Dominican authorities did not have the military means to oppose a French attack and would quickly surrender to it, thereby providing the grounds for the feared military movement against Haiti. Boyer therefore immediately mobilized Haitian public opinion. At the beginning of 1822 he secured the authorization of the Haitian senate to march into the eastern sector of the island to support the pro-Haitian party, which had declared itself in favor of the union with Haiti in November, and to achieve insular unity in order to preserve Haitian independence.[13]

The Dominican authorities of Santo Domingo did not have the means to oppose Boyer's army of 12,000 soldiers and grudgingly surrendered to it on February 9, 1822. This had been the third Haitian invasion of the eastern part in twenty years. The other two were in 1801 and in 1805, and on both occasions the Dominican population reacted by leaving the island en masse for fear of a massacre of the white people, as was believed to have happened in Haiti during and after the revolution.[14] Beginning in 1822 a new wave of emigration started. But this time the purpose of the Haitian government headed by Boyer was a different one from that of Dessalines and Christophe. Boyer wanted to incorporate the Dominican population into the Haitian nation, and to this end he committed all his efforts and resources.

Boyer's first public decision after taking possession of the eastern part of the island was to order the abolition of slavery and to promise land denoted by the state to all the freed men to enable them to escape the control of their masters and to live as free agriculturists on their own parcels of land.[15] On February 11, 1822, Boyer sent a circular to the Haitian military commanders whom he had named to govern each of the eastern communities, instructing them that "it is necessary in the interest of the State as well as of our brothers who have just received their liberty, that they be obliged to work, cultivating the land on which their survival depends, and receiving a part of the income fixed for them by the regulations."[16] His commanders were to encourage agricultural activity among the ex-slaves, who were to grow coffee and foodstuffs. At the same time the inhabitants of the eastern part of the island were to be made aware of the property law in use in Haiti, which derived from French jurisprudence. Boyer understood that Spanish property law and the system of land tenure that had been practiced in Santo Domingo for three centuries were radically different from the Franco-Haitian legislation that provided for absolute private proprietorship guaranteed by titles issued by the state. In the Spanish part of the island, the predominant system had been, from the middle of the sixteenth century, that of *terrenos comuneros.*[17] Under this system there was multiple possession of land and an irregular system of landholding, which had been reinforced by the low population density, by the abundance of land, and by a pattern of extensive exploitation associated with cattle-raising and woodcutting.

The system of *terrenos comuneros* originated as the island became depopulated in the course of the sixteenth century, for it was useless to try to divide the land for purposes of inheritance when the whole Spanish population was no larger than seven thousand people for the whole island. Original owners of land had received it through grants from the Spanish Crown. These were legitimized by the issuance of a deed called *amparo real*, whereby the crown guaranteed the ownership rights to the original owner and his successors. When that person died, his land was divided among his wife and children in equal parts. It was neither surveyed nor partitioned. The Spanish colony of Santo Domingo did not have a single land surveyor for centuries, and the most people could do was to define certain rough limits for their lands according to the course of the rivers, mountains, trees, and other relevant landmarks. If the family did not migrate, its members usually stayed their holdings, but as they died, new heirs claimed their rights to the land. Then, a process of formal—not actual—division took place. To complicate matters further, when one of the new owners wanted to sell his rights to the land, he could freely do so by simply being paid in money the value equivalent to his land right in the original deed. The buyer guaranteed his claim by writing it down on the back of the original *amparo real* or, in its absence, by a notary act legalizing it.

With the passage of time, thousands of sales, inheritances, donations, transfers, and turnovers of land took place. Everybody seemed to know what his rights were and nobody seemed uncomfortable with the system, since the main economic occupation of the population was cattle-raising, done by using the land extensively and letting the herds roam around as freely as possible. Cultivation was mainly restricted to subsistence production of plantains and yams, plus some cocoa, and it functioned more as gathering than as agriculture. In some parts of the north several hundred patches were cultivated in tobacco, which was exported to Seville. The normal diet was meat, plantains, yams, beans, and milk; thus most of the land remained outside cultivation. While the French had been developing the most intensive plantation colony in the West Indies, Santo Domingo remained a cattle-raising territory, producing meat for consumption by the slave masses in the western part of the island. Through this process developed a nonplantation economy, which made it possible to function without a formal system of land tenure such as in the French and English colonies of the West Indies.

Land, therefore, remained undivided, although proprietorship developed quite legally under a traditional and customary land tenure system that could not be altered because of the enormous costs of surveying the land and the already well-established ways of exerting property rights. As time passed, the changes in the value of the Spanish currency also contributed to the definition of the *terrenos comuneros* system. With inflation in Spain and in the Indies, the Spanish peso declined in value. In searching for a permanent measure of value, the inhabitants of Santo Domingo devised what they called the *peso de tierra*, related to the pesos in which the original property was valued at the time of the first division. As landownership developed into co-ownership in the original contract between the early settler and the crown, the *peso de tierra* became an *acción de tierra*, and *acciones* and *pesos* thus became identified. Landownership came to be defined, therefore, as the ownership of *pesos* and *acciones de tierras*, which gave rights to use the land. Anyone who had a single *peso* had acquired the right to settle in any region or area within the limits of the original property that was not actually claimed or occupied by a previous *peso* holder. Years later, when woodcutting became a lucrative occupation, the landowners differentiated the *acciones de tierra* and assigned to them different values according to the use of the land. By this new development, land for cattle raising or for cultivation kept its original value, but woodcutting rights were limited only to those who owned at least two hundred *pesos* or *acciones de tierra*.[18]

For the Haitians, accustomed to the clear and systematic French legal system, the *terrenos comuneros* of the Spanish part of the island seemed an absurdity, confusing and backward. They saw in it an obstacle that should be removed at once in order to give land to those who needed them, particularly the recently emancipated slaves. In this regard, the question to be resolved was which land to distribute, since according to the tradition most of it had been in private hands since the early colonial years.

It was the determination of ownership of land in Santo Domingo that presented a problem. Proprietorship, however, could not be established immediately without alienating the class of proprietors, who because of their Spanish origin were hostile to the Haitian regime. The *libertos*, therefore, had to wait for some time before receiving the promised lands. On June 15, 1822, Boyer reaffirmed his promise, proclaiming that he would make good their right to acquire state land on which to grow coffee, cacao, sugar cane, cotton, tobacco, and foodstuffs.[19] Meanwhile, a new battalion—Battalion thirty-two—was created to absorb those ex-slaves who wanted to be immediately free of their masters. This battalion became the principal military force responsible for the security of the Spanish part of the island.[20] There is evidence suggesting that the *libertos* who were recruited into the armed forces may have been ill-treated slaves. According to a letter of Francisco Brenes, former proprietor of Santo Domingo, written in September 1822: "The freed men insult their masters [especially] the freed men who are a part of the Haitian army. Former masters were subject to frequent insult."[21] Since Boyer's policy was to bring about the unification of the island as quickly as possible and to make true Haitians of all its people—whether white, black, or mulatto—he obviously had no desire to see these tensions continue. His proclamation of June was followed on August 26 by the naming of a commission to investigate "according to the data submitted by the relevant authorities, the properties in the Spanish area which should fall to the State: first, those properties whose owners had abandoned the country for a long time before the events which had brought about the present changes; secondly, those properties whose owners had left with the authority of the government, but who had declared that they had no intention of returning, because they were opposed to the system of government; and thirdly, those properties which had been abandoned because encumbered mortgage or other debts had not been paid."[22]

After sitting for a few weeks, the commission submitted its report on October 12, declaring that the state was entitled to the following properties:

> Properties belonging to the Spanish government; the convents of Santo Domingo, San Francisco, La Merced, Regina, and Santa Clara, as well as the various houses, ranches, animals, lands and lots which belonged to them; the buildings and accessories of the hospitals of San Andres, San Lazaro, and San Nicolas, located in Santo Domingo, and the properties attached to them; the properties of Frenchmen seized by the Spanish government and which had not been restored to their owners; the properties of persons who co-operated in the conspiracy at Samana and who left with the French Squadron;[23] all the *capellanías* which through lapse or default had fallen into the hands of the Archbishop, and had been donated to be used as an income for priests who had died or where absent; and the mortgages raised in favor of the Cathedral; and all funds collected from construction.[24]

Boyer immediately submitted the report to the Chamber of Deputies and the Senate.[25] On November 7, both houses gave it their full approval, which General Borgella, the new Haitian commander and governor of Santo Domingo, took to mean that the report had the force of law. He proceeded to confiscate properties which apparently belonged to the church or the other corporations but had been in private hands for several decades. They were stripped of their possessions by the military governor, who gave them to the ex-slaves, sold them at low prices to friends, or gave them to soldiers, officials, and Haitian functionaries who sought lands or homes in the east. These decisions by Borgella caused some uneasiness and provoked reclamations by people who considered themselves unjustly treated. Boyer was moved to name a new commission on January 22, 1823, to study the problem and settle "the reclamations of the inhabitants of the East whose properties are in the power of the State."[26]

The problems of this commission were at once gigantic and delicate. The confusion into which ecclesiastical lands and properties had fallen over the preceding twenty-five years, following the abandonment of the island by the archbishop and the religious orders as a consequence of the Treaty of Basle, in 1795, had enabled many Dominicans to occupy those lands under the paternal eye of the Spanish governors of the following years.[27] In effect, when Boyer occupied Santo Domingo, possession of these properties had already been sanctioned by an occupation of over twenty years. Furthermore, the communal system of tenure gave to those occupants a guarantee of property far more valid than any official document could offer.[28]

There was clearly some confusion relating to the rights of the complainants who were in actual possession and the rights of the former owners, many of whom were away from the island. In order to clarify the issues and make a positive decision possible for the Haitian government, Boyer issued a decree on February 8, 1823, giving "a time limit of four months, starting from that date, to the proprietors of the Spanish side who had migrated before February 9, 1822, to return to the country to take up possession of their properties." The decree also empowered the military governors of Santo Domingo to confiscate the properties of "Dominicans who had not taken advantage of the permission to return to the country" by June 8, 1823.[29] The majority of émigrés did not return, and there is sufficient evidence to indicate that their properties were taken over by the state.[30] People in actual possession were understandably uneasy. Many of those occupants were relatives or friends of the absentees. They were not regarded as proprietors in terms of Haitian law since they had no property titles, but according to the system of *terrenos comuneros* they had already acquired property rights.

Tensions therefore continued. At that time the Haitian government was unable to maintain calm among the Dominican population with its hispanophile tendencies. Its land policies had already deeply hurt the interests of the white proprietors of Santo Domingo, among whom, in a fairly uncomfortable position, was the archbishop of Santo Domingo, who saw in Haitian legislation an imminent danger to the conservation of the church's properties. As time passed, many other people also showed a coolness to the Haitian government, especially over the matter of land.

The archbishop, for his part, could not conceal his annoyance at the policy of nationalization of ecclesiastical lands and properties, even less so in view of Boyer's order of January 5, 1823, suspending payment of the salaries that both he and other members of the ecclesiastical *cabildo* were accustomed to receive from the state. The Haitian government's opinion was that priests should maintain themselves on their ecclesiastical incomes. If these were not sufficient, they were to take charge of the parishes and pastorships on the southern coast, which were in great need of religious personnel. Archbishop Pedro de Valera also wished to name as his vicar for the whole of the western region Dr. Bernardo Correa y Cidrón, but Boyer, annoyed by the refusal of the archbishop to collaborate with the Haitian government, under the pretext "that he was nothing but a subject of King Ferdinand VII," declined to recognize his office of archbishop and refused to acknowledge the validity of his nominations until Valera "be considered Archbishop and a citizen of Haiti."[31] This crisis naturally provoked the resentment of the Dominican clergy, who, in addition, had lost their salaries and their employment at the Universidad de Santo Tomás after December 1823, when Boyer had given orders to his commanders in Santo Domingo to recruit all young men between the ages of sixteen and twenty-five to enlist them in the army. This recruitment came into the halls of the university, which, on losing its students, had no choice but to close down.[32]

THE LAW OF 1824

At the beginning of 1824, spirits among the Dominican groups who remained loyal to Spain were impassioned, and they would not willingly accept the Haitian regime. Part of this agitation sprang from widespread frustration. In fact, the Haitian government had uncovered at least three conspiracies in the preceding year and had crushed a revolt against Haitian troops who were supervising a group of workers cleaning the road from Santiago to Puerto Plata.[33] These conspiracies and the harshness with which they were suppressed startled a good many individuals whose pro-Spanish sentiments were known. Thus, before measures could be adopted against them, a group of families entered into exile, embarking for Puerto Rico. This group increased the migratory flood that had started right after Boyer's occupation of the eastern part of the island in February 1822. What these émigrés did not realize was that their departure from the country, far from hurting Boyer, favored his plans to obtain the greatest quantity of land possible to be shared among the ex-slaves, soldiers, government servants, and partisans of unification.

On July 8, 1824, Boyer ordered the promulgation of a "law to determine which are the movable and the real properties of the East which belong to the State, and to regulate with due deference to the peculiarities of that part, the law of territorial property, in conformity with the mode established in other parts of the Republic, and to fix the salaries of the high clergy of the Metropolitan Cabildo of the Cathedral of Santo Domingo and to see to the welfare of religious personnel whose convents have been suppressed."[34] This law was to crown all the other efforts that the Haitian government had undertaken from the time of the unification of the island to find a legal and practical solution that would bring about the change from the Spanish land legislation to the Haitian legislation of French origin, in order to alter the patterns of land tenure and the prevailing property system. With this law, according to the government, all the inhabitants of the republic would have the right to own their own lands, protected by a title given by the state. The church, which was to be the institution most

affected by the removal of their property rights, would be compensated by a
new offer of an annual salary to each of its functionaries connected to the
Cathedral of Santo Domingo. The same law incorporated into the property
of the state: first, all properties situated in the eastern part of the island,
which before February 9, 1822, did not belong to private owners; second,
"all the movable and real properties, all the territorial incomes and their
respective capital which belonged to the previous government of the said
eastern part, whether the property of religious convents, or monastery hos-
pitals, churches, or other ecclesiastical corporations"; third, "all the movable and real property which belong in the eastern part to individuals who,
being absent from the territory when the union was achieved, had not
returned by the 10th of June, 1823; that is, sixteen months after the said
union, or if they belong to those who have left the island at the time of
union, without having sworn allegiance to the Republic."

In addition, the state claimed the property of those who left after the
unification. The execution of the law required the definition of the boundaries of existing properties, for which Boyer authorized the naming of a
committee to undertake the implementation of a general land survey. This
survey would also indicate which properties would become permanently
attached to the state. Above all the articles of that law, however, was a fact
impossible to ignore, since it would present problems of a practical nature,
whose solution would involve the violation of the interests of a good part of
the Dominican landholding population: most of the land titles in Dominican hands from the colonial era were affected to a greater or lesser degree by
possession, division, usufruct, sale, and participation within the communal
land system. The determination of the proprietors was extremely difficult,
for in the Dominican system of land tenure the owner of a title was not
invariably the owner of all the land. The latter could be, and was, affected
by innumerable sales of *pesos* or *acciones de tierra*, which gave the right to
other individuals and corporations to exploit the land with the same legal
capability and the same rights as the holder of the title. Boyer thought that
this problem could be resolved by authorizing his agents to bring together
the property titles in existence in the Spanish part "in order to proceed to a
demarcation proportional to the property right of each person, so that the
right of full possession would be awarded to those who deserved the quantity of land which in justice belong to them, providing new titles in place of
the old ones."

According to the law, no new proprietor could have fewer than five
carreaux (approximately 15.5 acres), and in the event that a smaller quantity was received in the distribution, the new proprietors could ask the state
for the necessary quantity of land to reach this established minimum, a new
unit of measurement for the Dominicans that became known as a *boyerana*.
On their new properties, the owners were to produce mainly for the export
market. If a farmer failed to keep the whole unit in production, he was

required to surrender it to other proprietors, since the interest of the Haitian government was to have the land cultivated to produce exports. Hence pigs could not be reared nor could cattle be held on units of fewer than five *boyeranas* (approximately seventy-five acres), which was the minimum quantity necessary to raise cattle economically.

In short, the law of July 8, 1824 sought to eliminate the system of *terrenos comuneros* under which the landed property of Santo Domingo could not be controlled by the state. At the same time, it sought to make of each rural inhabitant a *campesino* who owned the land that he occupied and who was obliged to cultivate it. This law directly challenged the peculiar system of land tenure in Santo Domingo. The execution of this law meant that Dominicans with titles to large properties originating from grants of the Spanish Crown in colonial times would find their properties fragmented and partially shared with the real occupants of the land.

Many of these great proprietors were in debt because of the decline of the market for hides, which had served as the sustenance of the colonial economy in previous centuries. Boyer wished to win them over by reducing to one-third the debts that they had acquired when they mortgaged their properties with loans granted them by the cathedral and other religious corporations, whose properties were now passing into the hands of the state. To facilitate the payment of this new debt, Boyer granted them three years in which they were to cancel their mortgages and reimburse the state in six monthly installments for the money owed. To the monastic orders and the seculars attached to the cathedral, the state would give in compensation an annual salary of 240 pesos per person. The archbishop, whose interests had been particularly affected, would receive a salary of some 3,000 pesos per annum from the state. In spite of this, the archbishop never pardoned Boyer for the ruin of the Dominican church and continued to refuse the assigned salary, maintaining opposition to the Haitian government.[35]

To Boyer's surprise and the surprise of the other military commanders, it was not only the archbishop who refused to collaborate but also the *campesinos* of Spanish origin. These latter were not sympathetic to the orders to cultivate cacao, sugar cane, and cotton, preferring to pursue the economic activities that for several decades had proven more profitable because the products had an assured foreign market: the cutting of mahogany in the south, the planting of tobacco in the north, and the growing and herding of cattle in the east. The majority of the mahogany on the river banks and on the outlets close to the sea had been exhausted, so that many inhabitants of the south moved on to the lands that now belonged to the state but were seen as belonging to no one. They continued to fell mahogany without having to pay the 200 *pesos* or *acciones de tierras*, which in the old system of communal lands was what gave a person the right to undertake this very productive activity. News of these events annoyed Boyer; learning that similar things had been happening from the first months of the unification, he wrote immediately to the justices of the peace of the southern localities so that "they would indicate as soon as possible the lands which belonged to the state which had mahogany forests, with the aim of preventing their felling and selling without previous authorization."[36] Despite the restrictive measures repeatedly made by the Haitian government during the following years to prevent the illegal cutting of mahogany and its illicit sale at the mouths of the rivers of Santo Domingo, the proprietors of the south and east never abandoned their business. Several years later, Boyer had to give up by ending the prohibition, permitting the Dominican landowners to fell their mahogany trees as a legal economic activity.[37] With the exception of the cultivation of some necessary items for subsistence, they never did concern themselves with the products in which the Haitian government had an interest. Ten years later, in January 1834, the governor of the province of Santo Domingo declared that "if the country was not more flourishing, it was not through lack of effort, but because of the frivolity of that mahogany trade to which, unfortunately, the people have by preference devoted themselves."[38]

That the country did not flourish more (in the sense that the government wished to see it), however, had less to do with the illegal cutting and contraband in mahogany than with the socioeconomic consequences of the Haitian policy of distributing lands to all those who desired them. This policy led to the gradual fragmentation of the Haitian plantations and to the emergence of an independent Haitian peasantry, which had no obligation to work other people's land and preferred to dedicate itself to living peacefully on the foodstuffs that they produced on their small parcels. Petión was the patron of the Haitian peasantry, as Boyer was its patron in Santo Domingo. The policy of land distribution had been universally popular at first, even among the Haitian mulatto proprietary class. But with time it became clear that the state's impoverishment increased as plantation agriculture continued to suffer from the shortage of agricultural labor. In contrast, the system of compulsory paid labor had proved successful under the regimes of Toussaint, Dessalines, and Christophe. The Haitian mulatto elite grew increasingly disenchanted with the general situation and exercised its influence on Boyer to adopt corrective measures. Their argument was strengthened by the fact that the policy of promoting the export economy had achieved no success, even in Santo Domingo, where the population was not only smaller but subject to military government.

CODE RURAL

The refusal of the rural proprietors of the Spanish province to produce new products for export could be easily explained: economic activity had been traditionally restricted to rearing cattle, cutting wood, and planting tobacco. Moreover, the inhabitants of this part of the country were, according to the Haitians, "an indolent and entirely unindustrious people, who cutivate to meet their own needs and nothing more."[39] But in Haiti, which was precisely where the mulatto elite exercised control and held its most important properties, the necessary and obvious solution was to revert to the policy of compelling *campesinos* to do plantation work. On May 1, 1826, Boyer personally presented to the Haitian Senate a set of laws designed to reorganize the agricultural economy of Haiti on the principle that work for the *campesinos* on plantations was obligatory, under threat of punishment.[40]

The Code Rural, as this body of laws was called, was designed to enable the Haitian economy to recover the levels of productivity achieved under Dessalines. These provisions, it was hoped, would among other things overcome the problems of the seasonal shortage of labor and the tendency of farmers to evade work and leave the plantation to till their own land. The code established that no one was exempt from working the land, with the exception of government servants and citizens in recognized professions. No proprietor could abandon the plot on which he lived and to which he would be attached from then onward, without previous authorization from the local justice of the peace or military chief of the area. Children of agricultural workers were not to attend school at the expense of abandoning their parents' plot without the permission of the authorities, and no worker could leave countryside to engage in commerce under any circumstances. Nor, according to the code, could any worker construct his own dwelling and leave the plantation (on which he was supposed to work for a salary) with his family. The latter regulation was made rigorous by a provision that forbade workers to spend more than eight days outside the plantation— even with the permission of the plantation owner. Once an agriculturist was employed by a plantation owner, he was obliged to serve him for a minimum of three years, before which time he could not leave without incurring serious penalties in the form of fines, imprisonment, or forced labor. Vagrancy was absolutely forbidden. In order to apply these measures and several others directed toward binding the agriculturist to plantation labor, the army would assign soldiers to each of the plantations to supervise the workers. The soldiers would be fed and maintained by the plantation owners. Further, women were obliged to work up to the fourth month of pregnancy and to return to work four months after childbirth. All these measures were to apply equally to the mulatto-owned plantations of the west and to the great proprietors of the east, whose support, or at least neutrality, Boyer wanted to ensure.[41]

The code was considered a masterpiece of Haitian legislation at the time. It anticipated possible difficulties and prescribed solutions for the successful execution of the decrees which aimed to reinstitute the plantation system of colonial times. The mulattoes and the Haitian government were anxious to see them put into immediate effect, without further debate. However, the code did not work for a variety of reasons. The principal reason for its failure was that rural Haitian workers simply ignored the provisions of the code and invariably refused to obey any suggestions that would restore the servile status of Christophe's and Dessalines' time. During these years a phenomenon had occurred of which Boyer and his elite seem to have lost sight: the appearance of an independent Haitian peasantry, owners of their small parcels, whose sole interest was a comfortable subsistence. There was a contradiction between the interests of this *minifundist* peasantry and those of the *grande culture*, since the development of the latter depended on the work of laborers bound to the plantations. Boyer and the government could do nothing effective to oblige the peasants to work, simply because the majority of the Haitian people were owners of small parcels of land and very few were inclined to be employed as peons on other people's land.[42]

On the plantations that had never ceased to have their permanent labor force in spite of the division of land, the code did not work because, as with the ranches of the east, the exploitation of the land had assumed forms that reduced the exclusive dependence of the worker on the planter. The predominant forms of exploitation were already the *aparcería* and the *medianería*. One-third, at least, of the Haitian population worked on lands belonging to others (in addition to their own properties), but in these cases the workers preferred to focus their attention on their own cultivation within the plantations (mainly foodstuffs) rather than on the export crops in which the planters were interested. Boyer and his collaborators, therefore, soon discovered that there was no way of forcing the peasants to work. The army, which in theory should have been entrusted (together with the justices of the peace of the communes) with applying the code, was not in a position to enforce it for two reasons. First, the majority of the soldiers and their families were small proprietors of rural origin, and they would not take action against their own families in order to favor an elite of large proprietors. The other reason is that in the year preceding the publication of the code, in July 1825, the Haitian government had reached an accord with France whereby the latter recognized the independence of Haiti. This agreement removed from the army the weight that had burdened it since the revolution, the expectation of a French invasion that would one day come to reduce them all once more to servitude. This agreement removed the enemy that had served as a pretext to maintain army discipline. The soldiers, relieved of the need to keep themselves in a state of preparedness for a war that was expected sooner or later, began very promptly to relax their military habits and to occupy themselves with their personal affairs, their small properties, their families, and their small interests, rather than with policing the countryside. The consequence was that when the Code Rural was promulgated, the military discipline that was to have been responsible for enforcing it was undergoing a process of decline, from which it did not emerge for a century. The irony of all this was that the code had been conceived as the instrument that would lift the exported production of Haiti in order to pay France the 150 million francs that the agreement established as an indemnity to the former planters and as a condition for the recognition of independence.[43]

The anti-Haitian prejudice that Boyer had noted when he arrived in Santo Domingo in 1822 continued in 1830, at least among an important segment of the population.[44] The several causes for the continuation of this prejudice were too firmly implanted in the Dominican mentality of the time to be uprooted in a few years. The control exercised by the Haitians over the Dominicans was sustained more by military power than by the voluntary submission of the majority of a population who never identified fully with the Haitians, whose language and customs were different. However good the intentions of the president might have been when he explained to his military commanders that "the interest of the Republic demands that the people of the Eastern side change as quickly as possible their habits and customs to adopt those of the Republic, so that the union may be perfect and that the former differences . . . disappear soon,"[45] it was certain that Haitian political economy and the legal organization of property ownership and agricultural labor had alienated the greater part of the Dominican population.

In theory, the French system that Boyer wished to impose seems more just and more modern, insofar as it guaranteed (in theory) a title to each proprietor and a property to each person. Under the Spanish system of communal lands, however, the population of Santo Domingo was not pressed by necessity to have legal titles to land, for the system allowed the population to occupy, exploit, and enjoy the usufruct of all the land they needed without causing hardship to any of the actual proprietors. This was what Boyer and Haitian bureaucrats never came to understand and what helped to keep alive the germ of opposition in the eastern part of the island. Besides all this, it was natural that in a region where ranching had been for centuries the predominant economic activity, a policy designed to promote the distribution of land for agriculture proved unpopular. A resolution of June 12, 1828, and the law of July 28, 1828, which authorized agriculturists to kill, without fear of reprisal, the animals of other people that damaged their cultivation,[46] not only intensified anxiety about Haitian agricultural policy but also "gave rise to continual quarrels between the agriculturists and the cattle producers, and even to frequent murder and homicide."[47] Also unpopular had been the limitation imposed in 1826 on the celebration of traditional religious fiestas because "in the various parishes of the eastern part of the Republic considerable time was lost and precious time for work missed because of the numerous fiestas."[48] That decree clearly ignored the character of the Dominican, who preferred to lie in his hammock or have a cockfight with his neighbors than to busy himself in plantation labors in accordance with the French model.[49] Therefore, the resolution of Boyer in February 1830 to close the cockpits once and for all, "cockfighting being no longer permitted in the countryside except on Sundays and festive days," proved equally unpopular.[50]

Boyer's interest was centered more on agriculture than on any other economic activity, since both he and the rest of the Haitian elite were convinced that in a country such as Haiti, without developed industries or commerce, only agriculture could provide a lasting foundation of wealth. The Code Rural faithfully reflected this philosophy; so too did the official resolutions and circulars to the various commanders of the departments of both sides of the island, whom he never ceased to urge to plant export crops and all kinds of foodstuffs.[51] Of course, the protection that Boyer gave to agriculture did not in any way imply that farmers were exempt from fiscal controls on the part of the state, as could be seen in the laws of May 3, 1826, and December 23, 1830, which established that the farmers should pay to the state five percent of the products that were not for export each year, exports already being taxed. The owners of pottery shops, the woodcutters, matchmakers, and owners of saltworks had to pay a similar tax.[52] Of all the farmers, the cultivators of tobacco of the Cibao Valley in the old Spanish part must have been the most protected. In April 1830 the government arranged to purchase all their undressed tobacco each year, "at a reasonable price."[53] According to García,"this arrangement was the source of great abuse on the part of Haitian employees, who being merchants for the most part, and if not they, their wives, took advantage of their position to fleece the farmers, and to offer the workers the lowest possible prices for the tobacco which they cultivated with so much effort."[54]

If what García says is true, it is difficult to see why in the following years many Dominicans still sincerely favored union with Haiti. In the south the restrictions and the control of the authorities and Haitian officials over the cutting and sale of mahogany continually hindered that occupation. Taxes and contributions were required, and in order to escape this multiple fiscal restriction, a number of Dominicans had no scruples about dedicating themselves to contraband. When the Haitian government realized that mahogany cutting was escaping their control, Boyer reversed his policy and abolished the prohibition on cutting mahogany that had been established after the unification of the island.[55] In 1830 he issued a series of orders to his commanders with the aim of facilitating the creation of a legal wood market on the island, so that the state could profit through the collection of taxes.[56]

ECONOMIC AND POLITICAL DIFFICULTIES

By 1830, discontent was general on both sides of the island. To the natural rivalries that had for decades marked the relationship between the ruling

Haitian elite and the mass of the black population was added a new problem, the noticeable devaluation of money, which intensified the general crisis.

Devaluation of money led to a fictitious increase in coffee prices (which the government used as an indicator of economic progress), but there was no doubt that "commercial affairs and the position of each person were affected by the result produced by the financial system since the creation of paper money," which had been emitted to help pay for the expenses occasioned by the Ordinance of 1825. The uncertainty that clearly affected the interests of the Haitian elite finally found expression in the Senate and the Chamber of Representatives of the republic, where some young lawyers, influenced by the liberal ideas of the France of Louis Philippe, wished to alter, by means of parliamentary debate, some of the procedures of government in use in Haiti since the foundation of the republic. Many of the political tensions of the years before 1832 were released, not without violence, in the debates in the Haitian Congress between the parliamentary leaders of the opposition and the defenders of the Boyer government. Among the defenders of the Boyer government were representatives from the east, who always made positive contributions to the debate. [57] As the situation did not improve, the struggles among the representatives increased in strength and violence. The government decided in August 1833 to expel from the Congress the two main leaders of the opposition, who had been "systematically opposing the measures of the executive, and persisting in their demand for the publication of the expenditure of the government." [58]

In April 1835, however, the deputies returned to the attack. They referred to the unfavorable economic situation and argued that the improvement in coffee cultivation had not been accompanied by similar improvements in other crops. Furthermore, commerce, the "second source of public prosperity, was losing advantages day by day," on account of the devaluation of money; the inequality between exports and imports, which produced an unfavorable trade balance; and the poverty of cities, whose commercial activity was steadily losing ground to small establishments in the towns and villages. [59] The criticism of the government was as extensive as circumstances would permit, and the deputies revealed that "the difficulties which occasionally paralyzed the progress of public administration came less from the imperfection of our laws than from the negligence of the functionaries entrusted with their implementation." The retort of the defenders of the government was that the merchants were responsible for the depreciation of money. They were accused of systematically introducing into the country counterfeit and debased money, which threatened to ruin the economy. In 1836 the opposition sensed a gradual increase of support from the merchants in their struggle against the government, because of the deplorable economic situation affecting the Haitian economic elite in the cities. This support was given additional stimulus around midyear when Boyer ordered the passage of a law that closed five ports of the west to foreign commerce, affecting important trading houses whose business depended on the import and export trade. "This measure," says Ardouin, "generated opposition against Boyer. The businessmen and speculators in merchandise and imported foodstuffs, the wholesalers and retailers, all who depended upon direct commerce overseas, were disgruntled upon seeing themselves obliged to resort to supplies from traders in other more important cities and towns," where the costs were certainly higher and the benefits fewer.

At the end of 1836 a group of military men in northern Haiti, believing the time ripe to mobilize the "peasant masses" to rebellion against Boyer, organized a conspiracy. Colonel Izidor, the leader of the conspiracy, had been an officer in Christophe's army and a large landowner since the era of Christophe. He was particularly hostile to the agrarian policies of Petión and Boyer. In October of that year, Boyer received news of the conspiracy but, far from acting immediately, proceeded to arrest the betrayer of the conspiracy, declaring that Izidor had been libeled. By January 1837, however, it was already clear that there was a military movement in the north. Izidor issued an anti-government proclamation, in which he spoke strongly about the decadence of the regional economy, which he attributed to the fragmentation of the plantation into small parcels given to soldiers and farmers, therby ruining the great plantations and *ingenios*. He took the opportunity to criticize the lack of discipline among the soldiers of the republic, who preferred to remain on their plots rather than do military service of any kind. With that proclamation, Izidor made his first and last error; the soldiers, peasants, *carabineros*, and cultivators understood by it that the aim of the rebel chiefs was to restore the system of compulsory labor as in Christophe's times. Despite the fact that Izidor, like the majority of the northern population, was black, the mere spread of this proclamation caused general alarm and immediately "there began the disintegration of the forces to whom Izidor had given arms." They left their rifles and ammunition everywhere, and the leaders in a short time found themselves completely alone and without popular support. As expected, Boyer and the loyal troops liquidated the movement without difficulty.

Boyer interpreted the lack of popular support for the Izidor movement as "manifest proof of the good sense of the people and of their dedication to good order and their attachment to the constitutional government." In reality what had caused failure was a lack of political tact among the military leaders of the conspiracy. Opposition to the government visibly increased daily. The reelection to Congress of the opposing deputies who had been expelled by the government from the chambers was a clear example of the intensification of opposition. These deputies attended the session of

1837, their energies fortified by additional reasons for criticism of the government. The leaders of the opposition, H. Dumesle and D. Saint-Preux, made their presence felt at the opening sessions in April. Their pressures and demands on the government to "improve" the situation in the country reached their climax in June, when the commision that had been set up to review the national accounts was able to expose the continued stagnation in agricultural production. More importantly, coffee production, the base of the economy, had dropped alarmingly over the previous three years, from forty-eight million pounds in 1835 to thirty-seven million in 1837, and the current crop would not be better. (In fact, production dropped to thirty-one million pounds because of the drought which affected the country for the entire year.) Saint-Preux, the president of the commission, blamed the government for the decline in production, pointing out "the disuse into which the rural code had fallen, the invasion of idleness and apathy which the climate favors, the lazy and negligent rural police, and the exploitation established at the customs." These facts produced impassioned discussion within the Chamber of Deputies, which after several vehement speeches resolved to send a message to the president of the republic to explain to him the country's commercial situation due to the 1835 law requiring payment of import duties in foreign money. In this message the deputies explained to Boyer the urgent necessity of abrogating this law.

This law had seriously jeopardized the growth of Haiti's foreign trade with the United States and Europe. The leaders of the opposition, who alone seemed to have a clear idea of the situation, persuaded the deputies to send a memorandum to Boyer. This memorandum demanded that Boyer work "to improve the monetary system of the country because the financial crisis in Europe and the United States was having a telling effect on the commerce and industry of Haiti, and was depriving the people of items of prime necessity, threatening our monetary system with a baneful collapse." The chamber recommended the publication of a "law which would suspend the payment of customs duties in foreign money." Such a law would aid the recovery of the country's commerce, since it would remove the obligation of merchants to pay part of their income to the state in foreign exchange. The merchants' practice of evading payment by introducing counterfeit or debased coin into the country, accentuating the problem of devaluation, would thereby be removed.

At the end of July 1837, shortly after receiving the message from the deputies, Boyer responded with a proclamation that left no doubt that the diagnosis of the opposition was correct in explaining the causes of the commercial crisis. The economic situation of Haiti during this year was crucial, because of its effects on the interests of the merchants of the eastern part, who suffered from the same problems as did their western counterparts. Boyer's proclamation said, in effect, that the problem afflicting Haitian commerce was a consequence "above all of the financial crisis which was being suffered in Europe and the United States." He continued:

> The complete unavailability of overseas credit has resulted in import restrictions and the scarcity of articles of prime necessity (foodstuffs imported from the United States) has caused prices to rise. Subsistence has therefore become very difficult for the people. . . . To all this must be added another factor which has contributed in no small way to the aggravation of our problems. An extended drought has, so to speak, simultaneously chastised several parts of the territory of the Republic and has snatched from the people their principal resources. The consequence is a general affliction from which no class of the society has been immune, but whose origin has been maliciously attributed to other causes. . . . Among other nations, the crisis has been born of the drunkenness of speculation. . . . Among us, it has been the result of a reaction; it is the counter-blow of the commotion which still rocks foreign countries with whom we are closely connected. Could the government impede this evil? Of course not. . . . [60]

In similar tone, Boyer continued his proclamation, attacking the opposition and accusing it of "only seeking a popularity dangerous to the society." He pointed out that his government had given undivided attention to agriculture, revealed by the frequent instructions that he had sent to the relevant authorities to direct and increase the planting of necessary foodstuffs for the subsistence of the people. As expected, Boyer did not accept the demands of the Chamber of Deputies, which he believed was dominated by the opposition. He chose, instead, to persuade the Senate one week later to reject the proposals of the deputies on the law regarding the payment of customs dues in foreign currency. According to Ardouin, who witnessed all these events, among the most important reasons for Boyer's refusal to revoke the law "was the urgent and ever present necessity of assuring for the treasury of the Republic the resources needed to pay the national debt." By his resistance to the demands of the deputies, many of whom represented commercial interests, Boyer increased the alienation that had been growing over the past few months on both sides of the island among the mercantile establishment. These frustrations assumed additional force in the following year, in May 1838, when a group of soldiers opposed to the government tried to assassinate the president and his secretary-general, Minister Inginac, who was second in line only to Boyer.[61]

In the eastern half of the island meanwhile, other pretexts for new conspiracies were not difficult to find. During the previous sixteen years, too many events had proven to be contrary to the Dominican spirit and interest. Those events, possibly stimulated by the chain of conspiracies and revolts in the western half of the island, and fed by the commercial crisis of the previous two years, activated a group of young men in Santo Domingo, some of them merchants or sons of merchants, who met on July 16, 1838, to form a secret society pledged to organizing the Dominican resistance and to separating the eastern part of the island from Haiti. *La Trinitaria* (the name of the society) was led by the merchant Juan Pablo Duarte y Diez. It succeeded in attracting the majority of the youth of the city of Santo Domingo, whose families had been adversely affected in one way or another by the various legal or military measures of the Haitian government. [62]

REACTIONS TO LAND LEGISLATION

As we have seen, Boyer made a determined effort to force the proprietors of Santo Domingo to submit their titles to the authorities to facilitate the delimitation of the boundaries of their lands in accordance with the law of July 8, 1824, and the legal decisions that completed that law. However, they set up a strong and continous resistance, filtering their protest through prominent Dominicans attached to the Haitian government.[63] With these tactics, Boyer found it possible to incorporate into state property only what had belonged to the church and what had been confiscated from Dominican exiles who had not wished to return.

The greatest complaints about confiscation of land were raised by the families of the exiles who could not meet the demands of the government, since they did not have titles in their possession but considered themselves, in accordance with Dominican tradition, the legitimate owners of those lands.[64] Even after the separation from Haiti in 1844, expositions pleaded for the restoration of the lands that had belonged to these former owners and to the church.[65] Those proposals were immediately resisted by those Dominicans who had been high functionaries of the Haitian bureaucracy during the domination or who had benefited from the sale of national property and acquired lands and houses formerly belonging to the church or to the exiles by virtue of the laws of May 7, 1829, and July 8, 1824, which had put up for sale the state properties not reserved for public use.[66]

Until 1834, the Haitian government had not been able to persuade the great landowners to claim their titles, in spite of the insistent demands of President Boyer and other Haitian authorities.[67] Therefore, on April 7 of that year, Boyer dictated a circular setting a new date for the Dominican landowners and proprietors to attend public offices "to verify their titles." The whole text of that circular sums up the rationale behind Boyer's land policy, as defined by the law of July 8, 1824, and provides a recognition of the government's failure to enforce it, despite the fact that it had been promulgated ten years earlier. The new deadline imposed by Boyer was December 31, 1834, after which "all the rights will be lost" by those who failed to verify their land titles with the official commissions appointed for that purpose.[68] This circular was seen by the Dominicans as an ultimatum that threatened to extinguish once and for all their property rights with the ultimate purpose of abolishing the traditional system of the *terrenos comuneros*.[69] The large landowners of Santo Domingo became increasingly alarmed and immediately appealed to the authorities entrusted with its execution. Boyer wanted, above everything else, to avoid frictions. As expected, even before the new term had expired, he published another proclamation recognizing that there were real impediments to compliance with the law, especially since there were not enough surveyors in the country to undertake the enormous task of measuring all the private lands in order to assign to each proprietor a legal deed corresponding to a single plot of land.[70] That could not be done in six months, nor even in six years; while Boyer finally realized that, he kept insisting on the transformation of the land tenure system of Santo Domingo, declaring the need to realize a national land survey or cadastral evaluation, and forbidding the sales of rural properties in both parts of the island until the cadastral works were finished.[71]

Things remained unchanged in regard to the land question for the next several years, much to the disappointment of Boyer, who had planned to use the law of July 8, 1824, to increase the national patrimony by making as much land as possible part of the public domain.[72] As the land policy failed, Boyer's fiscal objectives in the east had to be accomplished by attempting to increase the state's share of the mahogany trade on which the Dominicans had been concentrating in recent years.[73] But in March 1838 Boyer went back again to his former position and decided to press for the enforcement of the law of July 8, 1824, issuing a new proclamation intended to force the proprietors to verify their titles and to let the authorities split the properties among the actual co-owners of the eastern lands held under the system of the *terrenos comuneros*. The deadline was fixed as July 1, 1838, but again the Dominican landowners resisted.[74]

What then occurred is known thanks to Tomás de Bobadilla, who was at that time a public attorney. He left a note about the incident in his *Hoja de Servicios*, written in 1867,[75] which was afterward certified in declarations written by Antonio Abad Alfau and Manuel Joaquín Delmonte, witnesses to the events.[76] Bobadilla says that the merchants and owners of rural property in Santo Domingo held a meeting in which he, along with Manuel Joaquín Delmonte, was elected to determine and defend the property and dominion that they and their ancestors had been entitled to,

and taking a very personal interest in the need for me to be the source of strong representation to assure that these rights reach the ear of the Haitian government, and in consideration of the state of affliction of my compatriots who had made the petition, I set out on a distance of over 100 leagues, with full powers accorded to me by the inhabitants of the Seybo, Baní, Azua, and Neyba to represent them. The result which I obtained was so favorable, that the execution of the law was suspended together with other expropriation measures, thus assuring respect for possession and the sacred right of property of the inhabitants of the former Spanish part of the island, which was without defense or protection, suffering the sad effects of abandonment and of a foreign domination.[77]

This tardy trimuph on the part of the Dominican proprietors brought relief only to those who feared the loss of a part of their lands that were to be surveyed, but offered satisfaction neither to the exiles nor to those who enjoyed the usufruct of their lands. There was no relief either for those who enjoyed the usufruct of Church lands. José María Bobadilla, brother of Tomás de Bobadilla, declared in a booklet written in 1845 that during those years

the lands of the Church were ruined, as well as the lands of those Dominicans who were away for several years, including those who migrated in the years of 1821 and 1822, to avoid the lash of western vandalism. The homes and haciendas of these people were granted as gifts to Haitians, or were sold to them, at very low prices; which when carefully considered were more derisory shams than agreements and covenants founded in reason. Houses valued at four, six, eight, ten, and twelve thousand pesos were sold for two or three hundred pesos in the money of the province; the result being that the Haitians took complete command, protected by the shadow of legitimate titles, to houses, goods, and properties, whether from the Church or from those unfortunate Dominicans who wandered aimlessly in search of asylum which would put them out of reach of Haitian oppression.[78]

There is evidence coming from the Haitian side that what J.M. Bobadilla wrote was true. As early as 1826 Boyer recognized that there had been "deterioration, loses or depreciation on the rural properties of the eastern part."[79] As late as 1843 Boyer's successor, General Charles Héard, while making a military tour on the eastern part to suppress a widespread conspiracy, found that in three towns of the eastern part of the island, at least, the Haitian administrators had taken advantage of their power and positions in order to dispossess many proprietors from their lands and houses. In his report about his tour, Hérard says that he took special care in removing those Haitian officers from their posts, and returned the properties to their traditional legitimate owners.[80]

CONCLUSIONS

But is was too late. Conspiracy had been ignited by the secret society *La Trinitaria*, which had been operating in the eastern part since 1838. It was partially, and temporarily, suppressed by Hérard. But the political uneasiness did not disappear, for the roots of Dominican dissatisfaction with the

Haitian regime went deeper than the single issue of land tenure in Santo Domingo. For about two centuries, two different societies had been developing independently in both parts of the island under very different ecological and economic conditions.[81] In the early nineteenth century it was already evident that two different nations coexisted, one beside the other, with their differences based not only on dissimilar economic systems but also on racial, cultural, and legal dissimilarities. That was evident to Boyer and to his aide, General Bonnet, who in 1830 pointed out that the Dominicans and the Haitians were as different from each other as the Flemish and the Wallons.[82] But Boyer persisted, and finally failed, not only because the Dominicans were opposed to his agrarian policies but because his own countrymen were also opposed to them. By this time, the Haitians had developed into a black peasantry much more interested in cultivating their own plots than in serving as salaried workers for the plantation owners. The ruin of the Haitian economy was already evident in 1826, when Charles Mackenzie was appointed counsul of Great Britian to Haiti. His classic book on the economic and social conditions of Haiti illustrated with statistics the decline of Haitian agricultural exports, related to the development of the peasantry who abandoned the planting of cane, indigo, and cotton.[83] That ruin brought political instability to Haiti as the mulatto planters and the merchant class were hurt by the devaluation of the currency, triggered by the printing of debased paper money, and by the falling of export prices during the economic crisis that hit the United States in 1837 and 1838. Instability grew as Boyer's regime proved incapable of tolerating political dissension within the Chamber of Deputies, alienating those mulattoes who exerted leadership in the south of Haiti. By expelling them from the Congress, Boyer left them with the only road open to gain access to power: a military plot. Boyer was overthrown by his own class in March 1843, at a moment when the Dominicans were already organized and ready to fill the political vacuum that ensured the fall of the regime.[84]

Thus Boyer's successor, General Hérard, wanted to please the Dominicans by restitution of the stolen lands. He did not want to see the country divided in the middle of a revolution that released most of Haiti's social and economic energies into the political arena. Once he realized how unpopular and unsuccessful were Boyer's measures among the Dominican population, Hérard finally abolished all the laws, circulars, and decrees that had piled up as a consequence of the famous law of July 8, 1824.[85] He also abolished other dispositions that had offended Dominicans for years, like that forbidding them to write public and legal documents in French. All these measures were promulgated in the very last days of December 1843, but it was too late.[86] On January 16, 1844, the Dominican leaders of *La Trinitaria* issued their Declaration of Independence, calling the rest of the population to support their movement in order to separate Santo Domingo from Haiti. One month and a half later, on February 27, 1844, the Dominicans staged a coup d'etat and expelled the Haitians from their territory. The *terrenos comuneros* continued intact as the main land tenure system of the Dominican Republic until well into the twentieth century, when the enormous changes brought about by the massive introduction of new foreign technology and capital into the sugar industry made the communal land system obsolete and dysfunctional. What Boyer could not accomplish by legal means was finally achieved by foreign capitalists who, in order to invest in the sugar industry, demanded clear and definite proof of their proprietorship on the land. In this respect, according to Boyer's own words in the law of July 8, 1824, he intended to "wipe out all traces of feudalism" from the old Spanish colony. But it was not until capitalism made its full entrance into the Dominican Republic, with the modernization of the sugar industry in the late nineteenth century, that the "feudal" remnants of the colonial land tenure system finally disappeared. But that is another story, beyond the scope of this paper.

NOTES

1. See Robert K. Lacerte, "The Evolution of Land and Labor in the Haitian Revolution, 1791–1820," *The Americas* 34, (1978): 449–54.
2. See James C. Leyburn, *The Haitian People* (New Haven: Yale University Press, 1966), pp. 32–42.
3. Leyburn, *The Haitian People*, pp.42–51. See also James Franklyn, *The Present State of Hayti (Santo Domingo) with Remarks on Its Agriculture, Commerce, Laws, Religion, Finances and Population, etc., etc.* (London, 1828), pp 118–22, 189–90.
4. Leyburn, *The Haitian People*, p. 54, n. 21, quoting Saint-Rémy, *Pétion et Haiti* (Paris, 1854–57).
5. Ibid., pp. 51–64.
6. Both Leyburn (*The Haitian People*, pp. 32–64) and Franklyn (*The Present State*, pp. 317–67) summarize the process. Both authors offer insights on the effects of land policies on the Haitian economy and society from the times of Toussaint to the death of Petión in 1818.
7. See "Communicación de Sebastián de Kindelán al Escmo. Secretario de Estado y del Despacho de la Gobernación de Ultramar," May 17, 1821. Secretaria de Estado de Relaciones Exteriores, República Dominicana, *Documentos Históricos Procedentes del Archivo de Indias* (Santo Domingo, 1928), vol 3, n.p.
8. Documents related to these two aborted attempts can be found in Antonio del Monte y Tejada, *Historia de Santo Domingo* (Ciudad Trujillo, 1953), vol. 3, pp. 282–300.
9. Kindelán's letter (see n. 7) refers to these rumors as circulating in Santo Domingo in 1820. On the preparations for the French invasion and the European intrigues, see Emiliano Jos, *Un Capítulo Inacabado de Historia de la Isla Española de 1819-20* (Seville, 1952), which contains information on some of the French adventurers.

10. See Guy-Joseph Bonnet, *Souvenirs Historiques* (Paris, 1864), pp. 313–324. Bonnet was Boyer's most trusted general and the commander of the Haitian troops that approached Santo Domingo in 1822. In a letter to Boyer early that year, he highlighted the importance of Haiti's possession of "natural frontiers." See also Emilio Rodríquez Demorizi, *Invasiones Haitianas de 1801, 1805 y 1822* (Ciudad Trujillo, 1955), pp. 273–82.

11. Emilio Rodríguez Demorizi, *Santo Domingo y la Gran Colombia Bolívar y Nuñez de Cáceres* (Santo Domingo, 1971), pp. 3–29.

12. Gustavo Adolfo Mejía, *El Estado Independiente del Haití Español* (Santiago, 1938), documents the process of the emancipation of Santo Domingo from Spain.

13. See Frank Moya Pons, "La Invasión de Boyer," *Renovación* 193 (February 15, 1972): 3–7.

14. Frank Moya Pons, *Historia Colonial de Santo Domingo* (Santiago, 1973), ch. 15.

15. Jean Pierre Boyer, "Proclamation, en français et en espagnol, au peuple à l'occasion de la réunion de l'Est à la République," Santo Domingo, February 9, 1822, in A. Linstant-Pradine, ed., *Recueil Général des Lois et Actes du Gouvernement d'Haiti* (Paris, 1860–88), 3:442. See also Charles Mackenzie, *Notes on Hayti, Made During a Residence in That Republic* (London, 1830), 2:241–44.

16. Boyer, "Circulaire, en forme d'instruction, du Président d'Haití, aux colonel Frémont, à Azua; Hogu, à Bani; Prézeau, à Seibe; et aux commandants Isnardy, à Saint-Jean; Saladin, à Lamate, sur les devoirs de leurs charges," Santo Domingo, February 11, 1822. *Recueil des Lois*, 3: 448–456. See also Jean Price Mars, *La República Dominicana y la Rupúlica de Haití* (Puerto Príncipe, 1953), 1:198–200, and José Gabriel García, *Compendio de la Historia de Santo Domingo* (Santo Domingo, 1968), 2:93–94, for comments on this circular. García is an important source. He was born in the 1820s, during the Haitian occupation of Santo Domingo.

17. On the origins and legal evolution of the *terrenos comuneros*, see José María Ots Capdequi, *El Régimen de la Tierra en la America Española* (Ciudad Trujillo, 1946), pp. 74 ff; Alcibíades Alburquerque, *Títulos de los Terrenos Comuneros de la República Dominicana* (Ciudad Trujillo, 1961), pp. 12–32; and Manuel Ramón Ruiz Tejada, *Estudio de la Propiedad Inmobiliaria en la República Dominicana* (Ciudad Trujillo, 1952). On the history of the *terrenos comuneros*, Samuel Hazard, *Santo Domingo, Past and Present, with a Glance to Hayti* (New York, 1873), pp. 481–84, gives an excellent account.

18. For a description of the functional relations between the economies of the French and the Spanish colonies of Santo Domingo during the eighteenth century, see Frank Moya Pons, *Historia Colonial de Santo Domingo*, ch. 12–15. A firsthand description of the *terrenos comuneros* and the social implications of that system was collected by a commission of American senators visiting the island in 1871. Their report has been published as the *Informe de la Comisión de los Estados Unidos en Santo Domingo* (Ciudad Trujillo, 1960), pp. 343–44. Another important commentary on the evolution and social implications of the *terrenos comuneros* is Pedro Francisco Bonó, "Cuestiones Sociales y Agrícolas," in Emilio Rodríguez Demorizi, ed., *Papeles de Bonó* (Santo Domingo, 1964), pp. 265–66,

and Bonó, "Apuntes Sobre las Clases Trabajadoras Dominicanas," *Papeles*, p. 496.

19. Boyer, "Proclamation, en français et en espagnol, renfermant certaines dispositions en faveur des habitants de la partie de l'Est de la Republique," Port-au-Prince, June 15, 1822. *Recueil de Lois*, 3:471–75.

20. Emilio Rodríguez Demorizi, "Actos del Gobierno Haitiano, 1821–1843," *Invasiones Haitianas*, pp. 306–07. See also Boyer's proclamation cited in n. 19.

21. See "Copia de la Memoria Presentada por D. Francisco Brenes sobre la Situación Politica de la Ysla de Sto. Domingo," Puerto Rico, September 16, 1822. *Documentos Históricos Procedentes del Archivo de Indias*, 2:75–76.

22. García, *Compendio*, 2:98–99. The official act of the appointment of the commission was not published by Linstant-Pradine. Apparently it was lost before 1864. García must have seen a copy in Santo Domingo when he wrote the *Compendio*.

23. This refers to the Dominicans who tried to help the French vessels that arrived at Samana Bay in February 1822, too late to disembark their troops.

24. García, *Compendio*, 2:99-100. The *capellanías* were special mortgage contracts established between the church and certain individuals who committed their properties for life and afterward to provide funds to specific parishes and priests, who, under the contract, agreed to perform perpetual religious services and funerals in favor of the souls of the owner, his relatives, and his descendents. In Hispaniola, the *capellanías* were very common during the colonial period, and with time became one of the main ways for the acquisition of enormous tracts of land on the part of the church. As a result, when the Haitians invaded Santo Domingo, the archbishop was already in possession of much of the best land for, as time passed, many *cappellanías* had been extinguished and it was provided that in that case the land would pass into the hand of the archbishop. See, for example, the "Fragmento Documental de un Expediente General Tocante a las Rentas, Diezmos y Obvenciones que Percibían los Curas Párrocos de la Isla Española, Cerrado en Santo Domingo el 2 de noviembre de 1784, Archivo General de Indias, Santo Domingo 988," published as "La Parroquia de Higuey," *Clío* 114 (January-April 1953): 56–65. On the institution of *capellanías* in America, see José María Ots Capdequi, *Manual de Hisotria de Derecho Español en Indias* (Buenos Aires, 1945), pp. 125–26.

25. Beaubrun Ardouin, *Etudes sur l'Histoire d'Haiti* (Paris, 1860) 9:147–48.

26. Boyer, "Arreté portant la creation d'une commission charge de statuer sur les reclamations des habitants de l'Est dont les biens sont sous la main-mise de l'Etat," *Recueil des Lois*, 3:547–75.

27. See J. Marino Incháustegui, *Documentos para Estudio. Marco de la Epoca y Problemas del Tratado de Basilea en la Parte Española de Santo Domingo* (Buenos Aires, 1957), 1 and 2.

28. Hazard, *Santo Domingo, Past and Present*, pp. 481–84..

29. Boyer, "Proclamation qui accorde un nouveau delai aux emigres de l'Est pour y rentrer et jouir de leur biens," Port-au-Prince, February 8, 1823. *Recueil de Lois*, 3:577–78.

30. See note 65.

31. García *Compendio*, 2:106–08.

32. See Boyer, "Circulaire du même (Boyer aux mêmes commandantes) qui designent les individus, propres a etre oncorpores dans la gendarmerie," Port-au-Prince, December 3, 1823, *Recueil des Lois*, 3:693. See also Rodríguez, *Invasiones Haitianas*, p. 310, who comments on the effects of that circular on the closing of the university.

33. See "Sentencias Penales de la Epoca de la Dominación Haitiana," *Boletín del Archivo General de la Nación* 79 (October-December 1953): 329-53; 80 (January-March 1954): 24-26; 81 (April-June 1954): 219-23; 82 (July-September 1954): 400-08; 84 (January-March 1955): 66-79; 85 (April-June 1955): 157-65; 86 (July-September 1955): 275-92; 87 (October-December 1955): 388-99.

34. "Loi qui détermine quels sont les biens mobiliers et immobiliers, situés dans la partie de l'Est, qui reviennent à l'égard des particuliers de cette partie, le droit de propriété territoriale, conformément au mode établi dans les autres parties de la République, et qui fixe les appointements du haut clergé du chapitre métropolitain de la cathédrale de Santo Domingo, et assure le sort des religieuses dont les convents ont été supprimés," Port-au-Prince, July 8, 1824, *Recueil des Lois*, 4:45-50. The quotation in this and the next paragraphs all come from this law.

35. See Carlos Nouel, *Historia Eclesiástica de Santo Domingo* (Santo Domingo, 1914), 2:257ff.

36. See the "Avis de 24 Avril 1825, de la Secrétairerie générale interdissant la coupe d'acajou dans la partie de l'Est," *Recueil des Lois*, 4.

37. See the "Avis du même (la Secrétairerie d'Etat) concernant le renouvellement des contrats pour la coupe des bois d'acajou dans la partie de l'Est," Port-au-Prince, January 11, 1835, *Recueil des Lois*, 6: 125.

38. García, *Compendio*, 2:113-14.

39. Bonnet, *Souvenirs Historiques*, pp. 323-24.

40. "Code Rural d'Haiti," Port-au-Prince, May 1, 1826, *Recueil des Lois*, 4:113-30. See also the "Code Rural," *Les Six Codes d'Haiti*, suivis d'une table raisonnée des matières (Port-au-Prince, 1828), pp. 661-96.

41. See the sources cited in note 40.

42. See Ardouin, *Etudes sur l'Histoire d'Haiti*, 10:6-8 and 15-29, for a discussion of the implications of the code and for its failure in both the western and the eastern parts of the island.

43. See Ardouin, *Etudes sur l'Histoire d'Haiti*, 10-11, for a detailed discussion of the history of the agreement with France and the impact of the agreement in weakening discipline in the army. See also Jean Baptiste Wallez, *Précis Historique des Negotiations entre la France et Saint Domingue suivi des Pièces Justificatives* (Paris, 1826).

44. See Bonnet, *Souvenirs Historiques*, pp. 313-24.

45. Boyer, "Proclamation, en français et en espagnol, au peuple à l'occasion de la réunion de l'Est à la République," Santo Domingo, February 9, 1822, *Recueil des Lois*, 3:452.

46. See the "Circular du même (President Boyer) aux commandants de l'arrondissements, concernant les bestiaux trouvés dans les champs cultivés," Port-au-Prince, June 12, 1828, and "Circulaire du Grand Juge provisoire, aux commissaires du gouvernement pres les tribunaux de la République, qui

permet d'abatre les bêtes à cornes trouvées dans les champs cultivés," Port-au-Prince, June 17, 1828, *Recueil des Lois*, 5:165–67, and "Loi sur les bêtes à cornes trouvées dans les champs cultivés," Port-au-Prince, August 29, 1828, *Recueil des Lois*, 5:219.

47. See García, *Compendio*. 2:132–33.
48. "Circular de Grand Juge, aux commissaires du gouvernement de Saint-Yague et de Santo Domingo concernant les fêtes à chomer," Port-au-Prince, August 24, 1826, *Recueil des Lois*, 4:497.
49. See Bonnet, *Souvenirs Historiques*, pp. 323-24.
50. Boyer, "Circulaire du Président d'Haiti, aux commandants des arrondissements de l'Est, concernant les fermes des Gayères," Port-au-Prince, February 17, 1830, and "Circulaire du Secrétairerie de l'Etat aux conseils de notables de la partie de l'Est, concernant le même objet," February 17, 1830, *Recueil des Lois*, 5:330–31.
51. See the numerous reports submitted by the commanders of the districts in the years 1839 and 1840, which account for the results of the application of the Code Rural on their dependencies, in response to Boyer's instructions for promoting the development of export crops, *Recueil des Lois*, 7:139–54, for the year 1839, and 6: 1–61, for 1840. The supplement for 1839 should have been published in volume 6 of the *Recueil* but is was not and, oddly, was incorporated as a first part of volume 7.
52. "Loi portant amendement à la loi du 3 mai 1826, qui impose un droit sur les valeurs locatives et produits des bein fonciers," Port-au-Prince, December 23, 1830. *Recueil des Lois*, 5:371-72.
53. Boyer, "Circulaire du même, aux commandants des arrondissements de l'Est, concernant les achats de tabac pour le compte de l'Etat," Port-au-Prince, April 5, 1830, *Recueil des Lois*, 5:335.
54. García, *Compendio*, 2:146.
55. Boyer, "Circulaire du Président d'Haiti, aux commandants des arrondissements, concernant les coupes de bois," Port-au-Prince, August 7, 1824, *Recueil des Lois*, 4:53.
56. See the "Avis officiel concernant la liberté d'aller sur les côtes chargés des bois d'acajou," Port-au-Prince, September 14, 1828, and the "Loi qui porte un augmentation sur l'imposition territoriale des bois d'acajou et d'espinille," September 15, 1828, Port-au-Prince, *Recueil des Lois*, 5: 234. In the following months, Boyer proceeded to regulate the cutting and trade of mahogany as can be seen in the following acts: "Circulaire du Président d'Haiti, aux commandants des arrondissements de Saint-Jean, de la Marmélade et du Mirébalais, défendant les coupes d'acajou sur les propriétés de l'Etat," December 24, 1828; "Circulaire du même aux Généraux Borgella, Jacques Simon, Beauvour, et au Colonel Bellegarde, relative à la prorogation de la permission accordée aux bâtiments étrangers d'aller sur les côtes charger les acajous," December 29, 1828; and "Circulaire du Secrétaire d'Etat, aux administrateurs des arrondissements de Santo-Domingo, Porte-Plate, Jérémie et Gonaives, qui autorise les bâtiments etrangers d'aller sur les côtes charger les bois d'acajou," January 5, 1829, *Recueil des Lois*, 5:271-74. Another administrative regulation came in early 1830, with the "Circulaire du Secrétaire d'Etat, aux administrateurs d'arrondissements, concernant le

mesurage des bois d'acajou destinés à l'exportation," February 12, 1830, *Recueil des Lois*, 5:329.

57. Ardouin, *Etudes sur l'Histoire d'Haiti*, 10: 168.

58. Jonathan Brown, *The History and Present Condition of St. Domingo* (Philadelphia, 1837), 2:260.

59. The discussion and quotations in this, and the next several paragraphs, are drawn from Ardouin, *Etudes sur l'Histoire d'Haiti*, 10:264–304.

60. Boyer, "Proclamation relative à la crise financière en Europe et aux Etats-Unis d'Amérique," Port-au-Prince, July 20, 1837, *Recueil des Lois*, 6:355–56.

61. See the "Proclamation à l'occasion de l'attentat contre la vie du général B. Inginac," Port-au-Prince, May 8, 1838, and the "Rapport fait au Sénat par la députation envoyée au Président d'Haiti, à l'occasion de l'attentat contre la vie du général B. Inginac," Port-au-Prince, May 21, 1838, *Recueil des Lois*, 6:380–82. Ardouin, *Etudes sur l'Histoire d'Haiti*, 11:303, gives firsthand details about the attempt against Inginac.

62. José María Serra, "Apuntes para la Historia de los Trinitarios, Fundadores de la República Dominicana," *Boletín del Archivo General de la Nación*, 32–33 (January-April 1944), 49–69, written by one of the two founders of this secret society, is the classic account of how the Dominicans finally managed to organize themselves to struggle politically to win their independence from the Haitians.

63. Ardouin, *Etudes sur l'Histoire d'Haiti*, 10: 59–60, gives an account of the manner in which the Dominicans brought their complaints to President Boyer, with the intention of annulling the law of July 8, 1824.

64. See, for example, the "Exposición hecha por los habitantes de la Parte Española de Santo Domingo al Gobierno Francés, solicitando la protección de Francia per convertirse en República Independiente. Ofrecen como compensación el abandono de la península de Samana," Port Républican, December 15, 1843. Gobierno Dominicano, ed., *Correspondencia de Levasseur y otros Agentes de Francia Relativa a la Proclamación de la República Dominicana 1843-1844* (Ciudad Trujillo, 1944), p. 253.

65. See José María Bobadilla, *Opinión Sobre el Derecho de las Iglesias y Dominicanos Emigrados, en los Bienes de que Fueron Despojados por el Gobierno Haitiano Durante su Ocupación en la Parte del Este de la Isla de Santo Domingo* (Santo Domingo, 1845), published under the pseudonym "Un Dominicano."

66. See, for example, Manuel María Valencia, *Homenaje a la Razón* (Santo Domingo, 1845), published under the pseudonym "Un Aprendiz."

67. The list of laws and circulars that followed that of July 8, 1824, is a long one: "Loi additionelle à la loi de 8 juillet 1824," Port-au-Prince, May 12, 1826, *Recueil des Lois*, 4:475–76; "Loi qui affranchit les propriétés urbaines de la partie de l'Est de certaines rédevances établies par les anciens usages, et additionelle aux lois des 8 juillet 1824 et 12 mai 1826," Port-au-Prince, May 15, 1827, *Recueil des Lois*, 5:44–46; "Circulaire du Président d'Haiti, aux commandants des arrondissements de la partie de l'Est, relative à ceux qui occupent sans titres les terres de l'Etat," Port-au-Prince, May 17, 1827, *Recueil des Lois*, 5:47–48; "Avis de la Secrétairerie de l'Etat concernant un nouveau délai accordé à ceux qui occupent sous (sic) titres les biens de l'Etat, pour faire

régulariser leur position," Port-au-Prince, April 19, 1834, *Recueil des Lois*, 6:8–9; "Circulaire de Président d'Haiti, aux commandants des arrondissements de la partie de l'Est, donnant aux habitants de cette partie un nouveau délai pour faire vérifier leur titres sur certaines terres," Port-au-Prince, April 7, 1834, *Recueil des Lois*, 6:5; "Proclamation au habitants de la Partie de l'Est, pour la continuation de la vérification des titres de propriété," Port-au-Prince, August 11, 1834, *Recueil des Lois* 6:111–12; "Avis de la Secrétairerie d'Etat, pour la suspension de toute aliénation de biens ruraux," Port-au-Prince, September 27, 1824, *Recueil des Lois*, 6:112; "Arrêté concernant la confection du cadastre des beines ruraux," Port-au-Prince, January 16, 1835, *Recueil des Lois*, 6:130; "Arrêté qui accorde aux personnes occupant sans titre les biens de l'Etat, un délai pour régulariser leur possession," Port-au-Prince January 26, 1835. *Recueil des Lois*, 6:131–32; "Circulaire du même (Boyer), aux Généraux Guerrier, Gardel et Riché, sur le nouveau délai accordé à ceux qui ont des droits ou actions de terre dans la partie de l'Est, pour faire valour leurs titres," Port-au-Prince, March 26, 1838, *Recueil des Lois*, 6:379–80. More than anything else, these and many other related measures taken by the Haitian government regarding the problem of the land in the eastern part of the island show the inability of Boyer to work out a way to break the resistance of the Dominican landowners and liquidate the system of *terrenos comuneros*.

68. Boyer, "Circulaire du Président d'Haiti, aux commandants des arrondissements de la partie de l'Est, donnant aux habitants de cette partie un nouveau délai pour faire vérifier leur titres sur certaines terres," Port-au-Prince, April 7, 1834, *Recueil des Lois*, 6:5. See also the "Avis de la Secrétairerie d'Etat, concernant un nouveau délai accordé à ceux qui occupent sous (sic) titres les biens de l'Etat, pour faire régulariser leur position," Port-au-Prince, April 19, 1834, *Recueil des Lois*, 6:8–9

69. See the "Esposición Hecha por los Habitantes de la Parte Española de la Isla de Santo Domingo al Gobierno Francés," *Correspondencia de Levasseur*, pp. 253–54.

70. Boyer, "Proclamation aux habitants de la Partie de l'Est, pour la continuation de la vérification des titres de propriété," Port-au-Prince, August 11, 1834, *Recueil des Lois*, 6:111–12.

71. "Avis de la Secrétairerie d'Etat, pour la suspension de toute aliénation de biens ruraux," Port-au-Prince, September 27, 1834, *Recueil des Lois*, 6:112, and "Arrêté concernant la confection du cadastre des biens ruraux," Port-au-Prince, January 16, 1835, *Recueil des Lois*, 6:130–31.

72. See Ardouin, *Etudes sur l'Histoire d'Haiti*, 10: 247. See also the "Avis de la Secrétairerie d'Etat, qui continue la suspension de la vente des domaines nationaux," Port-au-Prince, February 25, 1838, *Recueil des Lois*, 6:377–78.

73. See "Avis du même (la Secrétairerie d'Etat), concernant le renouvellement des contrats pour la coupe des bois d'acajou dans la partie de l'Est," Port-au-Prince, January 11, 1835, *Recueil des Lois*, 6:125.

74. Boyer, "Circulaire du même, au Généraux Guerrier, Gardel et Riché, sur le nouveau délai accordé à ceux qui ont des droits ou actions de terre dans la partie de l'Est, pour faire valoir leurs titres," Port-au-Prince March 26, 1838, *Recueil des Lois*, 6:379-80.

75. "Real Audiencia de Santo Domingo, Hoja de Servicios del Magistrado Don Tomás de Bobadilla," *Clío* 78 (September-December 1950): 98.

76. See the "Certificación dada a Bodadilla por don Antionio Abad Alfau," and the "Otras certificaciones confirmativas de la anterior, dadas a Bobadilla por los Señores Manuel Joaquín Delmonte y Domingo de la Rocha," *Boletín del Achivo General de la Nación* 68 (January-March 1951): 183–85.

77. "Hoja de Servicios del Magistrado Don Tomás de Bobadilla," cited in note 75.

78. José María Bobadilla, *Opinión Sobre el Derecho de las Iglesias y Dominicanos Emigrados*, p. 4.

79. See the "Loi additionelle à la loi du 8 juillet 1824," Port-au-Prince, May 12, 1826, *Recueil des Lois*, 4:475.

80. "Rapport du Général de division, Charles Hérard aîné, represéntant du gouvernement provisoire, et commandant en chef de l'armée expéditionaire en mouvement dans les parties du nord et de l'est de la République," 1843, *Recueil des Lois*, 7:312, 314, 317.

81. See Moya Pons, *Historia Colonial de Santo Domingo*, ch. 9–17.

82. See Bonnet, *Souvenirs Historiques*, p. 324.

83. See Charles Mackenzie, *Notes on Haiti Made During a Residence in That Republic*, (London, 1830), 2:133–97 and 298–303.

84. See Frank Moya Pons, "La Caída de Boyer: Conspiración y Reforma," *La Dominación Haitiana* (Santiago, 1973), pp. 111-44.

85. Hérard, "Décrit qui abroge différentes lois relatives aux droit de propriété dans la partie de l'Est," Port-Républican, December 27, 1843, *Recueil des Lois*, 7:133-37.

86. "Décret qui autorise les fonctionnaires de la partie de l'Est à rédiger leurs actes soit en espagnol, soit en français," Port-Républican, December 26, 1843, *Recueil des Lois*, 7:131-33, and the "Circulaire du Président d'Haiti, aux commandants des arrondissements de l'Est, portant défense d'écrire à l'avenir, en espagnol, les actes publics," Port-au-Prince, November 14, 1824, *Recueil des Lois*, 4:126, which was abolished. See also the final concession to the Dominican landowners on the wood trade question: "Décret qui permet l'exporation des bois de construction dans la partie de l'Est de la République," Port-Républican, December 28, 1843, *Recueil des Lois*, 7:137.

10. The Formation of the Dominican Sugar Industry: From Competition to Monopoly, from National Semiproletariat to Foreign Proletariat

José del Castillo

The final decades of the nineteenth century saw a considerable increase in international commerce. The centers of industrial production characteristically demanded raw materials, stimulating peripheral mining and agricultural-based economies. As a corollary to this process, massive exportation of manufactured goods and capital from the developed countries of Europe (and the United States) to Latin America, Asia, and Africa completed the integration of the world capitalistic system. Thus, the system had moved into a redefined regional specialization.[1]

Other factors besides these general tendencies interceded decisively in the resurgence of the sugar production in the Dominican Republic. The most important was the outbreak of the first Cuban War for Independence (1868–78), for it affected the production of the world's major producer-exporter and channeled an important wave of its emigrants to the Dominican Republic, where they were to play a significant role in the emergence of the modern Dominican sugar industry. Another factor was the war between France and Germany in 1870, which affected the major producers of beet sugar. Also, the Civil War in the United States, which had taken place a bit earlier, left a devastating mark on the sugar cane plantations of Louisiana.

These external factors combined to restimulate an activity that had led to colonial economic growth in the sixteenth century but had then declined sharply, to revive momentarily at the end of the eighteenth century, and then decline again, while always playing a role in certain zones of the country even through its declining years. For even in the bad years, sugar production met local needs and occasionally added to export lists.

Also, local elements must be added to the external factors that fostered the resurgence of sugar activities in the Dominican Republic. The industry was to be affected as much in its domestic and rural mode of production (exemplified in the family-size operation's mill) as in its modern industrial development form.[2] Along the way it would pass through an entire gamut of intermediate combinations that involved elements of the great sugar manufacturing era and the typical components of the Industrial Revolution.

Eighteen sixty-five marked the end of what is known as the War of Restoration, the second Dominican war for independence, fought against Spain. The year 1865 would see the beginnings of a period of relatively greater political stability. Even though during the first three years following this war confrontations between civil and military factions proliferated, in 1868 a six-year regime presided over by Buenaventura Báez was imposed. Its very prolongation must be considered a coalescing ingredient in the development of sugar production.

The growing preeminence of the liberal element of the Dominican political power structure, particularly manifested in the emergence of the governments of the *Partido Azul,* undoubtedly also contributed to the resurgence of sugar production. These governments produced a series of legislative measures geared at stimulating heavy capital investments in large-scale agricultural production. Among these measures were tariff exemptions for machinery and tools; exemptions from the payment of export taxes for a certain period, and government land concessions. Businessmen who decided to open sugar mills were given the most benevolent of treatments within the overwhelmingly liberal spirit during the *Partido Azul's* golden era.

In addition to these conditions within the juridical and political order were others of lesser significance. During preceding years the process had been one of accumulation of capital, supported by the development of tobacco exports from the central Cibao region of the country and the exportation of lumber and dyes, most especially from the region known as the *Southern Band.* This mercantile development had permitted the formation of a merchant class linked to its financing and commercialization. And this group found itself prepared for moving into the new modes of production. On the other hand, the production of lumber for export had been experiencing a progressive decline, a decline that fostered the reorientation of capital traditionally used in its financing toward new areas. Thus sugar activity became the beneficiary of this phenomenon of displacement of commercial lending capital.

The Dominican Republic possessed natural conditions propitious to sugar development. It had an abundance of readily available fertile lands, naturally irrigated by a vast network of streams, whose suitability in the production of sugar had already been demonstrated. Land was cheap, and vast virgin areas could still be found because of the scant agricultural development of the country and its low population density. Those people who lived in the countryside were easily attracted to jobs in the sugar mills, being independent men in a country where there was little demand for the salaried laborer. Of course, this attraction held only where the monetary salary represented a strong improvement over traditional activity.

THE THREE PHASES OF DEVELOPMENT

The Dominican sugar industry can be analyzed in its three development phases within the period of 1875 to 1930. Each of these periods presents distinct elements. The first we have called the *competitive phase*. It was characterized by the predominance of individual businesses, a semimechanized technology, a predominantly national (Dominican) labor force, and the existence of attractive salary levels. In this phase small and middle-sized production units predominated and their principal geographic zones can be defined. The area around the city of Santo Domingo was the first zone. The area around San Pedro de Macorís was second, and the Puerto Plato region third. Of lesser importance were the regions of Azua, Baní, Palenque, Ocoa, and Samaná. During this phase the *colono* system (independent growers tied to larger estates) as a form of division of labor in the sugar industry had a relatively restricted expression and was found—if at all— only on the largest production units.

With the expansion of sugar mills, commercial activities developed at rates never before seen. This, in turn, gave rise to greater urban development, which in turn led to the expansion of the city of Santo Domingo, the growth of Puerto Plata and certain other population centers, and the beginning of the transformation of the village of Macorís, which years later became a vigorous and cosmopolitan sugar town. Along with urban growth and the development of commerce, a certain increase in manufacturing occurred. This growth, stimulated by the sugar industry, was oriented toward the manufacture of chocolate, rum and other alcohols, cigars, bricks and tiles, beer, and matches.

With the crisis in sugar prices beginning in 1884, a process of reorganization of the sugar sector began. It was characterized by the bankruptcy of numerous propertyowners and the closing of their establishments. Those mills that continued to operate passed into the hands of a small group of businessmen. This second characteristic of the new phase, the *phase of transition*, was a concentration of capital. It is marked by a modernization of producing units, the increase of the factories' production capacities, the extension of railroad lines, and the multiplication of modes of transport. Along with this technological modernization came reduced costs and, as an indispensable corollary, increased dependence on the *colono* system as a way of sharing the investment risks and administrative responsibilities in a fast-expanding business.

Along with the reduction of costs through technological modernization and a widened production scale, another development became clear. The Dominican labor force had begun to experience a progressive withdrawal to its traditional agricultural plots (to which it has always maintained ties). A decrease in the real wage had made that group unwilling to accept the terms of employment offered by the sugar plantation. As a way of avoiding the developing dangerous situation, sugar producers resorted to the hiring of a foreign labor force. This new hiring trend was to culminate in the first years of this century with the predominance of the foreign bracero in the sugar cane harvest.

In this second phase San Pedro de Macorís became transformed into the main sugar zone of the country, eclipsing even Santo Domingo. At the same time it was a zone shaken by the bankruptcy of the majority of the producing units established there. The other sugar zones had similarly unbalanced developments. Samaná would disappear as a sugar production area. Likewise, Azua, where a large number of *trapiches* had developed before the crisis of 1884, had disappeared from the sugar map at the turn of the century despite the introduction of a few modern units. Puerto Plata, on the other hand, with its ups and downs, had survived as a sugar area, reviving at the turn of the century.

A third phase was marked by the emergence of enclaves within Dominican territory.[3] The characteristic of this phase, the concentration of capital, had been defining itself since the beginning of the century: the rise of sugar corporations under whose control would be grouped a number of sugar mills. Expressions of the fusion of banking capital and North American industrial capital, these corporations meant a multinational presence in the Caribbean. Thus, the corporate control of Dominican sugar production was the consequence of a slow process that was accelerated by the misfortune following World War I and the postwar boom. For when the boom ended, mills and *colonos* went bankrupt. As this happened, their lands and their company stores passed into the hands of the larger corporations. The shuffling meant a greater degree of vertical integration of activities related to sugar production, converting the sugar business into a powerful commercial enterprise that possessed a network of subsidiary company stores called *bodegas*. To supply those stores meant the direct importation of goods. This meant passing over the great urban importation houses, drastically reducing the volume of their operations. The decline of cities like San Pedro de Macorís resulted. The period also generated, among other things, the ruin of urban manufacturing, which quickly went under with the importation of lower priced goods.

The fact that they were handling considerable masses of captive consumers, geographically far from other options and tied to the credit system of the *bodega,* stimulated the sugar businesses to coin their own currencies. With this step they reduced their own needs for liquid assets and restricted even further the use of money wage payments.

With regard to the labor force, which was composed of a majority of foreigners by the beginning of the twentieth century, a change took place in both their places of origin and levels of payment. The Haitian labor force displaced the workers from the small islands of the Caribbean, called *cocolos.* The new labor force had become an ideal substitute in the depression period because of the favorable employment advantages it offered the sugar business, primarily in recruitment, transport, and wage costs.

Individual producing units underwent an important transformation during this third phase. Originally they were bolstered by the conditions of World War I. The capacity of the mills was increased, cane fields expanded along with pasture and reserve lands. Statistics show that this was the most important moment for capital investments in Dominican sugar, not only in the expansion of preexisting units but also in the incorporation of the new sugar giants like the Central Romana and the Central Barahona. This process was brought about through the seizure of enormous tracts of land. For this seizure various expedients were employed, among them the dispossession of small farmers, both owners and squatters.

During this third phase new sugar zones developed: La Romana, Boca Chica, and Barahona. Older zones persisted, although the Santo Domingo zone had been reduced to one single establishment. As for markets, Dominican sugar, which traditionally had the United States as its principal point of destination, became directed in some measure to England and later to Canada. This change in direction toward the latter two markets came about because access to United States markets had been blocked by import restrictions.

Even though setting precise time limits on processes that mainly suppose slow transformation is somewhat arbitrary, it is nevertheless possible to define cutoffs that provide a more ordered understanding of the development of the sugar industry. Thus the first phase can be located in the beginning of the 1870s. At this time the first experiences of modern producing units can be seen. Its true growth, of course, did not begin until about the middle of the decade. This phase would have its point of transformation in 1884, after which those changes that reached their maximum expression in the nineties had their beginnings. The second phase started in the years just before 1884, while its markedly defined characteristics can be seen most clearly at the beginning of the nineties. This phase continued until the beginning of World War I, the United States military occupation (1916–24), and the resulting sugar boom. At that period the third phase emerged, whose tendencies had been developing through the beginning years of this century. With the crisis of the twenties, a pattern of enclaves developed, with characteristics that have been prolonged for decades, virtually unaltered.

THE COMPETITIVE PHASE

This first phase was characterized by the prevalence of the individual proprietor as the basic form of sugar mill ownership, with a few cases of partnerships—of two or three partners, at the most. During this phase, businessmen of various nationalities built sugar mills: Cubans, North Americans, Dominicans, Puerto Ricans, Englishmen, Frenchmen, Germans, and Italians. These men assumed direct control of their properties and were the operators. No distinction existed in this phase, as later in the corporate stage, between the condition of owner and of operator. Nevertheless, in some cases, the association of sugar mill operators with one or two capitalistic partners, some of them absentee, can be found.

The Origin of Capital

The capital for the investment could have originated in various sources: (a) the sugar mill operator himself, (b) a capitalistic business partner, (c) local financing, and (d) in foreign financing. Some of this international capital was obtained through loans made by businessmen from other countries, most of them connected with sugar commerce and located in New York. It was also obtained in the form of credits given by manufacturers of sugar industry equipment or by sales agencies. These were located in the United States (particularly New York), England, and France, where the machinery that the Dominican mills employed had originated.

Working capital generally came from loans from local businessmen, as well as loans from foreigners involved in sugar marketing. Since land was cheap, the largest investments were in the acquisition and installation of equipment, in the development of the infrastructure—transportation, deposits, docks, housing, and water supply—and in the development of the sugar cane fields.

Local loans, which were the most accessible, were extended on terms that ranged about 15 percent annually. These loans were based on mortgages of the sugarmill property and on contracts for the sale of sugar. For this service, the local merchant charged a 5 percent commission. These agreements usually involved the sugar of one harvest, although in some cases they involved several harvests, depending on the amount of the loan and on the estimated production of the mill. In certain circumstances, contracts assigned the control of the acceptance bills to the businessman giving the loan. As a producer became indebted in many ways to the lender, he quickly found himself pinned down by his debts. This situation led to an almost sure loss of property, with foreclosure on the mortgage, especially during periods of price crisis.

In some cases the local source of working capital had also provided some of the capital for the original investment. This occurred especially with down payments for the manufactured equipment (usually corresponding to a third of its total value); later the lender would help the producer with the payments and interest due. The lender also provided the funds to cover the needs of the harvest. By such a set of transactions the sugar crop would be pledged. As indebtedness increased, the lender who at the same time supplied goods for the part of the upkeep on the mill, often gathered together the small debts of the sugar mill operation with other lenders. He thus consolidated the operator's debts into one large debt or at least guaranteed his own role as principal creditor. In this way, when situations became critical, the foreclosure on the mortgage became the procedure for the acquisition of the mill property by the lender.

The Land

During this first phase, diverse methods were used to obtain the land for the mill. The main method was the purchase of land from proprietors; however, cases of renting land from absentee owners and of government land donations can also be found. The first, and predominant, method usually involved the purchase of contiguous land, some belonging to inheritances whose portions had not been divided among the inheritors. These were often virgin lands, with no agricultural development (or at least no commercial agricultural development). On occasion the mill operator would use the services of those who knew the area better, who would buy lands and then transfer the cleared deeds to the purchased plots to the mill operator. For this service, these intermediaries earned a modest percentage of the original value. Less frequently, already planted sugar cane fields were purchased.

In certain cases independent cane growers would associate with sugar mill proprietors under the *colono* system. This arrangement existed in Pajarito, a traditional agricultural zone, among other places. Because of its soil characteristics, the zone around Pajarito probably shifted from preexisting agricultural forms based on other crops to the planting of sugar cane. This would not have been the case, however, in the development of the mills in the San Carlos community, where virgin forests had predominated beside some cattle-grazing fields.

In those sugar zones where the industrial phase of sugar production had been preceded by the development of primitive mills, the smaller land units were absorbed. Whether this step came at the moment of the foundation of the modern mills or some time afterward, it was the natural consequence of unequal competition.

Technology

Among the sugar mills started between the middle of the decade of the seventies and 1882, the semimechanized predominated. This type of mill generally consisted of a steam engine and horizontal iron rollers. Here the only evidence of the Industrial Revolution was in the cane crusher roller itself. The rest of the process remained within the old manufacturing technology. The final product when this process was employed was known on the local market as *muscovado*. It brought lower prices than the other sugars of lower sucrose content, containing less impurities.

Of the thirty-some mills functioning, or in the process of establishment, in 1882, nineteen were of the semimechanized type. Substantial technological details are known about eighteen of these nineteen. They all had the Jamaican train, ten of them with double trains and eight with a single train. Ten of the semimechanized mills were of the pure type, while the other eight had incorporated new industrial units into the fabrication process, thus altering the essential characteristics of some of their manufacturing stages. Specifically, seven of these mills had either Laffertey or Weston centrifuges. In this way they had modernized the last stage of production, bringing out an end product that was higher priced, the centrifugal sugar today known as *crudo*. Five of these mills possessed vertical vacuum pans and three had Wetzel's Pans. Thus they were able to shorten the concentration and crystallization process—something that in the pure manufacturing process had to be done in two stages—and reached greater levels of crystallization.

Eleven of the functioning mills were completely mechanized. At least seven of them had triple-effect systems, one a double-effect; two were equipped with a special system known as the *Fryer Concretor.* Only one of the semimechanized group, *ingenio* Angelina, was able to survive, evolving toward the complete mechanization of its processes. A large proportion of the mechanized mills are still operating, especially those with the triple effect. Not one of the mills that adopted the Fryer Concretor managed to survive, however.

As a consequence of these technologies, the country was exporting three types of sugar: muscovado sugar, centrifugal sugar (in two classes: prime class, with ninety-six degrees of polarization, and second class, with eighty-nine degrees of polarization), and concretor sugar (60 percent sugar and 40 percent molasses). It also exported a part of its final stage molasses, used in the making of rums and alcohols.

The Sugar Mills

For the middle of 1882, official records show twenty-one mills in full production. Eight of them were located in the province of Santo Domingo (five

Table 10.1   Changes in the Relative Importance of Production of the Three Main Sugar Zones (1882–92), by Province (percentage)

Province or District	Relative Weight by Year		
	1882	1892	Change
Santo Domingo	55	25	−30
San Pedro de Macorís	14	60	+46
Puerto Plata	12	2	−10

in San Carlos and three in Pajarito), two in San Cristóbal, two in Baní, one in Azua, two in Samaná, and four in Puerto Plata.

Of these twenty-one establishments, four could be classified as large mills (in the Dominican sugar world). They were producing an average of 22,312 quintals of sugar and had an average of 4,900 *tareas* cultivated in cane (1 quintal equals 112 pounds; 1 *tarea* equals about 629 square meters). Three of these four mills were in San Carlos (La Fe, Caridad, and Esperanza) and one was in San Pedro de Macorís (Porvenir). The La Fe mill was the largest, apparently, with a production of 34,500 quintals of sugar and 5,000 *tareas* planted. The others were more or less equal: Caridad, with 18,000 quintals and 6,000 *tareas;* Esperanza, with 18,000 quintals and 5,000 *tareas;* and Porvenir, with 18,750 quintals and 3,600 *tareas.*

Eight mills could be considered of medium size: four of them in Santo Domingo (two in San Carlos and two in Pajarito) and one each in San Cristóbal, Azua, San Pedro de Macorís, and Puerto Plata. The average sugar production of these units was 10,968 quintals, and they averaged 1,975 *tareas* of cultivated fields. The largest of this group, Calderón, produced 15,000 quintals and had 3,000 *tareas* under cultivation; the smallest, Asunción, barely produced 7,500 quintals of sugar and possessed 1,200 *tareas* of cultivated land. Ten of the mills were small units, with an average production of 3,216 quintals of sugar and an average of 806 *tareas* of cane. Of these, the largest, Santo Elena, produced 4,500 quintals of sugar and had 1,200 *tareas* under cultivation. The smallest, La Rosa, produced 2,100 quintals and had only 250 *tareas* under cultivation.

The four largest units were responsible for 43 percent of the total sugar production of the mills and had 46 percent of the land under cultivation. The eight medium units produced 43 percent of the sugar and had 37 percent of the cultivated lands. Thus these twelve largest units produced 86 percent of the "industrial" sugar and had 83 percent of the land planted in cane. The nine smallest units provided only 14 percent of the production and 17 percent of the cane land.

Sugar Zones

Table 10.1 demonstrates the relative importance of the principal sugar zones in production. It indicates the reorganization of the industry in one crucial decade of its existence. The prolonged depression in sugar prices on foreign markets had weakened the established mills around the city of Santo Domingo, thus reducing their dominant influence. From the onset of the nineties, San Pedro de Macorís had in turn become the major sugar-producing center of the country, with seven mills of considerable size. The advanced technologies of the Macorís mills and their greater production capacities, combined with such other factors as the relative cheapness of lands, possibilities for the expansion of cane frontiers, and the new character of investment, form the group of factors that determined the emergence of San Pedro de Macorís as the sugar zone par excellence.

THE PHASE OF TRANSITION

During the Cuban Ten Years' War that ended in 1878, European beet sugar had overtaken sugar cane in production, making Germany the world's largest sugar producer.[4] Working under a bounty system, European producers flooded the world market with sixty million tons of sugar between 1850 and 1900, selling it at prices below production costs. Between 1882 and 1900 alone, the rate of growth of European beet sugar production was on the order of 188 percent.[5] The protection of beet sugar destined for foreign markets was part of a battle fought by the European states for the control of world markets. That battle ended in 1902 with the signing of the Brussels Convention, the first international agreement concerning tropical raw materials.

The beet industry had undergone extraordinary technological development during the second half of the nineteenth century, with the developments in sugar-processing methods and in the obtaining of high agricultural yield levels by experimenting with beet varieties that were more resistant and had a greater percentage of sucrose.[6] In this regard the sugar cane industry had been lagging. The gap reached such proportions that for world sugar production in the 1899–1900 harvest, an estimated eight million tons, 31 percent was cane sugar and 69 percent was beet. This continual decline in the role of cane sugar in the world was strongly felt.[7] These factors combined to provoke one of the most acute and prolonged depressions in the sugar industry. In 1884 prices had already descended to levels not seen in forty years.

The effects of these conditions on the Dominican sugar industry were profound. They meant the disappearance of a large number of the sugar establishments that had begun in the previous phase, with the displacement of numerous pioneering businessmen and the concentration of properties. Some fourteen mills either went bankrupt or closed down operations between 1884 and 1900: Esperanza, Caridad, Dolores, Jainamosa, Duquesa, La Fe, Encarnación, San Luis, Constancia, Bella Vista, Stella, and Francia in Santo Domingo; San Marcos in Puerto Plata; Cabeza de Toro in Samaná; and several others of minor importance.

According to the testimony of William L. Bass, the North American businessman who owned the Consuelo mill at the beginning of the present century, "Only a few sugarmills survived, and those that did were on the verge of bankruptcy; their owners no longer minded admitting the truth." He added that the twelve mills still in existence required "quick help," if not, they would be "reaping their last harvest next year."

Bass supported the signing of a reciprocity agreement between the United States and the Dominican Republic, one that would exempt Dominican sugar from United States import restrictions. He claimed that Dominican *crudo* brought $3.50 a quintal. Of that, $1.65 had to cover United States import tariffs and $0.35 had to cover marketing operations. Only $1.50 was left, therefore, to cover costs and profits. In his words, this margin was "insufficient to permit a man to live in the Dominican sugar industry, much less prosper."[8]

Other factors made conditions for the Dominican sugar industry even more difficult. One was the preferential treatment that the other tropical sugar producers received on the United States market. Starting in 1902, Cuba enjoyed a 20 percent reduction in the tariff, by virtue of a reciprocity agreement signed with the United States. The Philippines would enjoy a total tariff exemption for up to three hundred thousand tons beginning in 1909 and an unlimited exemption beginning in 1914. Hawaii had a complete exemption since 1879, while Puerto Rico had enjoyed the same status after 1901.[9]

Another of the consequences of the sugar depression was the concentration of properties. One sugar businessman, a person who had acted as a supplier to these establishments, had taken over the control of ten mills during the period just after 1884. This process of consolidation would continue until, by 1907, of the fourteen functioning mills, four belonged to the General Industrial Company (the inheritor of the sugar properties of Juan Bautista Vicini), three belonged to Bartram Brothers and Associates, and two belonged to Hugh Kelly. These three propertyholdings represented 67 percent of the cultivated area of sugar cane. The participation of foreign capital in this period is seen by the fact that seven mills were controlled by North Americans and one by Cubans living in the United States. Of these eight establishments, four were in the hands of absentee owners (Bartram Brothers and the Nariño Sisters). The other four were integrated into the General Industrial Company; registered in New Jersey as a North American business, its capital belonged to the heirs of Juan Bautista Vicini. Of the foreign properties not in the hands of absentee owners, several were in the hands of the heirs of Juan Serralles, the Puerto Rican who had founded the Puerto Rico mill; some were in the hands of the heirs of J. Batlle and Company, the owners of the Mercedes mill in Puerto Plata. One common attribute of all of these businesses was their family or individual character— the corporate phenomenon that would appear later was still unknown.

The geographic distribution of the mills in 1907 centered on San Pedro de Macorís, which had seven units representing 67 percent of the cultivated lands. Three were in the Province of Santo Domingo, with 16 percent of the land in sugar cane. Three were in Azua, with 15 percent of the lands. And lastly, there was one mill in Puerto Plata, representing 2 percent of the cultivated sugar cane lands.[10]

Throughout the period following the onset of the crisis, the surviving units had introduced more modern technologies in an effort to lower production costs and expand their productive capacity. In this way they were able to increase both their productivity and their production scale. This process was clearly seen in the mills around San Pedro de Macorís, some of which had been started with the triple effect, or at the least with the double effect.

In the first years of the nineties, there was not only expansion of already established mills but also the incorporation of new units, such as the Quisqueya mill and other less successful projects. Along with the introduction of factory machinery to increase the capacity of the milling, the land for cane planting was expanded. Railroad lines were extended, and locomotives and other equipment added in order to serve the existing cane fields and the newly cleared lands. According to Ramiro Guerra, not only did the railroad make the transportation of cane more efficient, but it made the sugar latifundia a possibility, by facilitating the exploitation of cane plantings at considerable distances from the milling point.[11] In other words, with the development of the railroad came the possibility of the large modern central mill.

With these developments, the Macorisan mills began a period of sharp expansion of their sugar fields, based on the *colono* system. Under this system, the sugar mill operator would share the risks of investment and of administrative responsibilities. And given the conditions of the agreements made with the *colonos*, the relationship was an advantageous one for the mill owner.

With the elimination of the bounty system in 1903, the world sugar industry began to show signs of revival, with a new wave of investing and increased production.[12] The Dominican Republic was no exception. Beginning in 1905 this country's sugar exports increased, a tendency that would be interrupted only in 1910, when the market would plummet to 1905 levels. Prices during those years oscillated between a fraction more than four cents to a fraction more than six cents a kilogram for exported sugar.[13] In spite of this, Dominican sugar exports did not reach one hundred thousand tons until 1914. Prices rose, along with exports, even more in 1915, when the First World War provoked extraordinary rises.

The ability of the Dominican Republic to take advantage of increased world demands of that period was not a chance happening. The Dominican government favored the development of the sugar industry in various ways. This was especially true of the administration of President Ramon Cáceres (1905–11), whose era appears in marked contrast to the revolutionary period, set off by the assassination of President Heureaux in 1899, that imme-diately preceded it. This brief respite of peace and prosperity stood out in the period of general instability, which ended only with the United States military occupation of 1916. During the Cáceres administration there was an effort toward modernization of Dominican society led by the president himself. Within this context, a series of laws benefiting the sugar industry was enacted. Among these was the law regarding registration of land titles, which was designed to clarify the confusing situation of land tenancy pre-dominant especially in the sugar zones, i.e., the system of communal land tenancy. This law became necessary when the developing capitalistic system proved incompatible with the old tenancy form. Dominican authorities labeled the system "one of the principal causes of the backwardness of Dominican agriculture" and a source of continual conflicts among farmers.[14] Complicating the legal situation was the explosion in land specu-lation, particularly in the eastern region, where new sugar lands were being established. An extraordinary proliferation of false titles circulated, making the problem critical.[15]

Another law, called the Agricultural Franking Law of 1911, provided exemption from import tariffs for machinery, agricultural implements, and imported construction materials needed in the establishment of agricultural operations. That law was designed to free investors from tariffs for a period of eight years when exporting the products of their new establishments.[16] The ultimate benefits of this law went to the sugar mills. The Sugar Trust was particularly interested in taking advantage of one clause of this legisla-tion. Since raw or processed products of the mills could be exported duty free, the Central Romana was thus permitted to export its cane to Puerto Rico to the Guanica Central Mill for crushing, in accordance with associa-tions developed within the trust. In this way, the stern, restrictive United States tariffs were sidestepped and full advantage of Puerto Rico's duty-free privileges exploited. Other legal measures, these admittedly to a lesser degree, stimulated sugar production. One such was the Cattle Law, which was aimed at limiting open-range cattle-raising, by limiting the areas that could be used.[17]

THE LABOR FORCE IN SUGAR PRODUCTION

An anonymous member of the *Sociedad Literaria Amigos del Pais* esti-mated that in 1877 there were ten thousand laborers in the whole country available for employment in agricultural export activities (coffee, cocoa, tobacco, and sugar).[18] In 1884 Maria Eugenio de Hostos pointed out that the sugar industry employed some six thousand laborers, of whom fifty-five hundred were Dominicans.[19] According to the member of the *Sociedad*, in 1877, day laborers in the mills earned 50 centavos a day, "working from six to six, with only two hours of rest from eleven to one. They require no food, no clothes, nor do they stay on the farm when they are ill, except in the case of an illness originating in some dangerous job the owner had employed them in. Then it is the custom to pay them a full week's salary, and charity begs that they be cured." Further, "payments are made Saturday afternoons, and early on Monday morning the owner can fire anyone he considers has not worked well on the previous week, taking on others who apply for work on that day. This does not mean that the owner cannot fire a man on the day and at the moment he desires, nor the opposite. The laborer is free to walk out whenever he feels like it, too." The source continues: "In the clearing operations, the cutting and burning, fencing, and planting of the cane (and other jobs that are not those of the daily harvest type) advantageous contracts can be drawn up for the worker, taking into account the relative time he puts into the job. This is especially obvious if it is considered that the worker naturally wants to finish one job quickly so that he can quickly go on to other opportunities and greater earnings with other piecework contracts."[20]

These quotations permit some understanding of the characteristics of the labor force in the sugar industry in its early years. First of all, it was a local labor force. Second, a daily wage predominated for the cane cutters and the other workers involved in the harvest activities. For the hands, this meant a workday of twelve hours, with a two-hour break, and weekly pay. For the other agricultural tasks, a piecework system was employed, based on pre-work agreements reached between operators and the employees.

The development of the sugar industry brought the mobilization of those people in the countryside who had small garden plots. They moved toward the mills in search of pay for temporary work, which was attractive to them at that time. A significant part of the rural population around the mills was involved in this process, and there was some internal migration, particularly from Azua to Santo Domingo and Macorís, and from El Seibo to Macorís. These phenomena provoked Hostos and Bonó to warn against the abandonment of the garden plots, arguing that it would cause a shortage of food produced locally.[21]

The Dominican sugar industry also received laborers from the logging industry, by then in rapid decline. The profits of this industry diminished in direct proportion to the distance logging was being done from the rivers, since these were used to transport the logs to shipping points. Logging in this period had already exhausted most of the profitable areas, and layoffs were common. Another source of laborers was from the bankruptcy of the *trapiches* of the southern region, especially after 1884.

In general, the internal migration was a population shift in response to the new, dynamic parts of the sugar economy. The influx of a new populace worried the provincial authorities of Santo Domingo. The governor sent a circular to the mill administrators pointing out the "increase in crimes and misdemeanors" that went unpunished "because of the influx of people who come to the Capital from all over the country to work in the neighboring mills without having the corresponding passports."[22] That was in 1883. The same year President Ulises Heureaux excused his government for not having implemented the law that created a police force for the capital. His justifications follow: "Nobody accepts this voluntary service because they find more money and more future in the agricultural companies"; "The citizens prefer a hard-worked day with their hands to any other means of earning a living."[23]

Nominal wages were on the rise between 1880 and 1883.[24] In Santo Domingo they were fifty centavos in the first year and ninety centavos in the second, an eighty percent increase. In the rest of the country, the wage in 1883 was sixty centavos, up 20 percent from 1880. According to Juan J. Sánchez, these were high wages for the period and were explained "by the competition of many businesses of this kind where there was a labor shortage."[25]

Beginning with the crisis of 1884, however, the sugar industry went into a prolonged slump. The factors that had made possible the recruiting of a mostly national labor force became so altered that the new situation provoked the gradual withdrawal of Dominicans. Part of the reason for this withdrawal was that many of the laborers had maintained their ties to the land. They had become a semiproletarianized labor force, working in the mills only as long as the levels of pay gave them a return over and above their basic needs.[26]

The crisis due to the fall in sugar prices led to the ruin of many sugar producers. Along with the closing of some mills and the reduction of activities in other establishments, other factors influenced the real wages of the workers. One was the monetary fluctuations that marked the rest of the century, signifying the reduction in the buying power of the most widely used coin of the period, the silver Mexican peso, and increasing the prices of basic consumer goods. There were also reports of occasional reductions in the money wage during the depression. The general tendency, however, was that of maintenance of money wages, and even of some increases that actually doubled the money wage level.

Another result of the depression was the refusal of the local laborers to accept a daily wage. They preferred an apparently more convenient payment system, based on piecework. Information dealing with the harvest of 1892–93 demonstrates this. This system had always been used for certain types of work, such as the routine agricultural tasks and for the clearing of the land. (In this regard the tradition has been maintained down to the present day.) What was new was the extension of the piecework system as the means of payment for cane cutting. The Dominican *campesino* had always preferred the type of work paid by the piece because it was better paid and because he had accumulated experience in doing it.

Piecework payments for cane cutting provoked the protests of William L.

Bass, owner of the Consuelo Mill. He lamented the inconveniences of this type of payment system. According to Bass, in its beginnings the sugar industry used work crews of braceros. Nevertheless, "The shortage of laborers and the antagonism of local residents and the authorities alike against the custom of promoting the convenient immigration has made it impossible for the industry to hire the crews it needs. As a result the operators of sugar cane mills have had to resort to the expedient of dividing the agricultural tasks of the mill into 'colonias.' In their turn the managers of the colonias have to divide their tasks by contract." Bass claimed that "the contractors, in turn, have to subdivide the tasks among the laborers by what is called 'piecework.' And this is only achieved after long and heated debate." In the opinion of Bass, the piecework system is a "custom that has nothing good about it; it offers no advantages and is the tacit recognition that the laborer is in a position to impose his demands on the owner." Bass indicated one of the reasons for the use of the piecework system when he stated that "the violent monetary changes upset wages and made it impossible to entice a Dominican day laborer to work for a daily wage."[27]

As we have seen, the participation of the Dominican campesino as a wage worker in the sugar economy had meant abandoning his traditional living—the conuco—temporarily. This was especially true for those who moved to the sugar plantations from distant points. What this meant for the campesino was that his basic diet, met mostly before with the production of his conuco and his raising of animals and fowl, would have to be purchased in the bodegas of the mills. There prices were even higher than in the stores in the cities, which led the analyst of the Macorís newspaper El Mensajero to term the bodegas "stranglers." According to this writer, who had worked in the mills, when Saturday came, "the bodeguero sits beside the pay clerk, list and pen in hand. As the clerk calls, 'John Doe, $3.60,' the owner of the bodega calls out immediately, '$3.35 to the bodega'. Then came the disputes."[28] Naturally, the diet of the campesino was altered. Fresh meats were replaced by salted meats, both beef and pork (jerky and salt pork), and dried fish (particularly mackerel, herring, and cod). In the same way, locally grown tubers were replaced by imported cornmeal and flour.

During this period, basic consumer products were in large part composed of imported items. And these articles were affected by tariffs, many of the articles imported from the United States and Europe being valued for collection purposes at nearly double their normal prices. Thus the high rates of currency exchange combined with the grave tariff structure and speculative prices to make the consumer's lot a difficult one. This situation was further heightened when the bodegas enjoyed a captive consumer market because their customers were geographically isolated from other outlets and were left with no alternatives. Locally produced food items also suffered from the effects of the movement of the labor force toward the sugar mills.

To show this, a look at the price fluctuations for the traditional foods of the Dominican diet should suffice.

Rice, imported from Europe (both through England from India and from Spain), had cost the wholesaler $5.50 a quintal in 1879. In 1884, it cost him between $6.50 and $7.00. In 1894 its price had reached 10 centavos a pound for the ordinary class, 12 1/2 centavos for the *canilla* variety, and 15 for the *valenciano* variety. This represented an increase of 81 to 172 percent. Dried cod fish, an essential article of the caneworkers' diet, sold for $8 a quintal in 1879, for $11.50 and $12.00 in 1884, and $18 in 1885. In 1894 a pound was sold for 20 centavos. Lard, which was used for cooking, sold for $16 a quintal in 1879, retailing in 1894 at 50 centavos a pound. A bottle of milk rose from 5 centavos to 30 centavos between 1885 and 1894. Beef increased in price from 10 centavos a pound in 1879 to 30 centavos in 1894—an increase of 200 percent. Plantains, priced at 50 centavos a hundred in 1879, were being sold at 5 centavos each by 1894—an increase of 900 percent.

All of these factors combined to transform the conditions under which the Dominican sugar cane laborer had based his participation in the industry. The attractive dream of saving a little money went up in smoke before the erosion of the real wage. The response to this change was a return to the *conuco* by the *campesino*, who did not totally depend on the wage for a livelihood and who could still enjoy an option.

The workers' preference for the piecework system can likewise be considered a response to the wage problem, for it was one way of negotiating the terms of payment. Raising the real wage was one way to break the resistence that was bringing serious problems to the mills in a period so critical for their continued operation. However, increases in nominal wages never breached the gap that inflation and monetary devaluation had left in the buying power of wage earners.

THE BRACEROS

In the long run, the solution that would emerge for the industry was the large-scale importation of foreign braceros.[29] They were willing to accept lower wages and to work for time wages instead of pay by piecework. The progressive withdrawal of the Dominican labor force and the problems of recruiting hands for the harvest had created the need to import migrant laborers.

After a few failures with experiments using families from the Canary Islands and a few hundred Puerto Rican farmers as temporary braceros, a solution was found in workers from several small Caribbean islands (*cocolos*). These islands included St. Thomas, St. John, St. Kitts, Nevis, Anguilla, St. Maarten, and Antigua. By the turn of the century, the new laborers constituted the bulk of the labor force in the sugar fields of the east, arriving by ship by the thousands on the eve of a harvest. This movement would continue throughout the first three decades of the twentieth century, when the Haitian immigrations (begun in the first decade) would come to predominate, a phenomenon that has extended to the present day.

During the first years of this century, an estimated 3,000 to 4,000 *cocolo* braceros were landing in San Pedro de Marcorís. That does not include figures for Santo Domingo and Puerto Plata. In the 1902–03 harvest alone, an estimated 4,500 *cocolos* arrived in the country (not counting Puerto Plata). This situation led José Ramón López to comment, "If it had not been for the people of the Lesser Antilles in this country, the sugar harvests would have been an impossibility during these years of revolts and commotions."[30]

For the beginning years of the century, the press frequently complained of the depressive effect of immigration on wages. They referred to the *cocolo* as the cause of the "corruption of the wage," indicating that he was willing to work for such low salaries as twenty-five cents a day, both in Puerto Plata and San Pedro de Macorís. Actually this wage was equal to 50 percent of the typical wage in the period when the labor force was predominantly Dominican, if the corresponding adjustments are made for monetary fluctuations. Such wage levels would increase slowly with the recovery of the Dominican sugar industry over the next two decades, to decline again in the twenties as a consequence of the crisis provoked by the end of the sugar boom during World War I and the postwar period.

The immigration of *cocolos* as braceros was handled legally. They were brought in through the ports of Santo Domingo, San Pedro de Macorís, and Puerto Plata. The traffic was organized by the captains of small ships that covered the routes between the small islands and Dominican destinations. In the majority of the cases the captains worked under previous agreement with the mills. Most of the workers returned to the country of their origin at the end of the harvest, taking with them a part of their earnings in the form of savings. These savings, according to English sources, were considered sufficient to justify the continuation of the migratory movements. Nevertheless, a law passed in 1912 aimed at halting the annual importation of braceros. The law, however, had little effect because of a much invoked clause that allowed the executive branch to grant special permission to millowners for the importation of laborers. The authorities similarly tried in 1913 to Dominicanize the harvest, recruiting people from the countryside in the Cibao region as well as in other zones of the country. These people, however, did not long remain in the cane fields. A satisfactory—to the millowners—solution to the labor problem awaited the arrival of the Haitian laborers, which began during the period of United States military occupation, at a time when Haiti was also occupied by the United States. Things were to change, with the ascent of Trujullio and later, but the recourse to foreign labor has survived to the present as an indispensable component of the sugar harvest.

NOTES

This chapter is a condensed version of the paper presented at the conference, which contains more detail and further references. For this volume the discussion of the post-World War I period has been eliminated. The translation was done by Kathleen Alfonso.

1. See F. H. Hinsley, ed., *Material Progress and World-Wide Problems, 1870-1898*, vol. 11 of *The New Cambridge Modern History* (London: Cambridge University Press, 1976); and W. Arthur Lewis, ed., *Tropical Development 1880-1913: Studies in Economic Progress* (Evanston: Northwestern University Press, 1970). For a more detailed version of this process in Latin American societies, see Leslie Manigat, *L'Amérique Latine au XXe Siècle 1889-1920* (Paris: Université de Paris, Editions Richelieu, 1973), and Roberto Cortés Conde, *The First Stages of Modernization in Spanish America* (New York: Harper & Row, 1974).

2. José del Castillo, "El resurgimiento de la producción azucarera dominicana como sector de exportación: los límites del trapiche," *Inazucar*, no. 28 (November-December 1980): 41–50.

3. Manuel Moreno Fraginals, *El ingenio: complejo económico social cubano del azúcar* (Havana: Editorial de Ciencias Sociales, 1978), 1:88.

4. This section is based, in large measure, on José del Castillo and Walter Cordero, *La Economía Dominicana durante el Primer Cuarto del Siglo XX* (Santo Domingo: Ediciones Fundación Garcia Avévalo, 1979), pp. 20–23, 25, 37, 40–42.

5. Charles Stover, "Tropical Exports," in Lewis, ed., *Tropical Development 1880-1913*, p. 55.

6. H. C. Prinsen Geerligs, "La situación de la industria de azúcar durante los últimos viente años," *Revista de Agricultura* 9, no. 10, (February 1914): 695–705.

7. Yves Guyot, *The Sugar Question in 1901* (London: Hugh Rees, 1901), pp. 58–59.

8. William L. Bass, *Reciprocidad* (Santo Domingo: Imprenta La Cuna de América, 1902), pp. 39–40.

9. Paul Mutto, "La Economía de Exportación de la República Dominicana 1900–1930," *Eme Eme: Estudios Dominicanos* 3, no. 15 (November-December 1974): 80.

10. The Dominican Republic, Promotion Division of the Public Works Department for the Jamestown Tri-Centennial Exposition, 1907, p. 50.

11. Ramiro Guerra y Sánchez, *Azúcar y Población en las Antillas* (Havana: Editorial de Ciencias Sociales, 1970).

12. Prinsen Geerligs, "La situación de la industria de azúcar durante los últimos veinte años."

13. Wilfredo Lozano, *La dominación imperialista en la República Dominicana, 1900-1930* (Santo Domingo: Editora de la UASD, 1976), p. 278.

14. *Memoria de la Secretaría de Estado de Agricultura e Inmigración* (Santo Domingo: Imprenta Vda. García, 1909), p. 40.

15. José Ramón López, "La Caña de Azúcar en San Pedro de Marcorís, desde el bosque virgen hasta el mercado," *Ciencia* 2, no. 3 (July-September 1975):

128–32. See also Alcibíades Alburquerque, *Títulos de los Terranos Comuneros en la República Dominicana* (Ciudad Trujillo: Impresora Dominicana, 1961).

16. Ley de Franquicias Agrarias, *Revista de Agricultura* 7, no. 4 (July 1911): 98–102.

17. Ley de Crianza de 1911, *Revista de Agricultura* 7, no. 2 (April 1911): 38–42.

18. "En la elaboración del azúcar está la salvacíon del país," *Gaceta Oficial,* nos. 177, 178, 180, 181, 182 (June 25, July 1, 16, 23, and August 2, 1877).

19. Eugenio M. Hostos, "Falsa Alarma, Crisis Agrícola," in Emilio Rodríguez Demorizi, ed., *Hostos en Santo Domingo* (Ciudad Trujillo: Imprenta Vda. García, 1939), 1:160.

20. See note 18.

21. Del Castillo, "El resurgimiento de la producción azucarera dominicana como sector de exportación: los límites del trapiche."

22. "Circular a los Señores Administradores de Establecimientos de Agricultura de esta Provincia," *Gaceta Oficial,* no. 451, February 3, 1883.

23. "Mensaje del Presidente de la República al Congreso Nacional en 1883," *Gaceta Oficial,* no. 456, March 17, 1883.

24. Casimiro N. De Moya, "Alcance al n. 43 de 'El Eco de la Opinión,'" *El Eco de la Opinión,* March 12, 1880, and "Emigracion Belga," *El Eco de la Opinión,* December 1, 1883.

25. Juan J. Sánchez, *La caña en Santo Domingo* (Santo Domingo: Imprenta García Hermanos, 1893), p. 31.

26. In a dispatch from San Pedro de Macorís signed J. A. (undoubtedly Juan Amechazurra, founder of the Angelina Mill and at the moment *colono* of the Consuelo Mill) the following was stated: "We have no hands. The farms are expanding and the braceros breaking free of the farms. *Here we don't have any real day laborers: all are property owners." El Eco de la Opinión,* June 2, 1892 (emphasis added).

27. Bass, *Reciprocidad,* pp. 78–79.

28. *El Mensajero,* September 29, 1884.

29. See also José del Castillo, *La Inmigración de Braceros Azucareros en la República Dominicana, 1800-1930* (Santo Domingo: Cuadernos del CENDIA, UASD, 1978), and Patrick Bryan, "En torno a la recepcion de los cocolos en la República Dominicana," UASD (Santo Domingo, 1973).

30. Ramón López, "La Caña de Azucar en San Pedro de Macorís, desde el bosque virgen hasta el mercado," p. 134.

11. The Question of Labor in the Sugar Industry of the Dominican Republic in the Late Nineteenth and Early Twentieth Centuries

Patrick E. Bryan

The economy of the Dominican Republic became increasingly export-oriented toward the end of the nineteenth century. North of the Cordillera Central, export production was dominated by tobacco and cacao cultivated by Dominican *campesinos*. South of the Cordillera Central, on the south coastal plains, the dynamism of the export economy was most evident in the plantation sector.

There were revolutionary changes in the reorganization of the sugar plantations in the south. Sugar had been only a minor crop, cultivated unsystematically with little capital. But with the contribution of capital and technology from Cuba and the United States, France and Italy, the sugar industry was transformed from individually directed mixed cultivation to a modern, monocultural, technologically oriented, and highly capitalized mode of production.

Even before the nineteenth century drew to a close, the sugar plantations had established themselves firmly on the flat lands of the south and southeast of the republic. Their level of technology was at least on a par with, even outstripped, the rest of the host community in terms of technical facilities: railroads, electricity, water supply. Under the impact of foreign investment, and in spite of the difficulties that the sugar industry encountered during and after the 1884 international sugar crisis, production soared in the last fifteen years of the nineteenth century. During the first two decades of the twentieth century exports increased even more dramatically.

From 5,834,385 kilograms in 1881, exports rose to over 20 million kilograms in 1889. The 1889 figure was doubled again by 1905 with total sugar exports exceeding 48,169,279 kilograms. In 1916, the figure had climbed to over 120 million, and in 1920 over 158,803,584 kilograms.[1] Land under sugar cultivation radically increased during the period, creating a virtual agrarian revolution and setting a pattern of landholding that weakened the traditional *comunero* system and substituted individual or corporate owned latifundia.

THE SHORTAGE OF LABOR

But plantations require cheap and abundant labor, particularly during the *zafra* (harvest), when cane is reaped by gangs of laborers. For approximately six months the job of cutting and transporting cane to the strategically located factory continues. However much the planters had sought to modernize their factories in order to reduce the quantities of labor needed, there was no obvious way in the absence of cane-cutting machinery to do away with hundreds of field laborers. The much vaunted shortage of labor in the Dominican sugar industry referred primarily to the harvest, between December and June.

At first labor for the sugar estates came from the Dominican Republic itself. One source within the republic was the vagrants in the southern ports.[2] Another source was the mahogany cutters, also from the south, whose source of employment was becoming less capable of providing them with a living. With the constant felling of the mahogany forests near to the coast, and the inability to transport timber from further inland, a large number of workers found themselves without employment.[3] There were plans, it is true, to establish a railway line that would facilitate the movement of timber from inland with a view to reviving the mahogany business; meanwhile other gainful means of employment had to be found.

The Dominican smallholders of the south were also attracted by the cash income provided by the plantations in the years of expansion between the mid-1870s and 1884. The large-scale movement of small cultivators to the sugar plantations disrupted local food supplies and created some anxiety in government. Even this source of labor was not deemed sufficient. In 1883 the view was expressed that "the natives will . . . be sufficient to carry on the works in the plantations now in existence, yet, should they increase in number, it will be indispensable to take steps for the introduction of foreign labor."[4] In fact, the planters had by that year begun to find labor costs prohibitive. In 1884, the year of the Dominican Republic's first serious sugar crisis, planters unilaterally reduced wages in an effort to reduce costs. Workers in the sugar industry in San Pedro de Macorís went on strike.

In the first decade of the twentieth century attempts were made to coerce labor. Between 1906 and 1911, vagrancy laws were passed. In 1908 the

Dominican government ordered the *Jefes Comunales* to force all vagrants or reputed vagrants to work. All commitments to labor were to be recorded in a *libro de registro*. One of the chief functions of the *Jefe Superior de la Guardia Republicana* was to identify persons who had no visible means of subsistence and "form part of the current of individuals reputed to be thieves, vicious people, and disorderly individuals." Such people were to be handed over to the relevant authorities and found work to do. Gambling, cockfighting, and all other rural amusements during the week were forbidden.[5]

There is no indication, in quantitative terms, of how successful these press-gang tactics were. It is certain, though, that "vagrants" would have done their utmost to evade the forces of the law, especially as the coercive forces of the Dominican Republic were also involved with recruiting for the army. The rough and ready justice of the smaller outlying plantations would not have made the sugar plantations attractive sources of employment for the Dominican worker. The fate of his colleagues in the plantations would have been additional discouragement: "Sugar holds first place, and still the people in the southern part of the island . . . are much poorer than those on the northern side who plant cocoa, coffee, and tobacco. In the south, the sugar estates have taken up a vast extent of lands which have been bought from the small landholders. These last have lost their independency (sic) to become common peons, and their producing value reduced to 50 cents to 60 cents a day during the sugar season. They are obliged to live abjectly and miserably."[6]

Dominican authorities never ceased attempts to secure Dominican labor. In 1913, for example, the governor of San Pedro de Macorís called a meeting of estate owners and administrators to discuss the wider use of Dominican labor on sugar plantations, so that the wages paid by the sugar industry would benefit Dominicans rather than foreign laborers who took such wages out of the country. The contract would have provided Dominicans with the same wages offered to foreign labor, one or two pesos per day, depending on the physical capability of the laborer. The Dominican laborer would be given free passage from any point in the republic, subsistence, and medical attention, provided that the laborer completed the harvest. The immediate fruit of this policy was to bring fifteen days later two ships the *Oliva* and the *Victoria* to San Pedro de Macorís with 107 workers coming from the commune of San Cristóbal. A few days later the *Viking* brought 162 Dominican *braceros* for the estates Consuelo, Angelina, and Santa Fe.[7]

Dominican labor proved insufficient. The common report was that the Dominican was too lazy to perform such labor. Persuasion, coercion, and recruitment obviously failed to lift the number of Dominicans working on sugar estates. The second option of the Dominican planter was to raise the level of wages. This option was rejected outright. Ever since 1884 there had been an insistence that wages should be made to rise and fall with demand

and supply factors. The Dominican planters were also determined to keep wages down to ensure the "viability" of the sugar industry in competition with Cuba. Immigration of workers was identified as one method of cheapening wages. In 1884, Dominican workers had gone on strike, refusing to work for the wages offered. The argument then, had been simply that the wages received could not supply such basic necessities as mackerel and butter.[8]

It has been noted that the "basic condition for success of plantation development is the low wages that [plantations] pay their labor."[9] The Dominican plantations were no exception. The question was the source of that labor, when for various reasons the numbers of available Dominicans were limited, and white immigrants were not to be put to work on sugar estates. The fundamental assumption behind plantation development had to be faced—the assumption that it was not the welfare of labor that mattered or the color of labor, but the maximization of profit. If the Dominican hispanophile elite were unhappy at that, the planters—most of them expatriate—were quite content to accept labor from any source. The overriding consideration was that labor should be cheap.

The demands of the sugar industry—another way of saying the demands of foreign capital—overcame the objections of the Dominican elite, who for various racial, cultural, and nationalist reasons showed great reservations about importing British West Indian labor. Perhaps to say that the objections were overcome is to overstate; the objections to British West Indian (and Hatian) labor were never fully overcome. But the laws passed by the Dominican government to contain or ban the immigration of British West Indians became dead letters.

BRITISH WEST INDIAN MIGRATION

Against a background of Dominican labor "shortage" and intense reservations about the importation of colored labor the British West Indian went to work in the Dominican Republic on the expanding United States owned plantations. The British Caribbean was viewed as an "Africanized" area, and the introduction of British West Indian labor was seen as a threat to the mulatto homogeneity of the Dominican Republic. The entry of British West Indians into the Dominican Republic was in direct contradiction to the republic's policy of immigration, which favored white immigration. Yet, the Dominican mulatto elite that dominated Dominican society and the formal institutions of government were caught in a dilemma. Exclusion acts directed against the entry of black immigrants could be viewed as offensive to the colored Dominican.[10] Caught between the realities of Dominican socioracial structure and the aspiration to alter those realities, and trapped between their own policies of collaboration with foreign capital and the demands made by the southern enclave on the mulatto image of society, the Dominican politicians were forced to temporize and to pursue virtually contradictory policies. In 1882, approaches had been made, by way of compromise, to the British government to begin an immigration of Asian Indians. But the Foreign Office was obliged to turn down the request, on account of reports reaching the India Office on conditions prevailing in the Dominican Republic.[11]

The immigration of British West Indians to the Dominican Republic's plantations was, at first, spontaneous rather than organized. According to Joaquín Balaguer, workers were employed from the neighboring Antilles for the first time in 1879: "The establishment of the first sugar factories made necessary by 1879 the employment of workers from the neighboring Antilles. To facilitate the flow of workers demanded by the new industry, a decree was dictated by General Cesareo Guillermo in his capacity as president of the *Consejo de Secretario de Estado* on January 18, 1879, offering a series of concessions to all immigrants who would enter the country under contract to some proprietor of a rural establishment."[12] This decree was not, however, aimed specifically at West Indians. Rather, there was always a preference for Canary Islanders who would enter Santo Domingo as *colonos* attached to a large estate. There had been British West Indians in the Dominican Republic for varying periods before 1879. Some had entered the republic as artisans. In fact, even after the sugar industry began its great boom, sugar harvesting and estate work was but one of several occupations pursued by British West Indians. Some were employed on the larger cacao farms in Samaná, others were employed as lightermen and boatmen in Puerto Plata. In San Pedro de Marcorís a number became substantial tradesmen. Others were money lenders. By 1916 about four thousand British West Indians had "settled more or less definitely in the Republic."[13] The occupations of these four thousand "comprise practically all branches of unskilled and semi-skilled labor, but may be said to fall into two principal divisions, viz. employment on the sugar estates, as cane-cutters, millhands, engine drivers, etc., and employed in connection with the ports as wharf-laborers, lightermen, boatmen, and to a certain extent fishermen."[14]

Apart from these four thousand permanently settled West Indians (or *cocolos* as they were called in the Dominican Republic), another two thousand or twenty-five hundred Leeward Islanders came to the country every year for the sugar crop between December and June. These seasonal workers were almost all cane cutters, paid by piecework. By 1917 about nine hundred, or roughly 10 percent, of the inhabitants of the town of Puerto Plata were British, mostly coming from the Turks and Caicos Islands. The consul had a fairly favorable report on these immigrants: "It is worthy of note that, although the Province of Puerto Plata is generally considered to contain the most intelligent and industrious type of Dominican, the town is almost entirely dependent on these British residents for its best craftsmen and laborers."[15] In 1914, between 17.5 and 20 percent of the population of

Montecristy (about four thousand) were British subjects. In Sanchez, the site of the terminus of the British Railroad, there were about six hundred British West Indians; in Samaná, in 1891, there were approximately two hundred working as artisans, mechanics, shopkeepers, and farmers.[16] One adventurous West Indian resident in the Dominican Republic since 1871 was a rancher of dubious honesty.[17]

British West Indian labor, then, was not confined to sugar enterprises, and while perhaps the majority of *cocolos* settled in and around the principal sugar-producing area of San Pedro de Macorís, there were a significant number scattered at some of the principal commercial and agricultural centers of the republic. Some laborers came seasonally, others stayed. Those who stayed in the southern plantation area were apparently a source of agony to the British authorities. The seasonal laborers were a different matter. They gave the consuls less work—seasonal work.

There were by the first decade of the twentieth century sufficient *cocolos* to constitute a very visible colored-black element. The British representative was concerned that "in the minds of the great mass of Dominicans an Englishman is a native of the British West Indies, while British subjects (sic) are popularly classed as Americans, and British prestige suffers as a result."[18] In 1884, it was calculated that 500 workers from outside the republic were involved with the sugar industry. In 1912 there were 4,000 foreign workers in San Pedro de Macorís alone. In 1895 the British (foreign) workers were seeking consular representation. In that year a petition was signed by four hundred British West Indians for such representation, which very appropriately ended with a prayer for the queen.[19]

The inability of the crumbling plantation economies of the Windward and Leeward islands to support a growing population that faced the prospect of a life without employment stimulated a mass movement to Panama to construct the canal, to the United States for general opportunities, to Central America for work in the banana industry, and to Cuba for work on the sugar estates. The policy of the colonial West Indian governments had become one of exporting blacks in the twentieth century—the converse of the slave-trade policy of the seventeenth to the nineteenth century. The one thing in common between these two policies was that they both were designed to defend the social and economic status of the British Caribbean planter class.

For the most part, the *cocolos* came from the islands of St. Kitts, Nevis, and Anguilla. A number also arrived from the Turks and Caicos Islands, Dominica, British Guiana, and Barbados. According to Proudfoot, "Cuba and the Dominican Republic were the major markets for labor from the Caribbean territories from about 1912 until the boom years ended in the 1920's."[20]

Virgin Islanders, for the most part a seafaring population, also performed seasonal labor in the Dominican Republic, returning home with an average of 10 pounds per person, considered a good wage, at least by the Colonial Office. In 1905 some five hundred men from the Virgin Islands worked on Dominican plantations, and from the tone of the colonial reports of the period, that was the average number of Virgin Islanders who worked every year in the Dominican Republic.

About 90 percent of the male population of Anguilla also migrated on a seasonal basis to the plantations of the Dominican Republic in some years. In 1926 it was reported that there were "hardly a dozen young men in the place [Anguilla] because of the 6,000 inhabitants every available man had gone off as usual to work for the four or five month season on the sugar cane estates in the semi-Spanish territory of Santo Domingo."[21] The same writer reports that the Anguillans received good wages in Santo Domingo, and "*mirabile dictu,* bring back the money each year and with it they built houses or employed it in other useful ways at home."[22]

Emigration from St. Kitts appears to have been most permanent. Between 1900 and 1910, the population fell 3,143 from 43,303, a drop explained by emigration to the Canal Zone, Costa Rica, and Santo Domingo. This migration was brought about primarily by lack of opportunities in the Leeward Islands. In a petition sent to the king in 1905 some immigrants wrote, "The cause why we have left our native land and are in this island [Santo Domingo] is because the British islands failed to furnish us employment and yet were levying upon us taxes of the most exorbitant nature, consequently those who were unable to bear the condition in which they were placed come over to this country, as it is adjacent and passage cheap."[23] In 1899, Arneage of the Royal Institution of Great Britian declared in even stronger language, "Her Majesty's black and colored subjects in the West Indies . . . have to choose between death from starvation in their native islands and suffering and ill-treatment in St. Domingo, where many have sought employment under the circumstances that their native islands are merely Islands of Death."[24] West Indians, then, migrated for the main purpose of performing manual labor on the various sugar plantations, though they were involved in other activities as well. It would be useful to examine the nature of the contracts that they enjoyed. Unfortunately, however, documentation is sparse on this subject. Prospective workers were taken to St. Thomas (Virgin Islands), where private contracts were signed. When leaving the Windward and Leeward islands, the workers were not necessarily informed about the estate to which they would be committed for the harvest. The contracts were signed on behalf of particular sugar estates at St. Thomas and committed a laborer to a particular estate. The British authorities took no active part in the arrangement of contracts short of advising prospective workers in their island press to seek contracts from plantations within easy reach of consular services. (In 1884 a number of West Indians left the estates after "differences with the planters." Perhaps these workers enjoyed purely verbal contracts).[25]

Specific examples of contracts are absent. But generally the basic agreement was for seasonal labor. There were also specific arrangements for wages. In 1916, unskilled laborers earned 60 cents (2 shillings, 6 pence) to $1.00 (4 shillings) per day, "the latter being the usual wage for foremen of gangs." Semiskilled workmen such as carpenters, blacksmiths, mill mechanics, and engine drivers received $1.25 (5 shillings) to $2.00 (8 shillings) per day. Cane cutters were paid by the ton, and an average workman could earn $1.25 a day, others earned $1.50 (6 shillings), and up to $2.00 per day.[26] These wages were higher than the Windward and Leeward plantations could offer.

The estates also provided accommodation for workers. Medical facilities were poor. Until 1916 only one estate (which did not employ much British West Indian labor) had a competent resident doctor, "and the laborers are not entitled to any compensation for injuries arising out of their employment."[27]

THE REACTION TO THE COCOLOS

In 1910 the British consul, commenting on the hostility of Dominicans to the British West Indian laborers, made the point that the imported workers did their duties for "remuneration somewhat lower than the rate of wages exacted by the few natives willing to do that class of work."[28] The cocolos, and the Haitians as well, had little option but to accept the wages offered. Immigrant workers away from their homes and families are also easier to control. Dominicans still had options other than work on the sugar plantations. A further comment was made on the essential work done by the cocolos when the Dominican government passed a law to restrict their entry: "There can be no doubt that if permission to enter the country is denied to these laborers the sugar industry will be brought almost to a standstill as native Dominicans can rarely be induced to work on the plantations . . . I understand that some of the sugar plantations have presented petitions to the government to enable them to bring in for the next season a definite number of natives from European colonies in the West Indies and that these petitions have so far been granted."[29]

In 1912, the Dominican government passed a law that declared in part that "natives of European colonies in America, those of Asia or Africa and of Oceana, as also laborers of any race except the Caucasian, need prior permission to immigrate into the country . . . Immigrants referred to . . . who arrive without previous permit will be repatriated in the same ship which brought them in, and the captain of the vessel will be fined $100 for each one of the said immigrants."[30] This law was a clear response to increasing pressure to terminate the immigration of British West Indians. In that year a minister of government declared: "Three or four thousand of them come, like locusts, at the beginning of the harvest to dispute wages with the campesinos of the country and to live in the worst conditions of morality and hygiene, to return to their native soil with the savings from six months continuous labor. . . . Nothing is imposed on them, nothing is demanded. . . ." The minister suggested that a tax be imposed on the *cocolos* before they could gain entry into the Dominican Republic. The republic, he argued, could well afford to impose such a tax because "this is an immigration which is not needed, because of its inferior race and because of its ethnological quality." Furthermore, the immigrants brought with them their "race, customs, their religion, and language."[31]

The British representative rightly saw the law as part of an effort by the Dominican government to "improve the race by attracting white immigrants and Spanish West Indians and by restricting the immigration of natives of the European colonies in the West Indies."[32] On the other hand, the planters saw the law as prejudicial to their cheap labor supply. The United States minister, in a letter to Knox, indicated that the provisions of the law were "causing some concern to the sugar estates which employ almost exclusively negro laborers from the British West Indies."[33] The planters immediately protested to the Dominican government and the latter submitted to the will of the planters. In fact, in September 1912 Mr. Russell was able to report that "all the sugar estates have made satisfactory arrangements for importing all their negro laborers from the British West Indies."[34] The satisfactory solution to the impasse was a clear case of the influence which the sugar enclave exercised on national policy. It also indicated that the national government had resigned itself to showing a "tolerance" of the yearly "invasion" of the British West Indian workers, however dangerous that tolerance might prove for the society and "culture" of the Dominican Republic. The speedy resolution of the problem, however, was not so much an indication of a change of heart as of the economic ambitions of General Alfredo Victoria, minister of war and marine. This minister purchased in the United States a steamer for the Dominican coastwise trade and proceeded to draw up contracts with the sugar interests for the transportation of laborers from the British West Indies at the rate of $3.00 per head. Thus, "all probability of any difficulty in regard to their landing was . . . eliminated, the Executive granting petitions to this effect and there will now probably be no more trouble this year on account of the provisions of the law in question." Another steamer offered a similar service at the lower rate of $2.50, but according to the United States minister, "the assurance of their being allowed to land the laborers was not so definite as under the Victoria contract."[35] The quality of law had been strained by corruption.

The hostility of the Dominican mulatto elite to the immigration of *cocolos* was transmitted to the Dominican working class. It was not difficult for the Dominican worker to see, in any case, that the *cocolo* was an agent for lowering wages. (Ironically, in the British West Indies at a corresponding time, Asian labor was employed to maintain a low level of wages—in Trinidad, Jamaica, and British Guiana.) In 1911, there were anti-British laborer demonstrations at some of the larger estates—Consuelo, Santa Fe, and Angelina—and "pamphlets had been distributed which recommended the burning of the cane fields if foreign laborers further would be employed."[36] The government sent troops to quell the disturbances, but no serious damage resulted apart from the burning of some cane fields, "a fact which we have to count on every year."[37]

Just before the harvest in 1915, a society was founded in the Dominican Republic to agitate on behalf of Dominican labor. The first contingent of workers from Anguilla was greeted with a riot. The efforts of the society to encourage the use of Dominican labor led to widespread disturbances in the country districts and "gave rise to disorders and attempts to strike." The Dominican government took the necessary steps to protect the sugar industry, on the appeal of the planters. A government official admitted that such steps were necessary "to destroy tendencies which threatened to bring about a conflict of considerable gravity for the Dominican state out of a matter which required peaceful and judicious treatment."[38] According to the governor of the province of San Pedro de Macorís, the foreign laborers who "are brought over by the estates under the obligation of repatriating them, took advantage of this state of affairs and began to demand higher wages, threatening to strike if they failed to secure their demands." A British West Indian laborer, William Henry (alias Jacobo), was among those people sent to the city charged with "interfering with the work on the *colonia* of La Sierra on the *Porvenir* estate."[39]

The society was dissolved, the agitation stopped, and the crop continued. The British consul indicated that prominent Dominican politicians were partly responsible for stirring up disturbances.

If the conflict between West Indian workers and Dominican workers were generated by economic competition, the Dominican upper class objected for other reasons, which reflected strong cultural and racial prejudice. In 1912 the paper *El Tiempo,* through a correspondent, spoke of the "rain of cocolos," the immigration of "nigger locusts." The cocolos were isolated for blame for all the ills of Dominican society, for the majority of homicides and incidents of wounding, for attacks on local authorities, and for "outrages against modesty." They took the bread from the mouths of Dominicans and were the major public charges. Dominican society should cease to throw away charity on "such monkeys."

It is probable, suggests Hoetink, that "the sheer numerical growth and the increasing social consciousness of the national bourgeoisie increased the social relevance of the racial factor, if only because through it, the mechanism of social control could be manipulated more effectively."[40] Edgar Thompson, in his discussion of plantation society in the southern United States, concludes more generally that "the idea of race, wholly apart from its logical and anthropological validity, had pragmatic value and influence in social life."[41] For the Dominican Republic, it was the system of thought most widely used to rally the mass of Dominicans together in their struggle against the Haitians throughout the nineteenth century. In the early twentieth century it was extended to correspond to the rise of the sugar industry and the need for black imported labor. It was so used by the Dominican mulatto elite to preserve a social order in which, in theory at least, the black or brown Dominican was superior to non-Hispanic, non-Dominican blacks.

The point in question is not the relationship between the Dominican elite and the Dominican mass—for the relationship of subordination and superordination was obvious, ("He who is black, let him speak clearly.") The point is that it was used to manipulate the Dominican working class against the imported sugar workers, when the true problem to be tackled was not one of race but one of low wages serving a foreign enterprise that based its success on low wages that the Dominican laborer would not or could not accept. The *cocolo* and the Haitian, as a rule, proved excellent scapegoats. The British West Indian migrant workers encountered comparable experiences in other parts of Spanish America, leaving on record a supposed arrogance, aggressiveness, and some conceit as a member of the British Empire.[42] A consul in Costa Rica was quite sure that his ability to exercise some control over these "troublesome" immigrants was made possible only by his appeal to them as responsible members of the empire. It was pointed out that although Mexicans and Colombians had caused "numerous disturbances (in Central America) . . . the big problem is the Jamaican Negro, proud of being a British subject. When the latter, with his 'cocky' attitude, is placed under the eye of a white boss from south of the Mason and Dixon Line, trouble is likely to ensue."[43]

The vice-counsul at Macorís complained that West Indian cane cutters were not registering at the consulate and emphasized that it was absolutely necessary for them to do so in order that consular protection could be offered them "as British subjects if they get into trouble as so often happens."[44] West Indians were occasionally expelled from the Dominican Republic because of an inability to stay clear of politics.[45] A vice-consul in Santo Domingo complained in 1906 that he was near the point of "nervous prostration."

In spite of everything—the pleas for curtailment of West Indian migration, or its modification; the demands for a more stringent law of immigration, "which would obtain useful people and not the riff-raff which Haiti and other people provided"; the law passed in 1912 restricting colored immigration—the number of immigrants increased after the law restricting their entry was passed.

Immigration of West Indians into the Dominican Republic continued until the late 1920s, when the possibility of going to work in the oil fields of Curacao diverted migrants to another source of earnings. The depression years reversed the tide even more. The United States occupation (1916–24) had seen the climax of *cocolo* immigration. In 1932, Rafael Trujillo called a halt. The decree of Trujillo instituted stiff penalities including compulsory labor in the agricultural colonies of the state. The law was translated and published in the *St. Kitts-Nevis Gazette* with a warning that all emigration of laborers to the Dominican Republic had been suspended "for the present."[46]

THE PATTERN OF RACE RELATIONS

It has been noted that the "plantation represents one type of situation in which the labor and the race problem meet."[47] This assertion is as valid for the United States South as it is for Santo Domingo and the British Caribbean. The Dominican Republic—as Santo Domingo—had been one of the first sites for African slavery on sugar plantations in colonial America and had been the first to decline. The plantation system had revived briefly by the end of the eighteenth century, only to collapse by the end of the eighteenth and the beginning of the nineteenth century. The nature of productive relations—a cattle economy combined with easy access to land by a freed African group and by mulattoes during the colonial period—facilitated a relationship between white and colored that was generally without the rigidity and bitterness of race relations in the plantation economies and societies of the British and French Caribbean or the United States South. The relative absence of acerbity probably had much more to do with the prevailing mode of production than with the laws of Alfonso the Wise or any Spanish juridicial tradition. It has been suggested that Frank Tannenbaum in his work on race relations in the Americas[48] confused technology and culture and erred in "comparing technologies in the name of comparing cultures."[49] It would certainly appear that the transition of the economy from a land of small farms to large plantations in Cuba had a direct impact on the nature of race relations, which had become harsher and more akin to relations in other areas of the Caribbean.[50] The brutality with which slave insurrections were put down in the colony of Santo Domingo at the end of the eighteenth century and the early nineteenth century, when there was a greater commitment to slave plantations, suggests that there was no fundamental difference between the Spanish and the British planter. With the Haitian occupation (1822–44) came the abolition of slavery (1822) and the migration of the elite of Santo Domingo, who preferred exile to life under Haitian rule, which put them on terms of legal equality with their ex-slaves.[51] Such planters found a haven in the slave colonies of Cuba and Puerto Rico.

The nineteenth century saw an evolution of racial consciousness that was almost indistinguishable from anti-Haitianism. European sterotypes of Haiti were readily accepted by Dominicans, and their own experience of

Haitian domination in the political sense intensified the tendency to assert a culture that was to them the absolute opposite of Haiti's. A number of simplistic assertions were made with a view to underlining the Hispanic tradition, the mulatto tradition, and the anti-African tradition. Thus "the level of civilization and general culture of the Ibero-American peoples is measured by the greater or lesser number of African population which are sheltered within them,"[52] or the Dominican people should not fold their arms and see their disappearance, "absorbed by the African race which shares the island with us, and whose population is spilling over into the Republic."[53] In 1946 it was still considered that "race is the principal problem of the Republic";[54] in 1908 there was a plea for the Dominicanization of the frontier, "in order to avoid in this way that our nationals continue to receive the waters of baptism from Haiti."[55]

The Dominican hispanophile elite were never reconciled to the inflow of Haitians across the border. The reason had partly to do with the organization of insurrectionary activity but also to do with the attempt to restrain the cultural influence of Haiti, which was associated with non-Catholic religious practices. In the late nineteenth century, when the need for Haitian labor on Dominican plantations and elsewhere became necessary, there had been discussions in the press as to the viability of such immigration. The paper *El Eco del Pueblo* took the position—in opposition to another paper—that race "has little influence or no specific characteristic influence."[56] But, especially during the first decade of the twentieth century, immigration policy showed a marked preference for white immigration, and attempted to restrict nonwhite immigration by law.

In its desire to "civilize" by populating, and in its consistent concern with "Africanization," the Dominican Republic was not unlike other Latin American countries. The fear of Africanization in the Dominican Republic was associated not only with "biological thinking" but with social race as well. This concern was reinforced by the very real fact that despite the proclamations of the hispanophile elite, the Dominican Republic continued to possess cultural patterns that were not necessarily Hispanic and were certainly not Catholic.[57] In the first decade of the twentieth century serious efforts were made to eliminate cultural and religious practices that violated the Catholic and Hispanic traditions of the republic. A strong directive to the chief of the Republican Guard in 1908 was aimed at uprooting rural customs that were regarded as destructive of the "culture" and aspirations toward civilization of the Dominican elite. Religious worship outside the Catholic and formal Protestant churches was banned. "Non-Christian" worship was declared an excuse for vagrancy and various forms of corruption. Wakes, last prayers, coming of age ceremonies, and other acts "which under the pretense of unauthorized religious practices . . . are nothing but extremely irreligious acts, acts of savagery which were the occasion for drunkenness and improper amusement," were to be strictly forbidden.[58] So too were the practices of *baquinis* and *velorios*.[59] Some of these religious practices, such as spiritist meetings, led to the profanation of corpses—or so it was claimed.

Since it was thought that migration from the Spanish Caribbean would be less incompatible with Dominican cultural tradition, some consideration was given to the immigration of Puerto Ricans. In 1903 an estimated 198 Puerto Rican men, 73 Puerto Rican women, and 39 Puerto Rican children were on the sugar estates. There were altogether 832 residing in San Pedro de Macorís.[60] Serious suggestions were made for the resettlement of Puerto Rico's "surplus" population, in particular along the frontier between Haiti and the Dominican Republic,[61] but the Domincan government disapproved of a general program of mass resettlement of Puerto Ricans in Santo Domingo.[62] Even after the final exclusion of the *cocolos* in the 1930s, a considerable amount of labor for the plantations came from Haiti, much of it illegally, fundamentally because the conditions that had given rise to the need for imported labor could not be removed by legislation.

CONCLUSIONS

This chapter, then, has been concerned with the economic demand of the sugar industry for imported, cheap, seasonal labor, contrary to the racial and cultural prejudice of the Dominican elite. The *cocolo,* apart from his racial background, alienated the Dominican working class by contributing to the lowering of wages and thereby becoming willy-nilly an agent of the plantation enclave. This enclave, set up principally with North American capital, was worked by a group of foreigners who brought inevitably the cultural characteristics of language, religion (English and Protestantism), and even a touch of Antillean bush medicine. They earned money for their endeavors—and spent it elsewhere. Thus, in the Dominican Republic not even common labor for the plantations was recruited wholesale from the indigenous work force. The end product was a conflict between Dominicans and West Indians.

The labor and the race problem met forcefully in the Dominican Republic. The question of race and labor became associated with problems of nationalism, social integration, and racial aspirations toward a Caucasian somatic norm. But the issue of race was not a creation of the new plantations that emerged in the late nineteenth century, however much they may have contributed to its intensification. The racial consciousness of the republic had been evident from the earlier part of the nineteenth century, with the Haitian invasions and occupations, and especially the extended control over Santo Domingo between 1822 and 1844. Continuous border conflicts and international views of Haiti promoted a sterotype that ultimately militated against the generous reception of the English-speaking

West Indian laborer. Illicit Haitian labor was also used in large numbers, but there was always disquiet about the extensive use of Haitian labor. It is not improbable, either, that the entry of Cubans and North Americans in the late nineteenth and early twentieth century sharpened the racial issue. For not only were Cubans migrating from a slave society—albeit in full process of disintegration—but North Americans occasionally showed open resentment at the employment of cheap black labor in such areas as harbor works—where the North American expected to earn $150 per month, black labor accepted $12 per week.[63]

NOTES

This essay has been previously published in *Social and Economic Studies* 29 (July/September 1980): 275-91, and *Eme Eme: Estudios Dominicanos* 8 (March/April 1979): 57-77, and is reprinted by permission of the Institute of Social and Economic Research, University of the West Indies (Jamaica) and the editors of *Eme Eme*.

1. Bureau of the American Republics, *Handbook of Santo Domingo*, Bulletin 52, 1892 (revised March 1894), Executive Document Part 3, p. 15, and Dominican Customs Receivership, "Annual Report with a Summary of Commerce."
2. E. Rodríguez Demorizi, ed., *Papeles de Buenaventura Baez*, Academia Dominicana de la Historia (Santo Domingo, 1968), 21:232-33.
3. British Parliamentary Papers (hereafter PP), 1875, *Accounts and Papers*, 73, Report of Major Stuart on San Domingo, p. 432.
4. PP, 1884, *Accounts and Papers*, 80, Part 5, Report of Vice-Counsul Coen on San Domingo, p. 744.
5. Archivo General de la Nación (hereafter AGN), Secretaría de lo Interior y Policía (hearafter SIP), "Memoria que al Ciudadano Presidente presenta el Sec. de lo Interior y Policía," 1910, and ibid., 1908, Anexos 2 and 3.
6. Department of State (hereafter D/S), Decimal Files 18, 9943/3, M-862, Roll 711, Knowles to Secretary of State, March 28, 1910. Enclosure, Arthur Lithgow, "Subject Tobacco."
7. *El Tiempo*, January 1 and January 15, 1913.
8. *El Eco de la Opinión*, October 9, 1884.
9. George Beckford, *Persistent Poverty: Underdevelopment in Plantation Economies of the Third World* (New York: Oxford University Press, 1972), p. 40.
10. D/S., Records of the Department of State Relating to the Internal Affairs of the Dominican Republic, 1910-29 (Economic Matters), microfilm series 626, roll 68, "Immigration into the Dominican Republic," enclosure to no. 107, March 8, 1924.
11. Great Britain, Foreign Office (hereafter FO), 23/74, 1882, India Office to Secretary of State, August 31, 1882.
12. Joaquín Balaguer, *La Realidad Dominicana* (Buenos Aires: Ferrari Hermanos, 1947), p. 32.

13. Colonial Office (hereafter CO), 318/338, Fisher to Secretary of State, no. 39, June 19, 1916.
14. Ibid.
15. FO 371/3228, 1918, Fisher to Secretary of State, no. 68, November 28, 1917. Enclosure, "Report on Recent Tour through Consular District."
16. FO 23/87, 1891, Foreign Office memorandum (no date).
17. FO 23/88, 1892, Coen to Secretary of State, no. 12, December 12, 1892.
18. FO 369/729, 1914, Fisher to Secretary of State, no. 19, February 13, 1914, "Report on the Dominican Republic."
19. FO 23/92, 1896, Petition of British Subjects in San Pedro de Macorís for Consular Representation, May 1, 1895.
20. M. J. Proudfoot, *Population Movements in the Caribbean* (Port of Spain, Trinidad: Caribbean Commission, 1950), p. 92.
21. Sir. T. R. St. Johnston, *From a Colonial Governor's Notebook* (London, 1936), p. 134.
22. Ibid.
23. FO 371/81, 1906, C. P. Lucas (Downing Street) to Under-Secretary of State, March 24, 1906, f. 709, enclosing copy of petition from British subjects resident in San Pedro de Macorís.
24. FO 23/96, 1899, Charles Arneage on the Edward Morris Case, August 18, 1899.
25. FO 23/76, 1884, Coen to Secretary of State, no. 2, January 25, 1884.
26. CO 318/338, Fisher to Secretary of State, no. 39, June 19, 1916.
27. Ibid.
28. Colonial Secretariat Records (hereafter CSR), Despatches from the Secretary of State (C.O.) to Governor of Jamaica. Enclosure to Despatch 331, Fisher to Sir Edward Grey, August 17, 1910.
29. CSR, Fisher to Grey, no. 236, August 17, 1912.
30. Enclosure in ibid.
31. AGN, SIP, Memorias, 1910, p. 86.
32. CSR, Fisher to Secretary of State, no. 237, June 27, 1912.
33. D/S, M-626, Internal Affairs, Roll 68, Russell to Knox, July 25, 1912 (no. 90).
34. Ibid., Russell to Knox, September 11, 1912, no. 205.
35. Ibid.
36. CO 318/342, 1917, Fisher to Secretary of State for Foreign Affairs. Enclosure to March 17, 1916.
37. FO 371/1132, 1911, Murray to Secretary of State, no. 25, April 15, 1911.
38. CO 318/342, 1917. Enclosure, Governor of San Pedro de Macorís to Fisher.
39. Ibid.
40. H. Hoetink, "The Dominican Republic in the Nineteenth Century; Some Notes on Stratification, Immigration and Race," in Magnus Mörner, ed., *Race and Class in Latin America* (New York and London: Columbia University Press, 1971), p. 120.
41. Edgar Thompson, *Plantation Societies, Race Relations and the South: The Regimentation of Populations, Selected Papers* (Durham, N.C.: Duke University Press, 1975), p. 95.
42. The reports from consuls in Tehuantepec, Mexico, in Costa Rica, and in

Panama are full of such suggestions. A number of these immigrants specifically requested to be recruited into British armies to participate in World War I. Such requests came from Santo Domingo and elsewhere.

43. Charles Kepner, *Social Aspects of the Banana Industry* (New York: Columbia University Press, 1936).
44. CSR, Enclosure to Despatch no. 49, February 2, 1910.
45. CSR, Enclosure to Despatch no. 62, 1914.
46. *St. Kitts-Nevis Gazette,* March 17, 1932.
47. Edgar Thompson, *Plantation Societies,* p. 36.
48. Frank Tannenbaum, *Slave and Citizen: The Negro in the Americas* (New York: Knopf, 1946).
49. R. Keith Aufhauser, "Slavery and Technological Change," *Journal of Economic History* 34 (March 1974): 45.
50. Franklin Knight, *Slave Society in Cuba during the Nineteenth Century* (Madison: University of Wisconsin Press, 1974).
51. Joaquín Balaguer, *El Cristo de la Libertad: Vida de Juan Pablo Duarte* (Santo Domingo, 1970).
52. *Listín Diario,* February 21, 1914.
53. Ibid.
54. Joaquín Balaguer, *La Realidad Dominicana,* p. 124.
55. AGN, SIP, Memorias y Anexos, 1908.
56. *El Eco del Pueblo,* April 23, 1885, editorial column.
57. For the nineteenth century see, for example, Sir Spencer St. John, *Hayti or the Black Republic* (1884) (London: Frank Cass Reprint, 1971), p. 163, where he describes Dominican "wakes."
58. AGN, SIP, Memoria, Anexo 13, 1908.
59. Ibid.
60. D/S, Consular Post Records, Despatches from Macorís Agency, 1895 to 1899 (2 vols.) and 1900 to 1906 (1 vol.), Reed to Dawson, No. 353, March 1, 1906, f. 253.
61. D/S, M-626, Internal Affairs, Roll 68 (Economic Matters), Yager to Wilson, October 2, 1915.
62. Ibid., Russell to Department of State, September 4, 1919, "Immigration into the Dominican Republic."
63. D/S, Numerical Files, M-862-442, Roll 67, Case 67, McCreery to Secretary of State, March 5, 1909.

Part Five
Perspectives

12. The Transition from Slave to Free Labor: Notes on a Comparative Economic Model

Herbert S. Klein & Stanley L. Engerman

One of the most fundamental changes in the world economy in the nineteenth century was the transition from slave to free labor in the Americas. It was a century-long process, beginning in the late eighteenth century and ending in 1888.[1] It was a process that reallocated and destroyed large amounts of capital, reduced commercial exports from America to Europe, shifted the centers of plantation agriculture in America, and transformed labor relations throughout the Western Hemisphere. Slave emancipation became the major impulse for the migration of Asian laborers to the Americas, as well as one of the important factors promoting the transatlantic migration of southern Europeans. It also profoundly reorganized peasant agriculture in many parts of the continent, just as it changed the nature of plantation agricultural labor itself. From being a supervised labor force organized in groups and employing women in all aspects of basic agricultural production, plantation labor shifted to family units of production in which control over actual working conditions shifted to the individual workers themselves. The transition also meant an increasing sexual division of labor, as women shifted out of plantation field labor. It affected the rhythm of agricultural production, as the marked seasonal occupation of labor during harvesting and planting became a more pronounced aspect of plantation agriculture in the Americas.

Yet despite its importance, the whole process of the transition from slave to free labor has been little studied from a comparative and international framework. Studies exist on individual processes of abolition, and more systematic work is being done with respect to emancipation and its aftermath in the United States, Brazil, Cuba, and elsewhere. But given the multiple outcomes, few have attempted to present a comparative analysis or to propose an explanatory model by which to account for the numerous variables that influenced the different emancipation processes and results. It is the aim of this paper to undertake such a statement of basic principles.

The transition from slave labor in the areas dominated by large plantations presented a number of variations within the Western hemisphere. Yet despite this diversity of post-emancipation arrangements, there was a common set of demands and constraints that operated everywhere, with the differing outcomes being determined by a combination of local circumstances and world market conditions. It appears that the black ex-slaves had similar interests when confronting the planter class. The planters also had clearly defined aims, which they hoped to achieve despite the change in the legal status of their labor force. The governments, for their part, frequently seemed to be supporting the planters, but at times they sought to balance the interests of these two essentially conflicting groups.[2] Given the differences in crops, in land availability, and in international markets, the clash of interests of planters and ex-slaves led to a quite complex and varied set of outcomes. It is the aim of this paper to offer some possible explanations for these differing results.

POSTEMANCIPATION CONFLICTS

In general, the ex-slaves demanded control over their own labor and access to their own lands to use for the production of food and other crops. Given the opportunity, ex-slaves withdrew from the production of sugar and other commercial plantation crops on the lands of the planters, preferring self-employment and the production of crops on their own lands. Thus, where possible, the ex-slaves withdrew their families and themselves from plantation field labor, especially when it was organized in the gang labor system, though not necessarily from the labor force, and they attempted to obtain direct control over land.

The planters in most areas were primarily concerned with maintaining the plantation system. They, and their governmental representatives (often for different reasons), were intent on maintaining preemancipation levels of production and of preserving as much as possible of the plantation structure and patterns of land tenure. Although some abolitionists thought that the ex-slaves might effectively produce the traditional commercial crops on their own lands, most assumed that the emancipated slaves would remain as landless, industrial-style laborers on the estates of the whites. The planters would remain as managers of these factories in the fields. Although many of the arguments by abolitionists before emancipation may have been intended merely to dampen proslavery protests, they often reflected the general belief that with the end of slavery the slaves would be left as an "uncivilized" and uneducated group that still had a long way to go before being integrated into the body politic. No major group of planters, and few government officials, in any of the ex-slave societies accepted as legitimate the ex-slave demands for land and the imposed end to the plantation regime.

Given these conflicting views of what the postemancipation societies should look like, bitterly fought battles resulted. Depending on circumstances, neither planters nor ex-slaves would fully dominate the outcome, and the relative political and economic power of the ex-slaves, the nature of power of the local authorities, and, finally, international market conditions for the plantation products, influenced the resulting arrangements.[3] In the majority of cases the ex-slaves would not be able to satisfy all of their demands, nor would the planters totally achieve their objectives. In general, some middle position was achieved, with the planters and the ex-slaves each being forced to compromise their most basic demands, although the frequent maintenance of planter class political power meant that there were limits on what was obtainable by the ex-slaves.

To begin the task of delineating the various factors that influenced the relative outcomes of these struggles, we can list several general categories of factors. These are land and natural resources, demographic characteristics and the land-labor ratio, government policies and their determinants, world market conditions, and technologies of crop production.

Land and Natural Resources

The quality of the soil and its history of usage influenced the costs of production on the plantations. The quality of soil being used determined the relative profitability of commercial crops at the time of emancipation. Equally, the amount of virgin soils determined future potential for profit. Finally, the relative availability of unused lands, its terrain and water requirements, and the ability to limit access, all influenced the potential development of small-scale freehold agriculture by ex-slaves. Thus, in societies such as British Guiana and Trinidad, with large quantities of virgin land just entering into sugar production, strong pressure for the maintenance of plantation agriculture was generated, while in older areas, such as Jamaica, such pressures were more limited. Even in such states as Brazil with an open frontier in even the coffee plantation regions, it was relatively easy for ex-slaves to obtain land, even if only as squatters. And on islands such as Barbados, with little available nonplantation-owned land, the plantation system was able to continue without interruption.

Demographic Characteristics and the Land-Labor Ratio

The ratio of whites to blacks in the population influenced the relative occupational opportunities open to the ex-slaves. Similarly, the ratio of arable land to labor influenced the available opportunities for independent settlement by the ex-slaves outside the plantation sector and thus the relative availability of labor to the planters. These, in turn, influenced the wage rates and the costs of production for the planters. Thus, for example, the high population density of Barbados meant that plantation sugar production persisted after emancipation, and the Antiguan planters were even willing to do without the period of enforced apprenticeship. These islands were frequently pointed to as the successful examples of what emancipation would accomplish.

A subset of factors related to the postemancipation possibilities for attracting more labor by immigration. The availability of indentured labor provided a basis for the maintenance of the plantation system in those cases where ex-slave labor costs were high or their labor not readily available.[4] The possibility of this in-migration depended on cheap and mobile sources of labor (as from India and China), reduced transportation costs, government subsidies, and governmental willingness to enforce indenture contracts.

A further set of constraints influencing ex-slave opportunities and their wage rates on the plantations were the possibilities to migrate out of the plantation region (e.g., from the southern states to the north in the United States, from the northeast to the south in Brazil, and from Barbados to elsewhere in the West Indies), but such movements were frequently long-delayed.

Government Policies and Their Determinants

In most cases it would appear that at the time of emancipation metropolitan governments were willing to provide some form of compensation to the slaveowners, in terms of labor commitments under a period of apprenticeship or some direct financial compensation or, more frequently, both. Among the major plantation areas, only in the United States and Brazil, both independent political regimes, was large-scale emancipation begun without any compensation to the resident planter class. Haiti was, of course, a case with no compensation paid to landowners, almost all of whom left or died with the revolution. Some indemnity was paid to France years later.

After emancipation there seems little significant difference in the attitudes of either colonial or independent governments toward the blacks, with again the obvious exception of the Haitian case. Most governments tried, at least initially, to maintain protected markets, provide for the continuity of the plantation structure, and undertake policies that helped reduce wage costs for the planters, either by limiting the bargaining power of the ex-slaves or by subsidizing alternative sources of labor (such as indentured labor). Yet the British government soon ended the special protection of its West Indian sugar producers, and it is argued that the end of the discriminatory sugar duties, not emancipation, generated the large-scale exodus from the Jamaican plantations, and limited the pace of recovery in the British West Indies.[5]

World Market Conditions

The greater the world market demand for the plantation crops, the greater the tendency either for the plantation system to be maintained or for the production of the export commodities to be continued with some modifications of the production arrangements. World market conditions would be influenced by the availability of alternative sources of supply or alternative crops. The different circumstances of cane sugar (where there was competition not only from East Indian sugar but also from the development of beet sugar in Europe), coffee, and cotton left a significant impact on the differing economic circumstances of the U.S. South and the Brazilian center-south, where economic recovery was more rapid, and on the Caribbean in the nineteenth century.

Technologies of Crop Production

The profitability of the plantation regimes would be influenced by the relative costs of the factors of production. The larger the efficient scale of production, the more necessary would be the maintenance of the plantation system. The possibilities of production on smaller units could, however, permit maintenance of the production of the export crop albeit at some reduced level of productive efficiency. Such adjustment was possible in the production of coffee, cotton, and tobacco, among other crops, but in general was not immediately possible for sugar and rice.[6] The late-nineteenth-century shift to smaller-scale sugar farms around a central mill might have been a response induced by the end of slavery, and it did limit the dependence on indentured labor in the Caribbean (as well as in the expanding sugar areas of Australia).

PATTERNS IN TRANSITIONS

In looking at the transition experiences, it seems clear that the Haitian case is the one instance in which ex-slaves, or at least their leaders, achieved success and satisfaction of their most basic demands. The internal divisions between radicals and moderates, and between whites and mulattoes, provided a setting in which conflict led to the eventual elevation of the ex-slaves to a dominant power position. Slaves thus not only achieved freedom, but they seized power and destroyed much of the capital invested in the plantation economy, as well as most of the planter class. Despite the initial attempts of the republican regimes to restore some aspects of the plantation economy, the land reforms of the 1810s and 1820s led to the establishment of small, peasant-owned farms. The general collapse of an effective export agriculture and the relatively limited nature of the national

Table 12.1 Changes in Average Annual Sugar Production in the British West Indies before and after Emancipation

	Percentage Change 1824–33 to 1839–46	Period in Which Pre-emancipation Level Regained
Barbados	+5.5	—
Antigua	+8.7	—
St. Kitts	+3.8	—
Trinidad	+21.7[a]	—
British Guiana	−43.0	1857–66
Jamaica	−51.2	1930s
St. Vincent	−47.3	never
Grenada	−55.9	never
Dominica	−6.4	1847–56
St. Lucia	−21.8	1857–66
Montserrat	−43.7	1867–76
Nevis	−43.1	1867–76
Tobago	−47.5	[b]

Source: Noel Deerr, *The History of Sugar* (London: Chapman and Hall, 1949–50), pp. 377, 199, 201.

[a] Trinidad output did decline slightly after the end of apprenticeship, and it was not until 1845 that the 1834 level was regained.

[b] Data merged with Trinidad after 1891. The 1877–86 level was two-thirds that of 1824–33.

market meant that no major influences were pulling the ex-slaves into a wage-labor system. This does not mean that they were outside the market economy—far from it. The existence of thriving local markets for foodstuffs and other commodities attests to the freedmen's willingness to respond to market incentives. The ex-slaves can be seen to have reacted as typical peasants, who can be drawn from their lands only if wages are high enough to provide a substantial income above the "subsistence" level that could be achieved by production on their own plots.[7]

Compared to the Haitian experience, the transition histories of the sugar islands of the British West Indies saw a greater maintenance of export production and the plantation system. In these British possessions three different patterns can be discerned, early detailed by the Oxford economist, Herman Merivale, in 1841.[8] On islands such as Barbados and Antigua, a lack of opportunity for land ownership precluded the large-scale withdrawal of ex-slave labor from sugar production. On these islands, sugar output continued to expand after emancipation (table 12.1). These were the areas from which, when sugar demand slowed and population increased, there was outmigration of labor to the expanding parts of the West Indies.

A second pattern was found in those regions undergoing rapid economic expansion at the end of the slave era, Trinidad and British Guiana (table 12.2). These areas were relatively "underpopulated" (with high slave prices

Table 12.2 Population, per Capita Income, Sugar Production, and Output Structure, Jamaica and British Guiana, Post-1832

Year	Population (000)	Per Capita Income	Sugar Production (000 tons)	Percentage of Exports in Total Output
Jamaica				
1832	370.0[a]	£15.6	72	43.5
1850	400.5[a]	12.2	29	24.3
1870	506.1	11.9	25	20.2
1890	639.5	12.4	17	19.1
1910	831.4	13.7	20	22.6
1930	1017.2[a]	15.7	65	19.8
British Guiana				
1832	98.0	£23.9	55	43.3
1852	127.7	19.9	49	22.3
1871	193.5	—	92	—
1891	270.9	—	114	—
1911	289.1	—	86	—

Sources:
Column 1 Gisela Eisner, *Jamaica, 1830-1930* (Manchester: University of Manchester Press, 1961), pp. 134, 289; Jay Mandle, *The Plantation Economy* (Philadelphia: Temple University Press, 1973), p. 19. The population estimates are for census years different from the year of output estimates in several cases, but these differ by only one or two years.
Column 2 Eisner, p. 289; Michael Moohr, "The Economic Impact of Slave Emancipation in British Guiana, 1832-1852," *Economic History Review* 25 (November 1972): 589; Mandle, p. 19. Jamaica incomes are in 1910 prices, those for British Guiana in 1913 prices.
Column 3 Noel Deerr, *The History of Sugar* (London: Chapman and Hall, 1949-50), pp. 198-99, 203.
Column 4 Eisner, p. 237; Moohr, p. 589. The Jamaican shares are based on current prices, those for British Guiana based on constant prices.
[a] Computed by using Eisner's estimates of total product and per capita product.

in the 1820s and 1830s). With emancipation, the ex-slaves generally either moved to unsettled land or to abandoned plantations, or else increased their labor input on the "provision grounds" from the period of slavery, and total sugar output declined. These declines were reversed within two decades in British Guiana, more rapidly within Trinidad; an expanding plantation sector reemerged, based on specialization in sugar production. The attempts to restrict the ownership of land by ex-slaves were, however, generally unsuccessful, and the new basis for estate labor was indentured labor, drawn mainly from India, under governmental subsidy and regulation.

The third pattern was typified by Jamaica. Sugar output fell dramatically, and this shortfall persisted for at least several decades (in Jamaica for about one century). Moreover the availability of lands, either from the decline of estates or from available public lands, allowed the ex-slaves to develop

Table 12.3   Average Annual Sugar Production before and after Emancipation (000 tons)

	Five Years before Abolition	Five Years after End of Restrictions[a]	Percentage Change	Period in Which Pre-Emancipation Level Regained
Haiti	71.7	[b] 1.2	−98.3	1960s
Martinique	29.1	(1847) 20.5	−29.6	1857–61
Guadeloupe	31.9	(1847) 17.7	−44.5	1868–72
St. Croix	9.7[c]	(1848) 7.3	−24.7	c. 1890
Louisiana[d]	177.1	(1865) 44.0	−75.2	1887–91
Surinam	15.7	(1873) 9.7	−38.2	1927–31
Puerto Rico	94.0	(1876) 74.4	−20.9	1900–04
Cuba	595.4	(1886) 745.7	+25.2	—
Brazil	254.0	(1888) 170.6	−32.8	1905–09

Source: Noel Deerr, The History of Sugar (London: Chapman and Hall, 1949–50), pp. 112, 126, 131, 212, 235, 236, 240, 245, and 250.

[a] Date either of abolition or end of "apprenticeship" controls, except for Martinique and Guadeloupe, where emancipation occurred in April 1848; Louisiana, where it was the end of the Civil War; and Haiti (note b).

[b] The first column relates to the period ending 1791. The second column relates to the first years for which postrevolutionary data are shown (1818–22).

[c] Output in 1840.

[d] Shown here are the averages for 1857–61 (which includes the high output recorded for 1861—the highest of any antebellum year) and 1866–70. The 1856–60 average, which includes the very low output of 1856, was 132.4. If an additional two years were allowed for readjustment, the 1868–72 average was 62.8—still a substantial decline for whatever combination of years are chosen.

rapidly a peasantlike economic base, free from plantation requirements. The increasing costs of production rendered the Jamaican estates less competitive than plantations in the new regions (British Guiana and Trinidad) or those that had better control over their labor force (Barbados, Antigua, and St. Kitts). Other islands in the British group such as St. Vincent and Grenada had a pattern similar to that in Jamaica. On these islands, the declining relative productivity of the sugar economy meant that planters were unable to replace slaves with contract laborers from Asia, while, at the same time, the continued importance of plantation organization for sugar production meant that a viable system of sharecropping could not be developed.[9]

The pattern in the French West Indian colonies of Martinique and Guadeloupe combined aspects of several of the British islands (table 12.3). As in most other societies producing sugar, there was an immediate drop in production as the plantation system adjusted to the end of slave labor. Unlike the Jamaican experience, however, production returned to preabolition levels within approximately one to two decades. But while the planters were able to use various mechanisms to maintain production, including the attraction of engagés (indentured labor), mainly from Africa, production over the next half-century did not increase as dramatically as in the newer British areas, and the relatively lesser importance of indentured labor meant a greater need for some type of arrangement to be worked out with the ex-slaves.

In the Dutch West Indies, above all in the plantation sugar society of Surinam, the Jamaican pattern also dominated, with production taking over a half-century to recover its preemancipation levels. This was brought about with the use of contract labor, imported from Asia for work in the fields, but clearly this area suffered a prolonged economic decline with emancipation.

The final abolition history among the smaller Caribbean producers worth noting is the case of Puerto Rico. Though the island's relatively small number of slaves were concentrated in the sugar industry and production was profitable to the end, the sugar industry was in decline from the middle of the nineteenth century. Thus the late nineteenth century saw the relative decline of sugar, and a shift to coffee with a reorientation of Puerto Rico's international trade back to Spain. When abolition occurred, therefore, the economy was in a process of reorganization. The relatively low demand for labor and the availability of a large labor pool due to the extraordinary population growth in the nineteenth century meant that when the sugar industry revived in the postabolition period, it could provide itself with abundant labor at low costs without the need to import workers. The crown was not reluctant to assist the planters with special vagrancy laws and other mechanisms that cut down on the mobility of the rural laborers and limited their ability to respond to alternative opportunities.[10]

In turning to the larger plantation slave economies of Brazil and Cuba, their post-emancipation experiences—at least in the earliest stages—seem to resemble the Trinidad-British Guiana pattern (type 2 among the British West Indies). In southern and central Brazil the threat of serious efforts at abolition led in the 1870s to a systematic effort at government organization and financing of a contract labor system. Unlike the West Indies, the Brazilians tried European immigrant labor in contract arrangements. But the rapid increase in dependence of the Rio de Janeiro and São Paulo coffee planters on Italian laborers rendered them extremely vulnerable to labor pressure, as the Italians felt that the contract system was close to slave arrangements and offered them inadequate compensation for the several years of labor demanded.[11] Able to find alternative employment in the cities or in other American nations, the Italians refused to accept indentured contracts, and the planters were forced to a compromise. Moreover, the technical nature of coffee production was such that the shift from gang labor to more acceptable sharing and piece-wage arrangements could be made without loss of productivity or any serious change in total output. Having worried about allowing Italians into favorable contracts for fear of their becoming competitors, by the last decade of the nineteenth century

Brazilian planters began to experience that competition, particularly as the coffee frontier continued to expand into the west paulista plains and slowly moved toward Paraná in the twentieth century.

In the Brazilian northeast, the history of emancipation fitted more closely to the Jamaican (type 3) model. Here the process of emancipation occurred while the economy was experiencing relative stagnation, due both to increased competition in the sugar markets of Europe because of the expansion of beet sugar and increased competition for slave labor because of the expansion of coffee production in the south. Moreover, the availability of land allowed the ex-slaves to move off the plantations quickly into small-scale commercial, as well as subsistence, agriculture. While the plantation system in the Brazilian northeast remained intact, planters were forced to work out complex wage agreements with the ex-slaves to attract them into plantation labor. This region was probably the last major sugar area in the Americas to introduce modern steam mills and the central (*usina*) type of organization, this taking place only in the first decades of the twentieth century.[12]

The Cuban case is an even more complex variant, for it involves a reorganization of the means of production, an introduction of foreign workers, and the successful incorporation of much of the ex-slave labor force into the sugar plantation industry—all in the context of the ongoing growth and expansion of the sugar economy.[13] As early as the 1840s, when Trinidad and British Guiana were turning toward East Indian laborers, the Cuban planters were beginning to import Yucatan Indians, and by the middle decades of the century large-scale importation of Chinese contract laborers had begun. Here the introduction of nonslave labor preceded the demise of slavery, and the transition had begun even before the ultimate legal end of slavery.

At the same time, the costs of conversion of the mills into modern steam-driven centrales led many of the planters to abandon direct control over the land and production of the cane, in return for maintaining control of milling and processing of sugar. Thus to some extent the great estates had become amalgams of subestate producing units in which intermediate-size farmers brought in their own work groups to till the land, and in which the ex-planters worked out controlled milling arrangements. Even before the final legal abolition of slavery in the 1880s (and especially after the Ten Years' War), free landless blacks, Chinese contract laborers, and slaves were working side by side on these complex units. By the time of emancipation, slave labor, while still dominant, was no longer the only source of the labor force even on the most advanced estates in the western half of the island.

Given the extraordinary vitality of the Cuban sugar industry, which dominated world sugar production by this time and was constantly expanding into the virgin areas of the western half of the island, the landowners were able to offer wages attractive enough to draw workers into the labor force.

Table 12.4 Per Capita Income and Share of Exports in Agricultural Output, U.S. South, 1860–1900

Year	Per Capita Income	Percentage of Exports in Agricultural Output	
1860	$93.9	37.9	—
1880	85.4	39.5	51.7
1900	116.1	—	48.4

Sources:
Column 2 Robert E. Gallman, "Gross National Product in the United States, 1834–1909," in Conference on Research in Income and Wealth, *Output, Employment and Productivity in the United States after 1800*, Studies in Income and Wealth, vol. 30 (New York: Columbia University Press, 1966), pp. 3–76, on 26; U.S. Bureau of the Census, *Historical Statistics of the United States* (Washington, D.C.: U.S. Government Printing Office, 1975), p. 8; and Richard A. Easterlin, "Regional Income Trends, 1840–1950," in Seymour Harris, ed., *American Economic History* (New York: McGraw-Hill, 1961), pp. 525–47, on 528. Income in 1860 prices.
Column 3 The ratio of cotton (and cottonseed), cane sugar (and molasses), tobacco, and rice output in 1879 prices to estimated value of southern agricultural output in 1879 prices. See Robert E. Gallman, "Commodity Output, 1839–1899," in Conference on Research in Income and Wealth, *Trends in the American Economy in the Nineteenth Century*, Studies in Income and Wealth, vol. 24, (Princeton: Princeton University Press, 1961), pp. 13–67, on 47–48; and worksheets underlying Stanley L. Engerman, "Some Economic Factors in Southern Backwardness in the Nineteenth Century," in John F. Kain and John R. Meyer, eds., *Essays in Regional Economics* (Cambridge: Harvard University Press, 1971), pp. 279–306.
Column 4 Gallman, "Commodity Output," pp. 46–47 (current prices); and Richard A. Easterlin, "Interregional Differences in per Capita Income, Population, and Total Income, 1840–1950," in *Trends in the American Economy*, pp. 73–140, on 100 and 103.
These estimates of southern agricultural output exclude Maryland, but this does not alter the general pattern.

Many of the ex-slaves found themselves working on the lands of their old plantations, and others worked on smaller farms providing cane for the *centrales* even though alternative land was available in the eastern part of the island for small-scale subsistence agriculture. Here many ex-slaves were able to obtain land, and by the twentieth century this region shared many features of peasant agriculture common to the other West Indian islands. But the dynamism of the sugar industry meant that in the western half wages were sufficiently high to keep many of the ex-slaves on the old estates.

The example of the United States shares several of the characteristics of other areas (table 12.4). A sharp decline in output and a withdrawal from the plantation labor force occurred, although unlike the outcome in most other areas, export production increased as a share of total southern agricultural output. While the continued vitality of the cotton market after abolition guaranteed that some type of persistence of the plantation would be attempted—since the cotton crop could be produced on smaller, nonplantation farms—it was possible to maintain output without a return to the plantation. This, however, was at a significant loss in productive efficiency. Similarly there were declines in production of other plantation crops, the extent of decline varying with the optimal scale of production in the antebellum period (table 12.5).[14]

The result in the United States, particularly in the case of cotton, was an apparent compromise, with the plantation lands being rented to ex-slave tenants and sharecroppers. They were provided land to work in cotton, in exchange for providing the landowner with a share of the cotton harvest. There was also a substantial increase in the amount of cotton production from the small white-owned and operated farms within the South, as well as some increase in the production of the other plantation crops by white labor in the late nineteenth century. The declines in output were most substantial in the states of the old Cotton Belt, with cotton production increasing dramatically in Texas in the late nineteenth century. After a period of moderate racial gains, legislative restrictions on voting, occupations, and education expenditures increased dramatically in the 1890s, a

Table 12.5 Changes in Output of Four Plantation Crops of the U.S. South

	Average Output 1856–60	Average Output 1867–71	Period in Which pre–Civil War Level Regained
Cotton (million lbs.)	1,720.2	1,323.6	1871–75
Tobacco (million lbs.)	434.2	284.3	1877–81
Rice (million lbs.)	123.3	47.9	1882–86
Sugar (thousand tons)	132.4	54.4	1884–88

Sources:

Cotton: George K. Holmes, *Cotton Crop of the United States, 1790-1911*, USDA Bureau of Statistics, Circular 32 (Washington, D.C., 1912).

Tobacco: George K. Holmes, *Tobacco Crop of the United States, 1612-1911*, USDA Bureau of Statistics, Circular 33 (Washington, D.C., 1912). Tobacco output in 1866 was 388.1 million pounds. There was a westward shift in tobacco production; e.g., Virginia did not regain the antebellum level until c. 1900.

Rice: George K. Holmes, *Rice Crop of the United States, 1712-1911*, USDA Bureau of Statistics, Circular 34 (Washington, D.C., 1912). There was a marked shift in the regional pattern of rice production, with Louisiana being the major producer after 1890. South Carolina's 1890 output was about one-quarter of its level in census year 1860.

Sugar: Noel Deerr, *The History of Sugar* (London: Chapman and Hall, 1949-50), p. 250 (Louisiana). The last crop before the Civil War was 264,161 tons, while the average for the four-year period of 1851-54 was 191,378 tons.

period of collapse in the cotton market. Yet even though the northward migration did not begin on a major scale until World War I and the subsequent restrictions on foreign immigration, blacks' incomes increased throughout the postemancipation period. After the initial decline in output due to the end of the plantation system, southern output grew at what, by the standards of time, was a rather high rate. Despite obvious problems, the postbellum South was not a stagnant economy (table 12.6).

In several ways the system that developed in the U.S. South resembled what would later emerge in Brazil, on the São Paulo and Paraná coffee estates, although in the United States the ex-slaves and southern whites were the major sources of agricultural labor. In the United States, the South could not compete with the North and the West for immigrant labor, nor did it have the resources or power to force the central government to subsidize a flow of directed immigration, as in Brazil and in the various Caribbean areas.

CONCLUSIONS

Among the several patterns observed, a few general points are worth stressing. It is doubtful that, in any major case, slave emancipation, however achieved, reflected a prior decrease in the profitability in the use of slave labor on the plantations. Broadly considered, emancipation usually came at times of expanding production, not stagnation, and this influenced the planters' desires to maintain plantation production. Apparently, as far as sugar production was concerned, in those areas without extremely high population densities, only the use of contract labor could maintain that pace of expansion of production. In the coffee and cotton fields, production could be maintained or even expanded after emancipation without resort either to contract labor or to the plantation system.

Second, while the slaves, in only a few cases and under most extreme conditions, succeeded in capturing the land that they had previously worked as slaves, emancipation—however uncompensated it was for the

Table 12.6 Per Capita Income Relatives, U.S. South, 1840–1920 (as percentage of United States average)

	1840	1860	1880	1900	1920
All South	76[a]	72[a]	51	51	62
South Atlantic	70	65	45	45	59
East South Central	73	68	51	49	52
West South Central	144	115	60	61	72

Source: Richard A. Easterlin, "Regional Income Trends, 1840–1950," in Seymour Harris, ed., *American Economic History* (New York: McGraw Hill, 1961), pp. 525–47.

[a] If allowance were made for Texas in these years, the relatives for the South would be 77 and 80.

slaves—was unqualifiedly a highly desirable condition in itself. Though the ex-slaves remained poor and politically weak in the great majority of ex-slave societies, the ending of slavery made some considerable difference in their ability to choose living and working conditions and to obtain the benefits of freedom in their social and cultural lives. From the perspective of today, the gains from emancipation are at times regarded as limited; to the emancipated slaves however, these gains meant major improvements in their lives that they bitterly fought to maintain. After all, despite the political, economic, and social power arrayed against them, in no area in America were ex-slaves forced back into the plantation gang-labor system of work, and no society was ever permitted to curtail finally and definitely their social, economic, and geographic mobility.

NOTES

We have benefited from the comments of the participants at the Conference on Problems of Transition from Slavery to Free Labor in the Caribbean, particularly Franklin Knight and Sidney Mintz, as well as those of David Eltis. An earlier version of this essay appeared (in Spanish) in *HISLA: Revista Latinoamericana de Historia Económica y Social* 1(1983): 41–55, and is reprinted by permission of the editors.

1. This paper draws on arguments and detailed references to sources presented in Stanley L. Engerman, "Economic Adjustments to Emancipation in the United States and British West Indies," *Journal of Interdisciplinary History* 12 (Autumn 1982), and Herbert S. Klein, "Consideraciones sobre la vialidad de la esclavitud y las causas de la abolición in Cuba del siglo XIX," *La Torre* 21 (July–December, 1973).

2. It is necessary to consider the differences between independent nations (such as the United States and Brazil) and those subject to colonial rule. In the latter case it is necessary to allow for differences between the local governments in the colonies and the metropolitan power (and, in the case of the British West Indies, between colonies with local legislatures and crown colonies). In no case, however, except for Haiti, did the governments deliberately undertake major policies to promote the interests of the ex-slaves at the expense of the planters, although the metropolitan and national governments did undertake policies presumably in the long-term interests of freedmen that, in retrospect, appear to be more favorable to planter interests. And even in Haiti it is necessary to distinguish between different groups of ex-slaves, as well as between the ex-slaves and the free persons of color.

3. While, in most cases, the ex-slaves wanted to operate on their own land, there may have been differences in the willingness to respond to market incentives. Thus while some freedmen may have preferred to move into food production for self-sufficiency and local sales, others wanted land ownership to be able to control and profit from production for export markets.

4. See K. O. Laurence, *Immigration into the West Indies in the Nineteenth Century* (St. Lawrence, Barbados: Caribbean Universities Press, 1971). For a discussion of indentured labor, and further references to sources, see Stanley L. Engerman, "Servants to Slaves to Servants: Contract Labor and European Expansion," forthcoming in E. van den Boogart and P. C. Emmer, eds., *Colonialism and Migration: Indentured Labour Before and After Slavery*, University of Leiden, Comparative Studies in Overseas History, vol. 6.

5. For a discussion of British policy after emancipation, see William A. Green, *British Slave Emancipation* (Oxford: Clarendon Press, 1976), while for a discussion of Jamaica see, in particular, Douglas Hall, *Free Jamaica, 1838–1865* (New Haven: Yale University Press, 1965).

6. Although rice at times was grown on small farms, there was generally a need for heavy capital expenditures to control the water supply. For the development of the rice industry in British Guiana, after the arrival of indentured labor from India, see Jay R. Mandle, *The Plantation Economy* (Philadelphia: Temple University Press, 1973).

7. For discussions of the Haitian case, as well as of developments elsewhere in the Caribbean, see Sidney W. Mintz, *Caribbean Transformations* (Baltimore: Johns Hopkins University Press, 1984). For a general discussion of peasant production see the classic work of A. V. Chayanov, *The Theory of a Peasant Economy* (ed. by D. Thorner, B. Kerblay, and R.E.F. Smith) (Homewood: Richard D. Irwin, 1966).

8. Herman Merivale, *Lectures on Colonization and Colonies* (London: Longman, Green, Longman, & Roberts, 1841). Another useful contemporary source, making a similar distinction, is William G. Sewell, *The Ordeal of Free Labor in the British West Indies* (New York: Harper & Brothers, 1861).

9. Some variants of sharecropping had been tried, rather unsuccessfully, on St. Lucia and Tobago.

10. See the paper by Andrés A. Ramos Mattei in this volume.

11. See, most recently, Thomas H. Holloway, *Immigrants on the Land* (Chapel Hill: University of North Carolina Press, 1980). See also Chiara Vangelista, *Le braccia per la fazenda: Immigrati e "caipiras" nella formazione del mercato del lavoro paulista (1850–1930)* (Milan: Franco Angeli, 1982).

12. See Peter L. Eisenberg, *The Sugar Industry in Pernambuco* (Berkeley: University of California Press, 1974).

13. See the papers by Manuel Moreno Fraginals, Rebecca Scott, Fe Iglesias García, and Francisco López Segrera in this volume.

14. The immediate decline in sugar production in the United States was greater than anywhere in the Caribbean. See J. Caryle Sitterson, *Sugar Country* (Lexington: University of Kentucky Press, 1953). And when national tobacco and rice production recovered, it was on the basis of expanded production in different areas than had been the major regions in the antebellum period.

13. Epilogue:
The Divided Aftermaths of Freedom
Sidney W. Mintz

The chapters in this volume were predicated on two obvious features of Caribbean economic, political, and social history: first, that while the various colonies created by the European conquerors followed widely divergent paths of development, the hispanophone colonies shared enough features to make them usefully comparable with one another; and, second, that any existing commonality underlay equally important differences in their individual character and destiny.

In spite of early settlement and a Spanish hegemony that endured within the region until well into the seventeenth century, it would be the colonial achievements of Spain's enemies—England, France, and the Netherlands in particular—that made the Caribbean region important to Western Europe. Against the backdrop of those achievements, the generally laggard economic development of the hispanophone islands—paralleled by the growth of their indigenous post-Conquest populations between the early sixteenth and the end of the eighteenth centuries—is basic to any understanding of what would later occur. Differences in size, in geographical location, and in local resources mattered greatly, of course. In addition, Cuba and Puerto Rico were afforded different opportunities by the Crown and by the Cortes. (Santo Domingo, though culturally akin to Puerto Rico and to Cuba, and with a history to some extent parallel, had become politically sovereign—1844—at least in name by the time the sugar boom in Cuba and Puerto Rico had fully matured.)

At the same time, what Spain could and would do with its two remaining colonies and how the populations and power structures of those insular societies would respond, were phenomena always subject to forces of wider scope. Without taking full account of those wider fields, the analyst of local

events runs the risk of endowing such events with an intensity and significance that they may not always possess. This matter of weighing local events
against external forces is one of the principal problems with which this
volume's authors were compelled to grapple, in making their interpretations. Each author, working from an intimate knowledge of some particular
case in space and time, gazes upward and outward, seeking to integrate
specific data with the wider field. Of course the fit of each such case—its
integration with international forces, with the relationship of local colonial
interests to competing interests in the metropolis, with the vagaries of the
expanding international sugar market, with the struggle for and against
slavery, with the constantly growing North American presence—is in every
instance different and unique. Even though limited to three colonial societies and focused primarily on the nineteenth century (slavery ended in
Santo Domingo with the Haitian invasion of 1822; in Puerto Rico in 1873,
followed by three years of apprenticeship; and in Cuba in 1880, followed by
six years of continuing change), these authors could scratch only the surface
of comparative study.

We dare not lose sight of the fact that we are dealing here with three
complex societies, each standing in different relationships to the metropolis
during the so-called transition period and each differently constituted in
terms of its population and economy. To be sure, it is because these societies
shared significant features that their comparison can be so illuminating. Yet
it would be foolhardy to claim that these three societies provide a spectrum
wide enough to span the variant possible "solutions" to the labor problems
resulting from the transition from slavery to freedom. Too many alternative
outcomes, particularly as affected by local conditions, have marked the
history of forms of labor exaction to be reducible to any three such cases.

PUERTO RICO AND JAMAICA: A COMPARISON

If we momentarily contemplate the Antillean region as a whole, we must do
so in terms of the evolution of the world economy, divided by the imperial
interests of national states. That world economy was becoming progressively
unified by a system of world capitalism, and on an international scale. At
the same time the planters of Puerto Rico or of Cuba had to deal with their
colonial governments; with their commercial and political masters in Madrid; with the slaves, free people, and contract laborers who composed their
labor force; and with the growing shadow of North American economic
(and political) interest. Only if we take all of this into account can we
discern in what ways the hispanophone cases made up a series of comparable instances during the centuries preceding the emancipation movement,
and then another such series thereafter. An example may provide some
sense of the comparative instance.

From the point of view of the European colonial powers, in the sixteenth and seventeenth centuries the Caribbean region was a pioneering zone that they felt free to "develop" as they saw fit. But the development was uneven and disorderly, and the region remained a theater of war, even while the plantation system was unfolding. From the perspective of forms of labor exaction, Jamaica and Puerto Rico, on the eve of emancipation in the British Caribbean and immediately thereafter, illuminate each other.[1] Jamaica was governed by a small clique of bureaucrats, planters and attorneys, and the military. A mass of enslaved and nearly powerless Africans, controlled by a tiny European minority, was leavened only with a meager intermediate stratum of free colored or white professionals. Practically a colonial factory for the production of tropical staples, Jamaica could hardly be considered a separate society and lacked many of the economic, social, cultural, and political features commonly associated with an intact society today.[2] Puerto Rico was similarly governed by a small clique of European representatives of the Crown. But in striking contrast to the bustling activity of the Jamaican plantations, it was a largely unoccupied island; an overwhelming proportion of its population was free, and of mixed and European ancestry; and most of all, it produced essentially nothing for export, while importing even less. From the European perspective, then, Jamaica was developed, and Puerto Rico underdeveloped. In other words a great deal of money could be made in (and out of) Jamaica, and hardly any at all in (and out of) Puerto Rico. From a cultural perspective the differences between these two societies were equally striking.

In the ensuing decades Puerto Rico was converted in large measure into a plantation colony, while Jamaica evolved to some extent away from its concentration on slave-based production for export toward a mixed economy, comprised of a plantation system, now much diminished, and a peasant sector, this latter producing both subsistence and some exports. To sustain the emergent plantation system in Puerto Rico, the planters had secured from the Cortes legislation that enabled them to force their own free (but landless) fellow citizens to work on the plantations.[3] In contrast, to man their declining plantations as the newly freed tried to build a peasant adaptation in defiance of the plantation system, the Jamaican planters taxed essential imports and used the proceeds to import contracted Indian labor, thus forcing down local wages.[4] Eventually the Puerto Rican economy reluctantly surrendered its dependence on forced and coerced labor, but not for more than half a century. The Jamaican economy, of course, had to do the same but much sooner; nearly forty years (1838–76) separated the dates of emancipation in these two colonies.

If we were to convert these contrasting cases into crude renderings of ideal types, we might imagine on the one hand a frontier situation. In this context two quite different outcomes would be possible: either a slave system that tied the labor force firmly to the land (as with all the early Caribbean plantation enterprises) or a settler system, in which each colonist labored for himself. But these contrasting ideal alternatives actually represent only one pole of a wider contrast. At the other pole we would envision a labor-saturated situation in which the supply of available labor power exceeds local need, so that all work is done for wages, by free but landless workers—rural proletarians. Once naked coercion was outlawed, all systems would gradually incline toward this alternative.

THE HISPANIC CARIBBEAN

To be sure, none of these three abstract types is represented by any of the Hispanic cases. In contrast to the French and British Caribbean colonies, however, the Hispanic Caribbean colonies provide provocative contrasts because emancipation came at different times, and in somewhat different ways, to each of them. In both the French and British Caribbean, it is possible to measure the effects of *simultaneous* emancipation (France, 1848; Britain, ending in 1838) against variant local background conditions. Thus the heavily populated, lowland Barbadian case, for instance, can be silhouetted against the more sparsely populated, highland Jamaican case. Such neat comparisons are ruled out in the case of Santo Domingo, its few slaves freed by the 1822 Haitian invasion, or in the cases of Puerto Rico and Cuba, whose fates in this regard were determined both by the differing influence of their planter classes in the metropolis and by local conditions in the islands themselves. In each such case, differences and similarities enliven insight by providing the opportunity to move back and forth from case to case, testing the possible weight of different factors.

To state the matter somewhat differently, any attempt to portray the range of variation of the transitional bridge between slavery and freedom among Caribbean societies by using only the hispanophone cases would necessarily fail. Yet these cases do provide illuminating contrasts, both with each other and with other examples within the region. Particularly useful are comparisons that extend over a period lengthy enough so that the play of forces through time can be revealed. In each instance—with the exception only of revolutionary Saint Domingue (Haiti)—the progression toward freedom was circuitous and uneven. Formal emancipation, rather than ending coercion and its ideological accompaniments, was but one step (though an immensely important one) in the evolution of liberty.

The nineteenth century, then, was the century of emancipation in the Caribbean, even if it came reluctantly and imperfectly. But it was also a century that witnessed an astonishing expansion of plantation production worldwide, an equally staggering international transfer of labor power, and a technical transformation of the world sugar industry. These three developments came to be linked to the eventual freeing of labor, though not in any direct or immediate fashion. Technical change in the sugar industry, which ultimately involved a vast improvement in grinding and extraction methods, with much larger mills serving much larger average acreages, did not occur evenly worldwide, or even regionally, but it paced swiftly growing world sucrose consumption and accompanying demands for more labor, particularly in the agricultural (as opposed to factory) phase. World sugar production shot upward so that the Caribbean region, for centuries a disproportionately important producing area, became less so, even while continuing to make a significant contribution to world production figures. Rapid technical change came first to Cuba, among the three Hispanic societies, and last to Santo Domingo; all three of these societies were by now (1880–99) more deeply involved than ever before in multiplex relations with the United States.

At the same time it may be important to remember that such a transition from slave to free labor was not a mere coefficient of the sugar industry, without the rise of sugar production and the plantation system in the Caribbean between the first decades of the sixteenth century and the last decades of the nineteenth, slavery could never have achieved its transcendental importance there. Hence an attempt to disentangle forms of labor exaction in this complex region during the transition from enslaved labor to free labor must deal with the history of sugar.

At the same time it may be important to remember that such a transition, even if we confine our inquiry simply to the three Hispanic cases, is endowed with a spurious exactness by the counterposition of the words *enslaved* and *free*. Hardly at any point and only for the briefest period is it possible to speak of pure slavery in the Caribbean region.[5] Although most planters in most Antillean colonies would certainly have preferred a clear-cut system of slavery with which to provide and sustain the labor power of their plantations, this was difficult to manage for many reasons. Debt bondsmen and bondswomen, Irish revolutionaries, union organizers, petty thieves, indentured servants, American Indian "serfs," Maya "deportees" from the Caste Wars, Chinese and Indian contract laborers, free Africans, and contracted Canary Islanders and Portuguese were among those introduced to plantation labor preceding slavery, during slavery's decline, to shore up the system in periods of shortage, and otherwise.

Yet there was almost invariable planter resistance to the abolition of slavery for reasons beyond the purely economic. Because slavery—and particularly the enslavement of human beings of cultures and physiques different from those of their owners—was predicated on the absolute, life-and-death control of the owner, it automatically provided ideological justification for *all* forms of labor coercion and thus rationalized and supported these other devices, even when they seemed milder in form and in application. The transition, then, was from one fixed status (slave) to another (free) only in ideal terms. In practice it involved a series of ongoing adjustments intended to sustain the economic and political power of those who needed labor over those who provided it. For this reason it is even difficult in some cases (as in the case of Cuba) to say exactly *when* slavery ended, since its demise was gradual and murky—a kind of grudging loosening of restraints, one by one, that would still leave the planters in a position of considerable power, insofar as the securing of labor was concerned.

LABOR MIGRATION

The more one seeks to integrate the transition toward free labor with other background conditions (land tenure forms, insular class structures, the relationships of local government to the ruling power, etc.), the clearer it becomes that the question of slavery and freedom entails far more than the economics and politics of emancipation. It need hardly be added that without some overarching comparative treatment of labor migration and the transfer of labor power, our comparative insight must remain blunted.

While Africans, Indians, and Chinese, among others, were for a long time not welcome in such countries as Australia and the United States, they had been welcome for an equally long period as contracted laborers in the Caribbean region. Policies seeking unrestricted migration caused negative reactions in Cuba in the late eighteenth and the nineteenth centuries, however. Unlike the usual Caribbean colonial factory, Cuba, during its epoch of underdevelopment, had acquired a European and Creole nonslave population, and its people had at least a minimal voice in its demographic fate. All the same, and in addition to an immense importation of enslaved Africans, during the nineteenth century perhaps 125,000 Chinese were shipped to Cuba. In the same century half a million Indians were shipped to Trinidad, British Guiana, Suriname, Jamaica, Guadeloupe, Grenada, Martinique, and elsewhere. Large numbers of migrants reached other sugar-producing areas worldwide:

> Sugar, or rather the great commodity market which arose demanding it, has been one of the massive demographic forces in world history. Because of it, literally millions of enslaved Africans reached the New World, particularly the American South, the Caribbean and its littorals, the Guianas and Brazil. This migration was followed by those of East Indians, both Moslem and Hindu, Javanese, Chinese, Portuguese and many other peoples in the nineteenth century. It was sugar that sent East Indians to Natal . . . sugar that carried them to Mauritius and Fiji. Sugar brought a dozen different groups in staggering succession to Hawaii, and sugar still moves people about the Caribbean.[6]

Such movements, of course, were the very fabric of Caribbean history from the Conquest onward and were responsible for the region's becoming one of the ethnically most heterogeneous of its size in the world. But the history of Caribbean migration changed radically in the nineteenth century, and a principal cause of that change was the expansion of North American power into the region and its swift subsequent consolidation. The three hispanophone societies (memorialized by the proindependence Puerto Rican composer Rafael Hernández as "las tres hermanitas") had existed on different terms within the Spanish imperium—an imperium in the case of Santo Domingo that was more cultural and philosophical than economic or political. Once the United States had penetrated the region, these three societies (together with Hawaii and the Philippines) became integral components of the aggregation of productive forces that would then feed sugar to North America's growing population. Thus the nineteenth century in the Caribbean region was in addition a North American century. Not surprisingly, perhaps, Caribbean labor migration after 1898 was almost exclusively connected to North American activity: the migration of the Puerto Rican people from the coffee highlands to the sugar lowlands and—a migration little remembered—from Puerto Rico to Hawaii;[7] the migration of Haitian and Jamaican sugar-cane workers to Cuba; the migration of Jamaicans and other West Indians to Panama, for the building of the Canal, and to the banana plantations of Central America; and so on.

These movements were a general aspect of the spread of North American power—as was the building of the Canal itself. But within the region, most such migration was linked to the changing character of the plantation business, and the specificity of North American investment in it. Almost a quarter of a million Haitians and Jamaicans went to Cuba in a mere fifteen years (in open contravention of a ruling that North American beet sugar producers had successfully promoted at the time of the invasion)—merely a coefficient of the explosive development of the plantation system there by North American interests. (In Puerto Rico, which soon saw a parallel development of its sugar-producing potential, such migration was unnecessary, and in Santo Domingo, when its turn came, a convenient supply of its own rural poor was soon supplemented by Haitian workers from across the border.) In the period of 1880–84 the average annual per capita consumption of sucrose in the United States was 38 pounds; by 1887 it reached 60.9 pounds; after 1898 it soared steadily. The new American colonies in the Caribbean and the Pacific practically assured U.S. sugar needs for the twentieth century.

There are various linkages among these different assertions, but the general point is obvious enough: the evolution of forms of labor exaction is tied to migration and demography; in turn, these are tied to the changing nature of the world economy. The sociology of the modern world requires us to treat labor practices in different places as ongoing, related—even interdependent—phenomena. Accordingly, to the extent that the emigration of laborers formed part of the "solution" to labor shortages in plantation areas—or, at least, to situations where a labor force already resident was unwilling to give enough labor at going rates to satisfy the planters—the political and cultural position of the newcomers must be taken into account in analyzing the transition to free labor.

It may also be fair to contend that in considering the hispanophone cases, international political considerations should take precedence over the admittedly important variants that typify each case "on the ground." This assertion is based on the fact that North American penetration of the Caribbean region in the late nineteenth century was channeled in large measure by the prior presence (and at that point the internationally accepted presence) of other European powers, including the Danes, the Dutch, the British, and the French—and it was only on the Spanish possessions that the North Americans descended as aggressors. Though they were disposed of in somewhat different ways, at different times and at different rates, the productive potentialities of these hispanophone societies were matter-of-factly invoked by the North Americans at their pleasure. In only one case, Cuba, may migration be thought to have played a critical role in the transition, especially since the Chinese migration there largely preceded emancipation. But at a much later date, when North American interests pushed the development of a modern sugar industry in that same country, they turned to Jamaica and Haiti for labor. Later, when sugar was developed by the North Americans in the Dominican Republic, they were able to count on the Haitians for their labor supply. Even Puerto Rico sought to import labor—from India—but was frustrated by the Cortes. Thus emigration played a role in the subsequent development of the sugar industry in all three hispanophone societies, even if unevenly and tardily. Not at all surprisingly, in the two cases where emigration was permitted, the migrants were consigned to specific occupational slots in the receiving societies, from which they were able to escape only slowly and with difficulty.

In every such case the cultural characteristics of the migrants, and not simply their numbers or the time of their arrival, told importantly in their influence on the transition itself. If one sought to compare the role of the Chinese in Cuba, for instance, with that of the Indians in British Guiana, the differing backgrounds of these two migrant groups would figure noticeably in their respective adaptations to their new situations. So too would the attitudes of the planters, who were indifferent to the social and political status or future of their laborers, so long as they could count on extracting their labor. And even more important, perhaps, the prevailing societal attitudes toward newcomers would be revealed as radically different. In Cuba there were classes who violently objected to the introduction of more nonwhites. In British Guiana those who objected had no power at all, and they themselves were "colored."

In our interpretations of the transition, we are justifiably intent on the struggles of the newly free to find their place in societies where they were long disinherited. But when massive migration has further complicated that struggle, even such curious features of life as a disposition to eat (and to grow) rice, to defer consumption for purposes of investment, or to marry in a large public ceremony can influence the nature and tempo of class formation, the development of class consciousness, and the effectiveness of class resistance to the demands of the plantation system. These are, after all, cultural attributes, the weighing of which cannot be avoided if they are carried by migrants entering transitional situations of the nineteenth-century Caribbean sort. If one were to single out a major vacuum in the coverage of the conference, it might well be this: our need to reconstitute historically not merely legal but also genuinely cultural processes of emancipation, with due attention to group differences, and the place of such processes in the total picture. To state as much does not diminish at all the accomplishments of the conference. Here we see a pioneering effort to cast light on an obscure (and obscured) but vital chapter in the emergence of the modern world.

NOTES

The author thanks Stanley Engerman, Richard Price, and Rebecca Scott for helpful suggestions and criticisms of earlier drafts of this paper.
1. Sidney W. Mintz, "Labor and Sugar in Puerto Rico and Jamaica," *Comparative Studies in Society and History* 1 (1959):20–30.
2. John Stuart Mill, *Principles of Political Economy* (Boston: Charles C. Little & James Brown, 1848), pp. 234–35.
3. Sidney W. Mintz, *Caribbean Transformations* (Baltimore: Johns Hopkins University Press, 1984), pp. 82–94.
4. See Nigel Bolland, "Systems of Domination after Slavery: The Control of Land and Labor in the British West Indies after 1838," *Comparative Studies in Society and History* 22 (1981): 591–619; A.J.G. Knox, "Opportunities and Opposition: The Rise of Jamaica's Peasantry and the Nature of Peasant Resistance," *Canadian Review of Sociology and Anthropology* 14 (1977): 381–95; and Sidney W. Mintz, "Slavery and the Rise of Peasantries," *Historical Reflections* 6 (1979): 213–42.
5. Sidney W. Mintz, "Was the Plantation Slave a Proletarian?" *Review* 2 (1978): 81–98.
6. Sidney W. Mintz, "The Plantation as a Sociocultural Type," in *Plantation Systems of the New World* (Pan American Union Social Science Monographs, 7 [1959]), pp. 42–50.
7. Sidney W. Mintz, "Puerto Rican Migration: A Threefold Comparison," *Social and Economic Studies* 4 (1955): 311–25.

Contributors

PATRICK E. BRYAN is a senior lecturer and head of the Department of History, University of the West Indies (Mona). He received his Ph.D. from the University of London in 1977 and has published articles on economic change in the Dominican Republic, 1870–1916.

JOSÉ CURET is a professor of history at the University of Puerto Rico. He received his Ph.D. from Columbia University in 1980. His publications include *De la esclavitud a la abolición* (1979) and *Los Amos Hablan: Unas conversaciones entre un amo y su esclavo aparecidas en 'El Ponceno,' 1852–53* (forthcoming).

JOSÉ DEL CASTILLO is director of the Museo del Hombre Dominicano and research professor in the Department of Sociology of the Universidad Autónoma de Santo Domingo. Among his publications are *La Gulf and Western en la República Dominicana* (1974); *La inmigración de braceros azucareros en la República Dominicana, 1900-1930* (1978); *La economía dominicana durante el primer cuarto del siglo XX* (1979); and *Ensayos de Sociología Dominicana* (1981).

STANLEY L. ENGERMAN is a professor of economics and history at the University of Rochester. He is coauthor of *Time on the Cross* (with Robert W. Fogel, 1974) and coeditor of *The Reinterpretation of American Economic History* (with Robert W. Fogel, 1971); *Race and Slavery in the Western Hemisphere* (with Eugene D. Genovese, 1975); and a special issue of *Social Science History* on "Trends in Nutrition, Labor Welfare, and Labor Productivity" (with Robert W. Fogel, 1982).

FE IGLESIAS GARCÍA is a research scholar at the Institute of Social Sciences of the Academy of Sciences of Cuba. She received an advanced degree in history from the Martin Luther University in Halle-Wittenberg, German Democratic Republic, as well as one in sociology from the University of Havana. She has published essays on population, social classes, and aspects of the economic development of Cuba during the second half of the nineteenth century.

HERBERT S. KLEIN is a professor of history at Columbia University. He is the author of two comparative studies of slavery—*Slavery in the Americas* (1967) and *The Middle Passage* (1978)—and three works on various aspects of Bolivian history—*Parties and Political Change in Bolivia, 1880-1952* (1969); *Revolution and the Rebirth of Inequality* (with Jonathan Kelley, 1980); *Bolivia, the Evolution of a Multi-Ethnic Society* (1982)—and most recently he has edited (with John TePaske) a collection of primary materials on *The Royal Treasuries of the Spanish Empire in America* (1982).

FRANKLIN W. KNIGHT is professor of Latin American and Caribbean history at The Johns Hopkins University. His publications include *Slave Society in Cuba during the Nineteenth Century* (1970); *The African Dimension of Latin American Societies* (1974); *The Caribbean: The Genesis of a Fragmented Nationalism* (1978); and *Africa and the Caribbean: Legacies of a Link* (coedited with Margaret Crahan, 1979).

FRANCISCO LÓPEZ SEGRERA is the director of research and postgraduate courses of the Institute of International Relations in Havana. He has published widely in the fields of Cuban history and Cuban-U.S. relations, including *Cuba: capitalismo dependiente y subdesarrollo, 1510-1959* (1972) and *Raíces históricas de la revolución cubana, 1868-1959* (1980).

SIDNEY W. MINTZ is a professor of anthropology at The Johns Hopkins University. He has done fieldwork in Puerto Rico, Jamaica, and Haiti; his publications include *The People of Puerto Rico* (coauthored with J.H. Steward and others, 1956); *Worker in the Cane* (1960); *Caribbean Transformations* (1974); and, most recently, *Sweetness and Power* (1985).

MANUEL MORENO FRAGINALS was visiting professor at Columbia University when he and a group of colleagues decided to organize the conference that led to the publication of this book. He is professor of history at the University of Havana and author of many books and articles on the economic history of Cuba and the Caribbean in general. His book *El ingenio* (1978) won the American Historical Association's Clarence H. Haring prize for the best work on Latin American history for the period 1976–1981.

FRANK MOYA PONS is executive director of the Fondo para el Avance de las Ciencias Sociales in the Dominican Republic. He is the author of *La Dominación Haitiana* (1973) and *Manual de Historia Dominicana* (1977) and has taught and lectured in universities in the United States, Latin America, and Spain.

BENJAMÍN NISTAL-MORET is the historic architecture conservator for the National Park Service, Southeast Regional Office, Preservation Center (Atlanta). He received his Ph.D. from the State University of New York at Stony Brook and also holds a degree in historic preservation from Columbia University. He is the author of *El Cimarrón, 1845* (1979) and *Esclavos prófugos y cimarrones: Puerto Rico 1780-1873* (1984) and is a coeditor of *El proceso abolicionista en Puerto Rico,* volumes 1 and 2 (1974, 1979). He has taught at the University of Puerto Rico, S.U.N.Y.–Stony Brook, and the City University of New York, Brooklyn College.

ANDRÉS A. RAMOS MATTEI is a professor of history at the University of Puerto Rico. He received his Ph.D. from the University of London in 1977 and has published *La hacienda azucarera* (1981), as well as other works on the history of Puerto Rico.

REBECCA J. SCOTT is an assistant professor of history at the University of Michigan, Ann Arbor. Her publications on the social and economic history of nineteenth-century Cuba include several articles and a book, *Slave Emancipation in Cuba: The Transition to Free Labor, 1860-1899* (1985). Her current project is a comparative study of postemancipation society in the sugar regions of Brazil, Cuba, and the United States.

Index

Books in the Series

The Guiana Maroons: A Historical and Bibliographical Introduction
Richard Price

The Formation of a Colonial Society: Belize, from Conquest to Crown Colony
O. Nigel Bolland

Languages of the West Indies
Douglas Taylor

Peasant Politics: Struggle in a Dominican Village
Kenneth Evan Sharpe

The African Religions of Brazil: Toward a Sociology of the Interpenetration of Civilizations
Roger Bastide, translated by Helen Sebba

Africa and the Caribbean: The Legacies of a Link
edited by Margaret E. Crahan and Franklin W. Knight

Behold the Promised Land: A History of Afro-American Settler Society in Nineteenth-Century Liberia
Tom W. Shick

"Alas, Alas, Kongo": A Social History of Indentured African Immigration into Jamaica, 1841–1865
Monica Schuler

"We Come to Object": The Peasants of Morelos and the National State
Arturo Warman, translated by Stephen K. Ault

A History of the Guyanese Working People, 1881–1905
Walter Rodney

The Dominican People, 1850–1900: Notes for a Historical Sociology
H. Hoetink, translated by Stephen K. Ault

Self and Society in the Poetry of Nicholás Guillén
Lorna V. Williams

Atlantic Empires: The Network of Trade and Revolution, 1713–1826
Peggy K. Liss

Settlements, Trade, and Polities in the Seventeenth-Century Gold Coast
Ray A. Kea

Main Currents in Caribbean Thought: The Historical Evolution of Caribbean Society in Its Ideological Aspects, 1492–1900
Gordon K. Lewis

The Man-of-Words in the West Indies: Performance and the Emergence of Creole Culture
Roger D. Abrahams

First-Time: The Historical Vision of an Afro-American People
Richard Price

Slave Populations of the British Caribbean, 1807–1834
B. W. Higman

Caribbean Contours
edited by Sidney W. Mintz and Sally Price

Between Slavery and Free Labor: The Spanish-Speaking Caribbean in the Nineteenth Century
edited by Manuel Moreno Fraginals, Frank Moya Pons, and Stanley L. Engerman

The Johns Hopkins University Press
Between Slavery and Free Labor

This book was set in Garamond 49 text and display by BG Composition, Inc., from a design by Chris L. Smith. It was printed on S.D. Warren's 50-lb. Sebago Eggshell Offset paper and bound in Kivar 5 and Papan by the Maple Press Company.